DRAWN OUT

TOM SCOTT
DRAWN OUT

A SERIOUSLY FUNNY MEMOIR

ALLEN&UNWIN
SYDNEY·MELBOURNE·AUCKLAND·LONDON

First published in 2017

Copyright © Tom Scott, 2017

Allen & Unwin
Level 3, 228 Queen Street
Auckland 1010, New Zealand
Phone: (64 9) 377 3800

Email: info@allenandunwin.com
Web: www.allenandunwin.co.nz

83 Alexander Street
Crows Nest NSW 2065, Australia
Phone: (61 2) 8425 0100

A catalogue record for this book is available from the National Library of New Zealand.

ISBN 978 1 877505 91 1

Internal design by Carla Sy
Set in 10.4 pt Feijoa
Printed and bound in Australia by Griffin Press
10 9 8 7 6 5 4

MIX
Paper from
responsible sources
FSC
www.fsc.org
FSC® C009448

The paper in this book is FSC® certified. FSC® promotes environmentally responsible, socially beneficial and economically viable management of the world's forests.

To Averil, my magnetic north

CONTENTS

Me and Sue, the twins.

CHAPTER ONE

EGGHEAD HATCHES

TO START AT THE BEGINNING, my first memory is of being pink and naked. So is my twin sister, Sue. We are Rubens' cherubs without the wings. We are screaming in terror, which none of his cherubs ever appeared to be doing. Our screams are echoing off white tiles wet with steam. We are clawing at the walls, scrambling over one another to escape a piping hot bath. Amid the thrashing and wailing I am transfixed by steam settling on a metal tap and blistering off again. I can see it still. It is mysterious and oddly beautiful. For a brief moment, this strange transformation blanks out the frenzy and muffles the screaming. Sue and I are not yet eighteen months old . . .

Sue has no memory of this. I remember only because it became the recurring nightmare of my childhood. I returned to the white-tiled bathroom many nights and woke heart racing, gasping for air. Too frightened to go back to sleep, I lay perfectly still in the dark afterwards, waiting for what seemed like days for dawn to arrive before approaching my parents at the kitchen table—the kauri table my mother 'improved' by gluing imitation Formica vinyl on top to make it 'modern'.

'I had *that* dream again, Mum . . .'

Mum would look shifty and swallow nervously.

'Did we ever have a bathroom with white tiles, Mum?' I always addressed the question to her. There was little point asking my father anything. Getting a straight answer out of him was like picking up mercury with chopsticks. Chopsticks held in wicketkeeper's gloves, while blindfolded. Mission impossible, but we foolishly persisted.

One sodden Manawatū afternoon, when the view out of the windows was of sheets of rain compressing the landscape to a handful of paddocks with sheep huddling motionless under macrocarpa trees, we begged him to take us to the pictures. He had a thick Northern Irish brogue, harsh and metallic yet surprisingly nimble—think Fred Astaire tap-dancing in hobnail boots on sheets of corrugated iron—and he was never at a loss for words. Except when he was on the phone to clients, when speech deserted him and his stammering was painful to listen to. He needed some sort of Heimlich manoeuvre for sentences stuck in his throat. We hid from view to spare him witnessing us witnessing his humiliation—and to spare us his subsequent rages. On at least two occasions he rectified the situation mid-conversation through the simple expedient of ripping the phone, cables and all, from the wall. The picture request, though, caused him no problems.

'What do ye want pictures for?' he asked. 'Yee've got pictures on the wall!'

'Pictures that move!' we wailed in unison.

'In dat case, I'll move dis picture over there, and I'll move dat picture back here!'

His replies were quicker than a Nadal return of serve, almost as if they were waiting in ambush for us. They came in fusillades as well as single shots. For example, he rose from bed late one Anzac Day (he was never one for shivering to death at dawn parades; he believed that brave men had made the ultimate sacrifice so that other men could sleep in and this was his way of honouring their memory; besides, he drank at the RSA once or twice a week anyway) and I stupidly asked him what he did in the war. Without hesitation he responded, 'I was a hero. Your father, Egghead, was a hero!'

Just about all the dads on Kimbolton Road had served in the war. Some worked on their farms in summer in the faded flapping khaki shorts that had been part of their kit in the scorching sands of North Africa. They had seen good friends and close mates blown apart, showering them in blood, brains and shit. They didn't want to talk about the war. Not so Tom Scott Senior.

'When Churchill called for a volunteer to assassinate Hitler, I put me hand up. They flew me into Berlin under cover of darkness in a Lancaster bomber. I parachuted down, hitch-hiked to the Chancellery, shot around the back to the bunker, knocked on the door and who should answer but Herr Hitler hisself! I grabbed the little fucker and strangled him to death with me bare hands, I did! When I got back to London they wanted to give me swags of medals. I said, "No! No fuss! No medals for me! It's just something *any extraordinarily brave* man would have done in my place!"'

So there was no question, really, that all questions were better put to Mum. She always went as white as the tiles I was describing when I asked about the nightmare, though, insisting that it was just a silly dream and that I should pay it no mind, while my father looked on with a knowing look on his face, basking in her discomfort. It wasn't until I was in my last year at Feilding Agricultural High that I learned the truth.

TENSION MOUNTED MOST NIGHTS IN our house as pub closing time approached. Conversation stilled as we waited for the familiar sounds of Dad's Vauxhall Velox whining down the street, lurching into our pitted driveway and coming to a shuddering halt beside the massive palm outside the front steps.

The engine ran on, backfiring like a mortar for quite some time after the ignition had been switched off.

Dad was partial to fish and chips. When replete, he disposed of the greasy papers by throwing them over his shoulder into the back seat of his car. When that space was full to overflowing, he began stowing them in the front passenger seat, tamping down the piles when they threatened his visibility. Eventually there was barely enough room to wedge himself into the driver's seat and operate the handbrake and gears, much like a Formula 1 driver's cockpit today. Imagine fully inflated air-bags made of cellulose and beef dripping. Apart from the fire risk, it made him very safe. A goods train on any one of Feilding's multiple railway crossings could have slammed into him amidships and, apart from reeking of vinegar and a light coating of batter, he would have emerged without a mark on him.

Extricating himself from the car always took some time. There would be another delay if he elected to empty his bladder on the verandah steps. Provided the engine had finished coughing up phlegm, the next sounds were keys rattling in the front door and his heavy tread in the hall.

He rarely fully entered the lounge. He preferred to stand in the doorway, a swaying silhouette, asking with tart, exaggerated politeness, 'Did anyone ring for me? Did the Pope ring for me? Did the Holy Father *hisself* ring for me? Did the Pontiff, perchance, ring for me? The Duke of Edinburgh? The Duke of Argyll? The Queen Mother? The Shah of Iran? Frank Sinatra? Did Frank Sinatra ring for me?'

The list went on and on. It was truly impressive. He was mocking his own reduced circumstances, of course. And when he was done with that he turned on Mum. 'Christ Jesus, yer ugly, woman! Put yer teeth in. That might help! They are in? In dat case try taking them out!'

The pattern was repeated endlessly, with only minor variations. Mum would pretend it wasn't happening, obliging us to pretend it wasn't happening either, which was fine as none of us had the courage to confront him. It was easier to ride it out silently until he staggered off to his room: the front room, with four dead television sets stacked on top of each other, and blonde-oak twin beds with yellow candlewick bedspreads. Mum's half, long abandoned, was piled high with clothing and books, including encyclopedias and his treasured anthology of Robbie Burns poetry. A pump organ worked by a foot pedal, a purloined aluminium aircraft seat painted fluorescent green, tinkling Venetian blinds and frail dark-brown roller blinds that partially disintegrated into dust if released with too much force.

Thanks to labouring on the chain in the freezing works in the school holidays I was physically stronger and taller than my father—not that it would have ever come to a physical confrontation. Once when I wasn't big enough or strong enough and he was pushing Mum around in the kitchen in a different house I had nervously asked him not to.

'Or what?' he barked.

'You'll have to deal with me,' I said, blinking rapidly. It was his turn to blink. He took a step back and looked at me in astonishment.

'Well, well, look who's up on his hind legs! Look who's up on his hind legs!' He left it at that, which was a relief. A few weeks earlier, bellowing madly, he had chased me down the hall over something I had said that he considered insubordinate and probably was. I made it to my bedroom and slammed the door shut, wondering nervously what was going to happen next. I didn't have to wait long. With a splintering crash, his fist came straight through the timber, shocking us both. He retreated wordlessly.

Three years on, when I was big enough and strong enough to splinter doors myself if I chose to, I challenged him. I can't recall exactly what I said, but it must have been blunt.

Suddenly he was the one rearing up on his hind legs, whinnying and snorting.

'LET ME TELL YOU SOMETHING ABOUT YOUR PRECIOUS MOTHER, EGGHEAD! YOUR PRECIOUS MOTHER AND YOUR FUCKING DREAM!'

Mum gave a loud cry and collapsed back onto the sofa, sobbing, as he began spewing out a story he'd clearly been saving for a moment such as this.

It was 1949. The war had been over for four years. My father had been a Flight Sergeant and airframe engineer in the RAF before enlisting in the New Zealand Air Force. He was stationed at Ohakea airbase on the Manawatū coast when he got a letter from my mother, writing to him from London.

Mum, Sue and I were sharing a one-bedroom flat in Brixton with a woman Mum deemed, possibly uncharitably, to be *a prostitute*. To a good Irish Catholic girl in 1948, even a fallen one, the label prostitute was all-embracing, ranging from girls who sold their bodies for money through to girls who went to parties exposing too much cleavage. Whatever the case here, this poor girl needed lots of sleep—sleep denied her when, just a few feet away, sharing a single bed with Mum, Sue and I came down with chickenpox, scratching and crying continuously. It drove her mad.

In the small hours of the morning she persuaded Mum that total immersion in a hot bath would take the sting out of the pox and help us settle. A hot bath was run and Mum detailed in her letter how she looked on with mounting alarm as this girl, now quite crazed, held me underwater, kicking and struggling until I went limp. She ignored Mum's pleading to stop, and a wrestling match ensued. Mum needed all her strength to get me to the surface.

'YOUR PRECIOUS MOTHER, EGGHEAD, WATCHED YOU NEARLY GET DROWNED!'

Mum was howling now. My response wasn't what either of them was expecting.

'I knew I wasn't imagining it!' I declared jubilantly. 'There *was* a bathroom with white tiles and steam!'

I thanked Mum effusively for saving my life. Not for the first time, my father backed wordlessly out of the room.

CHAPTER TWO

IRISH WHAKAPAPA

I DIDN'T GET TO IRELAND, the land of my parents, until I was 30 years old. Apart from my Aunt Catherine, who helped Mum with Sue and me in London when we were very small, growing up in New Zealand, none of the Scott children ever met a single relative. It was as if our family had arrived in the Manawatū from another galaxy. We had no cousins, no aunties, no uncles, no sisters-in-law, no brothers-in-law and no grandmothers or grandfathers. It was just us—a small microclimate of Irish lunacy set in the dull and sober Manawatū landscape.

The only evidence of a wider family came from Mum's side— fuzzy photographs smaller than postcards, with a pinking-shear trim. People not much more than white dots for faces and black and grey splotches for clothes pose en masse on a mailman's dray or stand singly with a favourite dairy cow. Very *Borat*. A tall, gaunt man, splay-footed like Charlie Chaplin, with high cheekbones, cigarette in his mouth, wearing a rumpled suit, pullover and tie and a broad cloth cap on his head, was Mum's father, Michael Ronayne. 'Kindness itself' is how she described him. He picked her wildflowers, sang her songs and carried her on his shoulders along the banks of the Blackwater that flowed slow, deep and wide past their thatched cottage. White swans trailed silver wakes amongst golden reeds on their side. Castles and grand mansions half hidden in forests of Sherwood green rose up on the other.

Unlike Mum, our father never spoke of his family. The closest he came to acknowledging kith and kin of any sort was when declaring bitterly that our mother's brothers were thugs who deserved go to prison for assault and battery. He didn't elaborate, but it was clear he had been on the receiving end of some sort of thumping. He didn't celebrate birthdays or acknowledge anniversaries—though, to be fair, two years after I had been accredited University Entrance, he appeared in the living room one evening and chucked a watch in my direction, slurring, 'That's for passing University Entrance, Egghead.' Until very recently I had no idea he had two sisters, who visited Mum in London after Sue and I were born and were very kind to her.

Having no connection with the past is curiously liberating. I have no heritage defining or confining me. No family tree determining how far the fruit can fall. I grew up believing I was a blank cheque and I could fill in as many zeroes as I wanted, this number varying widely as my self-esteem waxed and waned.

The Māori concept of whakapapa has no meaning for me. As a political reporter, on numerous campaign trails I accompanied party leaders onto many marae in chilly weather. The welcomes were always elaborate and the protocols always strictly observed. This often meant standing in drizzle for hours or sitting on hard benches in drizzle for hours, as dignified elders on the edge of tears paid interminable homage to ancestors represented in beautiful carvings on the walls and ceilings. When I wasn't fretting about frostbite or deep-vein thrombosis I marvelled at their obsession with people and things that went before.

I did wonder if whakapapa would have more relevance and

make more sense to me on my first visit to Ireland in 1977. I pondered this and other things as I stood on the deck of the rail ferry taking me across a lumpy Irish Sea—aluminium-saucepan grey flecked with mashed-potato foam, a portent of the national dish slapped in front of me every night for the next week. Swimming in molten butter, it was usually accompanied by the strict instruction, 'Work away, boy. Ye must be famished! Work away!' Only the Irish treat eating like a weights session at the gym, where you push your body to the absolute limit, eating until you can't take another bite, but do anyway. It must be a genetic memory from the potato famine.

THE TRIP TO IRELAND WAS one I very nearly didn't make. After six months in England and France, I just wanted to hightail it back to New Zealand. Spring refused to arrive, daffodils refused to flower, robins refused to sing, snow refused to melt. The family had already departed and I was left desperately circling Australia House on the Strand in a badly dinged Commer campervan that I hoped to sell to another poor sucker like me. Ahead of me and behind me, a convoy of homesick Aussies and Kiwis in similarly dented VW Kombi vans were hoping to do the same, all of us shooed away like seagulls at an airport by aggressive policemen every time we threatened to settle. In the end I sold the lumbering lemon to a sweet middle-aged English couple on Hampstead Heath, who told me apologetically that it was a buyers' market and they had me over a barrel. Had they actually sodomised me I seriously doubt that it could have hurt more.

I spent some of the pitifully small bundle of notes on the train fare back to the Georgian manor with a gatehouse in rural Sussex which was the residence of my de-facto in-laws, the only people I have ever heard shout 'DON'T COME FOR LUNCH!' down a phone line when friends rang to say they were contemplating a spin in the countryside. That night I rang my sister Jane in Palmerston North—Mum was living in her tiny sunroom—to tell them I wouldn't be heading to Ireland this trip due to my straitened circumstances. Mum worked in a shirt factory and Jane was a talented artist living off the smell of an oily rag, albeit paint-splattered. Somehow they telexed me £160. How could I refuse them? I boarded the boat-train at Paddington filled with gratitude and not a little apprehension.

I'm glad I went, if only to confirm beyond all reasonable doubt that I was a New Zealander and didn't belong anywhere else. The magical, mystical land of my forebears proved to be neither.

Not that my welcome wasn't warm and my relatives weren't lovely. Cousin Richard picked me up from Cork station and drove me to Fermoy in his battered VW, through a landscape almost violently green. The main crop seemed to be Celtic crosses made of stone and the predominant livestock white horses so still they could have been hewed from the same rock. We pulled up outside Daly's store in High Street, opposite a handsome stone bridge with multiple arches and a rushing weir. This weir was where my grandmother's first husband, a publican, took a team of horses to drink when he'd had too much to drink himself, and they all drowned. On my return, my father asked me if Daly's store still smelled, in the great Irish tradition, of stale bacon and kerosene. It did. I was rushed behind the counter to a small lounge out the back where aunts, uncles and cousins were waiting; I was hugged and squeezed and bombarded with scores of questions about Mum. Auntie Chris, Mum's half-sister, kept exclaiming in high excitement, 'Dis is Joan's boy! Isn't he gorgeous, girls! Couldn't ye just eat him?'

For the next week, I was the prize in pass-the-parcel. Rushed hither and thither, from village to village, cottage to cottage, pub to pub, drinking pint after pint of Guinness until two in the morning, then lying down gingerly on rock-hard beds before pitching into a soothing, Guinness-tinged abyss. I got taken to kiss the Blarney Stone, to afternoon tea with chirpy Uncle Tom and his elegant wife in their grandly furnished quarters above their antiques shop in Fermoy, and to call in on sweet and subdued Uncle Bonnie and Aunt Queenie in their almost bare, terrace house in Aglish. It was empty of furniture because their angelic-looking boy with the eyes of a captured feral creature, who couldn't speak, was given to breaking things in a rage. Later in the pub next door he poured soft drink over his mother's head. 'Isn't he a beautiful boy, Tom?' Queenie asked me keenly, while Bonnie smiled a sad, weary smile. When my mum returned to Ireland she took Michael for long, rambling walks. She made a connection with him and he was as sweet as a kitten for her. When it was time for her return to New Zealand they both bawled their eyes out.

The thatched cottage on the edge of the Blackwater with the wild roses tumbling madly over the roof was what I wanted to see most. In the middle of the day Uncle Paddy, who had never married for reasons that quickly became obvious, lay fast asleep, fully dressed with his boots on under tousled, grimy sheets in the bed he'd been born in. This was the bed my mother had been born in as well. Paddy needed his sleep because most nights he and Bonnie went poaching salmon. Neither of them could swim, but they worked without lifejackets in the pitch black to avoid detection by river patrols. I declined their invitation to join them. In the morning, he lamented the size of the fish, declaring his support for stiffer penalties for poaching. I went with him in his battered Mini by back roads—to avoid the Garda—to the poultry factory. By law all fish in the river were the property of the British aristocrats and German industrialists who owned the castles and estates running down to the water's edge. Justice of sorts was served when the same people paid a fortune for Paddy's salmon when it was served up to them in fancy London restaurants. Clearly the Irish tribes could do with some dignified elders of their own demanding that their ancestors be honoured and their ancient fishing grounds respected.

Everyone remembered Mum. She was her siblings' favourite sister and her nieces' and nephews' favourite aunt. They used to run to meet her when she got off the train from Limerick, laden with presents. My cousin Anne, a lively, attractive woman, told me that Mum was a striking, glamorous, glorious force of nature. During the war, she worked as a fashion buyer for Roches department store in the centre of Limerick, a grand Victorian structure—Munster's answer to Harrods. There is a picture of her with Katharine Hepburn tresses, dark lipstick on full lips, wearing a stylish tweed hacking jacket and smart jodhpurs, sucking on a long cigarette. You could imagine any number of earls and a Mitford sister or two just out of frame. She looks confident, poised and carefree. Then she met my father...

In a rare moment of candour he told us once that he spent the war ice-skating in Canada. Thin ice, most probably. Photos taken at this time show a snappy dresser with his arm around a different pretty girl in every picture. He resembles a youthful Bill Clinton. His wavy hair is slicked back with Brylcreem and parted down the middle. There is another parting between his two front teeth, which my brother Michael inherited. It turned both of their smiles into teasing, knowing alarm signals—stand clear, a joke is coming. Dressed in his RAF uniform, Dad is only truly smitten in one photo—the one where he is tenderly cradling his rifle.

He was an airframe engineer stationed in places with colourful names like Winnipeg, Moose Jaw and Medicine Hat. He got to war-ravaged Europe after hostilities had ceased, as

Tom Scott Senior, my dad.

part of the Army of Occupation in Munich. He was in a beer hall one night when some Kiwi soldiers, who wore shorts in all sorts of weather, arrived and ordered beers. Things were going well until a barman called a Māori a monkey. His voice swelling with admiration, my father described how his Pākehā mates took exception and completely wrecked the joint. When British military policemen in their distinctive helmets and white spats came running, blowing their whistles and waving long batons, the Kiwis kicked the snot out of them as well, then, as casual as you like, strolled into the bar next door and ordered another round. My father was so impressed that he decided then and there that he would join the Royal New Zealand Air Force.

While waiting for his papers to come through, he helped build the Shannon airport on the outskirts of Limerick, which is where he met my mother Joan, who all for her sophisticated airs was completely unworldly in matters of the flesh. A good convent girl, everything below the neck and above the knees was as mysterious, as dangerous and as out of bounds as the Belgian Congo.

Many years later I took her to a play at Downstage Theatre in Wellington—*Tonite Let's All Make Love in London* by my good friend Dean Parker, a brilliant screenwriter (*Came a Hot Friday*), playwright and essayist. For much of the first act, the male lead padded around barefoot and completely naked. We were seated in the front row, virtually on stage. At one point the well-endowed young man came close enough for her to check if he had an inguinal hernia or a circumcision scar, which I feared she might be doing when she leaned forward keenly. In a stage whisper, she turned to me and said, 'I've only ever had your father's penis inside me!' Shocked gasps rippled through the auditorium. She topped this with, 'What a shocking waste of vagina!' We used to joke that Mum was so fertile she could get pregnant watching BBC documentaries on sperm whales. As a petite old lady with a pink rinse, sitting demurely at our dining table, surrounded by her grown children, who now had children of their own, she explained her fecundity as follows:

'I stuffed meself with toilet paper, but your father's sperm *always* got through!' My response was to tell her that attempting to stop spermatozoa with cellulose was the equivalent of expecting a pine plantation to act as a rabbit-proof fence. I have a degree in physiology, which I felt I must put to good use. Mum sniffed. 'Ye can't help yerself can ye? Ye always take tings too far!'

WHEN MY FLYING VISIT TO Ireland drew to a close, an honour guard of relatives formed outside Daly's store to wave me off. Brooking no argument, Uncle Tom pressed £50 onto me, and Chris another five, which she couldn't afford. It was a godsend, and I never thanked them properly. I regret not writing to them.

Chugging north through empty countryside, I imagined my mother taking the very same trip 30 years earlier as an unmarried woman, her belly swelling with two unborn children percolating inside her, sitting alone, hoping not to be noticed by the nuns and priests who seem to be permanent fixtures in every Irish railway carriage. Head pressed against a cool windowpane, she would see her fretting reflection mixed in with theirs. She would be sniffling and using the sleeves of the designer jacket that would never fit her properly again as a hanky. Tears of regret and shame would be causing her carefully applied make-up to run. She would be shivering with fear, wondering what lay in store. All she knew with a fierce clarity was that no one was taking her babies off her.

This was not easy in Ireland. Unmarried mothers were subjected to enormous pressure from the church to give their babies up for adoption. Sue could easily have ended up in Canada and me in Australia. Or we could have disappeared altogether— if not off the face of the Earth, then beneath it. Recent grisly discoveries of mass graves containing the remains of babies and small children in the grounds of former Catholic nursing homes and orphanages confirm what many always half suspected. Certainly Mum knew enough to take the afternoon train to Rosslare Harbour, to cross the Irish Sea in gathering darkness, to disembark at Fishguard Harbour in the middle of the night and board another train bound for Paddington, arriving just before daybreak. Her older half-sister, Catherine, tall and beautiful, was waiting on the platform. They fell into each other's arms, sobbing.

Catherine took generous and kind care of Mum right up until her confinement, and Mum desperately wanted me to pay her a visit before I flew home. It was the least I could do and hardly out of my way. Catherine and her husband, Herb, lived in Hounslow, below the flight path to Heathrow. Every few minutes a 747 rattled every cup and plate in the house.

She was still tall and beautiful. Mum must have mentioned in her letters that I was a cartoonist. Sensing a connection, Herb, who saw himself as something of a Bohemian in the tradition of Picasso and Chagall, rose from the table to fetch his latest oil. It was of a bull moose with huge antlers in full roar, standing in a clearing in the middle of a Canadian forest. Little islands of white unpainted canvas were dotted across it. 'Only three numbers to go!' he declared proudly.

Back in New Zealand I was meanly recounting this moment when Mum interrupted, demanding to know if her sister still had all her own teeth. It was more than idle curiosity on Mum's part. Catherine had borne witness to the most degrading, stinging humiliation of Mum's life—something she never really got over.

The winter of 1947 was the coldest on record. Freezing Arctic storms lashed the British Isles. Three years after the war London was still pock-marked with bomb craters fenced off with barbed wire and sandbags. Whole streets were missing. Frequent heavy snowfalls disguised much of the ugliness. On the rare occasions that watery sun broke through grey skies, and before the soot had a chance to settle again, London was briefly as pretty as an illustration from Dickens' A Christmas Carol.

When Mum's contractions gathered pace, Catherine took her to Hammersmith Hospital. I arrived first. Whenever the opportunity presented itself, and even when it didn't, Mum reminded me that squeezing me into the world was an excruciating experience. She lost a lot of blood and doesn't remember Sue coming out at all. Septicaemia set in. She was delirious for days, coming round to discover she had dentures, courtesy of a hospital dentist who had gone to work with pliers and done a simple Irish colleen a favour. Mum had been very proud of her teeth. She wept with grief at the loss while feeding Sue and me. Three of us in a narrow bed, all gnashing our gums.

The Magdalene home for fallen women was badly damaged in the Blitz. One end of the ward was a flapping blue tarpaulin. Mum woke many mornings with snow spilling across the stone floor. How she coped in the bitter cold in a foreign country still exhausted by the war, a big city crippled by strikes and coal shortages, with two small children, no husband, no income and no home of her own, I'll never know.

WHEN WE WERE BIG ENOUGH she got digs of her own opposite a Jewish primary school. They advertised for a cleaner and Mum knocked tentatively on their door. Seeing twins gurgling in a pram they took pity and employed her on the spot. She claims she didn't do much cleaning beyond pushing a sodden mop back and forth while Jewish women, some Holocaust survivors, played with Sue and me and made her cups of tea. Mum never forgot their kindness and wouldn't let us forget it either. When the movie *Exodus* came out she made Sue and me cycle four miles into Feilding with her to watch it. Starring Paul Newman, it was about Jewish boat people, refugees from civilisation's darkest chapter seeking a new homeland and being denied entry into Palestine by the Royal Navy.

Meanwhile, back in London, the streets teemed with maimed and crippled war veterans who'd helped defeat Nazi Germany. Mum's heart filled with dread whenever one hobbled towards us, because I would imitate their mannerisms and gait with an uncanny accuracy no less hurtful for being entirely innocent. The seeds of future caricature skills were being sown long before I could hold a pen.

It was around this time that my mother's brothers managed to track down my father. He had enlisted in the Royal New Zealand Air Force and was on the verge of boarding a boat for New Zealand on a single man's assisted passage. His friends were appalled. 'Two little rocks in the middle of the fucking sea! Where will ye go when the tide comes in?' With no time to lose, Mum's brothers manhandled him into the back of a car and delivered him to a registry office in Hammersmith, where Mum was waiting with Catherine, Sue and me. My father had been roughed up quite badly. The registrar had seen this sort of thing before and didn't bat an eyelid. Nor did my father. He couldn't. Both his eyes were swollen shut.

Despite this initial reluctance the briefest of honeymoons ensued, which must have gone well because affectionate letters were exchanged in the months it took to obtain the documentation necessary for us to join him. We set sail for New Zealand from Southampton in July 1949 aboard RMS *Tamaroa*—part of the once mighty Shaw Savill Line. Catherine came to see us off and collapsed with grief on the docks. A giant policeman lifted her over the barricade and let Mum and her sister hug one last time at the foot of the gangplank.

Mum describes the voyage as a nightmare. Sue and I were drawn continually to the rail, where sharks trailed the ship's wake. There was a children's party on 21 July. I know this because Mum kept the menu. Paper must have been still subject to post-war rationing because the document is barely the size of a credit card; it records poached eggs on toast, roast turkey, salad, bread and butter, preserves, cake and fruit jellies.

Steaming towards Panama there were whispers of an outbreak of lesbianism below decks. Mum thought it was a tropical disease and panicked because Sue and I hadn't been inoculated against it.

Crossing the Equator, she bought us our first ice cream. Vibrating with excitement, I slammed the cone smack into my forehead and dropped to the steel deck in a dead faint. It was a harbinger of many not dissimilar accidents to come.

Our father somehow persuaded the skipper of the pilot boat to take him out onto the Waitemata Harbour to board the *Tamaroa* and surprise Mum before the ship docked in Auckland. Anticipating another 40 minutes of prep time she had no make-up on and was wearing a drab nightie; her hair was in curlers and her false teeth were in a glass by the bed.

He entered without knocking. She screamed and lunged for the teeth. I screamed as well. While my father was reeling in shock, Sue had the presence of mind to totter towards him, smiling. I hid behind Mum and shat myself. He never forgave me.

CHAPTER THREE

LEARN BY DOING

ARRIVING IN THE MANAWATŪ, WE stayed on a dairy farm and piggery north of Bulls until the Air Force finished building our house on the base itself. There was a big effluent pit behind the cowshed covered in green slime that I mistook for grass and attempted to run across. I didn't get far. Two steps in, I plunged through the emerald crust into its foul depths.

Sue's screaming brought adults running. My father pulled me out by my hair, which was relatively clean. The rest of me was coated in a tempura batter of urine and shit. Everyone recoiled from the stench. My father availed himself of the only sensible option: grabbing the high-pressure yard hose, he let me have it full blast over Mum's shrill protestations. Bawling and gasping I careened around the concrete yard like a rag doll, but it cleaned me up nicely. Clean enough for Mum to hug me, at least.

Number 10 Ohakea Station had a front hedge, a white front

gate and a concrete path leading to a frosted-glass front door—the image quite possibly of a moose standing in a Canadian clearing. At the back, another concrete path led to a rotary clothesline, a garden shed and a lemon tree. Paradise! The kitchen had all the latest mod cons—toaster, Kelvinator and kettle. Every surface sparkled and gleamed. Mum was over the moon. There were three bedrooms.

I had worked out by then that I got on my father's nerves, so I kept out of his way and drew pictures. Then Michael was born. My father doted on him and I don't blame him in the slightest. Micky *was* pretty amazing. He toilet-trained himself before he was three. Climbing over the high sides of his cot, he dropped to the floor as lightly as a cat and made his way to the toilet down the hall in pitch dark because he couldn't yet reach the light switch.

If other Ohakea kids had had the same skills, we might have seen more pictures growing up other than just ones that hung on the wall. The officers' mess screened movies on Saturday afternoons. Our father took Sue and I to a black-and-white film about a runaway lawn mower. It ate flower beds and hedges. It was truly terrifying. The boy sitting on the other side of our father crapped his pants. My father stuck it out as long as he could, then, cursing and gagging, holding the boy stiffly at arms' length, carried him to the toilets to wash his bum and rinse out his underpants. That was it for him. Movies were off the menu.

There were plenty of other distractions in the neighbourhood—the forbidden junkyard of dead plane parts and munitions casings in the gully at the end of the runway, the swimming baths sitting beneath the turreted water tower that looked like it belonged on a giant chessboard. One day the pool was empty for cleaning. Sister Sue and I perched on the edge at the deep end, absorbed in the task of watching a man in overalls with a broom sweeping up brown sludge on the bottom—maybe the movie boy was a keen swimmer as well—when curiosity got the better of me.

I have always had a large skull. It partly accounts for my father calling me 'Egghead' and Mum's claims of an excruciating birth. My centre of balance is critically governed by where my cranium is positioned at any given moment. In this instance, it was cantilevered a smidgen too far forward, and I dropped six feet to the damp concrete below me. All I can remember after this is Mum screaming when I got home because blood

Mum at a fancy dress party at Rongotea Hall.

was streaming down my face and my right eye was rolling drunkenly in its socket. An optician in Bulls said I would need eye operations when I was older, and fitted me with wire-frame spectacles that slowed down the rotations, corrected my blurred vision and more importantly prevented others feeling seasick when looking in my direction.

Dad quit the Air Force shortly after this. For years, I proudly assumed he'd been thrown out for refusing to salute an officer that he didn't respect, but the truth was far less swashbuckling. Farming was booming and he wanted to start his own topdressing and weed-spraying business. We moved ten miles south to the dairy factory hamlet of Rongotea, which seemed to have more churches than people. My father claimed it was too small for a village idiot, so the locals took it in turns.

RONGOTEA PRIMARY SCHOOL WAS A grand hall of learning consisting of three classrooms at the end of a dusty street on the outskirts of the hamlet. Mum walked Sue and me there on our first day, which began with the raising of the Union Jack and singing of 'God Save the Queen'. It passed uneventfully until the last period, when we were allowed to draw on brown butcher's paper with waxy crayons. Other children drew stick figures and squiggles. I drew the Phantom, 'the ghost who walks', in this instance riding his horse Hero, with his trained wolf Devil running alongside. They were good likenesses, but it wasn't fair, really. I had been practising secretly in my bedroom.

The other kids gathered around dumbstruck. When the teacher saw what I had drawn she shrieked and ran from the room, returning moments later with the other two teachers, one of whom was also the headmaster. They too gasped in disbelief. The words 'child prodigy' may even have been bandied about. They certainly came later. And not just from me.

I loved the attention. I was in approval deficit at home, so it was hugely gratifying. Then I discovered I could make other kids laugh. I liked making other kids laugh. I became a revolting little show-off on multiple fronts.

This was my undoing one winter morning. I was larking about on the upper playground as another man in overalls mowed the lawn below us. I slipped on the frosty grass. Gathering speed, I shot feet first into the spinning blades.

Years later, in a vet-school physiology class, I discovered that I have negative buoyancy. It's very rare. My bone density is such that I don't float in water. Aqua jogging, even wearing two floatation vests, is risky and a snorkel is advisable as back-up. On planes, when they go through the safety procedures I surreptitiously check the passengers on either side of me to see who is the smallest, because in the event of an emergency that poor bastard is going without a lifejacket. When I swim, I send up plumes of spray like multiple depth-charges, yet I barely move forward. Any trajectory in water is diagonal rather than horizontal.

This rare phenomenon, coupled with my recurring nightmare, meant I lived in fear of swimming sports and avoided participation. In my last year at Lytton Street School in Feilding (the school motto was 'Learn by Doing'—bugger that!), I was forced against my will to participate in the all-comers, across-the-pool freestyle, an event dominated by new entrants. At

GREAT MOMENTS IN GENETIC ENGINEERING...

Feilding's aging municipal baths we lined up in order of height. Even crouching I towered head and shoulders above excited five-year-olds. I was big for my age, with a large purple scar on my left knee, which could pass for a duelling injury at a pinch, but there was no way I could pass for a teacher.

Burning with shame, I edged down the pool until I was opposite the high diving board, the deepest part. The water was essentially chowder in those days, with dead sheep substituting for clams. Without my glasses I couldn't see the bottom, which was a relief, but I knew it was down there somewhere.

The crowd in the stands behind me tittered as we got on our marks. They didn't know it, but I would soon wipe the smiles off their smug faces.

The gun went off. Paralysed with terror, I dropped like an anvil into the opaque depths. Later I would claim that I began walking briskly along the bottom and was making good time so what happened next was totally uncalled for, but that wasn't the case. Noticing my failure to surface, two fully dressed male teachers dived in to the rescue. Encasing both their arms up to the elbows for safekeeping were kids' watches. Hissed threats followed me across the playground for months afterwards, but nothing was as bad as the kid who, just when I thought the whole affair was safely behind me, yelled out in the street, 'Look, Mum—it's the boy who nearly drowned!'

Bone density is a huge plus when you fall into a lawn mower, however. I stalled the big machine dead in its tracks. There was no pain that I can remember. There was a lot of screaming and shouting, but not from me. I dimly recollect people carefully unthreading my left leg from the mower's maw. In an ambulance, I watched in fascination as a small red dot on a white woollen blanket spread slowly outwards as we wailed towards Palmerston North. I don't know how much blood I lost but I'd made a passable Japanese flag by the time we arrived at the hospital.

They saved my leg. The lawn mower had to be put down. I wore a calliper for the next six months. People assumed I had polio and detoured around me. Polio was the Zika virus of its day. Everyone was terrified of catching it. A boy around the corner was rumoured to have died from it. Even in my calliper I sprinted past his house. The fence, garage and verandah of his home were choked with a dark ivy that I have associated with death ever since.

WE LIVED IN A DEAD house of our own—dank and decaying living quarters at the rear of an abandoned shop, with an outside toilet with a can—the contents of which had to be buried in a back yard where the grass came up to my waist and sullen nectarine trees barely bore fruit. It was Mum's job to dig the holes, even when she was heavily pregnant with Jane.

This didn't stop her boarding a bus to Palmerston North with Sue and me, to stand for hours with thousands of others lining Featherston Street hoping for a glimpse of young Queen Elizabeth and Prince Philip on their 1953–54 Royal Tour of the Dominion. Excitement had been building for months. Every school-kid in the country got a concertina booklet that unfolded to show the Coronation procession, a special medallion attached to a blue ribbon and little Union Jacks on sticks.

After an interminable delay, word came down the line that the motorcade was approaching. Hushed conversation gave way to cheering. A forest of arms began frenziedly waving flags, obscuring my view. Within seconds they had passed and were gone. Pat Lawlor's writing in the *Evening Post* (15 January 1954) is supposed to have summed it up best: 'This slip of a girl has made flames leap as if from a mighty furnace . . . a woman has sat at the keyboard of our thoughts and her charm has made music in our hearts.' Shame I missed it.

Before going into the maternity home to have Jane, Mum bought a dozen new nappies, washed them to make them fluffy and stored them proudly in the hot-water cupboard. When she was gone I developed ringworm symptoms on my scalp. Working on the theory that ringworm was averse to sunlight, my father cut off all my hair with hand clippers—a laborious task that included terse instructions to keep still, accompanied by painful taps on the head with the flat of the blades if I transgressed. At the finish there were small hedgerows of mousy ginger curls that he had missed, along with nicks, cuts and a bruise or two. Thoroughly miserable, I stole a beret of Mum's and pulled it low over my ears like Frank Spencer would later do in *Some Mothers Do 'Ave 'Em*. Returning home with baby Jane, my mother let out a heart-rending howl when she discovered rats had chewed holes in every single nappy, and another piercing scream when she saw what was under the beret.

In the foreword to his recent biography, David Cornwell, who writes his bestselling spy novels under the pen-name John le

Carré, asks if true stories can ever be told from memory. He writes that truth to a lawyer is fact unadorned, but to the creative writer fact is just raw material—an instrument to be used and not a taskmaster. He argues that first you invent yourself—then you get to believe your invention. If this is the case, I had my first moment of self-invention shortly after my head was shaved.

Trudging to school in my wire-frame glasses, wearing the beret, scraping my calliper along the dusty gravel—a moment when my self-pity should have been off the charts—I started

Sue, me, Jane, Dad and Michael.

giggling. It suddenly occurred to me just how daft I must look. Other kids hurtled past hurling insults but rather than bursting into tears, my default setting at home, I exaggerated my limp and revelled in the laughter this generated. I was learning that self-deprecation takes the sting out of almost any embarrassment if applied swiftly enough to the affected area. Self-mockery makes you if not a redundant target, then a less satisfying one at least. To paraphrase the Dalai Lama—what is the point of taking the piss out of someone if he is already drenched in his own urine?

The house we lived in is no longer there. It was bulldozed long ago. There is just an empty section filled with weeds next to the Rongotea Town Hall, where we went to concerts and fancy-dress parties. Girls had dancing lessons there. The village policeman, Bow Pike, very kindly took it upon himself to teach boys Graeco-Roman wrestling there. When he wasn't tirelessly throwing himself around on the mats demonstrating various holds on boys in string singlets and loose shorts, he sat on a box at dusk outside his house and played the bagpipes. Across the road a blacksmith forged horseshoes in a furnace that glowed orange in the gathering gloom. Dairy-factory chimneys and more church steeples than Vatican City were silhouetted against lipstick sunsets. It was like living in a Constable painting.

At the back of his long section, Bow Pike had a small orchard heavily laden with fruit. When my calliper was removed I scaled a high fence to steal some. He caught me and dragged me to an outside toilet, locked me in and went off to fetch something. I wasn't overly familiar with police procedure at this point in my life, but this didn't seem right.

It was a classic shithouse door made from vertical planks attached to a double 'Z' frame with a narrow gap at the bottom for ventilation. Something told me I didn't want to be there when Bow returned. I lay on my back and kicked like mad at the vertical planking. Two boards broke away and, like Peter Rabbit escaping Mr McGregor's garden, I wriggled out and raced to the fence, expecting to hear running steps, fierce blasts on a policeman's whistle and shouts of '*Stop, thief!*', but there was nothing apart from the thumping of my own heart. I wasn't sure of the statute of limitations on stolen apples, so I avoided eye contact with Bow after that, which wasn't necessary. He was frantically avoiding mine. Years later I read in the *Manawatu Evening Standard* that he had been sent to prison for buggering small boys. What had he gone to fetch, I ask myself. Vaseline? On second thoughts, maybe it was more like living in a painting by Brueghel.

Shortly before we left Rongotea, Mum walked Sue and me to the rugby clubrooms, where an upright piano and an uptight piano teacher were waiting. Sue and I sat mute with incomprehension while she went on and on about the need to practise scales on our piano at home. Finally, Sue interrupted her. 'Please, miss, we don't have a piano at home.' The teacher leaped to her feet and slapped her temple, screaming, '*Maoris are always doing this to me!*'

Mum was quite unruffled on the long walk home. 'Yee've had a music lesson, kids. Don't let anyone ever tell ye otherwise. Yer mother has ticked dat box for ye!'

CHAPTER FOUR

TELLING STORIES

ON A CANAL-BOATING HOLIDAY IN England in the spring of 1997—the spring that never sprung—we travelled down the Grand Union Canal towards Stratford-upon-Avon on a long-boat, *Brummagem Lass*, at full throttle—a pace so glacial pensioners wielding Zimmer frames caught up with us easily and eventually disappeared around bends in the towpath ahead. I didn't mind. With deep snow carpeting meadows and weeping willows draped in hoar frost, it was a world of crystalline beauty and hushed tranquillity. I half expected Ratty and Mole—well wrapped up—to come around the corner in a skiff. Glimpsing stately homes through curtains of oak and ash reminded me of something that I couldn't quite place.

In the Bard's place of birth it was demoralising not being able to afford tickets to the Royal Shakespeare Company's production of *A Midsummer Night's Dream*. Somewhat disconsolate, I took

washing to a laundromat instead. Waiting for the dryer to finish
I picked up a copy of *Tatler* and read about a gymkhana and a
girl with a name something like Lady Priscilla Burke-Pounding
coming first on a pony called Little Nigger Boy. I laughed out
loud. And it came to me. This stretch of England reminded me
of arriving in Feilding for the very first time in 1954.

We drove in from the south, up a broad boulevard lined with
tall trees and grand mansions. Feilding regularly wins the title of
New Zealand's prettiest town. Before the arrival of the wrecking
ball it had two magisterial picture theatres and a square lined
on all four sides with exquisite two-storey colonial architecture.
After Rongotea, things were looking up.

But our topdressing truck laden high with possessions
didn't slow. We kept heading north, through town out into flat
countryside and a farmhouse with a rotting verandah, another
copper that needed firing up, another outside toilet with a
can that needed emptying, and a clothesline sharing a house
paddock with moulting hens and grumpy Southdown rams

with scrotums so grotesquely swollen they could barely walk.

There were no rats, but the house was a little the worse for wear. Real estate agents talk about places being tired—this place was exhausted. The linoleum in the bathroom had brown lakes in it where it had worn through to the floorboards. Mum put up with it for several years, then used free sample pots of Dulux pastels to approximate the original pattern. Unable to afford a paintbrush, she dabbed on the colours with Dad's shaving brush. The end result looked like someone had eaten copious quantities of Frosty Jack shocking pink and lime green ice cream washed down with Blue Lagoon soft drink and then been violently sick.

Mum couldn't afford turps either. Despite her best efforts with Sunlight soap and scalding water, the bristles of the shaving brush solidified into something approximating a lobe of diseased liver. Understandably, Dad went apeshit. I admired Mum's strenuous denial of any involvement, despite standing on the proof.

I was recounting this tale for neighbours who lived two miles up Kimbolton Road when something immensely gratifying happened. Rosemary Ogle, a tall, sweet-natured, elegant woman, who had been laughing hysterically, suddenly exclaimed in surprise, 'Oh my God—I'm peeing my pants!' There can be no higher accolade.

The Ogles had a Romney stud farm with a spreading, handsome homestead, a circular driveway, a grass tennis court, and a cosy cluster of white stables, a woolshed and a barn. Their huge kitchen had a walk-in pantry and a walk-in cool room, where carcasses of lamb hung from hooks. The contrast with our place could not have been greater, and I loved being invited up there. Mrs Ogle would lean forward and ask sweetly, 'What's happening at home, Tommy?' And I was off like a racehorse on starter's orders, snitching on my family for cheap laughs, her hot scones and delicious homemade quince jam.

I told numerous stories about Sidney, Dad's giant worker who dragged bags of slag and superphosphate to the rear of our topdressing truck and emptied them into the hopper. This was a demanding, dusty, choking job that my brother Michael and I took over on Sidney's weekends off, which meant we developed forearms like blacksmiths well before puberty.

I told them Sidney's personal hygiene skills were somewhat rudimentary. Like one of the witches in *Macbeth*, her favourite play, Mum would emerge out of the steam swirling from the wood-fired copper in the washhouse and wave a furry wooden paddle at me, dangling colossal underpants smeared in excrement. 'Look at dis, would ye! The filthy bastard can't wipe his arse properly!'

I also told them how Sidney was deadly with a shanghai and could shatter ceramic power-pole insulator cups from 50 yards, and how he once knocked a female possum clean out of a macrocarpa tree. Sister Sue found a bald, blind baby possum in its pouch that we brought home and fed with an eye-dropper.

The wallpaper in the kids' bedroom hung down like Everglades moss, which the possum loved running up as it got bigger, until it reached critical mass and started stripping the paper and hessian off entirely as it climbed, exposing bare dusty sarking.

Mum, Sue and I went to work with flour-and-water paste and newspaper and relined the room, transforming it into a papier-mâché cube. When it eventually dried, I painted the walls blue, added a coral reef, bright tropical fish and a pirates' chest spilling doubloons. My crowning touch was a large cardboard shark hanging from the ceiling. Kids up and down Kimbolton Road, who had swags of Meccano sets, Hornby trains, Enid Blyton books, *Rupert* annuals, dolls and dolls' houses, abandoned them in droves to visit my undersea world.

It was the same with the submarine Micky and I built in the house paddock out of a rusting, corrugated-iron water tank that we tipped on its side. The Ogles, Hoggards and Hennigans had rubbish dumps filled with treasure at the bottom of banks at the back of their farms. Rummaging around in the bush and blackberry that lined the meandering Oroua River we came home laden with old radios, lamps, engine parts, broken Douglas chairs—just what you need in a German U-boat. Most highly prized of all was a World War One gas mask, which obviously the captain of the submarine wore in case the rest of the crew were overcome with fumes—always a risk 10,000 leagues beneath the sea. Most of the fuming came from our father: 'Clean this shit up. It's like a Māori pa around here!'

Michael, Sally and me.

STORY-TELLING DIDN'T START WITH THE Ogles. In the primers when they called for morning talks, my hand was always the first up. One Monday I was describing how I had been to the planet Mars at the weekend. The teacher sighed and gently suggested that I might be exaggerating. I pointed to the dumbest boy in the class. 'Gary came with me, didn't you, Gary?' Thrilled to be included in this epic voyage into space, even if the details were of necessity somewhat hazy, Gary obligingly said yes. She gave up at this point.

I broke myself of this habit next spring when mother ducks followed by waddling trains of ducklings appeared on the Hennigans' pond just beyond the woolshed. I got up before dawn, crept into the flax bushes and kidnapped a tiny duckling for my morning talk. I carried it home carefully and tucked it just under the rim of a sack full of potatoes in the washhouse. I would smuggle it to school in my lunchbox later. It would be a triumph. It would make me a star.

Halfway through breakfast I sneaked out to check on it. It is not by accident that the term 'dead duck' has entered the lexicon. I rolled back the sacking and there it was—still cute, but stiff as a board with its tiny webbed feet pointing skyward. I disposed of the body in tears and returned to the table weighed down with remorse.

We didn't have many books at home, but we had a radio that I listened to faithfully every night after dinner right through to bedtime. After that, when a suitable interval had passed, I crept into the hall and lay on the floor next to the living-room door and listened some more to it blaring through the cracks. Often my laughter during *The Goon Show* gave me away, yet despite clips around the ears from my father, I was always back again the following night.

I loved knowing what was happening in the world. My favourite words were, 'To end the news, here are the main points again...' Most afternoons in Standard 3 we had a general knowledge quiz, which I loved. I was devastated when my classmates eventually complained that it wasn't fair because I knew all the answers. The teacher agreed and I was banned from taking part. It was the same when it came to telling jokes. I sulked badly when I was told I had to let other kids have a turn. My twin sister Sue, normally shy and retiring, was finally able to participate.

Sue is the life and soul of every party now, a terrific painter and a very funny woman, able to tell shocking stories against herself. After her first trip overseas she freely admitted she was staggered to find in France that they didn't speak English with a French accent. When I had finished laughing I asked her why she had thought that would be the case. 'That's how it is in the movies.' Then she grinned. 'It gets worse. When I got off the plane in Los Angeles on the way over, I was so proud that New Zealand companies like Coca-Cola, Hertz and Kellogg's had taken over the world.'

Very few photographs were taken of us together as children. Those that do exist depict me squinting cautiously at the camera, bracing myself for something, and Sue looking dazed, her mouth slightly agape, also expecting the worst. Half in jest, she says her school days were miserable because of me. Teachers kept asking her why she wasn't as clever as her brother Tommy. You would never tire of hearing it. I wasn't solely to blame. She was severely traumatised by the actions of a troubled boy I'll just call Paul, whose colossal, terrifying mother came to fetch him after school in shapeless hillbilly garments, gumboots and an apron made from a fraying sack.

One morning, Paul was shrieking repeatedly that he needed to do a poo. The teacher didn't believe him, refused to let him go to the toilet and exiled him to the cloakroom instead. Plastic was all the latest rage. Sue was very proud of her new plastic lunchbox, and come the midday bell raced into the cloakroom to find her lunch on the floor and a steaming turd in its place. It could have been worse. It could have been my lunchbox and with my eyesight I may not have noticed the switch until it was too late.

So when one day Sue announced shyly that she had a joke to tell it was an encouraging sign that she was finally coming out of her shell. I parked my frustration to one side and listened to her tell a story about a woman who had a dog called 'Tits Wobble'. One day, said Sue, Tits Wobble went missing, so this woman went to the police station. The teacher looked alarmed at this point and shot Sue a warning look, but she would not be denied. Not this time. In a surprisingly clear, strong voice, she described how the woman went up to the counter in the police station and asked the policeman if he had seen her Tits Wobble. 'No,' said the policeman. 'But I'd like to.'

That afternoon the school bus had barely slowed to a halt outside our driveway when I was off, streaking indoors to snitch on Sue. She got her own back some months later when Mum was waiting on the roadside in an agitated state to tell us that our father had been seriously hurt in an accident and rushed to hospital. I started blubbing, asking between racking sobs if he was going to die. Mum immediately downgraded the serious accident to a flesh wound. That night at the imitation Formica,

Sue turned to our father and said, 'Guess what, Dad? When Mum told us you were hurt in an accident, Tommy was the only one who cried.' I felt tears welling up again, but she wasn't done. 'And you don't even like him!' I started blubbing again. My father looked stricken with guilt before regaining his composure.

'Would someone fetch the weeping bowl for Egghead, please? The Royal Weeping Bowl with the diamonds and the rubies in the rim! Tis a grand weep he's having and he deserves only the finest weeping bowl!'

I was banished to my undersea world where, even as I was feeling sorry for myself, I marvelled at the richness of his language. Weeping bowl was brilliant!

THERE WERE MANY NIGHTS LIKE this. After my expulsion there would be a tapping on glass. Mum would have run around the house paddock in the dark, dodging rams and the U-boat to hand my unfinished meals in through a window.

When Woolworths announced a 'draw your dad' competition for Father's Day—first prize was goods to the value of ten shillings from its Feilding store—I just had to draw the man responsible for 'weeping bowl'. Sitting a discreet distance away, at an angle where he couldn't see me, I sketched him in pencil while he listened to the radio.

On the day the winners were announced, I cycled to Woollies after school and checked out the two dozen or so badly drawn entries displayed in their front window. Mine was clearly the best by several light years, but to my stinging disappointment a blob barely recognisable as a higher primate, let alone a human face, had won first prize. I wasn't even highly commended.

Feeling hard done by, I cycled home and complained bitterly to my mother. I felt a fresh stab of horror when Mum said she wasn't putting up with this, leaped on her bike and started pedalling furiously into town. I could barely keep up.

'It doesn't matter Mum, really...' I yelled as she crouched low over the handlebars like Lance Armstrong leading the peloton through the French Alps. When we arrived she flung her bike to the ground, pedals still spinning, and stomped indoors. I could hear shouting, then Mum emerged, hurling curses back into the interior. In disgust she reported that the manager's excuse was that no child my age could possibly have drawn that picture, and they didn't reward cheats.

I learned then that there is such a thing as being too good, or at least making it too obvious. Richard Prebble put it best when he said of a former Labour cabinet colleague, 'Michael Cullen is too clever by three quarters!' I learned this lesson again when my father taught me chess. I don't know why, but I boasted to friends at school that the pieces of our set were carved out of solid white ivory and very rare black ivory. They demanded proof, and I had to lie again, saying that the set was too precious to take out of the house. In fact, they were cheap plastic, and hollow, which was just as well. With increasing frequency, heart in mouth, I started whispering, 'Checkmate, Dad . . .' and he invariably swept the pieces off the table in a fury.

This meant I wasn't particularly looking forward to driving with him to Wellington for my long-promised eye operation. We didn't have a car then; our mode of transport was my father's khaki, ex-army, 4x4 Chev with weed-spraying booms folded over the front. It resembled a metallic insect at prayer.

The whole family came out to the gate to say goodbye. Mum tearfully handed me a ten-shilling note that she couldn't afford. Twenty seconds later, as we were reversing onto Kimbolton Road, I managed to lose it. I blurted this out to my father. He cuffed me angrily about the head and I began crying softly and didn't stop for ages. Not a word was exchanged between us the whole trip. The engine was so loud, conversation would have been difficult anyway, even without me whimpering and sniffling.

The Porirua motorway was under construction. Four-wheel-drive engaged, we slithered and slewed through slushy orange clay for what seemed like hours. When we finally arrived at Wellington Hospital my father handed me over monosyllabically to the staff. Clutching my pressed-cardboard school suitcase containing my pyjamas, a toothbrush and a packet of butterscotch hard-boiled sweets, I watched him depart, both of us dry-eyed. Doctors and nurses commended my courage and made a huge fuss of me, but in truth I felt only relief and something close to elation at seeing him go. I was soon busy endearing myself to older patients, soaking up their attention and approval like blotting paper.

Before the ether general anaesthetic I was given a spoonful of strawberry jam that aroused suspicion. It hid a bitter pill, a sedative. I don't know why, but even today I can be eating a croissant and jam and the same bitter taste will flood my mouth. By the same token, in moments of joy and elation my mouth fills with the taste of butterscotch. I have no explanation for this.

Egghead at Rongotea – 11/4/1952

After the operation my eyes were swathed in bandages, rendering me sightless for two weeks, one of which was spent at Calvary Hospital in Wellington. There is no painless way to remove sticking plaster from eyebrows, and I dreaded having my bandages changed by nurses and nuns, who realised it had to be done in one swift yank. I had no visitors. Feilding was too far away. Parents of local children adopted me and I amused them with Sidney stories as well. I was in full pluck mode. I didn't need to actually see people laughing. All I needed was to hear it.

I STILL NEEDED GLASSES, BUT afterwards my eyesight was good enough to play rugby without them. Half-blind, I tended to run unwittingly into other boys, which delighted teachers and parents on the sideline because they saw it as naked aggression. Working on the topdressing truck in the weekends meant I was stronger than other boys my age, and whenever a rugby ball swum into focus I could pretty much wrench it off anyone or out of any maul. I had no other skills but these two attributes alone marked me as a player of potential.

Mr Sullivan, my teacher in Standard 5, a thoroughly decent, roly-poly man, who sometimes drove the school bus and always smelled as if he hadn't washed his hands thoroughly after going to the toilet, was determined to get me in the top team, but I would have to go on a strict diet to meet the weight requirements. Two weeks of agonising denial followed. I woke on the morning of the big weigh-in so hungry I could have eaten my own underpants, only to discover they were in the wash. I only had the one pair. It meant secretly borrowing a pair of my father's voluminous Y-fronts. Their buttery appearance unnerved me, but Mum assured me they were not Sidney's.

I pulled them on with a heavy heart. There seemed to be yards and yards of surplus cloth, which I tied up in a big knot at the front. They bunched between my legs and almost reached my knees. I looked like Gandhi in his dhoti if you can imagine Gandhi with legs like a Russian shot-putter. It was a struggle pulling my shorts over the top.

At school, Mr Sullivan marched us to the grocery store down the road. In the shed out the back there were Avery platform scales with a side-arm and sliding weights. On these scales sacks of sugar, flour and salt were measured out into smaller brown paper bags. We lined up in bare feet to stand on the tray. I hung back while other boys passed easily.

Finally, it was my turn. As I feared, bone density came into play again. The instant I stepped on the platform, the side-arm jerked skywards. 'Take off your shirt!' boomed Sullivan. It made no difference. 'Take off your singlet!' It still made no difference. 'Off with your shorts, lad!' I was most reluctant. 'Come on, boy, I haven't got all day!' Utterly heartsick, I began tugging and wrestling down my tight shorts.

I'll always be grateful to Mr Sullivan for what happened next. When previously compressed fabric, relishing its freedom, began billowing from my crotch much like those CGI reenactments of the Big Bang you see on astronomy documentaries, he started screaming, 'Pull them up! Pull them up!'

It meant that as an eleven-year-old I played rugby against teenagers from local high schools. My voice wouldn't drop for another three years and then only to the tones of a strangled tenor, yet here I was sharing changing sheds with guys with chests carpeted in Velcro and genitals that thwacked against their thighs. One huge boy used to push into the hottest part of the showers, bellowing, 'I can stand the shit if you can stand the pain.' People tended to get out of his way. Coming back on the bus from rep team trials held on vast Ongley Park, not that much smaller than the Serengeti, in Palmerston North, rather than calling for a toilet stop to get rid of the illicit beer he had guzzled, he insisted that we lift him flush against a narrow skylight in the roof so he could pee with the jet-stream. Unfortunately, gravity proved the stronger force and urine sprayed back into the coach.

CHAPTER FIVE

THE ONLY BOY WITH COURAGE

LATER THAT WINTER I SPENT two weekends in hospital with concussion, and a very wise doctor advised that I give rugby away. This gave me more time to devote to my morbid fear that the world was on the edge of nuclear annihilation—Soviet premier Nikita Khrushchev had just banged his shoe on the table at the UN General Assembly, saying warm and cuddly things like, 'We will bury you!' Other kids may have known how babies were made; I certainly didn't, but in Standard 6 I knew the difference between nuclear fission and nuclear fusion, and I knew that the Enola Gay, the B-29 Superfortress that dropped the atomic bomb on Hiroshima, was named after the mother of the pilot, Colonel Paul Tibbets. And I loved Albert Einstein's grim joke that he didn't know what weapons would be used in World War Three, but he was pretty sure he knew what would be used in World War Four: sticks and stones. I was discovering that humour could be used to make a serious point. I tucked that trick away.

I answered to Tommy, Junior and Egghead at home, and my nicknames at school included Four Eyes, Professor and Teacher's Pet. There was some truth in the latter in Mr Goodwin's class. He took a shine to me, delighting in my endless queries about isotopes of uranium even though he couldn't answer any of them. I had my own box of coloured chalks under the lift-up lid of my desk. When other teachers came calling on my services to draw Captain Cook's *Endeavour* or a fortified Māori pā on their blackboards, Goody waved me off proudly, no doubt relieved to get some respite. He had been in Bomber Command in the war and suffered from what we now call post-traumatic stress disorder.

Lots of teachers came back from with the war with injuries. An English teacher at my high school had lost an eye and was called 'Bung' Evans. He made us squeeze into one side of the classroom where he could see us all. Our gym teacher, Doug Thorley, like Hitler, had only one ball—the other had been shot off in the Battle of Arnhem. He wasn't called anything because we liked him and he taught boxing. If you gave him any cheek he insisted you glove up, then smacked the snot out of you while pretending to offer coaching tips. Brilliant!

They were both completely sane. Poor old Goody went 'doolally' from time to time—slang I learned later derived from an Indian town famous for its military sanatorium. There was no warning. One minute he was at the blackboard, perfectly normal—the next he was under his desk whimpering about Messerschmitts at ten o'clock. Our tall, gaunt headmaster, who walked stiffly like a whooping crane, would gently lead him away like one of his chicks, and return with a relieving teacher.

These changes in routine affected a boy called Mervin, who had one leg withered by polio. Perhaps in unconscious pursuit of healing calcium, he would dazzle us by drinking half a crate of warm school milk on his own. One relief teacher was exceptionally pretty, and in a macho display Merv polished off an entire crate. Staggering back to his desk after the bell, his limp more pronounced than ever, Merv spewed close to half a drum of curds and whey onto the floor. Despite a massive mopping-up operation the classroom stank like a third-world cheese factory in a power outage.

Merv was banished to the storeroom, where there was a hole in the wall just below the blackboard. Grabbing a broom, Merv inserted the handle through the opening and with uncanny timing, considering he was unsighted, pelvic-thrusted it at her when her backside faced the blackboard. I only dimly appreciated the sexual connotations of this act, but I joined in the laughter anyway. I also joined in the chant of, 'We want Goody! We want Goody!', accompanied by loud slapping on our desks. It was tremendous fun until she fled in tears and a guilty silence descended.

Our headmaster, bending low, went down the first row of desks asking every child in turn, 'Did you chant, "We want Goody"?' All he got was a shaking of heads and whispered denials. This continued when he headed down the second row towards me. He knew all about my box of coloured chalks and paused hopefully before me.

'Tommy, did you chant, "We want Goody"?'

'No,' I lied.

Disappointed, he turned to the boy beside me, Reon, who collapsed in sobs before the question was even asked.

'I did! I did! And so did everyone else! It wasn't just me! It wasn't just me! Everyone did!'

Tears streamed down his face and snot blasted out of his nostrils and dangled from his quivering lips. In an Oscar-worthy performance, the headmaster patted Reon's convulsing shoulders, squared his own, straightened to his considerable full height and declared in ringing tones, '*The only boy with courage!*'

MY STANDARD 6 YEAR WAS the year that Peter Snell won gold in the mile at the Rome Olympics. The commentary was replayed over and over on the radio. The truly fortunate saw it in black and white on the *Movietone News* before the main feature at the pictures. It was a magical, wondrous triumph. The *Weekly News* devoted the whole of its pink front cover to Snell breaching the tape, while the reigning world champion, the mighty Roger Moens, looked across in despair and disbelief. Snell's arms are outstretched, his head is tilted back, his eyes are shut, his mouth agape—it is exactly the same as the look on the face of Bernini's masterpiece *The Ecstasy of St Teresa*. Marble made flesh, housed in a glorious chapel just a few miles from the Olympic stadium. All of New Zealand shared in the ecstasy as well.

I studied that pink cover for hours and painstakingly drew a pencil copy in my school exercise book. When I showed it to the class I was besieged with requests for copies. This was before Xerox machines. I spent the next two weeks drawing Peter Snell. It was the perfect way to end my days at primary school.

Our Kimbolton Road days were drawing to an end as well. We were poorer than everyone else, but apart from the Ogles no one seemed conspicuously wealthy. Other mums dropped off fruit, vegetables and surplus clothing but they did it in such a way that it felt like incidental kindness rather than charity.

Christmas Days could be jarring, however. Other kids got presents galore and we got one thing each, unwrapped, accompanied by an orange. One Christmas I got a toy rifle that fired caps. I was chuffed.

That afternoon the Mason family paid a visit. Betty Mason came out to New Zealand on the *Tamaroa* with Mum, Sue and me. Betty was a blunt Yorkshirewoman given to saying things like 'There's nowt queer as folk', but she had a good heart. We referred to her fondly as 'Aunty Betty'. Her husband, Eric, who had been in the RNZAF with Dad, was a constant moaner, and we delighted in our father's private nickname for him: 'Uncle Ear-ache'.

Their oldest boy, Trevor, was a bit of a tearaway. While the parents drank beer, sipped sherry and nibbled Christmas cake, we headed off to the Hennigans' pond to scare the ducks. Trevor quickly realised that caps were of no real use in close-quarter, human-to-duck combat so, holding my new rifle by the barrel, he used the stock as a club on a fleeing drake, snapping the gun in two and leaving the bird dazed but still in one piece. I trudged home disconsolately with my dismembered gun. It was barely four o'clock in the afternoon.

'Never mind,' said my father tartly. 'It lasted and lasted.'

Birthdays weren't much chop either. One year Sue and I each got a book of morality tales for children that Mum had purchased from Mormon missionaries who went door to door. The books were the print equivalent of cod-liver oil. We both burst into tears and were inconsolable little shits. Mum apologised frantically as we boarded the school bus, pleading that it was all she could afford. When we got home we discovered she had push-biked into town to buy us another, more acceptable present each—an eight-mile return trip—and had prepared a lavish birthday tea of ice cream *and* jelly.

Suitably mollified, I got into bed that night and out of idle curiosity reached for the book that I didn't want a bar of earlier. The very first tale was called *The Dog in the Manger*. A chill swept through me. I was familiar with Aesop's fable about the selfish dog who wouldn't let tired oxen eat any of the straw in the barn, even though he couldn't eat it himself. The story was about a self-centred boy who was mean to his mother. I lay awake for hours sick with guilt.

It was a more innocent age then. The Whooping Crane called one assembly to tell us that someone had been murdered in New Zealand, but we weren't to worry—because it was in the South Island. The Scott kids roamed freely between the Kiwitea Stream to the west, which ran beside Battersby's bush, home to an escaped boar we could hear crashing in the fern, and the Oroua River to the west, home to Johnson's bush and Scout huts that we were forever trying to break into with no luck. We came home many nights after dark. No search parties were ever sent out.

It was even better in the rain. Dry gullies became creeks, and streams raging rivers. A boy called Grant Major, who proudly wore a lemon-squeezer hat, a green shirt festooned with merit badges and a neckerchief tied with a bone toggle to school one day a week, every week, all through primary school, forgot the Scout's motto, *be prepared*, in his final year. He crossed a swing bridge over the Oroua River in flood and was swept to his death.

This didn't slow us down. Many an afternoon when we shot off exploring, John Ridd, who owned the farm we lived on, would be leaning on his staff on the sloping ground below our kitchen window talking to Mum. He would still be there three hours later, hanging on her every trilled word, laughing at her stories in the gathering dusk, clearly in no hurry to go to his brand-new, sprawling mansion up the road. At the time, we thought nothing of the fact that Mr Ridd could lean on his shepherd's crook and talk to our mother for hours nearly every day. Looking back, it is obvious now that he was fixated on her, and Mum was flattered by the attention. Years later, she hinted to me and my sister Sue that John Ridd overstepped the mark on occasion. It was an open secret that our father's drinking was getting worse and Mum wasn't happy. Mr Ridd offered to take her away from it all. She must have been sorely tempted. He was a very wealthy man. Our father got wind of this, however, words were exchanged and Dad did the taking away—to a run-down farm cottage on Makino Road.

Cream with a brown trim where the paint hadn't peeled, it huddled beneath morose pines in a damp hollow. In the paddock next door were rotting pigsties, a prolapsed cowshed and farm implements rusting in long grass. Our landlord was Stan Beezer, who believed that aliens built the Pyramid of Cheops and they were coming back soon to take over the planet, so fixing things made no sense but charging rent did. In heavy rain the house leaked so badly that every spare Agee preserving jar and every pot and pan had to be strategically placed to catch the drips.

Our father's drinking got worse. Lawns stopped being mowed and broken windows were boarded up. Some mornings, trudging up the drive to catch the school bus, we passed vomit dripping from the windowsill of the marital chamber. Poor Mum. With the arrival of Robbie, then Sal, there were six kids to feed and clothe. She complained bitterly about not being able to afford knickers for herself, which of course my father would have misinterpreted. She went into a trance-like state listening to ball-by-ball cricket commentaries coming from Lord's and Trent Bridge. It briefly transported her back to soft English summers. Many a night I went to bed wondering what I could do to make her life better, then I would remind myself, hey, I'm still a boy. There was nothing I could do but help with the dishes, hang out washing and pick the daffodils that grew wild near the creek and place them in Agee jars to brighten the gloomy lounge.

WITH HIGH SCHOOL BECKONING, OUR father announced that he wouldn't mind paying for high-school uniforms if they weren't compulsory, but because they were, Feilding Agricultural High School could get fucked as far as he was concerned. It wasn't the money, he insisted, it was the principle. Mum dispatched Sue and I off to Cobbs' department store in Feilding's square. A woman in a black dress and white blouse with a ruffle collar, who could have stepped straight out of *Are You Being Served?*, helped us with the fittings, then asked us how we were going to pay for the uniforms. Sue shrank back and let me do the talking. I still had traces of a bad stutter. I took a deep breath.

'Mum wants you to put it on her account.'

'Your mother doesn't have an account with us.'

'That's the other thing. Mum wants to open an account . . .'

Sue was dragooned into accompanying me to elocution lessons to cure my stutter. She protested loudly the whole bike ride to the speech therapist in Feilding. 'It's not fair. I'm not the spastic!'

The woman had shocking halitosis. Clive James has described someone's halitosis as being so bad it started undoing his tie. Her breath started melting the enamel in my teeth. She pressed her face close to mine and shouted, 'REPEAT AFTER ME: HOW NOW BROWN COW!', spraying me with fine particulate matter into the bargain. I'm not sure if they were available back then, but I would liken the effect to her having eaten half a chub of garlic-flavoured dog sausage. I cycled home with Sue, vowing to never go back, and my stutter, that had been getting progressively worse as puberty beckoned, vanished without trace overnight.

CHAPTER SIX

EGGHEAD HAS FAILED!

AT HIGH SCHOOL, SUE WAS shunted into home craft and I was drafted into the top academic stream, 3P1, where I hardly knew a soul. To my class-conscious eyes they seemed to me to be the spawn of Feilding's aristocracy, if a small country town can have such a thing. Confident, carefree children of doctors, dentists, lawyers, accountants, bank managers, haberdashers, header-harvester salesmen, seed and grain merchants, freezing-works bosses, plus a few heirs to vast pastoral estates. For the first time I felt out of place in the one place I had always felt right at home—school. It didn't help that I was assigned another boy with thick glasses as my desk mate—Wesley Bell, the short, chubby son of a Methodist minister. We were both nerdy and my guess is the teachers felt we'd be good company for each other, and this seating arrangement wouldn't punish two other kids unnecessarily.

Wes asked me in a whisper if I had been invited to Russell McLean's party. Russell was a tall, plump boy with no discernible knees. His legs were like wedges of camembert cheese. The thick ends of the wedge emerged from his long shorts and the sharp ends vanished into his socks—which were always pulled up. He was the son of 'Fatty' McLean, the headmaster. They lived in the two-storey residence attached to the boarding school in the school grounds.

I hadn't been invited to Russell's party. Nor had Wes. Everyone else in 3P1 had. This pattern was repeated right through to the seventh form, with Wes and I sharing the Cinderella role. Russell's dad didn't like me much either. Reading out the list of pupils accredited University Entrance, Fatty glowered when he got to me and said that the following name gave him no pleasure at all. What had I ever done to him?

Oh yes, at the end of every term every form gave an end-of-term report in front of the whole school. In spite of feeling like the class leper, I must have amused my classmates because they nominated me for the task at the end of the first term in that first year, and they kept nominating me every term for the rest of my time at Feilding Ag. Other class spokespeople talked earnestly about trips to nature reserves, teachers who had just gotten engaged, or someone in their form excelling in some external music exam or gymnastic event—all very dull to most pupils, who would never excel in anything except stealing cars and teenage pregnancy. I shamelessly ransacked *Reader's Digest* for jokes, made up some of my own, and did three minutes of stand-up where I mocked teachers and classmates who shone. The assembly loved it. The staff and Fatty hated it.

I was in full flight one assembly condemning the 'cheek and audacity' of a teacher when Fatty spotted his chance to deliver some comeuppance. Rising to his feet—always a struggle—and adjusting his black gown like an obese raven flapping its wings, he loftily asked me to explain the difference between cheek and audacity. 'Spelling, mainly!' I responded cheerfully, to loud laughter and foot stomping from the school.

Fatty got his own back at prizegiving in my final year—

making sure I wasn't given any. There were about fourteen of us in the seventh form. Classmate after classmate got prize after prize, award after award. Some were vanishing from view behind stalagmites of books such as Winston Churchill's *A History of the English-Speaking Peoples* and the collected works of Charles Dickens. I got nothing, a fact not lost on the rest of the school. Everyone in the seventh form, however, got Higher Leaving Certificate no matter what, so when my name was finally called and I walked cockily to the stage, the packed stadium went crazy. The applause from pupils seemed to roll on and on while Fatty went puce and called for order. I was wondering if I had imagined this, until a few days later a local clergyman clutched me in the street to express his astonishment and congratulate me. He didn't say it was the second coming exactly but that was the inference I took.

I have been the guest speaker at two Feilding Ag prizegiving evenings since then. I disgraced myself on the second occasion and I doubt that I'll be invited back. Pointing to the gleaming kauri honours boards hung around the walls bearing students' names written in gold, I told the assembly that they wouldn't see my name on any of them and they wouldn't recognise any of the other names, 'because these kids peaked in high school!' I added quickly that ideally you should peak on your deathbed, but it was too late for the appalled staff on stage with me. Heresy had been committed. I could hear ice crystals tinkling in the air. Somewhere Fatty McLean is still spinning in his grave. Well, revolving slowly at least.

I CUT AN ABJECT, LONELY figure in my early weeks at high school. It was a stinking-hot summer. There was a teaching hiatus during which staff battled to set the timetable. Boys had military drill, disassembling Bren guns and drinking warm lemon cordial from metal milk urns, while in an adjacent sports field the girls tucked their skirts into their knickers and danced with hoops. We had separate swimming sessions in the school baths. This puzzled me until I stepped inside the eight-foot-high wall surrounding the swimming pool and saw hairy masters and boys frolicking together, buck naked. In shock I huddled as inconspicuously as I could high in the stands alongside a doughy boy, who introduced himself as Anderton the younger. His older brother was a prefect in the boarding house and his duties included wank patrols of the dormitories after lights out. I was thirteen, but had absolutely no idea what he was talking about.

'What's a wank?' Anderton shifted uncomfortably when he could see I wasn't having him on. He lowered his voice.

'You play with your cock until stuff comes out.' I reeled back in disgust.

'What's the fun in that?'

Deciding not to be too hasty, I gave it a try that night. I thought for a few terrifying moments that I was bleeding and that I might be anaemic, but the panic was fleeting. I quickly realised that if I dedicated myself to the task and was prepared to put in the hours like an aspiring concert pianist or tennis professional, this was something at which I could excel. And so it proved to be, if only to a rapt, appreciative gallery of one.

At primary school, during what I call my Peter Snell period, it baffled me when high-school boys on the bus twisted my arms up my back, demanding I draw pictures of naked women with legs akimbo for them. They insisted on anatomical precision. Luckily their knowledge in these matters was as imprecise as mine, and they went weak at the knees at anything circular. After my bringing-up-to-speed from Anderton Minor their appetite for such imagery made more sense.

Apart from the *Daily Mirror* comic strip 'Jane', about a gorgeous, leggy ingénue constantly falling out of her clothing, only available in intermittent airmail omnibus editions, there was no virtually no pornography of any kind readily available. One day I noticed that full-page ads for women's lingerie in the *Manawatu Evening Standard* were printed so badly that bra and knicker tones were barely distinguishable from the surrounding flesh. With a few deft strokes of my trusty 2B pencil I was able to fashion nipples and alluring triangles of pubic hair. These were immediately put to good use, and when I had sufficiently recovered I destroyed the evidence lest it fall into the wrong hands. Homemade erotica can only take you so far.

One afternoon in the abandoned cowshed I found an old milking cup with rubber lips that I thought, suitably lubricated, might approximate the real thing. Years later I was able to confirm what I suspected at the time—it didn't. Not even close. I'll spare you the details, but I climbed out of the iron vat I'd been hiding in and traipsed home wretched with guilt, self-loathing and despair.

A week later I noticed for the very first time tiny, slightly raised lumps, not quite pimples, on either side of the dorsal vein of my penis where it emerged from the pot-scrub of ginger hair. Sebaceous glands are common in adolescent males and become more visible when skin is stretched for whatever reason. A ten-year-old boy with access to internet porn knows this now. I did not know this back then. All I knew was that a suitable incubation period had passed since the hugely disappointing milking-cup experiment and I trembled with terror. It was blindingly obvious. I had caught venereal disease. Worse, I was still a virgin. It was doubly wounding and humiliating. How could I explain this to our family doctor?

Dear old Doc Mowbray made house calls when we were kids. He gave me one of his fountain pens that smelled deliciously of his pipe tobacco. He had diagnosed my inflamed appendix and had me rushed to hospital just as it was about to burst. I was still alive in significant measure due to him. How could I sit opposite him while he carefully put away his magnifying glass before turning back to me, eyes brimming with tears, to report that I had the pox? And not just any old pox, in this instance cow pox. It implied bestiality—a criminal act as well as a sin. It was a deeply scalding, shameful secret that I would have to take to my grave.

It meant girlfriends were out of the question. There were other factors that made this prohibition easier for me than it would have been for other boys (apart from Wes, obviously). I had mousy curls bordering on ginger. I wore heavy glasses that refused to sit straight on my head. I was badly knock-kneed, with a scythe-like sweep of my right leg—even today I can be crossing a street and see a ridiculous reflection in a shop window, start to giggle, then realise with horror that it is my own.

BUT I WASN'T GOING TO let venereal disease completely destroy my life. I went to the first high-school dance because I still had long pants that fitted (only just—they stopped just below my shins). Dad drove us there in his newly purchased second-hand Vauxhall Velox, with his old Air Force chum, Jock Laidlaw, in the front passenger seat, both of them giggling drunk. Sue and I sat nervously in the back.

Fatty's imposing house was attached to the boarding school and had a circular drive that Dad thought we should drive around, tooting the horn. In the middle of the circuit he decided to park at the front door, still tooting furiously. Jock was in hysterics. Sue and I were horrified. Fatty's unmistakable silhouette approached down a corridor towards the glass door then, like an eclipse of the sun, blocked all the light apart from a thin corona. The door opened. Fatty stepped out. My father fumbled with the keys. Fatty waddled towards us. The car stalled. Fatty gathered speed—no mean feat in itself. The Velox kicked into life and we lurched off with Fatty shaking his fist at our departing tail-lights. Jock was paralytic with laughter and Dad was slumped over the steering wheel, gasping for breath. They had had such a good time they decided to do it again, tooting the horn continuously but not stopping this time. Sue and I asked to be let out down the road so we could not be linked to this incident, and slunk into the school hall.

I was having a great time until I couldn't find my dance partner. The hall was partitioned with planters filled with shrubbery. Soaked to the skin in sweat, I was rehydrating with soft drink when I heard her voice coming from the other side of the greenery. 'Don't dance with Tommy Scott. He's a terrible dancer!' It was a knife to the heart. I sat out high-school dances after this, and have avoided dancing to this day.

Sue had a great night though, and was keen to go the following year. Mum helped her make a new frock specially, which took weeks. Sue kept asking our father, 'You will take me, won't you, Dad? You won't forget?' He got irritated.

'How many times do I have to say yes, for shit's sake?'

On the night, Sue was ready with her hair beautifully done by six. At seven there was no sign of our father. At eight we feared the worst. At nine Sue took off her frock, folded it away neatly, went to bed and cried herself to sleep. The next day I told our father he owed Sue an apology and he hurled a plate of food against the wall—which brought this particular topic of discussion to a close.

IN THE FOURTH AND FIFTH forms, my school clothes were pretty much the only clothes I owned. On mufti day, when you could wear what you liked, the only kids turning up in school uniform were Māori kids and me. To break this trend in the fifth form, on mufti day, after my father had left for work, I borrowed his tweed jacket, corduroy pants and brown brogues. It was before my growth spurt, so nothing fitted properly. Everything was outsized and baggy like a clown's outfit.

No one said a thing all day. I thought I had pulled it off until the very last period, when Christine Wilson suddenly blurted out, 'Tommy's wearing his father's clothes!' Every head swivelled. She was a lovely girl incapable of cruelty. It must have been shock that triggered her announcement. She later wrote the screenplay of one of the great Australian films, *Rabbit-Proof Fence*, under her married name, Christine Olsen.

I didn't socialise with anyone in my class. Not making the cut to Russell's parties still stung, so I made sure I rejected the other kids before they had a chance to reject me. After school I cycled straight home, dawdling for hours if necessary if other kids on bikes were with me because I didn't want anyone seeing where we lived.

My father had spent much of the previous winter soldering up and assembling a kitset transistor radio the size of a sewing machine, which had pride of place in the master bedroom, home now to brand-new twin beds with blonde-oak headrests with shelving, the candlewick bedspreads always immaculately made up. The local radio station started playing pop-chart songs late in the afternoons. At the appointed hour I crept in. To leave no trace of my intrusion, I lay on the floor between the beds and switched on the transistor. It was from this prone position that I heard something that made me sit bolt upright with a feeling approaching pure joy coursing through my body.

It was instantly familiar yet stunningly different. It had a shuffle beat, raw, urgent harmonica and glorious harmonies infused with yearning. It was *Love Me Do* by a group I'd never heard of—The Beatles.

Their sudden global ascension was the one shaft of sunlight in a year made dark by the assassination of President Kennedy, which was also Fatty's finest hour. He told sobbing girls in assembly that a terrible thing had happened but America would survive this tragedy and the world wasn't coming to an end. It made up for the time he told assembly that there had been too much thieving from lockers, that he knew who was responsible, he was going to stamp it out—and could all the Māori pupils stay behind please.

In the wake of the assassination I fantasised that I was a brilliant brain surgeon, able to piece Kennedy's cerebral cortex back together and make the whole world happy again. It was my own cerebral cortex that needed fixing. I was swimming laps in a pool of my own sorrow. Photos exist of me smiling happily with baby brother Rob on my knee, then a few years later, baby Sal, yet such was my self-absorption in the Makino Road years I barely remember my siblings at all.

Michael was cheerful and robust. He fell in love with The Beatles as well and somehow acquired an acoustic guitar and devoted most of his time to learning that. Together we built a two-storey tree hut in a spreading macrocarpa and beautiful little Jane was allowed to play with us in that. She came with us on raiding parties over the hill to Feilding's lawn cemetery to loot marble angels that we brought home in triumph—which had Mum frantically crossing herself and wailing that we would all burn in hell.

Robbie was approaching school age and I read him stories before he went to sleep. I thought he was a gifted child because he would take the book off me and read it back word for word. In fact, he was profoundly dyslexic and just had a prodigious memory.

My memory is not prodigious at all when it comes to my sister Sally Anne at that time. She is a kind, funny, pretty, supremely well-adjusted woman today so I'm picking she can't remember her Makino Road days either.

Sue, who was always far lovelier than she ever allowed herself to feel, attracted the attention of a slick young man who owned a Jag, which both thrilled and alarmed Mum. Sue wouldn't let him anywhere near the house. He had to park on the road, toot his horn and wait there while she tottered up the gravel drive in her high heels to meet him. It was the same after the movies or a dance. Regardless of the hour or the weather, he had to drop her off at the top of the drive. One night Mum, who was a Neighbourhood Watch group of one, decided they had been parked up far too long, so the spoilsport, the virgin with VD, was dispatched into the dead of night to tap on the fogged-up windows.

Sue left high school within a nanosecond of turning fifteen to work as a nurse aide in Feilding Maternity Hospital and board in the nurses' home. I always thought it was because she couldn't wait to escape but only recently she told me that Mum encouraged her to quit school and earn money.

She had barely settled in when she got a distraught phone call from Mum. Out of the blue, relatives from Ireland had contacted her to say they were on their way to see us. They had just landed in Auckland and were staying with friends for a few days before hiring a rental car and driving down in the weekend. In tears, Mum begged Sue to head them off. Barely fifteen, she cycled to Feilding railway station, caught the Limited at ten o'clock, spent a nervous, chilly night wide awake in a click-clacking carriage, arrived in Auckland before dawn, caught a bus to the suburb of

Westmere, walked for miles alongside tidal flats to a stranger's address, knocked on the door and told cousins she didn't know that her mother and father had gone away, she wasn't sure where or when they would be returning, so they couldn't come to Feilding. And they didn't.

SUE CAME HOME SOME WEEKENDS lugging one of her very first purchases—a portable, battery-operated gramophone and two long-playing records: Johnny Tillotson of 'Talk Back Trembling Lips' fame, and The Beatles' first album. I listened to one song on side two over and over until the batteries went flat: 'There's A Place'. Attributed to Lennon and McCartney, it was written by John. No matter what was happening or how bad he felt there was always somewhere he could go, it was his mind, and no time was he alone . . .

That song spoke to me more than any other song had ever done before. My classmates went around humming 'Four Strong Winds' and 'Tom Dooley', which was another good reason for hanging out with coarser types in the woodwork and metalcraft streams who were into The Animals, The Kinks, The Rolling Stones and Manfred Mann. Walking across the quad some lunchtimes there could be up to ten scruffy boys, socks around the ankles, singing 'Doo Wah Diddy Diddy' in joyous, ragged unison.

Metalcraft came in really handy. The Beatles had Vox speakers so these guys spent a lot of time in class working furtively and feverishly with hacksaws and sheets of metal to fashion impressively realistic Vox insignias to screw on the front of their crappy old amps and rubbish speakers.

The late, great American comedian Rodney Dangerfield once described going into a gay bar as follows: 'It was amazing! There were two guys for every guy.' Almost overnight in Feilding there were two bands for every band member. A sweet, shy, retiring, bespectacled boy called Len Sithebottom, arriving from Liverpool with a trunk full of War Picture Library comics, was dragooned into playing drums in a band while still jet-lagged, purely on the

basis of his Scouse accent. Only dead people and I had poorer timing than Len. I was tone deaf as well. I make Leonard Cohen sound like Pavarotti. With the wisdom of vet-school-acquired hindsight I now blame the bone density of the hammer, anvil and stirrup in my middle ears. This limited my contribution to the rock-music revolution sweeping the world to carrying amps and painting the names of bands on the drum kits. This kept me busy, as they were always changing. My favourites were Rommel's Lake and Atomic Porridge.

The Atomic Porridge story is a darkly comic, absurdist saga worthy of another book at another time, but it would be remiss of me not to pay homage to Ray Fiddler, one of the lead singers. Ray sounded like a cross between Paul McCartney and John Lennon. He had such stage presence that when the drummer vanished from the stage, which he did frequently to deflower schoolgirls behind the back curtains, Ray, armed only with a tambourine or maracas, kept the band driving forward, winking knowingly at me, the wistful, envious virgin with VD, taking money at the door.

Ray's parents were hip and sophisticated. They had *Esquire* and *Life* magazines placed casually on a coffee table. They had a drinks cabinet. After school, if his mother was out, Ray poured his mates hefty tumblers of Bacardi and Coke. There were occasions when some of them reeled outside and chundered on the Fiddlers' immaculate back lawn. They had a radiogram with jazz albums stacked neatly against the wall. I first heard Dave Brubeck's cool classic 'Take Five' in their living room. I was able to listen over and over again to *Bridge on the River Wye* starring my comic heroes Spike Milligan and Peter Sellers—doing a genius impersonation of Alec Guinness. Mrs Fiddler kindly insisted I stay for meals and I cycled back to Makino Road in the dark, no light, no helmet, guided by starlight on fence wire, shouting out in character my favourite Milligan lines, startling sleeping cattle who stampeded in the dark, crashing with a spronging sound into distant wire fencing, with me laughing my head off. I did a near perfect Major Dennis Bloodnok, Ind. Arm. Rtd., coward and bar.

The laughter stopped at home. The clothing situation was getting grim. I began roaming surrounding farms in search of dead sheep to pluck. If they weren't ripe, I dragged them into thickets of gorse or stands of bush, coming back a few days later when they had bloated, their bellies blue and stinking to high heaven. I had to battle nausea, but the wool came off much easier. I sold numerous sackfuls to a wool merchant in Feilding and bought my first pair of black jeans, a sports coat and a shirt with a button-down collar like Michael Caine's in *Alfie*.

School Certificate was looming. I took it very seriously. On the morning of the English exam, Mum fed me fish because it was good for the brain. I hated her fish because she favoured the rolling-boil method—you throw the fish into a bubbling pot, jam on the lid, come back in an hour's time and strain the flakes. Rather than cycle to high school, I chose this morning to take the bus to do some extra swat. The bus was late and I was very nearly locked out. Damp with anxiety, I sat down and began answering the comprehension question. To my horror, I couldn't remember how to spell the three-letter word used to join two parts of a sentence together. I scribbled the three options in the margin of my exam paper, now sodden with perspiration and cobwebbed with spreading ink:

nad

dan

and

They all looked correct. I picked one at random and soldiered on, close to tears.

LATE IN JANUARY THE FOLLOWING year word went out that the exam results were due any moment. I was still in bed when my father collected the mail from the letterbox at the gate. There was a terrible, theatrical wail from the kitchen.

'Oh no! Oh dear! Woe is us! Someone fetch the sackcloth and ashes!' shouted my father, loud enough for the whole house to hear. 'EGGHEAD HAS FAILED!'

I went numb and couldn't move for an hour. Mum eventually crept into my bedroom with a cup of tea and a piece of toast. What was I going to do? Would I repeat the fifth-form year? My life expectations had already shrunk to sub-atomic proportions at this point. We couldn't afford that. I would accept my fate and settle for a life on the chain or in lamb-cuts in Borthwicks' Feilding freezing works. I knew lots of good people who worked there. Some of them owned their own homes and speedboats before they were 30. It would be OK. 'Don't worry, Mum, I'll be fine . . .' I sniffed.

It was after one in the afternoon when I eventually shuffled like a zombie into the kitchen and reached for the opened envelope resting on the mantel above the coal range. I had passed, thanks to good marks in Biology, Chemistry and Mathematics. I got only 47 in School Certificate English—which meant I could never be a journalist, screenwriter or author. Those are the breaks.

IT WAS A HUGE RELIEF being a sixth-former. The ranks had thinned and there were only enough pupils left for two professional classes. Mum was very proud of me and decided to attend a parent-teacher evening in a fierce thunderstorm. I put the other kids to bed, listened to some National Radio, probably Manuel and his Music of the Mountains, for a couple of hours, looking out our curtain-less windows for some sign of her push-bike light bobbing in the downpour. She got home close to ten, completely saturated, reporting indignantly that my English teacher thought that I was a complete idiot who would never amount to anything. I sighed and handed her a cup of tea.

'Don't you worry, Junior! I got back at the bastard quick as a flash!' She beamed proudly—which worried me. 'I said to him straight, don't think yer shit doesn't stink, Sonny Jim!'

Later that year we moved out of Makino Road to a nice house in the borough of Feilding itself. We had the freezing works over the river, the wool scourer across the railway lines and the largest saleyards in New Zealand down the road—an olfactory Bermuda Triangle where fresh air vanished without trace.

I got a job in the school holidays working as a labourer on the cooling floor in Borthwicks. Mum saw an ad in the *Feilding Herald*—Farrell's shirt factory wanted trained machinists or women willing to learn. To the collective horror of her children, she applied. This was well before the feminist revolution. We were in no position to be snobs but we implored her to reconsider and spare us the shame and humiliation of having a mother who worked. I don't know where this objection came from. Doing the washing in a wood-fired copper and wringing the sheets through a hand-cranked mangle meant she was already a manual labourer. Our shame and humiliation vanished magically with the arrival of the television set that she managed to scrape together a down-payment for.

In the high-school library there was always a queue of boys waiting to look up the meaning of 'vagina' in a heavy, leather-bound dictionary. It sprang open automatically to this greasy, well-thumbed page in the gentlest of breezes. While waiting my turn, I rifled through the shelves and came across *Three Men in a Boat* by Jerome K. Jerome, which made me laugh out loud from the very first paragraph. It was a revelation discovering just how amusing the printed word could be. In the 1950s and '60s, publicly at least, New Zealand was probably the most humourless country on the planet. I'd put money on Holland being funnier. We gave the impression of being gloomier than Vladivostok in winter.

Frank S. Anthony's *Me and Gus* stories, written in the 1920s about likeable losers trying to establish dairy farms in harsh inhospitable swamp-land at the base of Mount Taranaki after coming back from the Great War, have a bleak charm and were once very popular but have long since fallen from view. In the 1950s there was a limp, patronising and racist column in *Truth* called 'Half-Gallon Jar', written by a Pākehā taxi driver who used the pen-name 'Hori'. On radio there was the Howard Morrison Quartet singing 'My Old Man's an All Black'—a lame play on Lonnie Donegan's already lame 'My Old Man's a Dustman'. A song called 'Taumarunui on the Main Trunk Line' by Peter Cape was demanded by a comedy-starved populace at every single request session and never failed to depress me. This doesn't mean that Kiwis weren't funny. When you read World War Two biographies there is a plenty of evidence of a wry, ironic and understated New Zealand sensibility—we made each other laugh out loud. There just wasn't much public expression of it.

This was before Barry Crump's comic novel *A Good Keen Man* hit the country like a thunderclap in 1960. Along with everyone else, I delighted in the novelty of the rollicking slapstick, the vivid, visceral accounts of life in rugged bush country and the sound of the Kiwi vernacular coming off the page, but there was a darkness and nihilism in there as well—especially in his unsympathetic depiction of women. Men didn't divorce wives or go to marriage guidance to mend relationships— they simply 'shot through'. Years later it emerged that, when intoxicated, Crump could be an abusive and angry husband and father to his wives and children. He may well also have been sexually conflicted. The outrageously camp Auckland actor Peter Varley loved recounting how he was once locked in intimate union with the famous author and star of the brilliant Toyota Hilux television commercials and, being exceptionally well endowed, leaned over the great man's broad shoulders and enquired solicitously, 'I'm not hurting you, am I, Barry?' The reply came from damp lips dangling a roll-your-own, 'Nah, she's beaut, mate.'

Later, *Puckoon* by Spike Milligan and *Catch-22* by Joseph Heller would also reduce me to helpless laughter. I daydreamed fancifully about doing something vaguely similar one day. On a long bike ride with my brother Michael, sniffing out dead sheep to pluck and checking out orchards to raid, I found something in a long-abandoned Makino schoolhouse that would push me in that direction. The building was in ruins. All the windows were smashed, desks were upended, parts of the ceiling had caved in and the floor was strewn with sheep droppings. In a corner, hidden under a pile of sacking, was a soggy copy of a controversial magazine that had been banned by the Feilding mayor. On the full-colour cover was a well-drawn cartoon of a man dying of thirst in a burning desert with a mirage of a beer tanker shimmering just out of his reach. It was a Massey Agricultural College capping publication—*Masskerade* 59.

Ten years later I would edit *Masskerade* 69 and be threatened with prosecution for blasphemous libel. This edition did not mock religion directly but there were more than enough risqué jokes and filthy cartoons to give any man of the cloth conniptions. To borrow from another comedy hero of mine, Frank Muir, my flabbers were absolutely gasted. I knew intuitively I had struck gold. I tucked it inside my singlet and hid it when I got home.

Feilding Ag was quite enlightened for its time. Pupils had their own self-government. Every class had a representative on the school council, which met regularly in beautiful council chambers and did radical things like abolish caps. Having power of veto, the staff would immediately make them compulsory again. Half the school prefects were appointed by the staff, the other half were elected by school houses. My whānau, Rangitikei House, elected me.

The boy prefects and the girl prefects enjoyed separate common rooms in the lovely old school building, sadly long gone. Without ever revealing my mother lode, I told an endless stream of filthy jokes, which offended a huge boy called Warren who was deeply religious. Unable to stomach my obscenity any longer, he dragged me out the door and threw me down a flight of stone steps. Weak with laughter from a freshly delivered and, if I say so myself, perfectly timed punchline I was unable to offer any resistance. It didn't matter. I was so full of dopamine—a by-product of sex, which didn't apply in this instance, and laughter, which did—that I felt no pain. In seconds I had bounded back through the door to tell a joke about a gorilla sodomising some nuns. Warren gave up.

In the seventh form, out of the blue, some classmates asked me if I wanted to come with them to see a capping revue in Palmerston North's wonderful old Opera House, again sadly gone, making way for a shopping complex. (I am totally opposed to the death penalty—I think it is barbaric—except for property developers, town planners and architects.) The show was amazing and wonderfully funny. A tall, thin, ginger man, an Antipodean John Cleese called Tony Rimmer, stole the show. At one point he came dashing out in front of the curtain, wringing his hands in panic, to ask if there was a doctor in the house. A plant rose and said he was. 'Enjoying the show?' asked Rimmer. 'Very much so' was the reply, and the auditorium erupted in relieved laughter.

In the car on the way back to Feilding we were still bubbling with excitement. One of the girls—it might have been Christine Wilson—said quietly, 'You will write one of those shows one day, Tommy.' The others swiftly agreed. I sat in the back dazed and amazed at this vote of confidence.

They dropped me off where I had left my push-bike at the entrance to the school grounds and I cycled home mulling this over. Could something that wonderful ever happen to me? To Egghead?

CHAPTER SEVEN

DREAMING SPIRES

IN 2002, MASSEY UNIVERSITY AWARDED me an honorary doctorate in literature. The capping ceremony, held in Palmerston North's beautifully restored Regent Theatre, was surprisingly moving. I got to wear billowing robes and a floppy velvet cap modelled on those worn by courtiers attending Tudor monarchs. I imagined I bore a vague resemblance to Paul Scofield, who played Sir Thomas More in one of my favourite films, *A Man For All Seasons*. I got to give the graduation address and afterwards lead a stately procession of gowned graduates through the streets of a city to which I had just been given a key. Awaiting us in the square was a marquee with champagne and canapés. Pushing through the crowd towards me was a middle-aged man whom I didn't recognise. I hadn't seen him in over 40 years. It was Keith, a childhood friend from Kimbolton Road. Along with others we had played war games together up and down the willowed banks of the Makino Stream. His mother was a lovely woman and very kind to Mum.

My one-man play about my father, *The Daylight Atheist*, starring Grant Tilly, had just finished a successful season at the Regent Theatre:

> By turns gloriously funny and gut-wrenchingly moving, *Daylight Atheist* is a triumph not only for Scott, Tilly and Mulheron, but for fathers everywhere. *Daylight Atheist* is a truly international story and one that deserves the widest audience.
> — DON KAVANAGH, *MANAWATU EVENING STANDARD*, 29 MAY 2002

Keith was itching to tell me that his mum had seen the play and thought I had told whopping fibs and exaggerations—apparently our life was nothing like how I had dramatised it. I should have let it go and passed on my very best wishes to his mum and dad, but I didn't. My hackles rose and I responded acidly:

'Thanks, Keith—you have just solved a mystery that has been gnawing away at me for years. I always wondered who that woman was in the corner of our lounge—squatting there silently, saying nothing, just taking notes. For the life of me I could never place her! Now I know! It was your mum!'

There's more of my father in me than I care to admit. Poor Keith reeled away, blinking rapidly. Apart from this terse exchange it was a marvellous day. I started thinking wistfully that Mum would have loved it, especially the medieval pageantry.

In case you are wondering, I want to dispel any impression created here that Mum was dead at this juncture. She was alive and well and living in her granny flat under our home in Wellington, having a hissy fit. Since guest seating was at a premium I couldn't invite all of my family to the ceremony, so I didn't. My sister Jane rang me testily to complain when she discovered that my brother Michael had been invited and she hadn't. I explained that when news of my honorary doctorate was announced, Michael had rung to congratulate me.

'Oh, so that's the rule now, is it?' she snapped. 'If we don't kiss your arse we don't get invited!'

Jane is very quick. There's a lot of our father in Jane as well. But she was right. That's exactly what I was saying. I had no comeback.

On the big day, Mum said she really wanted to come but couldn't out of loyalty to Jane. There was no changing her mind. We drove away with her doubled over on her front steps sobbing her heart out.

There's a lot of our mother in Mum, but she is nothing if not consistent. Four years later, in 2006, when in the New Year Honours I was appointed an Officer of the New Zealand Order of Merit for services as a cartoonist, journalist and illustrator, Mum told me that all this recognition wasn't fair on my brothers and sisters. It would mean a lot to her if just once I came a 'gutser'.

It's not an uncommon phenomenon. When Prime Minister Rob Muldoon got an honorary doctorate in laws from the University of Seoul while on a state visit to South Korea, lots of MPs, including members of his own party, wore curdled expressions for days afterwards.

I worked in the Parliamentary Press Gallery at the time and my good friend, the comedian John Clarke, rang me with a brilliant idea. I duly arranged for Labour backbencher Russell Marshall to place a question on the order paper, and it played out like this:

> 'Question number three stands in the name of
> Russell Marshall.'
> 'Mr Speaker!'
> 'Mr Marshall!'
> 'Mr Speaker, my question is to the Prime
> Minister and asks, "Can he confirm that on his
> recent trip to Korea he received an honorary
> doctorate in laws from the University of Seoul,
> and does he see this as an honour not only for

him but an honour for New Zealand as a whole?"'

Muldoon, surprised but delighted nonetheless to get such a flattering, patsy question from a man he frequently dismissed as the 'Red Reverend', got to his feet beaming with pride.

'Mr Speaker!'

'Prime Minister!'

'Mr Speaker, I can confirm that I did receive an honorary doctorate in laws from the University of Seoul and I see it as both an honour for me personally and the nation as a whole.'

'Supplementary question, Mr Speaker!'

'Supplementary question, Mr Marshall.'

'Mr Speaker, can the Prime Minister tell the House, will he be using the title "Doctor" full-time as in Goebbels or part-time as in Jekyll?'

No one dared make fun of Muldoon like this. The Opposition benches erupted in shocked, rapturous laughter—a long drought of sorts had been broken. It was a moment not unlike those famous *Life* magazine shots taken by Brian Brake of Indian villagers delirious with joy at the first drops of monsoon rain running down their uplifted faces like diamonds. Government MPs struggled frantically to suppress their mirth lest their leader look around and catch them being disloyal. It's probably fair to say the Prime Minister and Red Reverend were both stunned by the whole exercise.

JUST AS I WAS TYPING this story, I got a phone call from Radio New Zealand informing me that John Clarke had died while on a bush walk in the beautiful Grampians National Park west of Melbourne. Scores of laudatory and richly deserved tributes were paid on both sides of the Tasman to this strikingly original talent, my own inarticulate speech of the heart amongst them. Four days passed before I could return to my computer and resume work on this book—four days filled with swirling disbelief, exhausting sadness and the swapping of outrageous yarns about John with friends over the phone. We are of an age when this is going to happen more and more. I can't imagine what it must have been like for our fathers' generation during the war who regularly lost three people they loved before lunch.

I had heard of John Clarke long before I met him. It was five years out from him becoming Fred Dagg, comedy icon and national treasure. I was a third-year vet student at Massey in Palmerston North and he was a second-year arts student at Victoria in Wellington, 160 kilometres to the south—which might just as well have been the dark side of the moon to me in those days without a car or driver's licence. Such were his stellar comic gifts, word of John's existence spread north. The beautiful Bieder twins, Penny and Jill, whose parents lived near our thumping music crash-pad, studied at Vic and returned home in the holidays as his most faithful disciples. Penny, for whom I had an unrequited love, told me that I would adore John—he was so funny and so creative, and I reminded her a wee bit of him. I didn't need to hear this. I assumed they were an item and secretly resented him even more.

Of course I too fell under his spell when we met. Long before Jeremy Clarkson made it unfashionable, John was a double-denim man, shirt and jeans, with elastic-sided riding boots and receding hair with a shoulder-length mullet. Speaking as your friendly neighbourhood cartoonist now, his eyebrows were almost always permanently arched and his eyes bulged in their sockets like a poor man's Marty Feldman, which meant they always caught the light, and as a consequence they did indeed sparkle. He had the same amused curl to his top lip as John Lennon and his prominent central incisors coupled with prominent canine teeth resulted in a wicked smile, as if savouring a private joke that, if you were very lucky, he would let you in on. And when he did, you felt more than lucky—you felt chosen.

I was in the early stages of becoming a second-eleven celebrity as a political columnist on the *Listener* and had promised the Massey University Students' Association that I would edit one final *Masskerade*. At a loose end until his beloved Helen shifted to Wellington, John offered to help. His contributions were beautifully observed, economically written, except when a baroque flourish was required, and they kept coming and coming. He read them out to me over the phone and had me on the floor in fits of laughter.

Like this ad for a used-car yard:

L.M.V.D. RATBAG MOTORS

Ron Ratbag Dave Bastard

57 HOLDEN—Fashionable cinnamon. Very tidy and smart. Extras: heater, four on the floor (they fell off). Also 1959 Bedford truck, 14 tons with 17 head of cattle. Bring a crowbar if you only want the truck. $8795.

52 MORRIS POXFORD—Touch of rust on this one. One previous owner (no flowers please). 2 speed box. Extras: heater, steering wheel, roof, engine. A steal at $4875 + nominal charge for ½ pound oranges in universal.

It wasn't filthy enough for Massey students though, and thousands remained unsold in my garage. If you can find a copy, grab it and read it. It still stands up today.

Along with the usual suspects—Milligan, Evelyn Waugh, P.G. Wodehouse and Flann O'Brien—John was a big fan of *The Harvard Lampoon* and the writing of P. J. O'Rourke. When the Indecent Publications Tribunal banned a batch of issues, John got me to drive to Gordon and Gotch's warehouse on Wellington's Adelaide Road where, with me trailing nervously in his wake, he swept past a security guard in a glass booth with a casual nod and an authoritative 'Story!' and strode into the body of the warehouse itself. Magazines were stacked floor to ceiling on shelves and on pallets in long rows. Identifying the offending issues he tucked them under his arm, handed me the overflow, and briskly retraced his steps. With another casual nod and 'Story!' to the puzzled security guard we were safely out on the pavement with our spoils.

This cool, almost detached, nonchalant courage infused the best of his writing and performing. Provided that he wasn't shot by firing squad for rank insubordination by his own side first, you could see that John had all the ingredients needed to be a war hero in any conflict (apart from Bomber Command or as a Battle of Britain Spitfire pilot—he had a terrible fear of flying).

In 1974 the state broadcaster, BCNZ, had a flagship current-affairs show called *Nationwide* that provided extensive coverage of the major political parties' annual conferences, which included nightly panel discussions with political scientists with moustache-less beards chaired by broadcasting's young rising star, Ian Fraser. We had to make our own fun back then. It was also a time when they used a still of the Freyberg boat harbour as a station break.

In March of that year the Prime Minister, Norman Kirk, was not a well man. In fact, he was dying. His absence cast a pall over proceedings at Labour's bun-fight in Wellington's old Town Hall. In a gallant but unwise effort to liven things up, Ian hired me and a relatively unknown revue actor, John Clarke, to make fun of the remits.

The remit book ran to 40 pages, many of them stone-cold loopy—one demanded the government set up a Workers Tobacco Company to provide the proletariat with cheaper cigarettes. Ian recalls that I wrote half of the material with him, which was then filmed in his flat, with John giving brilliant, one-take performances straight to camera—his great strength right from the outset.

John always said the role of the satirist was to find holes in the veneer through which fun could be poked—but this fun cut to the bone. After John's evisceration the party faithful struggled bravely to appear amused, but were unable to keep up the pretence—embers of resentment were fanned into flames by Federation of Labour boss Tom Skinner in a speech castigating *Nationwide*. Not realising their microphones were live and could be heard by the press benches, on stage party bosses and senior cabinet ministers argued bitterly over whether *Nationwide* should be evicted from the conference. The chairman of the Broadcasting Council, Sir Alister McIntosh, rang Ian demanding he apologise the next night on air—which he did, somewhat tardily. When a shockingly frail Norm Kirk shuffled on stage with the aid of a carved Māori walking stick and whispered additional condemnation, the conflagration became a firestorm. One incensed delegate adopted a kung-fu stance in front of a very pale Ian Fraser, screaming, 'You're dicing with death!'

Terribly excited by this response, I bounded into the *Nationwide* offices the following week, showering saliva like a spaniel, asking when we were doing it again. No one knew where to look. The producer, Bill Earle, walked me back down the stairs to the street explaining gently that, yes, they would be doing more, but John wanted to do them on his own from now on. John could have told me first. For a moment, I had an inkling of how Pete Best must have felt when Ringo replaced him in The Beatles.

As history attests, John was quite right. He didn't need me. Ten years later I got to put words into his mouth again when he played Wal in the animated feature film *Footrot Flats* that I co-wrote with Murray Ball, the cartoon strip's warm and brilliant creator. In a terrible confluence of events, after a long, slow descent into dementia, Murray died just a few weeks before John. While terribly sad, Murray's death was also a release that everyone who loved him was fully prepared for. John's departure was altogether more shocking and cruel for being so unexpected and so premature. Two countries united in grief feel equally robbed.

I have some skills as a mimic, but I was always too self-conscious to ever be a professional performer. Even if I wasn't, my dyslexia shreds lines as fast as I commit them to memory. I can't sing. I can't dance. I can't play a musical instrument. I draw and I write. That's it. And my writing was close enough in intention if not in tone to John's precise, perfectly weighted prose for there to be an undeclared competition between us, which I always regretted.

John came to the Australian premiere of my play *The Daylight Atheist* at the Melbourne Theatre Company on the banks of the Yarra. It would play to packed houses, garner great reviews and actor Richard Piper would win prizes for his performance, but none of this was a given in the dressing room after the first show. Champagne flowed and Australian acting luminaries, including Garry McDonald aka Norman Gunston, one half of Kath and Kim, Geoffrey Rush and Mark Mitchell, famous for 'Con the Fruiterer' and who also played David Lange in *Fallout* (the four-part TVNZ series that I co-wrote with Greg McGee), crowded around Richard and me, showering us with praise. Hanging back shyly was John. When the crowd thinned, he came forward and shook my hand warmly. 'Well done that man!' A few days later he sent me a rapturous critique from *The Age* headlined 'Laughter hides the hurt'. When my partner Averil and I returned to Melbourne at the end of the run for the final performance, we lunched the next day with Richard Piper and Peter Evans the director. John came as well and he could not have been happier for me. I felt chosen again.

In middle age, our respective testosterone levels dipped. We had less antler to lock and I saw more of John when I came to Melbourne. Observing him decide on a time and place to meet was like watching an old dog approaching a rug on the floor— there was lots of circling and jostling until he was perfectly aligned with the Earth's magnetic field before settling in for the duration, which could be hours. He gave me a priceless piece of information on Captain Charles Upham VC and Bar for a project I was working on, and generously introduced me to producers who could be of use to me with a trans-Tasman mini-series I was writing. He didn't rule out being in it. Mind you, this was his modus operandi—he hated disappointing anyone straight off the bat so he would agree to things that were never going to happen, like attending Sir Edmund Hillary's eightieth birthday party which I helped organise at Government House in Wellington. Fear of flying put paid to a lot of these events, but the possibility that he might turn up was always a thrill in itself.

There is an elegant bookshop in Melbourne called Hill of Content. John took me to it one dusk. Plucking a book off the shelves, he started reading passages out loud. It was *The Traveller's Tool* by Sir Les Patterson—the nom-de-plume of John's great friend and fellow comic genius, Barry Humphries. It was filth and vulgarity elevated to great art. John was a famous Australian by then, a television star and a celebrated author in his own right. We were laughing so loudly and so hysterically we were asked to leave.

It was 1973 all over again.

FORMER NEW ZEALAND PRIME MINISTER Mike Moore, just back from Geneva after a stint as head of the World Trade Organization, congratulated me on my honorary doctorate. I said it was no big deal really. My mate Ed Hillary had been awarded at least half a dozen by American universities—he only had to dash in to use a toilet and they slid one under the cubicle door. Perhaps missing my lame joke, Mike suddenly saw this as a contest. Puffing out his chest he said he'd lost count of how many honorary doctorates he'd received from Europe's finest universities. I guess if anything is going to put an honorary doctorate into perspective it has to be that.

When I first arrived there as a student in 1966, Massey University was little more than a vast, circular paddock festooned with white pegs marking out the sites of future tower blocks. Most of the teaching was confined to a grand, three-storey, ivy-covered art deco building overlooking a cricket oval bordered by hostels and the beautiful art deco refectory building. With a stream running through it and ringed by native bush and mature English trees, if not Oxford or Cambridge it was a reasonable approximation of Stanford. I could imagine the Manhattan Project being worked on in secret here.

I hadn't cut the umbilical cord to Feilding yet so I lived at home that first year, which was stressful, as I didn't have a driver's licence or own a motor vehicle. I got rides with friends, caught the train or hitch-hiked. Twice I got stranded in Palmerston North and slept on benches in the university grounds. At two in the morning with no coat and a chill mist rising off the stream, Massey's glorious parklands lost some of their charm.

I had worked out by then that I didn't have VD, but I was still a virgin. The '60s were famous for sex, drugs and rock and roll and I was spoiling the average. I hadn't even kissed a girl. I raged inwardly at my utter hopelessness on this front. The longer I left it, the more impossible it seemed to be.

One Saturday night when, at the very least, I should have been staggering through the square with other first-year students swilling Blackberry Nip from a bottle in a brown paper bag and leaving pools of crimson vomit in my wake, I was instead in Feilding watching *The Dean Martin Show* with Mum and my younger siblings when our father arrived home more abusive than normal. The other kids wisely melted away. I remained to act as a buffer between him and Mum, which he didn't take kindly to.

'You know what your problem is, Egghead?' he asked rhetorically. 'You are a *homosexual!*'

'That's a low blow, even for you,' I stammered, tears welling. 'I'm not even sexual.' He didn't have time to call for the weeping bowl. I had already left the room. Chest heaving, I sobbed as quietly as I could manage in my bedroom. They were the last tears I ever shed in connection with him.

Entering the tiered lecture theatre in the main building was torture if it meant sitting near a pretty girl. I felt myself going crimson, becoming breathless and feeling sick. I would turn on my heel and sit out the lesson in the foyer, frustrated and ashamed of my wretched existence. This shyness with girls, bordering on pathology, was one of the few things I shared with Sir Edmund Hillary. Many years later, working on a documentary for TVNZ, I interviewed George Lowe, Ed's great mate and climbing companion on many mountaineering adventures, including the 1953 conquest of Everest. George mentioned casually that they were both virgins on Everest and this accounted in part for their ferocious energy. George also told me that while Ed was quite rightly acclaimed for being the first man to step onto the highest point on planet Earth, some ten paces ahead of Tenzing, he himself held an altitude record that went largely unheralded—the highest ever act of masturbation. I never had the courage to ask Ed about any of this, though he spoke openly of his awkwardness with members of the opposite sex. He put it very delicately: 'I was OK on the fairway, but hopeless on the green.'

I wasn't even OK on the fairway. I was a hopeless romantic utterly hopeless at romance. In my early forties I washed up in the bar at Bellamy's in Parliament one night, a recently single and somewhat dishevelled father of three children by two different mothers (it's complicated), when a tall and tan, young and lovely, elegant woman swept in. It was broadcaster Carol Hirschfeld. To my own surprise, I didn't turn crimson and make a dash for the door. I bought her a drink and set about making her laugh. And what a laugh it was—smoky and rich like Lauren Bacall's. She was spoken for, but her beau lived in Auckland. We both had time on our hands and hung out for a couple of months. Sadly, it was all very innocent. When she saw that I was becoming besotted she told me off very crisply, 'Stop idealising me!'

It wasn't exactly something new. I fell madly in love with girls sitting two rows in front of me in lecture halls and thought them perfect in every conceivable way purely on the basis of the way curls tumbled down the nape of a neck, light caught their cheekbones, or a top button was undone on a blouse. It meant I spent much of my first term at Massey in a state of low-grade anxiety until I made my first close friend—Tom Quinlan.

In an age of flared denim and buckskin he wore ironed white shirts and ties, a burgundy jacket, pressed black slacks and shiny shoes. He was good-looking in a weepy Irish tenor way. He could easily have played Father Noel Furlong in *Father Ted*, the part that launched the career of Graham Norton.

Tom was very clever and supremely calm. He helped me out

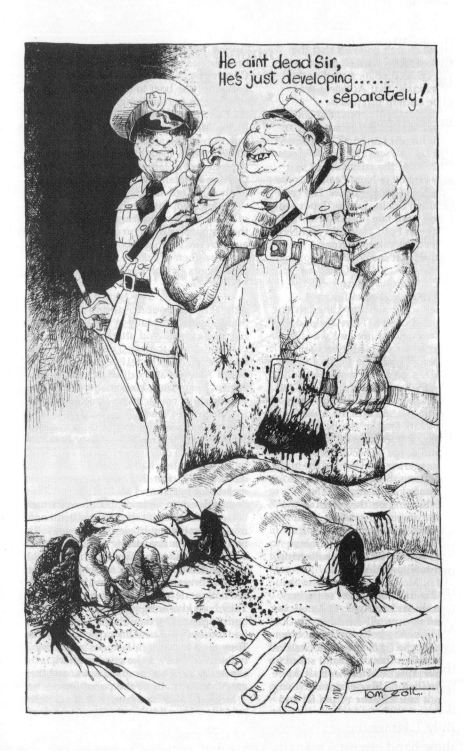

in chemistry labs when my spilling of hazardous chemicals threatened both our lives. The former mayor of Auckland, Dick Hubbard from Hubbard Foods fame, was the only person clumsier than me—if you come across half a test-tube in your muesli it may well be a remnant from this period.

The Vietnam War was at its height and the apartheid regime in South Africa was ever more brutally suppressing black activists seeking change. Quinny encouraged me in my early efforts at political cartooning. I cringe when I look at them now. I was still learning my craft and had a lot to learn. I submitted some to *Masskerade 66*. In his acknowledgements the editor, Chip Jones, a diminutive figure who wore ripple-sole brothel-creeper shoes, smoked a pipe, called everyone 'cock' and was way beyond cool, paid me this compliment:

> Not only an artist with formidable promise, but
> a figure well acquainted with the pulse of golden
> wit—originality.

Anderton Senior—he of Feilding Ag boarding-school dormitory after-dark patrol fame—was capping controller the next year and knew a 'wanker' when he saw one. In a rare honour for someone in their first year, I was tasked with editing *Masskerade 67*.

I WAS ON A HIGH all that summer, even standing for twelve hours a day, six days a week, in a refrigerated room surrounded by clanking machines and whirring saws. My job was trimming fat off racks of lamb. I didn't know how to sharpen my knife and was virtually pushing the fat off using brute strength until a big Māori guy said to me in sing-song fashion, 'Gizzus a look at ya knife, bro.' He made a great show of slapping the sharp edge of the blade into the palm of his huge hands, leaving nothing but temporary dents. 'Phew! Diz knife is bloody dangerous, eh. If it slipped you could give yourself a nasty bruise, eh.' It was pure Billy T. James ten years before Billy T. emerged from the Māori show-band circuit. This same guy, when he needed to go to the toilet, announced loudly, 'Won't be long fellahs, juz going out for a cave in, eh!'

On the other side of me on the line was a guy who had been a top shearer in his day, travelling the world for the Wool Board, giving demonstrations. He told me more outrageous jokes than anyone else before or since. I cycled home furiously in the gathering dusk to scribble down as many as I could remember.

This also was the summer that I met a short, powerfully built, matinee-idol-good-looking guy who was studying law at Auckland University—Brian Dreadon. His father was a hydatids control officer and the family had just moved to Feilding. Dreadon Senior, a lovely man, served in the New Zealand Forces in the ill-fated Greek and Crete campaigns. Pulling on a traditional Greek cap with a tassel, he would stand behind a minuscule bar that he'd built in their living room and offer us any drink we wanted—as long as it was retsina, which tastes of pine resin, and not even nice pine resin.

Brian was a surfer, who owned a yellow Mini. He insisted I get over my hang-ups about water and dragged me to Foxton Beach. Mum would come flying out onto the front verandah as we were departing to screech, 'Watch out for sharks, darling!' Brian was also a gifted rugby player—a silky runner with superb balance, a mile-wide sidestep and surprisingly strong in the tackle. (Not that surprising really, he was also a javelin champ.) When he came back to Feilding in his winter breaks I roped him into our social rugby team. Without him we lost on average by about 40 points a game. With him at first-five we were 40 points up by half-time. Best of all from my point of view, he was also a talented artist and drew a number of very fine cartoons for my first *Masskerade*—which I think I can claim with confidence was the best one ever—that is, until my others rolled off the assembly line over the next three years.

I was so pleased with myself that when Anderton Senior summonsed me to a meeting of the capping committee, I automatically assumed it was to shower me with praise and I preened myself accordingly, preparing a splendid jape and wheeze—an alarm clock set to go off in ten minutes and a phone.

When it sounded I would open my bag, take out the phone, chat into it briefly, say, 'It's for you . . .' and pass it to Anderton. Endless hilarity would ensue and my reputation as a wag would be further enhanced.

Instead, the mood in the committee room was distinctly chilly. I sat at one end of a long table while everyone else glared at me from the other. Anderton, perhaps remembering the bumptious third-former humiliating Fatty McLean in assembly, addressed me in stern, head-prefect tones. I had forgotten what an officious prick he was. Much to my horror, it worked. I started feeling like a third-former again.

According to Anderton, thousands of copies of *Masskerade* had been distributed illegally at Longburn freezing works. They were considering calling in the police and having me prosecuted for theft. What did I have to say for myself? The story was complete bullshit. No such thing had occurred. While I was catching my breath, the alarm clock went off in my bag. I pulled out the phone, mumbled into it briefly and passed it limply to Anderton. 'It's for you . . .' I wish I had added, 'It's Interpol, they've got some new leads!' but I was still reeling from the grotesque unfairness of it all. It was draw-your-dad-for-Father's-day revisited. I have learned over the years that New Zealand doesn't have a tall poppy syndrome; that's quite wrong. We have a tall lichen syndrome.

WITH QUINNY'S PATIENT TUTORING AND endless encouragement I passed Vet Intermediate and found myself locked into a career path I hadn't really given enough thought to. At Feilding Ag the teacher giving career advice, a dignified, handsome Sri Lankan man nicknamed 'Choko' Da Silva (it was a less enlightened time) gave me a questionnaire in which there was one question I couldn't complete: If I was sitting in a railway carriage, what would I look at most—my fellow passengers or the view from the window? My answer was both, equally.

'You must decide,' implored Choko. I wouldn't budge. Choko shook his head sadly. 'Then I am unable to advise you.'

A friend from high school was keen on veterinary science. I liked dogs and tagged along brainlessly. He dropped out, leaving me stranded in vet school.

I disliked almost every second of the place. The one consolation was making friends with astonishingly brilliant people. People undergoing knee-reconstruction surgery today probably don't appreciate that it was pioneered first in racehorses, then in grid-iron players by Wayne McIlwraith, who was in my class. Wayne introduced me to Bob Dylan's *John Wesley Harding* album and got an honorary doctorate from Massey a year after me, ha ha!

Greg Bunker was another genius—who quoted extensively from Tom Stoppard's only novel *Lord Malquist & Mr Moon* long before the rest of us had ever heard of the English playwright. In his third year he won the coveted Massey Chunder Bowl, never given lightly. Representing Massey at the Australasian Veterinary Students' Association conference in Melbourne, Bunker got comprehensively pissed and was being driven on a three-lane motorway with some Aussie vet students when he announced he needed to be sick.

'Out the window, mate! Stick your head out the window! This is Dad's car!' shouted the driver. Bunker started gulping and dry-retching. The driver went into a panic and started shouting.

'IT'S DAD'S CAR! STICK YOUR HEAD OUT OF THE WINDOW! BE SICK OUT THE WINDOW!'

Another passenger in the back wound down the window for Bunker, blasting him with fresh air, which seemed to help. The car eased out of the fast lane, changed lanes twice more and pulled over onto a grass verge. They shoved Bunker out and slammed the door shut after him. He weaved around for a bit, stood bolt upright as if remembering something of vital importance, then staggered back to the car, stuck his head in the window and projectile vomited into the interior.

A decade later, I listened mouth agape as he recounted how, while working for the UN, he was one of the first Westerners allowed into the Cambodian capital of Phnom Penh after Pol Pot was forcibly deposed. He told me strange autumn leaves blew down ghostly, silent streets, filling gutters and piling up against walls—banknotes. Both money and human life had no value under the murderous Khmer Rouge, who killed 25 per cent of Cambodia's population after resetting society to what they called 'year zero'.

CHAPTER EIGHT

LOVE AND DEATH

VET STUDENTS HAD LECTURES AND labs eight hours a day, five days a week, so I had no choice but to move to Palmerston North in my second year. I went flatting with one of the guys who gave me rides from Feilding to Massey—Johnny Blick. He wanted me to meet his folks. His father was a travelling salesman who drove a car that looked like a Hawker Siddeley until you looked closer. Mr Blick wore a yellow cravat, a check shirt, a tweed hacking jacket with leather patches on the elbows and smoked a pipe. They lived in a modest house in a dead-end street. While 'Mrs B', as he called his wife, toiled in the kitchen he leaned a leather— or possibly vinyl—patch on the mantelpiece and pointed with the stem of his pipe to a stack of *Man* magazines, a soft-porn Aussie publication long since extinct, on the floor.

'Johnny likes small tits and not much pubic hair. I'm the other way round. Give me big jugs and lots of undergrowth!' He winked at me, while Johnny opened a copy and pointed proudly at his father's preferred option—a woman with broad hips wearing what could have been the bottom half of a fur bikini.

'Mrs B. Wonderful woman, marvellous breasts for her age, very shy when I met her, quite a handful in the sack now. The trick you young chaps need to learn is that a woman must be fully lubricated before you insert your penis. To do that you get your hands wet like this . . .' He was about to spit into his pipe-less hand when mercifully Mrs B announced that dinner was served in the alcove. I picked at my food listlessly while they took it in turns to tell a dirty joke each. Maybe Johnny had told them I was the editor of *Masskerade*. Johnny went first. His petite sister was next, followed by Mrs B. It has to be said, Mr Blick won hands down.

'What sits on a wall, is hairy and smells like anchovy? Anyone? You'll kick yourselves! Humpty Cunt!' He beamed and sucked contentedly on his pipe while Mrs B looked on as proudly as if he'd just performed a Chopin solo piano recital at the Royal Albert Hall. He waved the stem of his pipe in my direction. 'Your turn, Tom!'

Masskerade 66 made me a star on campus. Pretty girls flirted with me at parties—at least, I think that's what they were doing, I had no real point of comparison. I alternated between being the life and soul of the party and the moody intellectual in the corner far too cool and preoccupied with world affairs to dance. In this latter state I would slip away and walk back to our flat alone and despairing.

One night a beautiful girl studying food technology was having none of this and invaded my bedroom—perhaps she wanted to borrow a cup of sugar and I am impugning her motives. The room was dark. As best I could tell she climbed onto my bed and hoisted her skirt. A boy with bad acne at high school, Bob Whitehead, had mesmerised a bunch of us with his description of how pubic hair felt under a girl's knickers. 'It's like a tablecloth on bracken, lads.' Two boys lapsed into a dead faint. With a deft unfastening and shimmy of her hips the food-technology girl was down to her breasts and bracken. For the first time in my life I touched nipples and pubic hair that I hadn't drawn with a 2B pencil. I have never put my hand into a woman's clutch purse awash in warm oil while blindfolded, but I imagine the revelation would not be dissimilar to what I experienced next. Sensing that this could take all night if she didn't take charge, she took charge.

There is a scene in Woody Allen's great movie, *Love and Death*, set in Czarist Russia where, after a sleepless night of wild sex, Diane Keaton's character asks Woody in amazement how come he is such a good lover. Head barely poking out from under the bed-covers he peers at her through thick glasses. 'I practise a lot on my own.'

Apart from the Czarist Russia setting it was a bit like that in the morning. She was in bed exhausted—teaching can really take it out of you when you have a slow learner—and I was making her toast and a mug of instant coffee when there was a loud rap on the back door. Towel around my waist, full of the joys of spring, I opened it. A nifty red sports car was parked in the driveway. The driver, a tall distinguished man in his late forties with an R.A.F. fighter-pilot's moustache and a military bearing, hissed at me, 'If my daughter is here, please tell her that her father called.'

We were a studious bunch in that first Carol Street flat. As exams approached, we worked at our desks in our bedrooms well past midnight most nights, huge coffee mugs hanging from cords around our necks like identity tags, waiting for someone else to crack first and boil the kettle. The Beatles and The Rolling Stones alternated on the record player in the lounge until Johnny insisted on some bluegrass—plunking banjo and screeching fiddle—which had the beneficial effect of driving us back to our rooms. We all passed with flying colours that year.

In subsequent years the music got louder and wilder and my marks lower and lower. The Doors, Cream, Vanilla Fudge, Steppenwolf and Jefferson Airplane blasted out morning, noon and night. Marijuana, morning-glory seeds, datura flowers, magic mushrooms and LSD eventually displaced caffeine. Trying desperately to bridge the widening gap between myself and microbiology, parasitology and pathology I discreetly avoided taking drugs. I had seen my father intoxicated too often for it to have any appeal. I maintained my hip credentials by painting giant murals of Jimi Hendrix, Lightnin' Hopkins and the formula of LSD on walls in fluorescent paint that gave off a ghostly luminescence under blue light. We had no blinds and the strange glow reduced cop cars to a crawl when they went past, which they seemed to do several times a night.

Before I got a motorbike of my own, Quinny took me to vet school on the back of his scooter, and fretted about my welfare. There were times when I fretted myself. One flatmate, Big Al, had colossal shoulders and even wider hips. He was shaped like a Russian doll with a razor-sharp butcher's knife in a scabbard on his belt. He owned several rifles and fierce pig-dogs. Feeding them was expensive so he placed an ad in the paper offering a good home for cats. Gareth Morgan would have approved, but we moved out swiftly. None of us wanted to be the stop-gap measure if the supply of moggies faltered.

In the next flat a cheerful guy called Geoff was repeating his intermediate year while working part-time at Glaxo Laboratories, where they boiled down huge quantities of bullock to make beef agar, which was then allowed to set in Petri dishes for bacteria or fungi to grow on. In lieu of rent one week, Geoff lugged back to the flat a damp, Father Christmas-size sack of mince boiled to exhaustion. It resembled white sand. A bunch of hippies from Wellington had crashed with us for nearly a fortnight. They never rose before noon, smoked joints the size of an elephant tampon and were always hungry. Geoff and I added four bottles of Worcestershire sauce, a dozen small cans of tomato concentrate, a brush-and-shovel-full of salt and pepper and served it up to them as part of a spaghetti bolognaise. When I got up next morning they had gone.

It seemed only weeks later that Geoff came roaring up the drive in an old farm truck. He was hitch-hiking back from Auckland and had got stuck north of Taihape in a downpour. Standing out of the rain under a macrocarpa in a woolshed paddock next to this truck, he noticed that the keys were still in it. Having stolen it he now had to dispose of it.

We had a flat conference. Geoff thought he might push it into the Manawatū Gorge in the dead of the night. A paranoia fuelled by cannabis gripped everyone in the room (except me— my paranoia occurs naturally). Terry thought the cops would be combing the country looking for this truck by now—especially in the dead of night. Then Geoff had a brainwave. He would saw it into pieces and dispose of them separately—a sump here, an exhaust there, a radiator somewhere else. He set to the next morning with a hacksaw and two days later was almost halfway through the chassis. On the third day he soldiered on manfully until the chassis suddenly gave way of its own accord and the truck collapsed like a scrum. Geoff was too exhausted to do any more and the truck could no longer be moved forward or back, driven or towed. The only solution was to stop mowing the lawn. When it reached elephant grass proportions and the truck was no longer visible our landlord paid a rare visit and had a fit.

WE GAVE NOTICE AND MOVED to the Palace of Versailles of student squalor—Nash Street: five bedrooms, a huge lounge and so dilapidated that keeping it tidy was pointless. It occupied the end of a short street in a semi-industrial zone, so there were no neighbours to consider. I put the finishing touches on *Masskerade* 69 here. Murray Bramwell and John Muirhead, two witty and erudite arts students who favoured black turtlenecks and long scarves, one of them short, the other tall, like Simon & Garfunkel on the cover of *Bookends,* helped with wry and sophisticated contributions. It was Murray who coined the adage 'Ags talk only to vets and vets talk only to God'. I also got more terrific writing and cartoons from the ever-reliable Brian Dreadon.

Brian was present when the Epitaph Riders blatted into our front yard on snarling Harleys and Triumphs and stomped inside to conduct some sort of drugs transaction with Terry. They had a midget with them wearing an identical black leather jacket with their insignia on the back.

'This is Stumpy, OK?' said the gang leader, standing beneath one of my murals. 'Any bastard who makes fun of him will have shit to pay! OK?' Stumpy went around the room introducing himself to everyone in turn, politely shaking hands and saying, 'Hi, I'm Stumpy.' We bowed like we were meeting royalty—partly nerves and partly on account of the height differential. He got to the second shortest person in the room, Brian, who flashed him a handsome smile from under his bushy handlebar moustache.

'Stumpy?' drawled Brian. 'How did you get a name like that?'

Through all this I was leading a double life. I was still dressing like a Mormon missionary and going to vet school every day, but my heart wasn't in it. There were small diversions. One lecturer wore shorts made from an old shot-silk ball gown, that presumably had previously belonged to his wife. They changed from green to purple depending on how the light struck him and you risked epilepsy if you sat in the front row and stared at them directly. I learned things I didn't want to know—like that male pattern baldness was a genetic trait that you inherited from your mother's father. I raced home next weekend on my gleaming BSA 650 motorbike, unbeknownst to me dubbed the 'chrome coffin' by bikies all over the Manawatū because several people had died while riding it, to ask Mum how much hair her dad had, and her answer was so depressing that I thought seriously about driving into a power pole myself on the way back. She said her dad had lovely thick hair above his ears, coming out of his ears and on the bulb of his nose. In mounting panic I asked her to describe the follicle situation on the top of his head. Her answer haunts me still: 'Like a billiard ball, he was.'

I also learned that dissecting diseased liver and staring down microscopes identifying worms in ruminant faeces never grew on me the way that I assumed it would. In one practical exam, asked to identify the origin of various tapeworms, I tossed in the towel completely and scribbled dementedly—*Nematodes 2 U*, *Nematodes Direct* and *Twenty-Four Hour Nematode—We never close!* It was a cry for help if there ever was one.

My dear friend, the late, great Christchurch humourist A.K.

Grant, rang me once complaining about Helen Clark's gloomy persona on television.

'I accept that she is an admirable woman in many respects,' he sighed down the phone, 'but why does she persist in looking as if permanently poised to announce the death of the poet Keats?' She did and still does, more so since losing the race for the job of Secretary-General of the UN, which she would have done very well. Our parasitology lecturer, Nobby Charleston, wore the same expression after marking our practical exam. Normally a decent, soft-spoken man, he started wailing and beating his breast the moment he entered the lecture theatre— in all his time teaching he had never known such impudence. There was someone in the class who thought he was funny, but he wasn't. He could see this person now, sitting right at the back, looking very pleased with himself, when this person really needed to wake his ideas up!

I hadn't joined the dots at this point and was wondering what anyone could possibly have done to rile Nobby like this, and looked around to discover that the only person sitting right at the back was me. It was Nobby, bless him, who first alerted me to the fact I wasn't cut out for veterinary science, and that I should quit and become a cartoonist or a writer. I didn't listen to him, however, and struggled on haplessly, wasting everyone's time for another year.

STRICTLY SPEAKING I WAS NOT expelled from vet school—just asked not to re-enrol. The shame and sense of failure was still crushing. I could hear my father's voice in my head: 'Egghead has failed . . .'

At Oxford and Cambridge disgraced undergraduates are 'sent down' and may not enter university buildings, or even travel within a certain distance of them. I came very close to being 'sent down' in the wake of *Masskerade 69*. The Vice Chancellor thought about it then thought better of it. This is a great shame—an exclusion zone around the vet school would have suited me down to the ground.

I had some inkling of the furore to come when I showed the very first copy off the printing press to Mum and she burst into tears. At peak outrage the beleaguered Professorial Board kicked for touch and referred it to the Indecent Publications Tribunal, who came back months later with this ruling.

> The dominant impression conveyed by *Masskerade* 69 is one of barely relieved vulgarity. In word and picture its content is coarse in conception and crude in expression. Its frequent resort to the subject of sex as prop for its humour, the tasteless attacks on religious forms and attitudes and a series of jokes involving disease, bestiality, and racial prejudice undoubtedly offend against normal standards of propriety and good taste.

This is simply not the case. It was actually a carefully thought-out and stylish publication for its time. Its only crime was making fun of things that were previously considered out of bounds, compounded by an obvious glee in doing so. It pre-dated Monty Python's scandalous (at the time) movie *Life of Brian* by ten years. It entered the same territory, albeit without their finesse, that Eddie Izzard and Ricky Gervais colonised in their monologues 40 years later. I am still fond of Jesus on the phone talking to Doubting Thomas about the loaves and fishes. 'Picnic? What picnic? How many coming? Five thousand people? That's a big picnic, Tom. What are we going to feed them? Seven fish and three loaves of bread! What are you expecting, Tom? A miracle?'

There is nothing Freudian happening here. I wasn't rebelling against a puritanical upbringing. My father was from Northern Ireland and nominally Protestant. When Feilding was hit by a spate of church arsons he was for a time one of the suspects. I'm not sure on what basis, but he was more than capable of claiming involvement as a joke. When Mum left him for good the neighbours commented that they hadn't seen Joan for a while. 'That's because I had her put down,' he responded matter-of-factly. They were shocked. 'Well, she was getting old and smelly, leaking and dripping, with me traipsing behind sliding newspaper under her arse.' They rang the cops, who turned up asking where Mum was. 'Palmerston North,' he replied, 'which if you believe John Cleese is as close to death as you can get without actually dying.'

Mum had a childhood steeped in fierce, florid Catholicism, which she later resented and rejected to the point that on her deathbed she made it plain she wanted no hymns, no scripture readings and no priests at her funeral. Instead a bottle of Jameson's was to be placed on top of her lilac coffin along with shot glasses and we were to drink a toast to her as we filed out into the Napier sun while Louis Armstrong sang 'What a Wonderful World'.

Masskerade 69 reflected the turbulent, querulous tenor of the era—the zeitgeist, as Bunker or Murray Bramwell would have put it. On the cover of the 8 April 1966 edition of *Time* magazine, in large, bold red type on a black background, the editors asked their famous question: 'Is God dead?' It was an age when everything was being questioned, though an old lady tagging along at the rear of an anti-Vietnam War march through Palmerston North provided an answer, at least to her own satisfaction, with a placard that read: *'God's not dead. He isn't even sick!'*

Massey students demanded more proof. One night in the refectory we held a symposium that picked up where the *Time* cover left off. We asked if God had ever existed in the first place. I went along with Bunker and Quinny. There were about 200 students, many of us barely out of our teens, struggling to grow beards, wearing roll-necked pullovers, corduroy jackets, moleskin strides and suede desert boots and smoking pipes. We crowded into a big upstairs room and listened to a procession of impassioned speakers insisting that all religion was hokum and irrelevant in the modern world. There was no dissent. Every condemnation of every denomination was cheered loudly until a monstrous, demented-looking older man with thinning blond hair tied back in a long ponytail, dressed in blue cleaner's overalls, armed with a mop which he pounded on the floor like a biblical staff, stormed the stage. Pushing a shocked speaker aside he snatched the microphone and in a thick Afrikaner accent began to berate the hall:

'Listen to yew! Yew are so brafe in your blasphemy! I call on any one of yew to cum up 'ere an' call on Gawd to proof he exist by strikin' yew det weeth a bolt of lightning! Hew among yew is brafe enuff to invite the wrath of the Lawd upon yew and be reduced to essh?'

I leaned over to the Bunker and said in a low voice that this was silly and he should take up the challenge.

'Fuck off,' he whispered back. I turned to Quinny, who shook his head.

'Any one of yew?' the man roared, his eyes blazing like lasers. Two hundred people lowered their gaze and shifted uncomfortably in their seats. Needless to say there were no takers.

WITH PERFECT TIMING, *MASSKERADE* 69 hit the streets just before Easter and all hell broke loose. The Vice Chancellor at the time, Dr Alan Stewart, was deeply offended, as was a Hawke's Bay priest, Father Duffy, who started a campaign to get *Masskerade* banned. Letters of outrage and disgust poured into the *Manawatu Evening Standard*. Overnight a fundraising appeal for student hostels was stalled in its tracks. The Students' Association was threatened with prosecution and heavy fines. *Gallery*, a current-affairs television programme hosted by Brian Edwards, wanted me to fly to Wellington to debate the issue with Father Duffy. The Student Union was aghast at the prospect of me being interviewed live on air. I guess they feared I might bring my bag, alarm clock and phone. RING! RING! 'It's for you, Father Duffy. God wants a quick word . . .' They told me bluntly that if I went on television against their wishes they would wash their hands of me entirely. I would be on my own in the dock if I got sued and they would not meet any of my legal costs. I caved in and declined the invite—more cowardice that I still regret.

I didn't miss out entirely on going head to head with an enraged priest—the Massey Catholic Students' Association invited me to their pastoral centre to debate the merits of my publication with Father Jim Kebbell—a rising star in the church and something of a heartthrob with devout Catholic girls and girls of atheist persuasion alike. About 30 students and I sat in awkward silence in the large lounge waiting for my interlocutor to arrive. He swept in, black cassock flying, in full Spanish Inquisition mode. With his sharp features and fierce eyes he looked terrifying. I was terrified. But it was soon obvious that his heart wasn't really in it and his diatribe petered out. By the end of the evening we were laughing like drains together and became good friends. This sometimes meant a knock after midnight and Jim asking if I wanted a game of chess.

Jim behaved like a devoted son to James K. Baxter, who spoke occasionally at Massey gatherings, but only ever recited one poem that I can recall. It was short but he intoned it slowly and grandly, savouring his own words like boiled lollies.

Sometimes . . . I feel . . . like a turd . . . in the . . .
arse pipe . . . of life

Not his best work. 'Hemi', as Baxter had taken to calling himself, inspired a deep reverence in many, but I always felt there was something phoney about him (not his poetry, which ranks amongst the finest of the twentieth century). He would wait until it was raining heavily before announcing softly that he was walking to his Jerusalem commune on the upper reaches of the Whanganui River. Pulling his old duffle coat tightly around his stooped shoulders, he would pad in bare feet to the door only to be beaten by ten people offering him a ride, one of them usually Jim.

Years later, when Jim effectively excommunicated himself from the Catholic Church by getting married, and I had been excommunicated from Prime Minister Rob Muldoon's official press party covering a Commonwealth Heads of Government Meeting in Delhi, Jim and I met up again. He was an adviser and punkah wallah for his old chum, Samoan Prime Minister Tupuola Efi, who insisted that I join them both for a nightcap and deep background conversations every night of the conference. Excluded from Muldoon's press briefings, I ended up knowing more than any other journalist—all thanks to *Masskerade* 69.

It was also thanks to *Masskerade* 69 that deputy Prime Minister and Attorney General Jack Marshall wrote to Vice Chancellor Stewart on 24 December 1970.

> Though some people might contend that blasphemous libel as a criminal act belongs to a past age and should no longer be treated as a crime, it is clear that Parliament has intended that it remain one. The Crimes Act of 1908 was repealed and replaced by the Crimes Act of 1961. The provisions as to blasphemous libel were substantially repeated, it remains law and it would be the duty of the Police in appropriate cases to prosecute . . .

He included a blunt warning—events at Massey University over the past few years were testing the tolerance of the community too far, and in the event of a repeat transgression he would use his authority to initiate proceedings.

Under the Crimes Act, anyone found guilty of blasphemous libel faced up to a year's imprisonment. The statute has rarely been invoked anywhere in the Commonwealth since the war poet Rupert Brooke, up to his neck in mud, shit and rotting corpses in Flanders Fields in World War One, dared to question the existence of a higher power and was charged with blasphemy, deftly escaping punishment by dying in battle.

Marshall's letter was passed to me illicitly and I published it in full in *Masskerade* 70. Alongside his letter I included this note:

> Every year decent people are offended by the contents of *Masskerade*. What is most frustrating to them is the feeling they have no way to prevent the reoccurrence of such material. 'There ought

to be a law against it!' is a familiar cry. Well,
there are laws against it and you should read Mr
Marshall's letter to acquaint yourself with them.
As proof of our concern we have included a letter
of protest to the Attorney General and all you
have to do is fill in the particulars and post it to
the Justice Department. Please print legibly in
ink. Nom de plumes will not be accepted.

The Students' Association was horrified at this provocation. I
argued that should we end up in the court we could call God as
a witness. If he didn't turn up we had no case to answer. If he did
turn up it was the biggest news story of all time.

In the event the Attorney General ignored us, as did everyone
else. The righteous fury of the year before was a soufflé that
didn't rise twice. Bugger.

CHAPTER NINE

LOCKED IN

AFTER MY IGNOMINIOUS DEPARTURE FROM vet school I had a year to kill before Massey set up physiology as a stage three unit, which I needed to complete a rather tatty Bachelor of Science degree. I did a philosophy paper and a biochemistry paper, but mostly I drew cartoons for the student newspaper *Chaff*, and was a judge of Miss Massey, held on the cricket oval in front of the refectory.

I can picture it now. It was a warm, still evening. The grass was the colour of emerald. The setting sun lent the terracotta art deco buildings a pink glow. Young girls, hair and make-up perfect, jewellery sparkling, wearing glamorous gowns, approached the oval in an excited giggling gaggle . . . falling silent when they saw the temporary drafting yard that some ag students had set up on the lawn. Guys in black bush-singlets, shorts and gumboots (and this was well before Fred Dagg), armed with whistles and rattles and assisted by yapping dogs, rounded them up into a holding pen, where they stood ashen-faced until another gate was thrown open and with a lot more shouting and barking they were unceremoniously herded down a narrow race, on either side of which guys in white coats armed with red and blue raddle marked them on the back as they tottered past in their high heels towards a drafting gate, to be culled into the clearly identified finalists' pen or the ugly pen. Dazed girls fought back tears when they examined ruined ball gowns, not to mention the more permanent, incalculable damage to their self-esteem if they ended up in the ugly pen.

I hasten to add here that I was not part of this pre-selection process. I was dressed sombrely in a tuxedo, as were a city councillor and the local MP, the rotund and jolly Joe Walding. We merely mingled with the finalists, deliberated in private, then declared a winner.

I know what you are thinking and I quite agree. We have gone backwards as a society.

At the cocktail party afterwards, Joe, who was not afraid of a knife and fork, was piling hors d'oeuvres onto two plates as if a bell were about to ring sounding that time was up, caught my eye and looked guilty. I repeated an Ambrose Bierce quote that an abstainer was a weak person who yielded to the temptation of denying himself a pleasure. He got very excited and made me hold his plates while he scrambled for a pen and paper to write it down.

Some years later, at a parliamentary reception for a visiting rugby team, where Joe was keeping pace with giant locks at the canapés table, matching them mouthful for mouthful, I witnessed him whip this note out of his pocket and recite it gleefully. On the campaign trail of the 1984 snap election, the Labour Party appointed Joe as David Lange's minder because he was very shrewd, had a calming presence and every time they sat down to dine together, Joe's eating habits made David's seem anorexic.

—

A REPORTER AND A PHOTOGRAPHER from the local paper usually covered Miss Massey. One of them told me the *Manawatu Evening Standard* was on the lookout for a cartoonist, and the editor, Denis Wederell, would like a word with me. Drenched in Old Spice and looking as much like a Young National as I could, I met Denis in his office. A very short, personable, bald man, he offered me a job on a trial basis for the princely sum of $5 a cartoon. That settled, we went downstairs to visit the paper's owner, the ancient and venerable N.A. Nash, in his gloomy, mahogany-lined office. The paper had been in the Nash family forever—more than a business, it was a dynasty unparalleled since Rameses. Old N.A., who was 90 in the shade, reached for my sample folder with a trembling, liver-spotted hand. Grabbing a cartoon at random, he fixed it with a watery stare for all of two seconds before pushing it away.

'One thing we're all tired of is students! You can't pick up a paper without students rioting somewhere—I want nothing about students, understand? And Vietnam. I'm sick of Vietnam. Just be funny.' To his credit, Denis suggested I be allowed a certain freedom of expression. This incensed N.A. I thought the old bugger was going to die. He started wheezing and shouting that the paper was worth millions and they weren't going to have me jeopardise it in any way. He asked me if I knew how much his paper was worth. I didn't.

'Lots,' he said. 'Do you know the Prime Minister's wife, Mrs Holyoake?' I didn't, as it happened. 'I do. Lovely woman!'

Following this illuminating chat, we returned upstairs, where Denis gamely opined that N.A. was a remarkable man. 'He can sound so wrong so much of the time, yet it's truly amazing how often he is right.'

I didn't mind—I had my first paying gig, and was assigned a tiny office off the newsroom. Every cartoon was preceded by an editorial conference.

'Has anyone got any ideas for Tom?' No one ever had any ideas for Tom. Denis would look in my direction.

'Any ideas, Tom?'

'Well, Mr Wederell—Denis, sir,' I would cough, 'I was half

wondering about these campus riots . . .' My voice would trail off as Denis's face lit up. 'Rail fares to Auckland! Gone up again. Preposterous! Go to town on that!'

The next day every newspaper in the country was full of stories about the All Black trials for the upcoming series against the Springboks and the arrest outside the grounds of demonstrators opposed to New Zealand rugby teams touring South Africa. I suggested a cartoon about this big news story and was stunned when Denis agreed. Twenty-four hours after publication, a shamefaced Wederell told me N.A. didn't get it (I think the old boy did) and my trial was terminated. I had lasted barely a week.

I wrote about this brief foray into newspaper cartooning for *Chaff*. In the article I said that Denis was the same height sitting as he was standing. He sued for libel. I wanted to go to trial and summons Denis to the witness box (I was an old hand at this now), and ask him to sit, then stand. 'No further questions your Honour. The Defence rests.' The Student Union settled out of court for $600 dollars. It could have been more, but the libel was contained. When the offending issue of *Chaff* was dropped off in bundles around the city, *Manawatu Evening Standard* reporters were dispatched like commandos in dawn raids to snatch as many copies as they could find before they fell into anyone else's hands. Their orders were then to destroy them.

The late, legendary head of TV3 News, Gordon McBride, was a print man early in his career and came up from Southland as a young reporter to work on the *Manawatu Evening Standard*. On his first day, the deputy editor waved him across to his desk, discreetly slid open a bottom drawer and winked. Expecting a copy of *Penthouse*, Gordon peered in all excited and saw instead the offending issue of *Chaff*, open to my article.

Denis Wederell had long since left the building. We had both moved to Wellington. I would sometimes see Denis on Lambton Quay in the mid '70s. When he saw me coming he would dash through traffic to get to the opposite pavement to avoid contact. I thought he was going to get himself killed, so I gave chase next time, cornered him in a doorway and told him that this was stupid and we shouldn't be enemies. He was very relieved and immediately offered me a job caricaturing captains of industry for a business publication he edited. I even drew him for one cover. Recently I got a sweet note from his daughter. He was very proud of the picture and the family used it on the programme for his funeral service.

After being sacked as a cartoonist, I washed windows part-time and became invisible. Standing on a stepladder inside a lawyer's office, I smeared suds across a glass pane and wiped it off again while seated below me a distressed farmer's wife seeking divorce detailed her husband's depraved sexual demands. A former flatmate could see me all too clearly. 'Locky' Smith, now Sir Alexander Lockwood Smith, former Speaker of the House of Representatives and former High Commissioner to the Court of St James's, told me he did sudden U-turns in his car when he saw me trudging the streets with my ladder and bucket because he didn't want to hurt my feelings by whizzing past in his brand-new Ford Escort. That's compassionate conservatism for you.

I also wrote and produced my last capping revue, starring my friend, Peter Hayden, who went on to become an award-winning presenter and producer of wildlife television documentaries, both here and overseas. Latterly, at an age when most people are taking fewer career risks, he chanced his arm at acting full-time and has made a success of that as well.

The revue also starred a very pretty, super-bright social-sciences student, Christine, who became my first serious girlfriend. When Palmerston North Hospital opened a separate psychiatric unit and called for student volunteers to work night shift, we both applied and made the cut, with about ten other students. The first television drama I ever wrote, *Inside Every Thin Girl*, was based on an anorexic patient we befriended—Peter Hayden starred as one of the student volunteers.

Early evening, they locked us in with the inmates and unlocked the doors the following morning. We made toast and cocoa for patients who couldn't sleep and played endless games of table tennis to keep ourselves awake. Apart from one young man smearing his faeces on the wall, nothing untoward ever happened.

The front-door buzzer sounded after midnight one night. When I went to check who it was, my father was swaying drunkenly in the security lighting. We talked awkwardly through an intercom.

'Egghead, I'd like a job here. I could do this.'

'It's not up to me, Dad,' I replied politely. 'You'll have to talk to the hospital authorities.' He nodded and weaved off into the darkness.

As you'd expect, there was less of a stigma against mental illness in such an institution—the threshold for going loopy was much lower. The senior staff seemed to take it in turns having breakdowns of one kind or another. Mild cases were called 'acting out'—they sought sedation and were put in a room with a 'do not disturb' sign on the door. I was always tempted to add in felt pen 'disturbed already'. Others had full-blown psychotic episodes, which meant one of two things—either they were never coming back, or rapid promotion.

The occupational therapist was on leave after a nervous breakdown. Word got out that I could draw. With no training whatsoever, I was promoted to acting occupational therapist and put in charge of twenty patients, half of whom were schizophrenic, which made it 30 patients in total (just joking). It could be challenging. If you gave them playdough or clay they tended to make erect penises, and you had to give them positive feedback without looking perverted yourself. Not having a clue how to weave a basket and desperate to keep them therapeutically occupied, one afternoon I put John Lennon's haunting, post-Beatles, primal-scream album on the turntable and asked them to draw what they felt. The first track was 'Mother'. Big mistake!

Over metronomic, thudding-heartbeat drumming, Lennon started wailing plaintively that his mother had left him but he had never left her, and that he wanted her but she never wanted him. Yes, I thought, nodding my head in time. This is great! Then I heard something else. It was quiet at first, then built in intensity. A low moaning accompanied by gentle swaying, which I interpreted as a good sign until it escalated rapidly into banshee wailing, howling and slapping of foreheads. I quickly lifted the needle off the vinyl as staff came running from all directions.

'What happened? What's going on?'

'I'm not sure. Something set them off . . .'

At a staff meeting one morning, with Christmas Day just a few weeks away, I suggested that I might get the patients to help me make a Christmas cake.

'What are you going to bake it in?' smirked the head psychiatrist. 'The kiln?' He started shrieking with laughter, which obliged the rest of the staff to nervously join in. I wondered then if mental illness might be contagious.

My relationship with Christine got a whole lot more serious when she became pregnant. We got married in a park and had the reception at our flat. Tom Quinlan was my best man. Having set a precedent with my twin sister's wedding, my father did not attend.

I WORKED IN THE FREEZING works one final summer while looking for a job that matched my exceedingly lacklustre qualifications. The School of Occupational Therapy in the Central Institute of Technology in Petone needed a tutor in physiology. Provided no one else bothered to apply and they were desperate, I had a slim, long-shot, outside chance of getting it. I drove down for the job interview in my brother Michael's 'Noddy car'—a cute Morris Eight Sports.

Michael was a mechanical wizard. When we lived in Owen Street we shared a big bedroom. I kept my half spotless— operating-theatre hygienic. You could safely eat a meal off every surface. His side was a pigsty. Guitars, amplifiers, greasy tools and smelly clothing were scattered everywhere. I had to step carefully around engine parts soaking in trays of oil to get to my bed. I only complained on one occasion and learned my lesson.

'Look, Tom, I find your anal-retentive ways deeply offensive. Your obsession with neatness and order drives me mad, but have I ever grizzled and complained? No! Out of respect for you I have kept these feelings to myself.'

There was a lot of our father in him as well.

When I was contemplating purchasing a motor vehicle, I naturally sought his advice. He was soaking in a bath at Owen Street. I had to invade his privacy because he could be in there for hours. Not that it made much difference—the grime just seemed to swap pores. I told him it was a Ford Prefect and was going to cost me 60 bucks. He whistled softly.

'I dunno, Tommy . . . My Ford only cost ten dollars and it goes like a dream. The Buick cost fifteen dollars and only needed new spark plugs. The Morrie Eight is perfect and only cost twenty dollars. I've always said—pay more than twenty bucks for a car and you're only buying trouble . . .'

I was tootling along in his Morris Eight when I encountered a torrential downpour coming down the Ngauranga Gorge, turning the snaking descent into a nightmare luge run. The canvas top started streaming water and the single windscreen wiper, which provided a small wedge of visibility, stopped working. The car's designers had anticipated this might happen and thoughtfully provided a tiny lever on the inside of the windscreen that you could use to manually operate the wiper. With one hand on the wheel, the other hand throbbing from the effort of creating a clear triangle in the deluge, I slid down to the Hutt Motorway, buffeted, rocked and sprayed by cars and lorries thundering past me. What was I letting myself in for?

Even the name—Central Institute of Technology—sounded like one of those asylums the former Soviet Union maintained high in the Arctic Circle exclusively for dissidents. There were times when it felt like it. But the students, all female, not much younger than me, were sweet and lovely. There were some awkward moments. When a very pretty girl asked, 'Please, sir, what's an orgasm?' I blushed crimson, which I hadn't done for ages, and told her to see me after class. Much to my relief when the bell sounded she was the first person out the door, which suggested she knew the answer and was winding me up. The staff were also lovely. Mostly spinsters of a certain age, they made a huge fuss of me, the only male on the staff. The head of the school had a leg so withered by polio it had to be encased in a plaster sarcophagus painted in flesh tones. Quite literally a drag, she had to heave it along as she walked. It struck things and was cratered and scratched. Tall and pretty, she lived with her mum and her cats. When her mum died she killed the cats and took her own life.

I knew how she felt. Sitting in my small office overlooking the playing field, watching seagulls wheel overhead, trying to plan lessons with a mountain of essays at my elbow waiting to be marked, I couldn't escape the feeling that life was passing me by. We lived in Eastbourne. On the bus home the words from the big hit of that year, 'A Horse with No Name' by America, kept repeating themselves in my head, about how good it felt to be out of the rain.

Except it was still raining, the Morris Eight had died and we didn't know a soul. Our small downstairs flat had been built into a bank at the rear of a house by our landlord, who lived upstairs. There was hardly any natural light. The only view was of concrete-block retaining walls. We had no television set and precious little furniture. It was worse for Christine—she had a brain the size of Africa, was stuck in the house all day and was heavily pregnant.

SHAUN WAS BORN ON THE seventh day of the seventh month of 1972. He was beautiful. I floated more than walked back to CIT in Petone in the soft morning light for my first lesson of the day, vowing that I would be the best father ever for him. I fell short all too often and in middle age tearfully confessed this to my mother, fully expecting her to take issue with this harsh assessment, or at the very least say something neutral yet vaguely consoling, like 'You were very young, darling, and you did the best you could.' Instead she swooped like a bird of prey spotting a lost lamb. 'Dat's right, ye were! Ye were a piss-poor father to dat poor boy!'

Most lunchtimes I took sandwiches or bought a pie and walked from the CIT campus to the windswept Petone foreshore, where seagulls huddled together for warmth, and stared longingly at the glittering capital city across the water. I felt like Nelson Mandela staring across at Cape Town from the prison rock of Robben Island. Apart from him being locked up at night in a small, damp concrete cell, sleeping on a straw mattress. Apart from him breaking rocks in a lime quarry by day without sunglasses and suffering permanent eye damage as a result. Apart from being allowed only a handful of visitors and denied access to newspapers. Apart from being denied permission to attend the funeral of his mother or his first-born son. Apart from being subjected to verbal and physical abuse from some Afrikaner guards—apart from all that—our experiences were identical.

One of the biggest thrills of my life was giving the after-dinner speech at the one-hundredth anniversary celebration of the Parliamentary Press Gallery in Wellington's old Town Hall, at which Nelson Mandela was the guest of honour. Earlier in the evening a high-school choir sang South Africa's new national anthem 'Nkosi Sikelel' iAfrika' beautifully and Mandela thanked each girl in turn, shaking their hands warmly as tears streamed down their faces. I got to present him with framed originals of two of my cartoons—one I drew on his release from Robben Island, the other I drew the day he became South Africa's first post-apartheid president.

The dinner was a great coup for my mate, chairman of the Press Gallery organising committee and private-radio titan, the gravel-voiced Barry Soper. Barry's contacts are so good he is able to report accurately what some politicians mumble in their sleep. When he heard whisper of a possible Mandela state visit to New Zealand, faster than the speed of light Barry dispatched a dinner invite via the ANC in Pretoria long before the apparatchiks who arrange such state visits at this end had even thought about their first gin and bitters for the day. Mandela consented partly as a thank you to the role the New Zealand news media had played in the struggle against apartheid. Foreign Affairs, Internal Affairs and the Prime Minister's Department grizzled into their riesling at being gazumped.

After their regular Wednesday interview in his ninth-floor office, a peeved Jim Bolger asked Barry to travel down in his private lift with him. (Prime Ministers have one for their exclusive use.)

'Look, Barry, I really think someone of my stature should introduce Mandela.' Barry said he'd get back to him. He did. The answer was no.

To be fair to Jim, he did lead the fight against the 1981 Springbok tour inside cabinet, persuading almost every minister, bar Prime Minister Rob Muldoon and maybe one other, that the rugby equivalent of coitus interruptus needed to be practised. Being outnumbered twenty to one was tantamount to a draw in Muldoon's book so, using his casting vote, the tour carried on. To their collective shame his cabinet colleagues maintained a sullen silence in public.

When Mandela died it was galling watching assorted dignitaries and luminaries scrambling for a seat on the RNZAF flight taking Prime Minister John Key to South Africa for the state funeral—none of whom I remember being part of the handful of protesters outside the Hutt Recreation Ground when a white South African team participated in the World Softball Champs in 1976. Ever so politely, the cops requested we move away. A dashing, romantic figure leaped on to the deck of a truck with a loud-hailer and in a fiery speech condemned jack-booted Gauleiters and the creeping fascism of the police state—it was the fledgling poet Gary McCormick, barely out of primary school. Nor were they in the bedraggled huddle outside Athletic Park, mumbling 'Amandla! Awetho!' while thousands of Pākehā males streamed into the ground to watch the trials for the 1976 All Black tour to the Republic, some of them yelling out to me in passing, 'Why are you with those commies and homos, Tom?'

It was a fair question. I asked the eternally reasonable Halt All Racist Tours (HART) leader, Trevor Richards, who was standing near me, if he ever felt like chucking it in. He shook his head and smiled benignly under his bushy walrus moustache. He replied that the massive crowd pouring past us were ill informed, on the wrong side of history, but essentially decent. They would see the light one day. That's how he spoke, and he was right.

When John Key was asked what his stance on the 1981 Springbok tour was in a televised leaders' debate with Helen Clark during the 2008 election—which he went on to win handsomely—he could only manage an uncomfortable, sickly smile and the feeble claim that he couldn't remember, which is about as plausible as being a sentient adult on 20 July 1969 and later claiming you couldn't remember the moon landing. No one would have held it against Key if he had admitted to being a young snot-head in favour of the tour. He would have earned even more points still had he invited Trevor Richards and John Minto to travel with him to Mandela's funeral, up the front in the VIP section of the Air Force plane.

WHEN CHRISTINE WAS OFFERED A good job with the University Students' Association in Wellington I quit my job at the CIT and became a full-time househusband and child-minder. With or without ovaries, no one knows how demanding and lonely

a task this can be until they have done it for eight hours a day, five days a week, for months and months on end. How my mother coped with my sister Sue and me in London on her own I'll never know.

At times, I zoned out playing with Shaun and would break out of a daze to find him staring at me curiously. How long had I been silent, I wondered. And was this why he was slow to talk? He said 'Mum' and 'Dad' and a few other simple words but was essentially monosyllabic. We were worried sick. It turned out he was biding his time. One lunchtime, I was offering him something or other, and in a surprisingly deep voice for his age, he said slowly and deliberately, 'Actually, I would prefer . . .' 'Actually' was actually his first word in his first actual sentence. He started calling me 'Tom' shortly after this. When I asked why this was the case he looked at me as if I was stupid. 'Everyone else does!' I had to accept that.

When he had his afternoon naps I raced to the dining-room table and drew cartoons for *HART News*, for no fee of course, wondering when a real cartooning job would come along. Bounding up the stairs to the HART offices one day I heard music that I had never heard before, yet I recognised immediately. One of the few joys of the CIT was having the library on the same corridor as my office. I ducked in to read copies of *Newsweek* all the time. One issue raved about a sensual, hallucinatory, mystical, jazz/blues/rock album by an Irishman who sang with a singular intensity and urgency. I burst into the room. A singer was howling about venturing in the slipstream between the viaducts of someone else's dream and being born again. It was Celtic mumbo jumbo. It made no sense and it made perfect sense.

'This is *Astral Weeks* by Van Morrison!' I shouted excitedly. They couldn't confirm it. It was on the turntable when they arrived and they had just pressed repeat. I reached for an album cover I had never seen before. It was *Astral Weeks*. This song was a sign.

I was about to be born again.

The capital enjoyed two daily papers back then. The *Evening*

Post cartoonist was the legendary Nevile Lodge. He had been there so long he qualified under the act as a living fossil. His *Sports Post* covers of All Black test matches were rightly famous. Astonishingly, they came out on the same day as the game. You could listen to the test match on the radio in the afternoon, go to the flicks at the Regent in the evening, head for the pie-cart in Feilding's square close to midnight and be intercepted by a paper boy yelling '*Sports Post! Sports Post!*' and there would be Nevile's cartoon on the cover of a kiwi and a springbok locked in titanic battle.

I have kept up his tradition, but I was never a big fan of his drawing style or stolid view of the world. He was a testy curmudgeon long past his best when he finally retired and I replaced him on the *Evening Post*. Come to think of it—I am close to that age now and must make more of an effort to wear revolving bow-ties and break into song-and-dance routines when I enter the controlled anarchy of the newsroom…Come to think of it—they don't have newsrooms any longer, just hushed workstations and the low pinging of computer keyboards. (I only ever heard the fabled cry of '*Stop the press!*' once. It was the morning of the stock-market crash of 1987. I was dropping off one of my first cartoons to the now departed *Evening Post* when the editor, Rick Neville, came running out of his office and yelled it out across the stunned newsroom, then, snatching an old manual typewriter, began pounding out the front-page lead himself. It was very impressive.)

Nevile Lodge can be excused some of his gloom—he spent the best years of his life behind wire in a concentration camp, as did Sid Scales, the much-loved, long-serving cartoonist on the *Otago Daily Times*, and the great British cartoonist/illustrator Ronald Searle. The wonderfully whimsical Carl Giles and the celebrated, hard-nosed American editorial cartoonist Herblock (Herbert Lawrence Block) both began their illustrious careers as war artists. Pulling on rectal gloves and inserting your hand up a cow's bum at vet school hardly counts.

Eric Heath, the cartoonist for the *Dominion*, was a kind man of sunny disposition so it's hardly surprising his cartoons lacked edge. He was a terrific painter of marine life but I was not a fan of his cartoon drawing style or his choice of subject matter. It was too domestic—trolley buses, cats trapped in trees and impish politicians. N.A. Nash would have loved him. To my haughty gaze, neither Eric nor Nevile could caricature politicians very well. I get disproportionately irritated by cartoonists identifying people they are drawing by using names on clothing, briefcases, desktops or doors—it's a device we all employ from time to time when a person is not well known. When I resort to it I end up irritating myself.

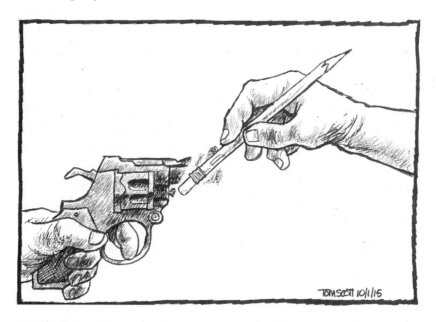

I grew up adoring the economy of line of the great Mort Drucker, who captured faces perfectly in *Mad* magazine's movie parodies. I also loved the spidery line and the assured cross-hatching depictions of writers, artists and politicians of David Levine in *The New York Review of Books*. Our very own Dunedin-based Murray Webb is one of the few cartoonists in the world to approach Levine's genius. I also admired the savage, jagged strokes and splattered ink of Gerald Scarfe and Ralph Steadman, who distorted politicians' faces to grotesque proportions while keeping them recognisable. And I have long been a fan of Bob

Brockie's wry, eccentric doodles in *The National Business Review*. His drawings in Victoria University capping magazines in the 1960s were a huge inspiration to me.

When Labour won the 1972 election and Norm Kirk became prime minister, none of the nation's cartoonists could draw him properly. There was something elusive about him. Like an explorer in a pith helmet searching for the source of the Nile, I went looking for the essence of Norm Kirk. I spent days, then weeks at my drawing board, growing weaker and weaker from hunger and thirst. I know memory is an unreliable thing but I'm pretty sure I came down with full-blown malaria and had a touch of dengue fever at one point (the same phenomenon occurred when my deadline loomed for *Listener* columns, then magically disappeared the next day). I began wondering if I should abandon this foolhardy, nightmare quest, when voilà! Norm appeared on the paper before me. Even now I am proud of this drawing, though the poor lettering in the speech bubble displeases me still. It was streets ahead of what everyone else was doing at the time and too good to waste on *HART News*—assuming they'd want it. Then I remembered that the *Post* and the *Dom* were not the only game in town—there was also the *Sunday Star*. Should I pay them a call?

CHAPTER TEN

DRAWING THE LINE

TUCKING MY KIRK CARTOON CAREFULLY in a folder and dropping Shaun off at day-care, I headed off with some trepidation for the *Dominion* building in downtown Wellington. It was a brooding neo-Gothic edifice. You could imagine gargoyles and a hunchback on the roof. The foyer was dark and echoing. I stood by the lifts for ages trying to summon up the courage to head for the offices of the *Sunday Star* three flights up. My nerve failed me and I returned to the pavement. It was a pathetic repeat of heading into a Massey University lecture theatre full of pretty girls then chickening out. I forced myself back to the lifts. 'Going up?' said a stranger, and I stepped in with him.

I told a receptionist on the third floor that I had something to show the editor. She told me to follow the bellowing. It came from a bear of a man who looked like a mob enforcer—the

The Reason Labour Won is Because We represent the Little man.

Scott.

late, great Frank Haden. He was genuinely scary. He took my drawing in a huge paw, glared at it through heavy horn-rimmed spectacles, nodded approval, demanded another one next week and waved me away. The audience was over. The rapture I felt at that moment was repeated four days later when I opened up the *Sunday Star* and saw my cartoon in pride of place. I was a published cartoonist in a national publication!

Years later, Frank and I were part of a press junket to Eastern Europe just as the Iron Curtain was coming down and countries released from 40 years of brutal Soviet subjugation were frenziedly changing the drapes. In a bar in Budapest we met a local musician who didn't speak a word of English but sang 'St. James Infirmary' beautifully, accompanying himself on harmonica between verses. To my surprise, Frank, now a jovial, cuddly bear of a man, joined in on the chorus. You think you know a guy!

Frank accepted another half-dozen cartoons and I settled joyfully into my new role, not realising that I was about to be reincarnated again. Across town in the offices of the *Listener* which, thanks to its monopoly on television-programme schedules, enjoyed a per capita circulation matched only by *Pravda* (more than a few people used to swear that in the right light you couldn't tell them apart), the social historian, trade unionist and contributor of blackly comic pieces to this publishing juggernaut Tony Simpson was informing the new editor, the towering, handsome-in-an-aging-film-star way, Ian Cross, that due to commitments in Stockholm these contributions would cease for a period. In desperation Ian asked him if he knew of anyone who could possibly fill in for him.

Tony and I had never met. I was illustrating articles for the New Zealand edition of *Rolling Stone*, edited by Alister Taylor, which Tony also wrote for (he was everywhere!). One day I told Alister I would dearly love to do a parody of Tony's idiosyncratic comic prose. This was duly passed on. Tony was flattered that some neophyte scribe wanted to mock his writing. When Ian Cross needed someone to come off the subs bench, Tony unhesitatingly selected me, for which I will be forever grateful and indebted.

Tony has just published an erudite, witty and wise memoir of his own, *Along for the Ride*, in which he recounts his slightly different version of the role he played in my becoming a *Listener* writer. He also adds a footnote to this story from his time working for Jim Anderton, in the deputy prime minister's capacity as a member of the honours and appointments cabinet committee. Tony was asked to check with me whether I wanted to be put up for an honour. Tony phoned and I consented, cautioning that it had also been proposed under the previous Lange government but had been turned down on the grounds that I made fun of them. Nevertheless, writes Tony, Jim's nomination went ahead and when the list was published my name was there. Tony commented on this to Jim, who grinned and said that mention of my name had triggered much the same response as earlier— 'He keeps laughing at us'—to which he had retorted, 'Of course he does, that's why we are giving it to him.' Everyone looked sheepishly at the table and my name went through.

John Key didn't ask for this cartoon.

I should declare here that Jim has purchased more originals of mine than any other politician—both the unflattering and the flattering ones. He only stopped when he ran out of wall space. Michael Laws, both as an MP and as mayor of Whanganui, kept my children in shoes with his purchases. John Key couldn't resist owning an original if it included President Obama in the drawing. He paid me in bottles of his own 'JK' pinot noir, which dazzled some guests at dinner parties and disgusted others. If Bill English starts collecting originals I guess I can look forward to pizza topped with Wattie's spaghetti from a can.

I was holidaying in Malaysia with Averil when the 2006 New Year Honours were announced. I had become an Officer of the New Zealand Order of Merit and I was thrilled. In some ways, I was very fortunate to make the investiture at Government House later that year. The day before the announcement was made we were in a huge enclosure housing thousands of feathered creatures. The heavens over Kuala Lumpur opened up like a spillway of a hydro dam, sending us scrambling for shelter under a spreading banyan tree. The tropical downpour was incredibly heavy and showed no sign of letting up, so gradually, one by one, flamingos, herons, ducks and pelicans took shelter with us, squeezing alongside, almost touching, avoiding eye contact like strangers on a crowded commuter train. Shaun, now a hefty six foot five with the lung capacity of a channel swimmer, asked forcefully but not unreasonably, 'Why are we standing in Asia's largest aviary at the height of the Asian bird flu epidemic?'

Radio stations and various news outlets tracked me down for comment. It is customary on these occasions to say that you see the award as a tribute to your profession as a whole, and that you accept on behalf of a team. I insisted the award was for me and for me alone—the cartooning fraternity could get their own bloody gong. It was obvious I was joking and that I was pretty chuffed by the whole exercise. I received warm letters of congratulation from the unlikeliest of people, which touched me.

My default setting of biting the hand I was supposed to kiss could account for the fact I have never been appointed to any statutory board or commission. Russell Marshall told me that shortly after Labour swept to office in the 1984 election, at an early cabinet meeting the subject of appointees to the board of broadcasting came up. Russell cheerfully suggested me and was shocked by the tsunami of fury that ensued. 'Not that bastard!' would best sum up the reaction. Nearly half his colleagues were smarting over something I had written or drawn. At the same enclave David Lange wanted a woman, a Māori and a South Islander for the board of Radio New Zealand. Judy Finn of Neudorf Vineyards fame in Upper Moutere was mentioned. Judy, Miss Massey the year I judged, had been a smart, witty broadcaster and lived in the South Island, thus ticking two boxes. Going for three in row, Lange wanted to know if she had any Māori blood at all. Mike Moore couldn't help himself. 'It is my understanding, Prime Minister, that from time to time she has a little Māori in her.' He was joking, everyone knew it and laughed heartily. Some jokes are just too tempting to ignore and truth doesn't come into it. When John Lennon was asked if Ringo was the best drummer in the '60s, he couldn't help himself either. 'Ringo wasn't even the best drummer in The Beatles.'

IAN CROSS'S RECOLLECTION OF OUR first meeting differs from mine. In the foreword to my collection of parliamentary columns, *Ten Years Inside*, Ian writes that I turned up in bare feet and blue jeans, a slightly bemused expression on my benign face exaggerated by the lopsided angle of spectacles held together by sticking plaster. I can't deny the latter because I don't stare into a hand-held mirror when I walk, only sitting down. But I most certainly was not barefooted. Exposure to James K. Baxter ensured I was only ever barefooted on a beach or in the shower.

What I do remember with a searing clarity is putting my cartoons in a folder, strapping Shaun into a baby seat and setting off in my Ford Cortina for the Charles Fergusson tower block adjacent to Parliament with Alice, our chihuahua-fox terrier cross, yapping and leaping between the front and back seats. I must have come down winding Glenmore Street too fast because cartoons sprayed from the folder and suddenly Alice was carsick. I pulled over, close to tears, and flicked chunks of partially digested dog food off the cartoons with an old beach towel, then mopped up the excess fluid, leaving straw-coloured stains on some of the drawings.

Ian was very good about it. While I paced about jiggling Shaun he opened the windows of his office to let in fresh air and placed my smelly folder on his desk. Turning the pages slowly he studied each cartoon in turn, silently and with intense concentration. After an interminable, unnerving wait, probably only ten minutes or so, he flashed me a lofty, patrician smile— somewhat inevitable when you stand well over six foot—and said, 'Young man, you are a writer! I have a small job for you . . .'

Cross had the vision of a South American condor when it came to spotting raw talent from a great distance—Geoff Chapple, Gordon Campbell, David Young and Rosemary McLeod were all hired by him and quickly became stylish feature writers or stylish columnists—in Gordon's case, both. They are all still doing great work today in plays, books and on websites.

That first writing assignment turned out to be a financial writers' seminar held by the New Zealand Society of Accountants at the James Cook Hotel called 'Fact, Figures and Fallacies'. Hold me back! I hoped that it would be held in a large ballroom with a standing-room-only crowd, allowing me to hide down the back, but it transpired that the Discovery Room at the Jimmy Cook was not much bigger than a large lounge and only three-quarters full. The intimate setting and my early arrival meant a full gauntlet of introductions. With my blond afro, flaming-red beard, platform-sole shoes and flared jeans I stood out from the chartered accountants and stockbrokers. Everyone was perfectly civil but it was long, dull day. This was my first job with the *Listener*, I was desperate to do well and here I was fighting to stay awake. All I could do was send it up, which may well have been Cross's intention all along. He could be very Machiavellian. It was part of his charm.

He was pleased with the piece and the next week I was sent off to cover the United Women's Convention in Auckland, with baby Shaun and Christine. It was so earnest and well intentioned it made fun of itself. All I had to do was write it down accurately. Cross was delighted with my mockery. Middling pieces on assorted topics of my own choosing followed and I chose poorly. My new career was in danger of dribbling to a halt until Cross set me another test—though he was too shrewd to frame it like that. I was dispatched to cover the Royal Opening of Parliament in February 1974.

The piece began with a true account of a conversation between middle-aged ladies and the gentlemen of military bearing, whose contribution was mainly body language, that I eavesdropped on in the foyer of Parliament Buildings as her Majesty entered.

'She's a country girl at heart.'

'Yes, she's a country girl at heart.'

'Spirited she can be too, just like her dear old dad, George.'

'Yes, just like her dad, a country girl at heart.'

'Mind you, there's a touch of Mary in there.'

'Oh yes, there's no denying that.'

I finished the article on the Queen hoving into view after exiting the old Legislative Council Chamber. A curious soft moaning emanated from the same watching women. I wrote that it was unlike any other sound that I'd heard before— exhaled from deep in the larynx, it could only be likened to the sound young children make when holding a kitten. It morphed into language as the Queen approached.

'Isn't she beautiful?'

'Oh, look at that.'

I wrote that as an infidel I had been witness to a very special communion.

I must have passed the test I didn't know I was sitting because Ian immediately made me the *Listener*'s parliamentary correspondent. I got my own column right up the front of the publication, emblazoned 'TOM SCOTT'S PARLIAMENT', with my photo printed alongside it. I am all hair and spectacles. I was once described in a comic debate televised live on a New Year's Eve, quite possibly by Jim Hopkins, as resembling a rat peering through a toilet brush, an apt description that was shouted out joyously in the streets by strangers for years afterwards. Muldoon even borrowed it once for a speech at a National Party conference, but with the inexorable passage of time the description no longer fits and it has fallen into disuse. I am no longer recognisable, and a hairless, neonatal possum peering through a toilet brush with white plastic bristles doesn't have the same ring to it.

BACK THEN YOU ONLY GOT to work in the Press Gallery if you had done tours of duty reporting on court proceedings, city council meetings, industrial disputes and the return of the much-feared Island Bay dog poisoner. Only a handful of elder statesmen—they were all men—got to write their own political columns. I was a virgin in a brothel with the instant status of a madam. It was galling for the older gallery members, some of whom made no effort to hide their dislike and suspicion of me.

Accreditation was confirmed annually. In what may have been just coincidence, when Muldoon came to power these older members challenged my membership at a Press Gallery AGM. I don't pay much attention to these things so I wasn't present to defend myself, but I did run into TV reporter Spencer Jolly shortly afterwards. He was still ropeable. 'It was an outrage, mate!' he railed. 'I bloody told them so! I said this is a kangaroo court! You are acting as judge and jury! If this vote goes ahead, I want my abstention recorded in the minutes!' Thanks, Spencer.

Years later I was made a life member of the gallery. If the mood takes me I can sling an identity tag with a magnetic strip on it around my neck and wander freely about the corridors of power, with the exception of a few hallowed sanctums like the Prime Minister's lift and the members' swimming pool—but then again, the last thing you really want to see is an MP in a string bikini or budgie smugglers.

Before I could begin my new life, I had to purchase a tie, get a haircut and trot down to the coin-operated photography booth in the foyer of the railway station in search of a suitable likeness for my first press card. When it arrived, Ian Cross guided me across to Parliament like a proud parent taking a child to their first day of school. We entered the building through an unattended rear door, of which there were several. There is only one entrance for members of the public today. You have to step through a metal detector and your bags are X-rayed. Ian knew the old building well and headed unerringly for Bellamy's. We went down back corridors that had peeling plaster ceilings and worn carpet. Shallow wooden boxes filled with sand serving as ashtrays lined the walls, along with mysterious dark bronze tulip structures which I later discovered were spittoons. What should have taken just a few minutes took almost an hour because we kept running into politicians he used to cover as a young reporter on the *Southern Cross* newspaper. They invariably greeted him like a long-lost friend, including former prime minister Sir Keith Holyoake, who boomed, 'Ian, dear boy, dear boy! How nice to see you!' He had an incredibly deep voice for such a small man. In one edition of *Masskerade,* beneath the bold headline 'TESTICLE TRANSPLANT FOR PM', I published a news photo of him holding two hairy kiwifruit in the palm of his hand. Given the rich baritone bouncing off the plaster and marble, they should have been coconuts at the very least. I was actually quite fond of old Keith by then. I had warmed to him ever since he told Brian Edwards on television that his favourite book of all time was *Origin of the Species* by Charles Dickens, and that the simultaneous worldwide eruption of student protest against the Vietnam War was due to sunspots.

We eventually made it to Bellamy's and caught up with Ian's old chums in the Press Gallery who could give me some pointers. Bellamy's back then was a ramshackle old wooden structure that leaned against the south wall of the main building. It was always busy. You came down rickety stairs through an air-lock of cooking smells, tobacco smoke, body odour and hops. Every evening it had the casual gaiety of a benign riot. The bar was one of those continuous-counter affairs that you can still find in the odd country racecourse. Thin partitions segregated the various castes. At the far end, messengers got a bare wooden floor. Next door to them, the press got greasy linoleum. The Members and Members and Guests bars graduated to carpet the colour of bile, sticky with spilled beer. Any pattern had long since been obliterated with cigarette burns. (Ironically, the adjacent dining rooms, similarly segregated on class lines, had grand kauri sideboards, gilded mirrors, crystal chandeliers, starched linen tablecloths, heavy silver cutlery and the finest china.) People entered the cubicle appropriate to their status, hung up coats, tucked briefcases against the walls, then checked the stainless-steel warming drawers to see what tasty morsels were left over from lunch. Sometimes there were crumbed oysters and sweetbreads but mostly it was fish in limp jackets of batter. Stomachs lined with carcinogenic lipids, they were ready to battle through a Japanese commuter crush to the bar where warm beer was served through a long hose.

That first afternoon I nursed a pint and stared about in wonder.

'Well, young man,' shouted Cross above the cacophony, 'what do you think?' It was amazing.

'I guess it will have to do.' I grinned back.

MY FIRST COLUMN APPEARED ON 9 March 1973. I acknowledged that, in appointing me their parliamentary correspondent, the Listener had avoided the pitfall of hiring an expert, and I would bring to the hallowed calling of political reportage much-needed bumpkin simplicity. My political philosophy could best be described as dynamic conservatism—which was akin to virile impotence. I was trying too hard.

I read those early columns today with a strange mixture of pride and embarrassment. In my own defence, they were like Bellamy's fish and chips—best consumed hot off the press before they had time to cool and congeal. They had a galumphing energy and innocence, which automatically made them different from what everyone else was doing at the time.

I didn't want to write the same column twice, which was

difficult because much of parliamentary life was repetitive. When the House was in recess I ransacked my childhood for columns. I wrote about my time at the CIT and grisly anatomy lessons conducted around a cadaver in dimly lit, chilled rooms at the back of Wellington Public Hospital. A morgue attendant with a macabre sense of humour played the same prank every week. I had to dash in first, crank the body out of the rust-coloured embalming fluid and rearrange the partially dissected hands before the innocent girls studying occupational therapy arrived and were confronted with a dead man masturbating. I got an official warning that the article breached the Human Tissues Act.

I was on a downward spiral. In a few short years, I had gone from libelling someone who had risen from the dead to someone who hadn't. Had I been prosecuted I would of course have gratefully written about the trial. I wrote about anything and everything that I thought might amuse my readers. I was still trying to get the hang of things and was in a near permanent state of high excitement and low-grade anxiety. Plus I was moonlighting on my final edition of *Masskerade* with John Clarke.

When John rang me from a second-hand clothing shop it provided the inspiration for one of my favourite pieces—The Dead Man's Coat. It was too good to waste so I later incorporated it into my stage play *The Daylight Atheist*, on the assumption that it is perfectly acceptable to plagiarise your own work.

> I'm now the proud owner-occupier of a dead
> man's coat. It's a very fine coat and must have
> once been very expensive. I was very pleased
> with myself when I handed the lady the $10.
> I said to John, 'The cloth alone is worth twice
> that!' 'Yes, you've got it very cheap, son, probably
> on account of him being dead and thus in no
> position to argue.' It was John who found it for
> me in one of those small second-hand shops
> in upper Cuba Street. 'I've got just the thing for
> you, lad. It's huge. It should fit you like a surgical

stocking.' It took three assistants to get it off the hanger and across my shoulders. I cooperated from below as best I could by stepping into it with a clean-and-jerk movement. It was truly magnificent. While rummaging through the pockets I came across a discreet label: *Anderson and Sheppard Limited*, 30 Cellar Road, London W1, and the owner's name. He'd been knighted. 'He must have been down on his luck to sell this,' I commented to John. 'He's dead,' said John. 'You don't come much unluckier than that.' There was no gainsaying that. 'Is it warm though?' he asked. 'As toast!' I replied. 'Crikey! He can't have been dead long!'

IN THE EARLY 1970s, Hunter S. Thompson's extraordinarily visceral and brutally candid *Fear and Loathing on the Campaign Trail '72*, covering the 1972 US presidential election, was the inspiration the world over for a whole generation of fledging political journalists, including me. The young Bill Ralston was an early disciple, and you can still see Thompson's influence in the gifted descriptive passages of Steve Braunias and the brilliant comic essays of Raybon Kan. Imitation is the sincerest form of flattery, except Hunter was impossible to imitate even though I tried. His book included these killer lines.

> Ed Muskie talked like a farmer with terminal cancer trying to borrow money on next year's crop.

> Humphrey is a treacherous, gutless old ward-heeler who should be put in a goddamn bottle and sent out with the Japanese Current.

Thompson's approach to journalism was to swamp his bloodstream with every legal and illegal mind- and mood-altering substance he could grab, then to deafening rock accompaniment pound away at the keyboard of an electric typewriter in a hallucinogenic frenzy before sending dazzling stream-of-consciousness prose to his editors, who were white with panic as deadlines ran over, on a new-fangled invention called a fax machine.

Muldoon had one on the 1978 campaign trail. It was a closely guarded secret. It was the size of a small chest freezer. I saw it being loaded into the boot of a car at Napier airport by two men wearing sunglasses. Granted it was a sunny day, but this added to the air of mystery and intrigue. Rumours swirled that it was a gift from the CIA. Over drinks in a bar that night I poured wine into Muldoon's press officer and he let slip that staff in National's election HQ in Wellington could draft speeches for his boss and then transmit them to him anywhere in New Zealand over a telephone line. Holy Toledo! We were shocked and dazzled. These were the days of miracles and wonders.

Thompson called his fax machine the 'mojo wire' and he dubbed his writing 'gonzo journalism'. The novelist Tom Wolfe called it 'the new journalism' and *The New York Review of Books,* which didn't approve, called it 'zoot suited prose'—which is a compliment in my book. Thompson was to baby boomers what F. Scott Fitzgerald was to pre-World War Two America—with not dissimilar tragic endings.

I hate seeing people out of control, stripped of dignity and talking gibberish when intoxicated, so I am averse to drug-taking of any description—apart from caffeine, the odd hefty slug of Jameson's and a glass or two of pinot. I have always maintained there is nothing wrong with double standards as long as they are high.

Christine had returned from a trip to China visiting collective farms, crèches and the like, convinced that Shaun should go into childcare. He was such an eccentric little boy, voluble and full of fun at home, but quite shy and timorous in the outside world. We tried placing him in a perfectly acceptable playcentre in Campbell Street, Karori.

'You go,' smiled an older woman running the show. 'He'll be fine.' He was racked with sobs by the time I got to the door. I crouched outside a window for twenty minutes listening to him howl. When my bawling got louder than his I went back indoors and took him away.

A group of like-minded friends was setting up a family group to look after each other's kids—Shaun had no problems with adults he knew and homes he was familiar with—so we joined. My turn in the child-minding barrel was Friday morning—as luck would have it, the same day as my *Listener* deadline. I was too busy chopping up apples, dispensing cartons of yoghurt and cleaning up after the odd toilet accident to be a wild and crazy guy. As far as I was concerned, gonzo wasn't feasible in God's Own.

The closest any of us ever got to fear and loathing was while covering Rob Muldoon at the height of his considerable powers. My first parliamentary exposure to him came when I was covering Roger Douglas's Superannuation Bill Select Committee in the old Parliamentary annex behind Broadcasting House. (Douglas was an innovative, reforming, democratic socialist long before he became an innovative, reforming neo-liberal. Only his polite, unswerving, deadly zeal never changed.) Close up I witnessed a nifty piece of footwork by Muldoon that completely blindsided hapless government MPs on the committee. I mentioned him in dispatches:

> Most of the Opposition members were on time
> but only two Government members had arrived.
> The deputy leader of the Opposition seized
> the moment. 'Your lot are late,' barked Muldoon.
> 'Standing orders say we start at ten. Where is
> your chairman?' His gravel-voiced delivery
> and his expression—a frown in the process
> of becoming a snarl—seemed to unnerve the
> forlorn Government members. 'If you lot
> don't nominate a chairman, then we will!'
> And he did . . .

—

IT WASN'T MY FIRST CLOSE encounter with Muldoon. I wrote a piece on him for *Chaff* after he addressed a capacity crowd of students at Massey and ran rings around anyone foolish enough to challenge any of his assertions. As an exercise in intimidation it was only bettered by Māori activist Dun Mihaka in the same lecture theatre some months later. Wearing heavy boots, short footy shorts exposing thighs and calves the size of tree trunks, and a torn white singlet, he paced back and forth like a caged big cat, except we were the ones feeling trapped. He tore strips off smug Pākehā liberals who thought they should be congratulated for all they had done for the tangata whenua. Despite being outnumbered 300 to one he kept us all cowed and trembling for well over an hour.

Years later we became friends when he asked me to draw a picture of Prince Charles and Lady Di in the back of a speeding Daimler witnessing him baring his tattooed buttocks—which actually happened as they left Wellington airport in a crisp southerly. Dun was very lucky the wind-chill factor didn't kill him. It was for the cover of his book *Whakapohane*, which someone should make into a film. When drawing the picture I discovered a tender side to Dun, which I hadn't expected. 'Make her, beautiful, eh!' he purred. 'She's a very pretty lady!'

When Sir Robert Jones founded the New Zealand Party in 1984 with the express intention of prising the clenched, arthritic fingers of his old chum Rob Muldoon off the levers of the economy, the party held its inaugural conference in Wellington. Dun, who had joined the party that day, tried to speak to a remit on prison reform. He was denied permission and was asked curtly to leave the stage. He started arguing with the chair. Jones left the stage to call the police. The delegates stared screaming, 'Out! Out! Out!' It was a terrible moment for a party congratulating itself on its tolerance—and not the most pleasant moment for Dun either, who listened to the animals baying for some time before turning his back on the hall and dropping his shorts. Horrified members and security guards surrounded him like hyenas nipping at a wounded rhino. From the press benches I could see hurt and a rare fear in Dun's eyes.

I got up and led him away before anything crazy happened, whispering to Dun that it wouldn't matter who threw the first punch—he would be the only one arrested. He was grateful.

Ironically, when Labour won in a landslide a few weeks later I met a delegation of Māori elders milling about one evening in Parliament's foyer. 'We've come down to talk sense into these new fellahs, eh,' said a silver-haired kaumātua with a carved walking stick. 'We've got to get Māori off the tit, Tom. We've got to get our young people off the tit of welfare.' There were affirming nods and murmurs all round. Then his handsome face clouded over. 'And you know what? We had to pay our own way here, eh! We had to pay for our own airfares!'

Dun's finest gate-crashing was the time he eased past Parliamentary security and made his way to the august offices of the Speaker of the House, Dr Gerry Wall, who also happened to be his local MP. Wall was shocked to see him. Half rising in his chair, he pointed to the door and demanded Dun leave. Dun replied that given the fact he lived in Wall's electorate, he had visiting rights. Differing views were exchanged on this matter. It got tense. Dun says he pushed Wall ever so lightly on the chest at this juncture and his ergonomic chair on rollers flew backwards, striking something and depositing the Speaker of the House of Representatives onto the carpet—across which he proceeded to crawl, reaching for the phone on his desk. Dun told me his mind started racing at a million miles an hour.

'I said to myself, think, Dun, think! You are in a power of shit now, boy! Think!' Wall's bony, nicotine-stained fingers were about to dial. 'Then it came to me!' Dun slapped his huge hand on Wall's, pinning it to the table. 'You tried to touch my cock!' Wall looked up at him, aghast.

'That's preposterous! I did no such thing . . .' Dun told me he could see horror and uncertainty on Wall's blood-drained face, which gave him some hope.

'I've heard about you Pākehā perverts who love brown cock!' Dun turned on his heels and exited. He expected running footsteps. Nothing. It was the same when he descended the front steps. No shouting, no ringing alarms. He reached his old van parked on the concourse and turned the keys, bracing himself for thumping on the door that never came. He drove off scarcely able to believe his luck.

I WAS PUSHING MY LUCK with Muldoon in the pages of the *Listener*. He was so confrontational and belligerent in the House that I had no choice but to write about him. Over the next ten years many people would ask me why the press didn't simply ignore him. My stock response was that would be like driving across the Desert Road on a clear day and refusing to look at Mount Ruapehu—it couldn't be done.

Shortly after Muldoon's psychological victory in the Superannuation Bill Select Committee, he was at it again in the chamber. After a Beehive banquet and a bellicose address from a visiting US Secretary of State on the evils of communism where, to borrow Denis Welch's great line, the Müller-Thurgau flowed like wine, Muldoon was more splenetic than usual during Question Time, accusing the elderly, amiable and somewhat bumbling Speaker Stanley Whitehead of shielding a minister. This is the parliamentary equivalent of a player shoving the referee—at minimum a sending-off offence. Hurt and rattled, Whitehead lamely requested that Muldoon withdraw and apologise. Instead he snarled that he'd had enough and was going to walk out, compounding the offence. His colleagues rushed to his defence, pleading clemency. Muldoon's scowl softened and with a knowing smirk he rose and said, 'I made it honestly. I withdraw and apologise.' Throughout the afternoon. Opposition members came across to speak to Muldoon. Grins and quiet pats on the back were exchanged.

I wrote that the Terror from Tāmaki had done it again, and that it was a schoolboy apology from Parliament's most famous schoolboy. Tiny hairline fractures began appearing in our relationship about this time. Two years later the wings fell off.

These days Winston Peters employs similar theatrics in the chamber but they lack his former role model's deadly menace. It doesn't help that at the height of his outrage Winston will sometimes wink at his bench-mates or flash a grin at journalists in the gallery.

When Winston was a relatively new, second-term Member of Parliament I was exposed to this bipolar skill shortly after I had mocked him in a cartoon. We bumped into each other in a back corridor and he immediately flew into a self-righteous, Old Testament fury—he knew exactly what game I was playing and he wasn't having it. I reminded him of Mark Twain's advice that you should never pick a fight with people who buy printer's ink by the barrel. I was looking for a cartoon idea and he just might feature again. At approximately twice the speed of light his molten rage morphed into silken charm and an infectious crocodile grin bisected his handsome face. I have cartooned him mercilessly and viciously many times since, yet we remain on friendly terms. He sure knows how to hurt a guy.

Most political parties in Parliament host drinks evenings for the Press Gallery, and the Press Gallery reciprocates with a huge omnibus piss-up/barbecue at the end of the year where normally mild-mannered people get absolutely shit-faced. It is estimated that the majority of the members of the Speaker's Chair Club gained entry to it in the murky aftermath of these Rabelaisian evenings.

The Speaker's Chair Club is the ground-level equivalent of aviation's famous Mile-High Club. To qualify you have to engage in an act of sexual congress in the Speaker's chair, and it has to be with a land mammal of some description. For obvious reasons this is frowned upon when the House is actually sitting. The practice began during the tenure of Speaker Richard Harrison, the loveliest and most genteel of men, a Hawke's Bay farmer who started the tradition of upholstering the Speaker's chair in lamb's fleece. It proved too tempting for the libidinous and Harrison could never figure out why the wool ended up with more lanolin than it ever had on the animal's back.

Sadly, I never qualified for this most secret of societies, but in March 1974 I was invited to drinks hosted by Her Majesty's Loyal Opposition in their caucus rooms on the ground floor of the old Parliamentary Library. Journalists and their partners waited in a line to be formally welcomed by the elegantly attired Leader of the Opposition, the former Prime Minister and Attorney General Jack Marshall. The man who once threatened me with blasphemous libel, the man who I had recently drawn declaring he'd set up a shadow cabinet and he was head shadow, greeted me so courteously and so effusively it was almost embarrassing. Equally warm and gracious was his wife Margaret, still a great beauty in late middle age. Next in line was Marshall's rumpled deputy, in an ill-fitting pale grey suit, white shirt stretched to breaking point on his billowing gut and a poorly knotted tie: Rob Muldoon. He took one look at me, shook his great dome of a head and refused to shake my extended hand.

I was shocked, but pretended to be quite unruffled—a lesson my father had taught me. Grabbing a fruit juice and a club sandwich I worked the room talking to surprisingly affable Opposition MPs until Marshall, with a little help from his friends, climbed unsteadily onto a red leather couch and in his soft, slow fashion and with a thin, damp-lipped smile, announced that next time we met for drinks National would be back in government. Gallery chairman Terry Carter sprang onto the same couch and said the press couldn't possibly wait that long, and could they bring the drinks forward a few years. This elicited good-natured laughter, but Gentleman Jack was not wrong—except he would not be the leader. Within weeks of that drinks night his deputy had deposed him.

Two years later Marshall invited me to be a guest on the pilot of a television show he was hosting called something like *After Dinner with Jack*. Towering John Roberts, the left-wing, loquacious and opinionated professor of political studies at Victoria University, was one of the other guests. We pretended to eat a meal until Jack pushed back his plate, tapped a glass of wine and asked our opinions on the great issues of the day. I remember a fun-, banter- and laughter-filled hour ensuing. Afterwards a BCNZ producer armed with a clipboard came dashing into the studio to declare himself thrilled, but could we do it all again please, and could we let Jack say something this time?

THE OPPOSITION HAS FORMED ITS'
SHADOW CABINET, AND I'M
HEAD SHADOW!

Marshall's demise came as no surprise to regular observers of the House. His aloof immobility contrasted starkly with Muldoon's constant interjections, endless points of order and withering contributions to debates. Even more telling was the incessant exchange of notes, secret signals and knowing grins that Muldoon exchanged with his colleagues. There was a feeling that Marshall was prepared to let things happen, whereas Muldoon would make them happen.

The Third Labour Government had enjoyed an extraordinary honeymoon in their first year back in office. The Prime Minister, Norm Kirk, was much lauded, both here and abroad, for New Zealand's fresh and independent voice in world affairs. In the House itself Kirk was an imperial, unassailable colossus. There was a feeling in National's ranks that to give themselves any chance in the next election they needed to be led by a bare-knuckle street-fighter with scant regard for the Marquess of Queensberry rules. The Member for Tāmaki fitted the bill—even when perfectly still, slumped in his seat, he appeared to be grinding his teeth together. Blessed with a splendidly fierce countenance he would occasionally slowly scan the government benches and this would invariably leave the observed looking queasy and uncomfortable, as if caught in the glare of a searchlight sweeping from a watchtower. In a prison movie Muldoon would be the one leading the rioting and the throwing of food.

About this time, perhaps by sheer coincidence, his first and best book *The Rise and Fall of a Young Turk* came on sale. I went to the launch in a Wellington bookshop. Devoted fans lined up for autographed copies, asking for dedications to themselves or for relatives. I waited patiently in line then slid my copy onto the desk in front of him. Muldoon looked up without expression.

'Could you inscribe it "to the fabulously talented, warm and witty Tom Scott"?' I smiled. He said nothing and wrote: 'I love your wit—such as it is.'

IN THE TWENTY YEARS THAT I covered politics for the *Listener*, the *Auckland Star* and the *Evening Post* (the latter two now deceased), I attended more party conferences than World Health Organization guidelines say is strictly good for you. Both major parties had their fair share of earnest lunacy. Put simply, Labour saw it as their sacred task to save the world, whereas National's sacred task was keeping Labour out of office. It meant Labour's annual get-togethers were like Lent and National's like Mardi Gras.

At one National Party conference in Christchurch I sat in the back seat of a rental car in Hagley Park on a wet Saturday afternoon watching a girls' hockey match, while in the front seat, the late Neil Roberts, a television reporter with more pirate charm than a flotilla of Johnny Depps, and Marilyn Waring, National's rebellious outspoken lesbian, passed a joint back and forth, debating which girl they would most like to take to bed— though they didn't express it quite that politely. I couldn't help thinking I was not in Feilding any more.

At an after-match function at a National Party conference in Dunedin's lovely old town, while music played and corks popped, I pointed to a not unattractive, blousy, Dolly Parton blonde across the crowded room and whispered to my colleagues that rumour had it she was Muldoon's mistress. At National's next conference one year later she pushed through the crowd, glowered fiercely and said she had a bone to pick with me.

'You told your mates that I was Muldoon's mistress!'

All wounded innocence, I insisted that I would never say such a dreadful thing and that she was completely mistaken.

'*Don't bullshit me!*' she hissed. '*I teach deaf children. I am a lip reader.*'

What are the odds?

This sort of weirdness just never happened at Labour conferences, which was a great shame. Federation of Labour conferences were never that weird either, but they could get pretty whacky.

I was at their forty-third annual conference in Wellington's old Town Hall when newly elected chairman Jim Knox, famous for his mangling of the English language, rose to his feet and announced proudly, 'Fellow delegates! I have been coming to Federayshun of Labour conferences now for twenty-five years in concussion.' It was hard to disagree with him.

That was the year his secretary mistakenly stapled two copies of the same address together and Jim didn't twig to the suspicious thickness. Even at single thickness Jim's speeches were not noted for their linear precision and clarity. Tossing caution and the rules of pronunciation to the wind, he would attempt ad libs. The effect was much like a stereo needle on a dirty LP—halfway through one train of thought the needle in Jim's brain would skid and he would suddenly be ranting about something entirely different.

On this occasion his improvisations had pushed the speech out beyond the critical 60-minute mark. Bladders were filling, blood-sugar levels were falling, hairpieces were itching, nicotine cravings were kicking in and appointments for casual adultery in nearby hotels were fast approaching (in that regard, they had more in common with National than Labour). Delegates began shifting restlessly in their seats craving the magical words, 'In conclusion ...'

They waited. They waited. And they waited some more. Finally, there was a collective sigh of relief when Jim simultaneously bellowed and mumbled—something only he could do, 'In conclusion, fellow delegates, lemme say thish! We're not on a collishion course wiv the Gummerment! The Gummerment are on a collishion course with us! Thank you! Thank you very mush!' Severe leg cramps prevented most of them from leaping immediately to their feet to applaud, and in that critical micro-hiatus Jim turned the page.

'Fellow delegates! I have been coming to Federayshun of Labour conferences now for twenty-five years in concussion ...' It was too late. He was already reading the entire speech again. I stole this incident for my screenplay *Separation City*.

The weirdest National conference of all was just after Marshall's dumping by his own caucus. The party at large didn't know it was coming. They weren't consulted and were still sentimentally attached to their former leader. Matters weren't helped at their Sunday church service when Muldoon gave the sermon and quoted scripture to the effect that if a limb was diseased it needed to be cut off, while the Marshalls sat stoic and stony-faced in a pew below him.

It was more of a poor man's Sodom and Gomorrah back at the South Pacific Hotel at the bottom of Queen Street, where most of the press and National MPs were staying. The BCNZ's silver-haired and utterly charming current-affairs maestro Des Monaghan used the company cheque book to shout a huge swag of us to a raucous meal at the ritzy rooftop restaurant. Wild parties spilled down the corridor I was staying on. I remember being shocked when people poured champagne they couldn't be bothered finishing down the ventilator shafts. One MP's wife, half out of her frock, rolled around in a wardrobe with a young reporter. Pat Talboys, the wife of the gentlemanly, universally well-regarded former senior cabinet minister Brian Talboys, slurred tipsily, 'I hope we don't get back into government. Our sex life is so much better now we're in opposition.'

'Darling, darling . . .' demurred the horrified Talboys. So much for power being the ultimate aphrodisiac. You got the feeling National had done something precipitate that they felt slightly ashamed of.

CHAPTER ELEVEN

GOING ONCE . . .

BACK IN WELLINGTON THE FOLLOWING Monday, I braced myself for my first ever prime ministerial press conference. It hadn't been possible earlier because Norm Kirk had been absent overseas or convalescing after varicose-vein surgery. At the appointed hour the Press Gallery trooped upstairs to the Prime Minister's suite on the third floor of the old Parliament Building and loitered nervously in the marble and columned foyer like novitiate priests waiting for an audience with the Pope. I never saw this degree of caution with any other Prime Minister. With Lange there was always excitement, and with Muldoon apprehension, but nothing on the scale Kirk induced.

Twenty minutes of low, stilted conversation took place before we were ushered down a gold-carpeted corridor and allowed into a large office with windows that looked down on a drab internal courtyard with olive-green walls. It reminded me of

Colditz. The windowsills were carpeted in pigeon droppings.

We waited silently in this room, notebooks, tape recorders, lights and cameras at the ready, for quite some time before a door at the back of the room opened and a big man entered and shuffled slowly to a huge brown desk, where he lowered himself gingerly into a chair. He had one foot in a large, shiny, black leather shoe, the other in a sock and sandal.

I had never been this close to him before. I was shocked by his appearance. You didn't need half a degree in veterinary science to see that this man, if not terminally ill, was close. He was chalky white. His hair was plastered to his temples by sweat. It wasn't a hot day and he was the only person in the room perspiring. When people asked questions he spoke so slowly and the gaps between sentences were so protracted there was room for whole separate conversations, had anyone dared.

At the finish, Ian Templeton from the *Auckland Star,* a dear man and shrewd journalist with impeccable sources, rose and said, 'Prime Minister, I'd like you to meet a new member of the gallery.' I approached the Prime Minister's desk and put my hand out to shake his. Wearily, he raised his giant hand off the desk. It was damp and limp.

Outside in the safety of the corridor I expressed an alarm that none of the other reporters seemed to share. Kirk's health had been deteriorating slowly and inexorably for so long the gallery barely registered the decline any more.

I never saw Norm Kirk at anywhere near full strength, but even unwell he was a commanding figure in the House. His mere presence seemed to charge the air of the chamber with a strange tension and expectation. He always entered the floor of the House through the side door and they were especially grand arrivals, as he did so behind an escort of shorter colleagues. He would pause to joke with people like Joe Walding. Even when in considerable pain he would reach his bench grinning broadly, and before taking his seat he would turn and give an exaggerated wink to those in the back rows behind him. It was a performance of a captain telling his men they had nothing to worry about.

If he rose to speak he was granted an immediate respectful silence. Few dared to interject. Even Muldoon was cautious. Members from both sides of the House sat up straight and paid close attention to what he had to say. Should he begin to shout, the Press Gallery filled to overflowing as if by magic. Reporters denied desks to write at would stand about exchanging grins, happy just to share in the excitement.

Kirk never warmed to the concept of journalists looking down on politicians—he thought it should be the other way around. Journalists should cover Parliament from a deep pit in the floor. I'm glad this never happened. Imagine the shock of looking up a cabinet minister's nostrils and seeing nothing but daylight.

The only other parliamentarian who could pull a crowd like Kirk was David Lange, whose press conferences in the Beehive theatre were must-see events. There was a suspicion that numbers were swelling due to senior civil servants sneaking in to catch the vaudeville.

As Kirk's health deteriorated his triumphant entries into the chamber became less and less frequent. His last lap began with varicose-vein surgery in April 1974. Eager to return to work, he denied himself an adequate recovery period and complication followed complication. As his strength eroded, so did party morale. Kirk felt this keenly and in private he would rage at the terrible fatigue that dogged him. He took to shooting the pigeons soiling his windowsills with an air rifle, contributing to rumours that he was half martyr and half fruit loop.

Not long after the Labour Party conference where Kirk had castigated the news media, *Inquiry* reporter George Andrews met him in the car park beneath Parliament. Laden with a couple of briefcases and some notes, Kirk moved with a slowness that was painful to watch. George plucked up the courage to offer assistance. Kirk shook his head. 'George, I'll carry these bloody things even if it kills me.'

In June he was cleared for full duties but this failed to quell growing public anxiety. Aware of the wild conjecture, Kirk joked grimly with reporters following minor surgery to treat an ingrown toenail that the same incision had been cunningly used to remove assorted cysts, growths and cancerous tumours.

On 28 August, Kirk entered Our Lady's Home of Compassion in Island Bay for complete rest. The next day, at a parliamentary reception for a visiting sports team, I grilled junior government whip Jonathan Hunt on the real state of his leader's health. Jonathan was more interested in dropping hints about a big story he was intending to go public on the following week, and assured me loftily that the Prime Minister was on the mend.

Kirk died two days later, on Saturday, 31 August, after a seizure. He was 51 years old and had been Prime Minister for barely 21 months.

The week after his death was the most extraordinary I ever witnessed on the Hill. Rain began falling constantly in the capital, and with it came a cloudburst of grief of stunning intensity. That grief, like the rain, seemed to endure for about a week, then abate as suddenly as it had come.

SORROW IS LIKE A SPLINTER in the heart, and I have often wondered if Labour would have fared better in the '75 election if a little piece of the splinter had been left in place and wiggled at appropriate moments, or if they had called a snap election straight after Kirk's death, when the grief was the size of a vampire stake.

Instead Labour were desperate to paint a picture of business as usual, and put Kirk behind them—as if his death were of no great consequence. He was hardly mentioned by Labour on the hustings. Significantly, on the campaign trail in Rotorua, Rob Muldoon made a well-publicised detour to pay his respects to Kirk's widow, Dame Ruth. If there was any legacy to tap, Muldoon wasn't going to pass up the opportunity.

After Kirk's death, his government driver told me a sad story. Very near the end of his life, Kirk had an engagement at a Catholic school in Palmerston North. Several times on the two-hour drive from Wellington they had to stop for the Prime Minister of New Zealand to get out of the car, lower his trousers, squat on the side of the road and purge himself of bloody diarrhoea. Pale, shivering and humiliated, he got back into the LTD apologising profusely. What struck the driver was how alone Kirk was.

Kirk's death came as no surprise to his driver. I learned through a terse, jarring *Sunday Star* headline: 'KIRK DIES AGED 51'. I read it over and over again in disbelief. I hurried down to Parliament on Monday morning, pen and notebook at the ready. In the marble foyer there was an air of hushed, reverent chaos. Workmen in shorts and boots had been there since four in the morning making preparations for Kirk to lie in state. They jostled for space with messengers and television crews. Outside on the concourse, a crowd began to assemble quietly. As the hearse drove up the first strains of a Māori lament moved the base of public grief from one of polite containment to one of free expression. Then Pacific Island groups started singing soaring hymns. Polynesian New Zealand began acting as a catalyst and poultice for diffident Pākehā sorrow. Anyone within hearing distance who had any feelings on the matter could feel them being tugged to the surface.

Norm Kirk's body in its huge coffin was placed in the foyer of Parliament with a New Zealand flag draped over it and potted ferns placed around it. Soldiers from all the forces stood at attention at each corner, their rifles upside down. People queued well into the night, three nights in a row, in steadily falling rain, for a chance to pay their respects. Some brought young children with them, awestruck and silenced by their parents' grief. A few asked hushed questions.

'What are the soldiers doing, Mum?'

'They are changing the guard, Michael.'

'Is that anything to do with Christopher Robin?'

'No, dear, it has nothing to do with Christopher Robin.'

When I enquired why they had brought their kids out at such a late hour in such bad weather, the standard response was that this was a piece of history. They wanted them to pay their respects and say goodbye to a great man who would be talked about and remembered for many years.

That hasn't been the case. Kirk slipped off the radar relatively quickly and is seldom mentioned now. The scale and the depth of the mourning for him forced many commentators into new assessments of the man, but this frenzy of post-mortem punditry—I indulged in it myself—died away with the subsidence of the unprecedented sorrow.

That sorrow subsided faster for some than for others. I stood watching mourners file past the coffin for the best part of a day. I was there when Kirk's Labour Party colleagues came to pay their respects. The queue had slowed and a small bunch of them paused within earshot. They were grinning and delighting in the fact they had the numbers to ensure that Kirk's deputy, Hugh Watt, wouldn't become leader. With Kirk lying just a few feet away, there was something shocking and harsh about their pragmatism.

I was still there when it was Sir Keith Holyoake's turn. He stood in front of Kirk's coffin booming, 'Farewell, Norm, farewell!' He wasn't being theatrical or attention-seeking. There were tears in his eyes. It was a genuine and touching salute to a respected political opponent. Sometimes it is easier to pay tribute to a fallen foe than your own comrades. The French have a saying that no man is a hero to his valet.

On the Tuesday afternoon the House paid tribute to the fallen Prime Minister. Three of the most moving speeches came from Opposition spokesmen. 'Fifty-one,' said a pale Brian Talboys, 'is too young to die.'

'I find it very difficult to accept that the big man will not walk through that door and enter this chamber again,' said Holyoake.

'He graced the office of Prime Minister,' said Jack Marshall, adding, 'We treated each other with mutual respect, which is probably mystifying to our more rabid supporters.' Through all the implied rebukes, Muldoon stared sourly straight ahead.

Kirk's coffin was so heavy the pallbearers almost lost control carrying it down Parliament's steep steps. It lurched forward and they had to step quickly to keep up with it. He was loaded into a hearse, driven to Wellington airport and loaded with full military honours into the belly of a Royal New Zealand Air Force Hercules, which is probably still flying today. They took off in a terrible storm bound for Timaru, the closest airport to Waimate, where he was to be buried. The weather was so bad Timaru airport was closed, and the Hercules was forced to turn back to Christchurch. The coffin was swiftly unloaded and without ceremony shoved into the back of a revving hearse, and with one police car in front and another behind, the funeral cortège accelerated south into the lashing maelstrom. My locking partner from social rugby, Phil Melchior, a reporter for NZPA, and other pool journalists followed in two additional cars. Through whipped-up spray and sheets of rain they chased screaming sirens and flashing red lights. Police on motorbikes blocked off side-roads as the convoy hurtled south, well in excess of the speed limit, to get to the Waimate cemetery before nightfall.

Phil told me that racing through small country towns was quite off-putting. Local radio stations had reported that the Prime Minister's body was coming. Heads bowed and hats removed, citizens lined main streets that had become shallow lakes. Not slowing, the convoy raced past, sending up walls of water like Moses parting the Red Sea. Mourners would have seen very little and been left drenched.

They got to Waimate cemetery just as the rain eased off and the last rays of the setting sun struck the burial plot where the Prime Minister was finally laid to rest. Almost as soon as the earth hit the top of his coffin, the Labour Party began pretending he never existed. They didn't know it yet—no one did—but their re-election chances were being buried with him.

IN JULY 1975 I WAS wildly excited as well as nervous when Qantas offered to fly me to Australia as its guest on its inaugural flight from Sydney to Belgrade, in what is now Serbia. Apart from one trip to Auckland and back on an Air New Zealand flight, still within sight of land, I had never left New Zealand soil.

I didn't possess a passport. When I applied, I found to my dismay that I wasn't entitled to one. I arrived here as a toddler and it was remiss of my twin sister Sue and me not to correct our parents' oversight and apply for New Zealand citizenship the instant we stepped off the gangplank. At the age of 28 I had to traipse to the British High Commission in Thorndon with my birth certificate in exchange for the dubious glory of a United Kingdom of Great Britain and Northern Ireland passport—which for years to come put me at the head of the queue should a plane get hijacked and they started executing passengers.

Back then the first Boeing 747s with their distinctive bubble were just starting to roll off assembly lines in Seattle in huge numbers. With the onset of the jumbo-jet age, passenger numbers soared exponentially as well. New Zealand, once described by Rudyard Kipling as last, loneliest and loveliest, all of a sudden seemed closer to the rest of the world. I wrote at the time:

> Does constant rubbing of the shoulders with
> people draped in Spanish leather, Italian
> suede, French velvet, American denim, English
> check, Mexican saddle cloth, Bolivian llama
> hide, Japanese silk, Bali batiks, Indian saris,
> Mao tunics and camouflage jackets from the
> Indochina war zone tend to put you, in your
> Hugh Wright's winter clearance sale viyella
> creams, a little on the defensive? When others
> talk of lovemaking with beautiful strangers on
> the Côte d'Azur, moonlight poetry readings at
> the Acropolis, being shot at by rebel tribesmen
> in Iran, more fornication in Vienna, dysentery
> in Damascus, alcohol poisoning in Munich, still
> more fornication in Rome and broken axles
> in Islamabad, do you keep your slap and tickle
> stories from the Foxton sand dunes to yourself?
> Do you also automatically assume that people
> are no longer interested in the time your scooter
> broke down in the rain opposite the Palmerston
> North gasworks?
> If you do, you are suffering from what my
> sophisticated friends call OE deprivation.

OE, of course, is the abbreviation for overseas experience—and no New Zealander, it is claimed, is complete without it. As well as being vital to emotional, intellectual and sexual development, OE very nicely fills that awkward gap between high school and marriage. In fact, OE must be pursued when young and is often used to force reluctant partners into marriage or as compensation when marriage plans fall through . . .

My sophisticated friends using the term 'OE deprivation' were in fact only one man, John Muirhead, my chum from *Masskerade* and *Chaff* days. I have falsely been given the credit ever since. Things even out.

In another *Listener* piece I wrote that when New Zealanders moved to Australia it raised the IQ of both countries. Muldoon helped himself to this line at a press conference a week later and it has been cited for years as proof of his droll genius. My joke! I have no real cause for complaint—I had refashioned it from a Will Rogers line in the first place. Besides, I was chuffed that Muldoon was reading my columns.

The Qantas trip could not have come at a better time. Another old chum from Massey, Greg Bunker, then earning a king's ransom prescribing pills to pampered poodles in Manhattan, put it best when he warned, 'At your present rate, you'll get here playing mah-jong on the sun deck of the *Mariposa*.'

I was a nervous traveller. Getting out of the Manawatū was a wrench. So what if the world was my oyster? With my luck I would be allergic to shellfish.

It helped that in Sydney all the journalists on the Belgrade junket were given a guided tour of the Qantas base at Mascot. When I discussed safety issues with a man from Qantas he said I had nothing to fear—my worries about flying were groundless. I said it was the groundless bit that worried me. To demonstrate the principles of flight, he blew across a piece of paper. 'There,' he said proudly, as the far edge rose, 'the Venturi effect—that's what keeps these seven hundred thousand pound babies forty thousand feet aloft.'

Shortly after take-off, most of the press party had managed the spiral staircase to the Captain Cook lounge in the bubble. Before we had left Australian air-space, they had drunk the bar dry of beer. It was thirsty work flying for hours over parched sand and rock, albeit hidden in inky blackness far below us. Then they uncomplainingly switched to spirits and that was all gone before we reached Singapore. It was my first exposure to the Aussie media and you couldn't help but love them.

Apart from Australia, which barely counts, and Singapore, which was just a stopover, the former Yugoslavia was the first country I ever visited. Much like a duckling or gosling believing that it is the same species as the first living creature it sees on hatching, I imprinted on Yugoslavia. I want to return to Lake Bled and Dubrovnik and take Averil with me. George Bernard Shaw once said that if there is a heaven on Earth, it is Dubrovnik.

I came close to heaven when I played in a doubles match on clay in Dubrovnik with the great John Newcombe, Ken Rosewall and Rod Laver. I partnered 'Rocket' and it was largely thanks to his speed around the court that we won the first set seven games to five. We were no match for Newcombe and Rosewall in the second and third sets, however.

The match was played on a private court in an exclusive suburb of Dubrovnik before a highly partisan but surprisingly knowledgeable crowd consisting of two ball boys, a whitewash-application man and a suspicious head groundsman. They watched us in contemptuous silence. The tennis wasn't worth keeping an eye on, but the hired sandshoes and expensive hired racquets were.

I should point out that for the purposes of the match I was Tony Roche, and my new Aussie mates played the other Aussie tennis greats. We had to stay in character the whole match. I should have been completely outclassed, but being Tony Roche for the morning I lifted my game to previously unscaled heights. In short, it was the most enjoyable tennis match I have ever played.

I was impressed with the Australians' ability to weave and

sustain an elaborate schoolboy fantasy. It eventually got to the stage where Rosewall began to argue with an imaginary linesman, and Newcombe began shouting his hotel room number to imaginary girls in an imaginary crowd. The whole trip, the guy playing Newcombe had only one answer when you asked him how he was: 'I'll be OK, mate, when I've had a root.' When we drove through the streets of Zagreb in a bus he crouched at the front like Queequeg, the harpoonist in *Moby Dick*, spotting attractive girls and awarding points out of ten. 'Nine pointer on starboard, boys! Holy fuck! Eleven pointer on port!'

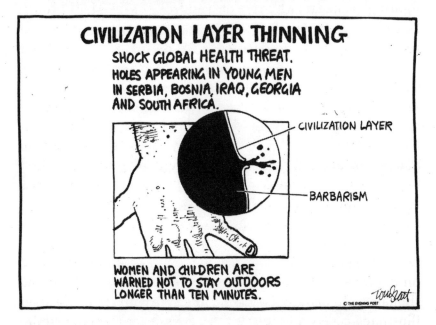

Watching the news fifteen or more years later, it was horrifying seeing beautiful landscapes and glorious medieval towns that had seemed calm enough to our naive gaze descend into sectarian violence, 'ethnic cleansing' and a genocidal barbarism unmatched since the charnel houses of World War Two. I did some of my better cartoon work on this more recent bloody chapter in European history.

If you want to be sickened again, read *Slaughterhouse: Bosnia and the Failure of the West* by David Rieff. He recounts a chilling moment for members of my generation in particular, who believed in the redemptive power of music, where Serbian troops head off for another day of rape and butchery with Bob Dylan blasting through their Sony Walkmans.

I DIDN'T TAKE THE QANTAS flight back to Sydney with the other journalists. Instead I flew on to London, where I hung out with friends on Fleet Street and spent an afternoon in the Press Gallery in the British Houses of Parliament. It was hardly an in-depth investigation, yet when I got back to New Zealand, fighting back tears when we descended over the Marlborough Sounds on a crystal-clear morning towards Wellington's dear rugged coast, Ian Cross decided to put me on the *Listener* cover. I am wearing the tan suede jacket Christine bought me in China, I am sucking a cigar Winston Churchill fashion, I am saluting, I am wearing a pith helmet, and I am photographed against a large Union Jack. The tagline is 'Tom Scott and other New Zealanders in London'. Visually it was cheesy overkill and, given the ordinary copy I submitted, quite unmerited, but Ian was determined to milk whatever star status I had. And if I didn't have any star status he was determined to manufacture some.

To my shame, I was a more than willing accomplice. Over a two-year period either my cartoons or my likeness appeared on the cover of the *Listener* nine times. There was a head and shoulders photograph, two cartoon versions of me, and five other illustrated covers on subjects as various as the Commonwealth Games in Christchurch and Muldoon's first prime-ministerial trip to the People's Republic of China—in which I depicted him striking a heroic, Mao-like pose on a wall poster, in the bottom right-hand corner of which some creature has recently emptied its bladder.

It was very nearly ten covers. Ian commissioned an election-year cover then rejected it as too provocative. I drew a movie poster with a jovial Muldoon as King Kong on the top of the old Parliament Buildings, snatching biplanes out of the sky, while in the foreground an equally jovial Bill Rowling pilots

a circling Sopwith Camel. The tagline was: 'NOW SHOWING: PARLIAMENT. G. Certificate'.

Ian was absolutely right on one thing—the censor's rating was far too lenient. That year in politics there were scenes of graphic violence, coarse language and naked, full-frontal appeals to greed and fear. Ian could see coming what the rest of us couldn't—Muldoon was shaping up to overturn Labour's seemingly impregnable majority, so there was little to be gained depicting the next Prime Minister as a giant ape and pissing him off unnecessarily.

I was the one pissed off. I decided to print it as a poster that would make me rich and teach the *Listener* a lesson. I ended up with a pile of them in my garage sitting alongside the stacks of unwanted copies of *Masskerade* 73. They came in handy as gifts and I have only one badly creased copy left.

AFTER KIRK'S DEATH, ON 6 September 1974 the Labour caucus voted for Bill Rowling to be their next leader, with Bob Tizard as his deputy. They were the best choice at the time. It was impossible to dislike Bill, but harder to be impressed by him. With Bob it was the other way around.

During the 1975 election campaign, I was with Prime Minister Bill Rowling when he opened a new gymnasium at a high school in Tokoroa. Afterwards, as people were streaming out, I must have looked lost because he asked me how I was getting to his rally in Taupō that night. In those days, the *Listener*'s largesse extended to typewriter ribbon, litres of white-out, modest hotel accommodation and airfares, but not rental cars. I replied sheepishly that I was hitch-hiking and he immediately offered me a lift in his LTD. I became wildly excited—here I was, little Tommy Scott from Feilding, riding in the Prime Minister's limousine!

As we crawled through cheering crowds in the school grounds, a local Highland pipe band formed a guard of honour on either side. Accompanied by the stirring skirl of bagpipes, we swung out onto the street. Heroically they kept pace with us as we gathered speed, almost sprinting in the end, not fluffing a note until oxygen debt kicked in and they fell away one by one.

It was then that I felt a joke coming on that I just had to share with my new best friend.

'Have you noticed, Bill,' I beamed, 'the only two things they pipe out of town are politicians and sewage!' The car rocked with hearty laughter. I was too busy slapping my thighs and dabbing my eyes to appreciate that it was coming only from me and the snickering driver. My new best friend had gone puce with indignation.

'Fuck you, Scott! I've a bloody good mind to make you get out and walk from here!'

It was in Rotorua that I realised for the first time that Labour could lose the election. We were sitting in the bar next to a steaming hot pool when one of National's campaign ads came on television. To ringing balalaika music, animated Cossacks danced across the screen. A hook snatched away a ballot box, while a voiceover asked what freedoms were safe under Labour.

All the National Party ads were in this vein—extremely slick, very accomplished for their time and like nothing New Zealand had ever seen before. While undeniably clever, they were also fear-mongering, red-baiting and black propaganda—they should have been slapped with injunctions the first time they slithered out from under a rock.

Rowling's people came into the bar shortly afterwards. They hadn't seen the ads and they weren't particularly bothered—everything was tracking nicely according to the feedback they were receiving. There was just no way the country would vote for Muldoon. Their smugness and naivety were deeply disturbing to witness.

It was a wild, giddy, emotionally charged, high-stakes election. On the campaign trail with Muldoon in Napier I called in to see twin sister Sue. Noticing my jittery state, she enquired gently into my wellbeing. I replied that I was hardly getting any sleep and that I was exhausted. Larry, her husband, whose contracting firm was carting boulders for the extension of the Napier breakwater, put things neatly into perspective for me. 'Yeah, those fountain pens can get pretty heavy.'

I suggested to friends appalled at the prospect of a Muldoon ministry that they should dress as sweet, demure nuns and pack the front two rows of the Founders Theatre in Hamilton on the night of his campaign launch. When the red light came on indicating that he was being broadcast live into a million homes, they were to rise as one, chanting in unison, 'MULDOON'S A CUNT!' But no one listens to me. I also suggested filling a bike pump or water gun of some description with a mixture of cream-style sweet corn and ripe Roquefort or Stinking Bishop cheese and, when Muldoon was in full flight, splattering it across the front of his shirt, creating the impression that he'd just vomited on himself. With a bit of luck this would trigger a chain reaction of projectile vomiting throughout the hall of Monty Python's Mr Creosote proportions, and the broadcast itself would have to be halted and replaced with a still of the Freyberg boat harbour.

It is now a matter of record that Muldoon never chundered

over his own clothing at his campaign opening, but instead went on to win the election in a landslide. There were many reasons for this. The tide had gone out on Labour, National's election bribes were bigger and better sold, but mostly Rob Muldoon had simply more intellectual firepower, more physical stamina, and was vastly more ruthless than his opponents—which sadly many found appealing. No blow was too low, no taunt too cruel. He had been on the receiving end of cruelty and abuse all through his school days and was determined as an adult to get his retaliation in first. Muldoon would never have offered me a lift. If he had I may not have accepted. What I know for sure is that I would never have dared make that joke.

With Muldoon's stunning victory, Parliament, already fractious and fiercely tribal, became even more bitter and partisan. Had Rowling stepped down as leader at this point, which Geoffrey Palmer and Bill English did when their governments were heavily defeated, it is hard to imagine Muldoon endorsing let alone enthusiastically campaigning for him to get a top job at the UN—which John Key did unstintingly for Helen Clark after he defeated her.

Shortly after his big win, I met the new Prime Minister in a Parliamentary corridor—always a scary experience. He had a colleague in tow, and as much for his benefit as for mine, Muldoon paused to bark, 'Ahhh, Scott isn't it? I read an article of yours in the *Listener*! I didn't know *you* could write!'

A voice, not my own, jauntily and foolishly replied, 'I didn't know *you* could read!'

His colleague grinned. 'He's got you there, Rob—' then instantly regretted it when Muldoon glowered at him. We were both on the outer, though my time in the gulag lasted a little longer.

THE NAME SOWETO HAS A lovely Swahili cadence to it, but in fact it is an acronym for the South West Townships—shanty suburbs for black South African workers, servants and their families that sprawl endlessly across brown barren plains outside of Johannesburg. On the morning of 17 June 1976, Sowetan students gathered in the street to protest the introduction of Afrikaans as the official language of instruction in local schools. Their 20,000-strong peaceful protest was halted in its tracks by ferocious police brutality and murderous fire. The official death toll of young blacks killed by the police was 176. Other estimates put it as high as 700. Less than two weeks later the All Blacks, who were travelling with the blessing of newly elected Rob Muldoon, touched down in the Republic to play a four-test series and provide comfort and distraction for the ruling white minority.

Like many others, I was appalled. I wrote an angry column about a Pākehā student uprising in New Zealand, where an oppressed white majority are subjugated by a brutal Māori minority.

> Today Otara still smoulders. Many buildings couldn't be saved, while others were deliberately left to burn. Soldiers and policemen, ironically many of them Pakeha, cautiously patrol the rubble-strewn streets. The worst of the rioting and destruction have died down now. No one seems to know how many people have died. 'Well,' Rangi Nathan, the Minister of Police, told a press conference in Wellington, 'with Pakeha it's always hard to tell.' And the foreign press crews smiled politely.
>   'I know you boys have deadlines to meet,' he continued. 'If you want an official death count I'd put it at seven. Remember too, one of the seven fell under a tank and the other six died of natural causes.' 'Natural causes?' exclaimed the grizzled API Reuters correspondent. 'Our information is that most of the dead were shot through the heart at point-blank range!' The Minister merely grinned. 'Gentlemen, I put it to you, what is more natural than to die when you've been shot

through the heart at point-blank range?'

Unofficial sources put the death toll at over a hundred, with the number of wounded running into the thousands. The situation is complicated as Otara has no hospital or morgue of its own. The final toll will depend on what the army and police clean-up units find buried in the corrugated ruins of the three gutted primary schools.

The most vicious rioting in New Zealand's history lasted over three days and at times spread as far north as Queen St. Often there was no purpose to it as young Pakeha gangs rampaged through the streets, smashing windows and stealing luxury items like television sets, food and clothing. The electrical goods were a popular if mystifying choice as Otara is still without power. 'Most Pakeha don't earn enough money yet to pay enough tax to justify such capital expenditure,' explains Koro Rolls, the Minister of Social Welfare . . .

I knew Cross would hate it, so I didn't hang around long when I dropped it off at the subs desk. I am a tireless, fearless warrior for freedom—just not *that* fearless.

About an hour later I was back in Karori when I got a phone call from Ian, during which he accused me of continually challenging his authority and writing deliberately provocative material that pushed my own point of view rather than mocking the views of others. He said he wouldn't print it. I said sadly that it seemed like a parting of the ways then. Just as sadly he agreed—adding that I left him little choice. There could only be one editor and he was it. We said goodbye civilly to each other and I hung up.

I wanted to cry. Working on the *Listener* had become the best thing that ever happened to me. It was too good to be true, it couldn't last, it was time for things to return to normal. I would go back to teaching or something . . .

I looked out the window. It had started to snow, something that hadn't happened in Karori for years. Slowly the valley was whiting out. I cheered up enormously. The symbolism could not have been more perfect—anyone who could be fired and then have a freak snowfall hit seconds later was born to write. That night I was to be the first speaker in Ngaio's winter lecture series and I hadn't yet written a speech. That didn't matter—I could tell them how I had just been dismissed and wallow publicly in my martyrdom. Outside in the snow-blanketed street children wrapped warmly against the cold spun deliriously amongst the falling flakes, shrieking and laughing. I started laughing too.

Later that evening my good friend, the cartoonist Burton Silver of *Bogor* comic-strip fame, came to pick me up in his battered, rusting, draughty Morris van and we drove cautiously along slushy streets to the Ngaio Hall, wondering how many people would brave the snow, sleet and bitter cold to attend. In the event the place was full of loyal column-readers, little old ladies in the main, one of whom grabbed my arm tightly in her gloved hand and told me proudly she'd driven all the way from Upper Hutt. In this crowd I could do no wrong. There were gasps and anguished angry cries when I told them I had been fired from the *Listener* that afternoon. I kept them waiting a few moments, then added that Ian rang back 30 minutes later to holler down the line, 'Damn you, boy! I'm going to print it after all.' The hall erupted in cheers and relieved applause. Not half as relieved as I felt.

CHAPTER TWELVE

GOODNIGHT, DEAR BOY

AFTER I GOT FIRED FROM the *Listener* a second time in 1981, several newsagents told me that loyal readers of my column were announcing angrily in their shops that they were boycotting the publication until I got my job back. Apparently this stance was most pronounced in New Plymouth—these were the loyal fans after all who had cheered wildly and shouted my name when I tagged along at the rear of the Royal walkabout on Devon Street in 1976. I don't know how long this boycott would have lasted. Mercifully it was never put to the test.

A number of prominent academics, writers, artists, some judges and a few MPs wrote letters to the editor expressing alarm and dismay at my sacking. Sam Hunt wrote saying he would never submit another poem. Gary McCormick said the *Listener* never published any of his poems anyway, but from now on they wouldn't even get the chance to reject him, as he was boycotting them. The tipping point undoubtedly was Christchurch satirist A.K. Grant's resignation in solidarity with me. I knew how much Allan's weekly column meant to him, both emotionally and financially, so I rang to thank him and urged him to change his mind. He got quite cross with me and wouldn't have a bar of it. The *Listener* concluded they could lose one humourist, but not two, so with Gordon Campbell playing the Henry Kissinger role, feelers were sent out to see if I would return. I did, on better terms and conditions than before. It was all due to Allan's principled courage.

When you get to a certain age you suffer from the conceit that there are no new flavours in the world—only variations and combinations on the old ones. One of the joys of my first trip to Asia in 1975 was coming down to breakfast in my Bangkok hotel and being presented with a bowl of fresh fruit I had never seen before—mango, papaya, lychees and langsat—and being gobsmacked by the astonishing new tastes.

I had much the same sense of discovery when I stumbled upon the work of A.K. Grant in the late 1960s. I was sitting in the student cafe at Massey University when a friend approached with a copy of the Canterbury student newspaper *Canta* and insisted on reading aloud from an article printed on the inside of the back cover. It was a piece on the Otago gold-rush.

> Gold was one of New Zealand's main exports
> during the latter half of the century, especially
> after the advent of refrigerated shipping enabled
> it to be transported to England without going
> bad in the tropics. Treasury and the Bank of
> England were fulsome in their praise of the first
> consignment to arrive at Threadneedle Street
> though their enthusiasm was moderated slightly
> by the discovery of a dead rat in one of the bars . . .

I was blown away. As a fledgling comic myself, it was both an exhilarating and a painful moment. These were jokes that didn't come from England or America. They were homegrown and they were brilliant. I memorised the writer's name. I knew instinctively he was a force to be reckoned with. I cut out all his articles and read them many times, always with the same mixture of mirth and envy.

He disappeared from view for several years, and the next I heard or saw of Allan was when I switched on the television one night and caught a dismal panel game featuring a plump, tweedy man introduced as A.K. Grant. I leaned forward keenly and was shattered to discover he was wearing a cravat. Satire and cravats didn't go together, I thought, or perhaps they did and that depressed me. He looked exactly like what he was at the time—a respectable Christchurch lawyer and drawing-room wit—nothing at all like the man I had imagined responsible for the blazing invention I kept in a folder.

I actually made it onto the *Listener* a few years ahead of Allan, an accident of history despite him being my senior by seven years. It gave me the temporary advantage of being the magazine's elder statesman of comedy. When we finally met in person I was relieved to see he was wearing an open-necked shirt and a battered brown leather jacket. He was short, rotund and jolly—Sancho Panza to the tall, slim, solemn Roger Hall's Don Quixote, who came in with him. After a polite exchange, the three of us retired to a bar. Roger had to depart early. Left on our own, Allan and I discovered we enjoyed each other's company enormously through the simple expedient of laughing uproariously at each other's jokes. He was booked on a late flight back to Christchurch but I persuaded him to ring his wife Liz and explain he was coming up to my home to meet my second wife, Helen. He thought her adorable, and she found him charming as well. That night, long after Helen had retired, we talked over a bottle of whisky about comedy writing and our favourite comedians.

Comedy writing is a peculiar business. The intention is simple enough, but the task itself is daunting: triggering mirth. Laughter is one of the most complex and singular of all human responses, second only to orgasm. If you have just made love to a beautiful woman, given it your best shot so to speak, and she laughs in your face, this is still a considerable achievement in itself. When a sad movie fails to make you burst into tears you don't feel the same sense of betrayal as when a comedy movie fails to make you laugh. Allan's betrayal rate in his columns was one of the lowest in the game. I never ceased to admire his craft, his invention, his scholarship, his dogged Christchurch integrity and his dancing wit. His collection of pieces *The Bedside Grant* loses nothing in comparison with the writing of comic giants of yesteryear such as Jerome K. Jerome, P.G. Wodehouse, Evelyn Waugh, Alan Coren, and more latterly, Woody Allen, Clive James, P.J. O'Rourke and David Sedaris. He was that good.

I am not alone in thinking this. The celebrated English wit, comedy scriptwriter, and radio and television personality Frank Muir happened across Allan's *The Day of The Possum*, in which he describes a hideous possum-skinning competition first in the tone-perfect prose style of Raymond Chandler, then Katherine Mansfield, Frank Sargeson, Norman Mailer, T.S. Eliot and Ernest Hemingway. It is brilliantly funny even if you are not familiar with the writers being parodied. Muir was so impressed he immediately included it in a tome he was compiling, *The Oxford Book of Comic Prose*. This article should be a permanent part of the English curriculum and taught in schools.

I treasure one piece in particular of Allan's because it captured perfectly the excruciating dilemma I faced every Monday—how to piece together another thousand words in some sort of order that made sense and was hopefully amusing. Allan channelled this familiar agony through a vicar wrestling with writing a sermon:

> From the window of my study I can see a clump
> of tall pine trees. They grow in a corner of the
> local golf course, and magpies nest in them at
> nesting time. The other day I watched as a solitary
> golfer lined up a shot near the trees. Suddenly a
> magpie swooped down out of the trees and flew
> past the golfer's ear, startling him and disturbing
> his concentration.

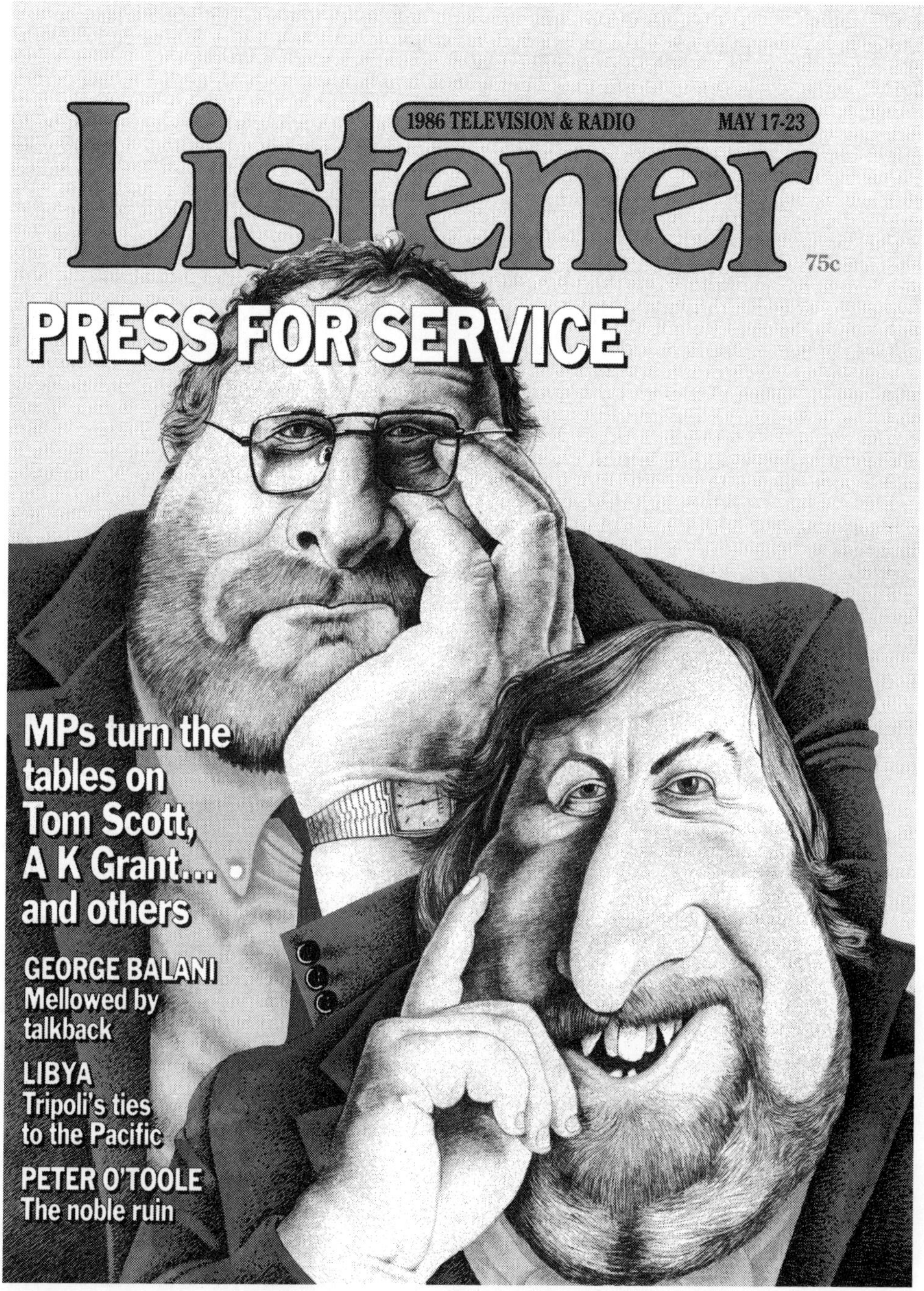

1986 TELEVISION & RADIO   MAY 17-23

Listener

75c

PRESS FOR SERVICE

MPs turn the
tables on
Tom Scott,
A K Grant...
and others

GEORGE BALANI
Mellowed by
talkback

LIBYA
Tripoli's ties
to the Pacific

PETER O'TOOLE
The noble ruin

Angrily he waved his club at the magpie, just as you or I might have done. Then he concentrated on his shot again. And back came the magpie soaring past the golfer's other ear. Absorbed, I watched the struggle between golfer and magpie, until it was time for me to attend to other duties. But as I went about these duties, my mind kept going back to the golfer and the magpie. Because, when you think about it, every one of us is either a golfer or a magpie.

Some of us concentrate on the daily tasks at hand, oblivious of all other considerations except the desperate need to improve our performance. Such are the golfers of this life. Others of us soar aloft on wings of imagination, and then attack people. Those are the magpies of this world.

And many of us, whether golfers or magpies, are unaware that there is Someone watching us, just as the golfer and the magpie were unaware of me, in my study, watching them, as I scrabbled round desperately for a laboured analogy with which to illustrate my Faith for Today . . .

ALLAN DESERVES TO BE AS celebrated and honoured today as Janet Frame, Jane Campion, Roger Hall, Billy T. James and John Clarke, yet he is largely forgotten. It is partly because there were never any cameras around to capture him at his anarchic, freewheeling, unguarded best.

I take some pride in encouraging him to step out of the shadows and finally become a solo comic performer. It was at a fundraising event for Amnesty International, based on the English model of Comic Relief, held in Wellington's lovely Muppet Theatre, the Opera House. I organised it with Ian Fraser, I designed the poster, was one of the MCs alongside Ian, and I wrote the ensemble sketch with Allan that closed the show. But my single most important contribution was persuading Allan to put his white shirt on back to front and walk out into the spotlight and simply read his 'Faith for Today' sermon.

He stepped out nervously and his awkwardness became a hysterical component of the performance. Two paragraphs in and the audience was roaring with laughter. He was one of the highlights of the night. He came off stage and hugged me in the wings, exclaiming he wanted to walk back on and do it again.

Dave Dobbyn was also on the bill. Accompanying himself on acoustic guitar, he sang 'Loyal' for the first time in public. It was a magical moment. My son Samuel Flynn Scott and Lukasz Buda (stalwarts of The Phoenix Foundation) produced Dave's 2016 album *Harmony House*, which is fantastic. I wonder if Dave remembers being in the same show with five-year-old Sam?

Helen had made a superb, very realistic, slightly larger than life-size papier-mâché mask of Muldoon. We put it on Sam, dressed him in a jacket with sleeves hitting the floor and got him to walk on stage while David McPhail, famous for his Muldoon impersonation, stood at a microphone in the wings doing the Prime Minister's mirthless cackle. Sam stood rooted to the spot when the applause finished and I had to dash out and gently lead him off, which prompted David to ad-lib, 'Oh no, Mr Scott! Security! Security!'—much the same words Muldoon had used when he had me escorted from his post-cabinet press conference. 'Take your hands off me! Don't touch me, Mr Scott! Don't touch me!' The crowd went wild.

Allan and I wrote a television sitcom together, the critically panned *Press for Service*. Noam Pitlik, the American actor and director who won an Emmy for Outstanding Direction for the hugely successful and ground-breaking sitcom series *Barney Miller*, was brought out to New Zealand by the BCNZ to conduct a workshop on how to make television comedy in 1988. It was held out at Avalon Studios. Allan and I were 'Exhibit A' in the 'what not to do' category. I attended on my own, with a heavy heart. Big, burly, witty and charismatic, Noam announced that he was going to play three sitcom episodes back-to-back—*Barney Miller* and our own *Gliding On*, both of which were deemed successful, and *Press for Service*, which wasn't. At the rear of the room I sank low in my chair.

In the event, judging by the laughter, what Allan and I wrote more than held its own. Afterwards, Noam made a beeline for me and shook my hand.

'I don't know why they told me that yours stank. It's pretty darn good. You're a funny guy.' We hung out during the rest of his visit. He and his gorgeous wife, Susan, fell in love with New Zealand and for a time lived in Auckland and worked here briefly. When my relationship with Helen foundered for the first time they took me on holiday with them to Taupō. It rained a lot, which made it miserable enough in the sea-grass-matting lodge, and with my self-pity needle on full I made it even worse. I think all three of us were ready to slit our wrists by the end but they were far too gracious to let on. I caught up with them whenever I went to Los Angeles. It was a sad day for me when Noam died in 1999.

Allan and I also wrote the first draft of a screenplay together called *Happy Families* for Sam Pillsbury, now a vintner making gold-medal-winning Grenache and Shiraz wines in Arizona, but back then a whirling, twirling Energizer Bunny director and producer responsible for the provincial Gothic masterpiece *The Scarecrow*, still one of my favourite Kiwi films. Sam rented a bach for us at Waikanae Beach right on the sands, and with Allan thrashing away at the keyboard of an electronic typewriter, in less than a week we bashed out a screenplay that we at least thought was fantastic.

Sam drove down and took us out to a fancy restaurant for a celebratory lunch, ordering a bottle of their finest Chardonnay— the first Chardonnay I had ever tasted, big and buttery. While Sauvignon Blanc and Pinot Gris have roared in and out of fashion I have remained steadfastly besotted with this grape and this particular style ever since.

I knew that our script had a vulgar energy, but I didn't know how vulgar others would find it until some months later when I attended drinks at the Film Commission and a woman who assessed scripts for them, Helene Wong (now a film critic on the *Listener*), approached and asked if I was Tom Scott. I had just worked all through the night on a long article for the *Auckland Star* and was too bone-weary to appreciate how frosty and disapproving she was, otherwise I would have denied it, or at least braced myself for what was coming. When I confirmed that I was, she launched into a blunt and bruising critique that left me winded. She had just read the script that Allan and I wrote together. I can't recall her exact words but what I took from the terse exchange was that she thought the screenplay was sexist and disgusting and that I should be ashamed of myself. It's a bit late now, but if it helps I feel ashamed of myself on a fairly regular basis. My guess is that one of Allan's great lines did the damage. He gleefully wrote that there was no such thing as premature ejaculation—only delayed orgasm, and that the sooner women sought professional help for this surprisingly common condition the better. Most men punch the air at this line, while women roll their eyes.

I LOVED ALLAN. IT WAS heartbreaking for everyone who cared about him watching him descend ever deeper into alcoholism. He claimed he drank because he woke up every morning feeling depressed. I told him he woke up every morning hungover. The Japanese have a proverb—the man takes a drink, then the drink takes a drink, then the drink takes the man. This was never more true than in Allan's case. He loved his wife and daughters beyond measure, but this love was no match for his addiction.

When his marriage folded, he moved into a dark, cramped, soulless flat in a block of apartments near Hagley Park. Gary McCormick, who is a very kind man beneath his sometimes testy alpha-male persona, flew back and forth to Christchurch solely to take Allan out to dinner and get food into him. Allan, of course, would only agree to a restaurant with a liquor licence.

Whenever he stayed with Averil and me, he would head upstairs with a full glass of red wine and a cheerful cry of, 'Goodnight, dear boy.' I had a 9 a.m. deadline for my *Evening Post* cartoons back then, so I was an early riser and more often than not I would find him in the front room sitting contentedly in the low morning sun reading a novel with a freshly opened bottle of wine and a full glass on the coffee table in front of him. If he'd already been to the lavatory the bathroom was out of bounds for days. I would joke with him that he must have eaten a badger that was off. It was proof, if any were needed, that his liver was feeling the strain.

He was briefly engaged to Jane, a lovely, pretty, generously proportioned woman who favoured riotously coloured kaftans. It was Allan himself who told me about introducing Jane to his friends in the Woolston Working Men's Club. As he was wont to do, Allan theatrically rotated his left arm about like a tarmac marshal guiding a taxiing plane into docking position. 'I present to you this dear woman! This divine creature is my fiancé!' There was a cough on Allan's right. It was Jane. 'I'm over here, Allan. That is a pokie machine . . .'

After that it was pretty much all over bar the shouting, which he still insisted on doing at his second home, The Brewers Arms in Merivale. He rang me in a state of considerable excitement one morning. A buxom barmaid had invited him to share her bedchamber the night before. He remembered lots of amorous grappling but for the life of him he couldn't recall if penetration had occurred. It would mean a lot to him if it had. Should he ask her for confirmation of consummation? I said the minimum compliment you can pay any woman who has granted you the gift of her body is to remember this fact. Under no circumstances was he to ask her. Two days later I got another call, this time wistful, rueful and tinged with regret. 'I should have listened to you, old boy. She's not talking to me now.'

It was similar to a call my son Shaun made one night. He asked me to hand the phone to Averil, which he always did when affairs of the heart were involved.

'What's the rule about sleeping with your best mate's girlfriend, who you've always fancied, after they have split up? How long do you have to wait? When is it acceptable?' There was a palpable urgency in his voice.

'Just a second,' said Averil dryly. 'I'll consult the manual. Here it is. Never. Never do that.'

There was a pregnant silence, then, 'Bugger! My question was retrospective in nature.'

IN LATE MARCH 2000, ALLAN was admitted to Christchurch Hospital. I flew down the moment I heard. I wasn't prepared for what I found. It was a pitiful, shocking sight. His beard was long and clotted, his face sallow, his plump cheeks now hollow, he had a mad, terrified stare and the whites of his eyes were daffodil yellow. He couldn't talk so I prattled on. I would come back next week with a CD player, headphones and his favourite Bob Dylan bootleg compilations. When it was time to leave I leaned over to hug him. It wasn't easy. He smelled dreadful, like he was already decomposing. Holding my breath, I kissed his stubbly cheek. His eyes focused properly for the first time and he finally spoke a few words, hissing in my ear, 'Bring a bottle of vodka!'

Out in the corridor I passed a senior nurse on her way into his room.

'He's dying, isn't he?'

'I'm sorry, sir, I cannot divulge such information.' Back in Wellington I rang Trevor Grice, with whom I had written *The Great Brain Robbery*, a book warning teenagers about the dangers of drug and alcohol use—the book that prompted Allan to comment sadly when it was published, 'I'm afraid, dear boy, you've really fallen off your perch here.' When I told Trevor about Allan's yellow eyes, he didn't muck round. 'His liver's rooted. He's fucked.'

Three weeks later Allan was dead. When I rang my daughter Rosie in Melbourne she was devastated for me. 'Oh, Dad, he was your kindest friend . . .'

The packed, standing-room-only memorial service was held in a large chapel and crematorium complex on the outskirts of the city. After Allan's immediate family had spoken, David McPhail came forward. Close to tears, he barely made it through his tender and generous eulogy. Next up was Gary McCormick. Utterly incapacitated by grief, he couldn't finish and returned to his seat beside me, racked with sobs.

Averil patted my leg. It was my turn. I was walked to the lectern, looking down at my hand-written notes. The first line was, 'Oh, Dad, he was your kindest friend ...' I knew there was no way I could say that without dissolving into tears myself. I had to think of something else.

> Let's be honest here, we all know Allan liked a drink. He was a very heavy drinker, no question. Not to put too fine a point on it, he was an alcoholic. I'd hate to guess how much alcohol there was in his bloodstream when he died, so I feel I have to ask—is cremation really the safest option? When that coffin goes through those curtains I'm going out that front door before the fireball engulfs the whole place!

I said it for me, but the whole chapel erupted in grateful laughter. Allan would have approved. I was then able to read what I had prepared.

That night, back in Wellington, I was falling asleep when a familiar voice called out from the stairs, 'Goodnight, dear boy.'

'Did you hear that?' I whispered to Averil, wondering if I had imagined it.

'Yes. I heard it,' she replied softly. 'Allan is wishing you goodnight.'

Goodnight to you too, dear boy ...

CHAPTER THIRTEEN

THE SPY WHO CAME IN FROM THE WARM

ON 14 FEBRUARY 2014, AMID press coverage and speculation about former computer mogul Kim Dotcom's boast that he would play a spoiling role in the New Zealand elections at the end of the year, I drew a cartoon of John Key in a trench coat spying on Dotcom's mansion through field glasses. A soldier assisting Key is suggesting to the Prime Minister that he really should leave this sort of thing to the GCSB.

Within hours of publication, I received an email from a familiar source, an 'Arch Pol', requesting the original. Arch had purchased a good number of cartoons over the years. Every time I did anything related to espionage, Arch would contact me and I would send it to him with an invoice to a nondescript P.O. Box number. This time I got a phone call as well.

'Hi, Tom, this is Arch Pol. You have probably guessed by now that this name is a pseudonym.' I told him I had no idea, confirming, if any proof were needed, that I was gormless as well as harmless. 'We have a collection of your cartoons here at the GCSB,' he continued. 'Would you like to come and see them and have afternoon tea with the director?' You bet!

I arrived ahead of the appointed hour, stepped through a security X-ray machine, had my cell phone confiscated, was given a special card and told to wait for someone to come and fetch me. Someone did. I was taken up in a lift to the foyer of the GCSB section. In pride of place was an Enigma machine from World War Two. Around the walls were framed cartoons by every newspaper and magazine cartoonist in the country. A good many were mine.

Arch ushered me into an inner sanctum to have afternoon tea. 'We keep the ones we don't think are suitable for public display in here.' Hanging in this small boardroom were cartoons highly critical and mocking of the SIS and the GCSB. They were entirely mine.

The director arrived. Tea was poured and convivial conversation ensued. I said something to the effect that they would have been run off their feet spying on me way back in the '70s.

They exchanged knowing looks and giggled.

I don't blame them if they were. At that time Christine worked for the New Zealand University Students' Association. Most of the organisers were members of the Wellington Marxist Leninist Organisation, which later became the Workers' Communist League. Communism, like the world's other great religions, had deep schisms. Christianity split into Protestant and Catholic wings, Islam into Shia and Sunni faiths, and Marxist-Leninist doctrine into the Russian industrial model and the Chinese agrarian model. The University Students' Association comrades were Maoist. These reds weren't under the bed. They were sitting at the desks and answering the phones. They were austere, severe and sincere, a deeply committed cadre fired with a migraine-inducing zeal—everything I'm not.

You can't be a fellow traveller when you are travelling in opposite directions, and Christine and I were moving in opposite directions. As a court jester, no matter how rude I was to the king, I was part of the established order that Christine and her chums were opposed to and wanted to replace. She told me that a colleague and his wife had taken to reading the collected works of Lenin out loud to each other in bed, and it had brought them closer together. She wanted me to consider this. Small wonder then that when I started working at Parliament our mail began being opened surreptitiously with a blunt breadknife, and when I picked up the phone the line would snap, crackle and pop like Kellogg's Rice Bubbles. Sometimes it was so noisy you half expected a man wearing a raincoat and headphones parked in a van at the end of the street to ask you politely to speak up.

It must have been a nightmare breaking the elaborate codes. 'If it's raining I'll take the kids to the museum. If it's not, Christine will take them to Scorching Bay. Ollie's allergic to peanut butter, right? Or is it strawberries?' Anyone monitoring my conversations would have quickly determined that—apart from to Ollie, obviously—I was no threat to anyone.

But Muldoon wasn't taking any chances. Shortly into his first ministry, a Parliamentary security guard took me aside and lowered his voice. 'Don't ever misbehave in this building, Tom. They want us to keep an eye on you. If you're ever drunk or disorderly, the ninth floor wants to know about it.' I thanked him and he shot away. I hadn't been planning to misbehave, but I took his advice seriously, which ruled out adventures in the Speaker's chair.

I remember one wet, miserable afternoon in Karori when Christine's friends were around and the conversation turned to Cambodia and the genocidal Pol Pot regime, which was ostensibly Maoist and thus allowed a degree of artistic licence. Things got heated when I protested that he had butchered two million of his own people. An otherwise perfectly reasonable young woman replied along the lines that you couldn't make an omelette without breaking a few eggs, adding that the real figure was one million, tops. I knew right then that our marriage was doomed.

Had I been more honest and more courageous we would have parted painfully but honourably then. I wasn't and we didn't, so it was a train wreck when it finally happened.

The child-minding family group dined together once a week, rotating the duty. They were messy, high-decibel affairs. The kids loved them, and if parents guzzled enough cask wine we had a great time as well.

It was at Kevin and Margaret's home in Wilton on a wet Sunday that I met Helen for the very first time. She was visiting from Auckland with her three cute kids. She was tall and beautiful, funny and smart. I was smitten the instant I saw her, just as I had been with Christine. My heart is the only thing remotely reckless about me. I hardly said a word to her that night. I couldn't look her in the eye. So I poured a huge effort into entertaining the room hoping to impress her indirectly.

My mate Kev reported later that Helen had asked lots of questions about me, and said that she found me interesting and amusing. It could have gone either way. On the evidence presented she could just as easily have found me shrill and tragic. As a result, I couldn't get her out of my mind.

—

THERE WAS A TWO-WEEK ROYAL TOUR of the country in February and March 1977 and Ian Cross assigned me to follow it in full. The *Listener* devoted four pages to my story and put me on the cover, which they asked me to draw.

My copy wasn't memorable, but Muldoon's ability to greet the Queen everywhere she went surely was. He would wave her off at one airport and greet her descending the steps at the next. She could have been forgiven for thinking he had cloned himself. Fleet Street scribes were appalled at first then eventually amused, joking that should Her Majesty require a gynaecological examination on tour she should brace herself while on the examination table with her feet in stirrups for the very real possibility that the doctor would lower his mask and it would be Muldoon.

I met Her Majesty in person on a clear and warm Auckland evening at a cocktail party on the Royal yacht *Britannia*. After passing a rigorous vetting on the jetty, the media joined a queue on the scrubbed breadboard decks to be introduced to the Royal couple. Flip and facetious conversation died away to nervous silence as the queue shortened.

The Queen took my suddenly damp palm and gave me a warm smile and disconcertingly shrewd gaze. As everyone comments, she was smaller than expected and more attractive and animated than her photographs and film footage suggest. It was a weird experience to meet up close the person whose face is on every banknote, every coin and every second *Woman's Weekly* cover. (I am not alone in thinking this. After performing in a royal variety concert at the Albert Hall, the singer Glen Campbell was formally introduced to Her Majesty back stage. In his soft southern drawl, Campbell commented later, 'I'd seen her face on so many stamps I had to fight the urge to lick the back of her head . . .')

The media could have stayed and drunk hefty gin and tonics all night, but the Royal Navy whisked us off with a courteous but steely resolve when our allotted time was up. As arranged I caught up with Helen for a drink. She was wearing a long, figure-hugging, dark green frock. On a lithe, tanned arm she had a silver bracelet that could have been from the Andes or Tibet. The metal embraced a turquoise stone mottled like an ancient map of the world. Everything about her was exquisite and beautiful. It was just like 'Norwegian Wood'—apart from the 'time for bed' bit.

I had severe abdominal cramps all evening and desperately needed to go to the toilet. In great pain, I gabbled incessantly for hours. In the foyer, in mounting agony, I waited desperately for Helen's cab to arrive, pecked her demurely on the cheek when it did, then raced for a ground-floor loo. The detonation left me semi-concussed. The only consolation was that if it had happened on the *Britannia*, the Special Forces who guard the Queen would have riddled the toilet cubicle with gunfire.

The next morning the press contingent assembled at Whenuapai airbase for a Hercules flight to Whangarei. Inside the cargo bay our Hercules had a decidedly unfinished look. Wiring, cables and piping flowed everywhere like a da Vinci sketch of a dissected arm. Already nervous, the British press were taken aback when advised there were no lavatories in the accepted sense, just a wide funnel and a tube leading to the exterior of the plane, and that paper bags were available if anyone got sick, along with earplugs if we couldn't tolerate the deafening noise.

'Any parachutes?' someone joked.

'No,' said the commander, equal to the task. 'But, if the worst comes to the worst, hold your nose and put a cross on your head—that way we'll know where to dig.'

My chum Phil Melchior, who had flown with Kirk's coffin in this very cargo hold, nonchalantly strapped himself into his webbing seat and with a knowing smile leaned across to me. 'OK. How did it go last night?'

'I'm in love,' I whispered.

The rest of the trip passed without incident, though in a walkabout down New Plymouth's Devon Street the crowd made almost as much fuss of me as the Queen—squealing and shouting out my name. They were kidding, of course. It was the verbal equivalent of a Mexican wave—they were doing it to amuse themselves. Still, the Fleet Street hacks were astonished and the *Telegraph's* royal correspondent wrote about it at some length in her next piece on the tour. There wasn't a lot happening; much like the Devon Street crowd, the press were also clutching at straws.

I returned to Wellington and was somewhat distant with Christine, who wanted to know why. I am a member of a particularly shallow generation. To allay suspicion, I played her 'There is Someone Else', a cheesy Boz Scaggs ballad from his cheesy *Silk Degrees* album, which I still play from time to time. It implied that the 'someone else' I'd finally found was her. Christine was thrilled, but it was a calculated, dishonest diversion measure that shames me still.

We had moved to Thorndon by then, within walking distance of Parliament, which was perfect, and just around the corner from the Katherine Mansfield Memorial Park with its scented garden for the blind. I played there most afternoons with Shaun, laughing and being silly together until it got too dark to see and the air was filled with scent. Shaun was happy and that delighted me.

IN TIME FOR THE CHRISTMAS market in 1977, my first book, *Tom Scott's Life and Times*, was published. The celebrated poet Brian Turner, a man with a wit so dry it should come with a fire warning, did a brilliant job editing and assembling a collection of my better writing and drawings. In some ways, it was a stocktake of my career to date, and if you took my personal life into consideration it was a fire clearance sale as well.

Back in the days before Wellington coffee bars and bistros burst into existence there were very few places for families to eat out in the city. A church hall in Mount Victoria that sold lasagne, pumpkin soup and garlic bread had queues of parents and kids queuing around the block on Friday nights. That's how desperate we were for novel cuisine. We launched the book there. Being in the presence of a famous, published author did not overawe Shaun and the rest of the kids from the family group who wrestled at my feet, tugged my jeans and asked for drinks as I was giving a speech and their parents were studiously pretending it wasn't happening. The book sold very well.

One night I was drawing a cartoon for a *Listener* cover of the Parliamentary chamber in pandemonium and riot. It was four in the morning, just five hours until my deadline, and I was nowhere near finished. There was an urgent tapping on the door. The live-in nurse and housekeeper from upstairs who looked after a very old lady was intoxicated and crying—could I come and help?

I followed her upstairs and she waved me into the old lady's bedroom, remaining outside herself. The old lady was frail, had lost almost all of her hair and was the same colour as her sheets. Clearly on death's door, she was fretting about something. Mumbling something in a barely audible whisper, she kept pointing to a glass of what I took to be cloudy orange juice on her bedside table.

I thought she wanted a sip, and lifted it up to her lips. She recoiled in horror and shook her head. I took a sniff. It was urine. She'd had a last little pee into the glass. I asked her quietly, 'Would you like me to flush this down the toilet for you?' She nodded, sank back into her pillows and gave me, a complete stranger, a relieved smile. Her last smile probably. She died that night. An ambulance and her adult children were on the way and she wanted to keep what little dignity she had left intact.

There were photographs of her as a beautiful, stylish young woman covering the walls. I returned to my desk noting to myself that we pass this way but once and there are very few happy endings.

Many nights after this I spent my last waking moments before tipping into sleep wondering if I would ever see Helen again. But events not of my making set in train almost a year earlier in the debating chamber would change everything with a brutal swiftness that I accept responsibility for.

CHAPTER FOURTEEN

THE SEEDS OF A DOWNFALL

IN THE MIDDLE OF 1976, Speaker Richard Harrison, who liked my columns, called me into his office and poured me a Scotch. Something was preying on his mind. It was a recent conversation he'd had with the Prime Minister concerning Labour's Colin Moyle. A handsome man with pompadour hair and a Kirk Douglas dimpled chin, Moyle was easily the Opposition's best performer in the House, fuelling rumours that he would soon replace Bill Rowling as leader, which would not be good news for National. According to Harrison, Muldoon had chuckled and said that was never going to happen. He had the goods on Moyle, which he would reveal when the time was right. 'When things get heated in the House,' said a pale Harrison, 'I think to myself, is this it? And I feel sick. What can it possibly be?'

I didn't know either, but we would both find out on the evening of 4 November 1976. During a bad-tempered, three-hour debate on the supplementary estimates, and amid a flurry of competing points of order, Muldoon thought mocking laughter had come from Moyle. He responded, 'I shall forgive the effeminate giggles of the Member for Mangere, because I know his background.' Ignoring the implied threat, an angry Moyle walked into an ambush, asking if it would be in order to accuse the Prime Minister of being a member of a dishonest accountancy firm. Muldoon, who had been drinking, lowered the boom. 'Would it be in order for me to accuse the Member of being picked up by the police for homosexual activity?'

Both sides of the House were stunned and sickened by Muldoon's behaviour. When I checked out Rowling's office after the House had risen, Moyle was curled up in a foetal ball on a couch, weeping—a broken man. Who knows how things would have turned out had he crossed the floor of the chamber and smacked Muldoon or risen to make a point of personal explanation, as Standing Orders allow: 'Mr Speaker, I would like to assure the Honourable Member for Tāmaki that he is so physically unattractive he has nothing to fear on my account.'

A year earlier, in a seedy part of Wellington, late at night Moyle invited an undercover policeman into his ministerial car—not a good look at the time. As absurd and as cruel as it sounds today, homosexual acts between consenting adults were deemed shameful, sinful and criminal back then. When the late British actor Denholm Elliott, who specialised in playing sweating district commissioners, died of AIDS, his widow was asked how this could have happened. She responded cheerfully, 'Having a bloody good time, I imagine.' Incapable of such sangfroid, Moyle offered three differing and increasingly tortuous explanations. In the wake of an official inquiry that scolded him, he resigned his safe Mangere seat so he could contest it in a by-election and return to politics with a fresh mandate. Under pressure from his own party and under intense media scrutiny, he subsequently pulled out of the by-election. The candidate nod went to a human dirigible in a black kaftan cut in the shape of a suit, a jaw-droppingly obese defence lawyer with a pudding-bowl haircut, heavy horn-rimmed spectacles, a booming voice and an astonishing, rollicking, mischievous, rapier wit—David Lange.

Lange was the last of twelve people seeking the Labour nomination for the safe seat. At the end of the long night, the chair of the meeting introduced him as the man who'd had the longest wait. 'And I've got the biggest weight!' he boomed. The hall erupted in cheers and laughter. Mike Moore, who was also seeking the nomination, whispered to his wife, Yvonne, 'It's all over, he's got it ...'

The man who would eventually defeat Muldoon became a Member of Parliament because of him. In true Shakespearian fashion, Muldoon's dark deed set in motion events that would lead to his eventual downfall.

Two weeks after the Royal Tour had ended, Muldoon was

scheduled to open National's by-election campaign in Mangere. Ian Cross never visited Parliament, but quite by chance that very afternoon I ran into him strolling down a corridor with some cabinet ministers. On the spur of the moment, I said I really should cover the Prime Minister's speech that night. Not ideally placed to refuse, Ian consented and two hours later I was on a flight to Auckland and a short cab ride from the Mangere hall.

All I remember from the meeting is that Muldoon was more bellicose than normal and when a young Samoan reporter, Fraser Folster, crept across the stage to adjust some recording gear, the muttering and hostility from the Pākehā audience was obvious. Even more painful to witness was Fraser's acute discomfort and embarrassment at this reaction. At the close of the meeting I caught another cab, to St Mary's Bay in Auckland, and spent the night with Helen. The next day I returned to Wellington and with a heedless regard for the consequences pulled the plug on my marriage and my *Listener* column—sending my life and the lives of others into free-fall.

HELEN AND HER THREE CHILDREN, Emily, Jacob and Ned, had been heading for England when I arrived in their lives. I dragged them down to Wellington to live in a tiny, squalid rented flat in Mount Victoria, but their trip to stay with Helen's dad, Michael Forlong, a successful documentary film-maker now living in Surrey, couldn't be delayed any longer. I decided to tag along.

Going overseas was still a big deal. Burton Silver and Peter Hayden organised a surprise farewell party. People assembled at Burton's quaint Scorching Bay cottage and he led a convoy of cars on a magical mystery tour around the Miramar Peninsula to Shelly Bay, then still an air-force base whose gates normally closed at ten, but Burton persuaded them to leave them open. He herded everyone onto a jetty where a coastal trader was waiting, with more guests hiding under the hatches. Burton, who combines comic genius and lateral thinking with meticulous preparation, handed out souvenir boxes of matches emblazoned TOM SCOTT CRUISES. There was music, food and wine. It was a balmy, starry night. Out on the water we passed a Japanese fishing boat at anchor and Ian Fraser yelled out, 'What about some squid pro quo?' which we all thought was hugely jolly.

I was quite overcome that Burton and Peter had gone to such elaborate lengths on my behalf until I detected a mood swing and a swelling mutiny below decks. The more militant of the feminists in our midst had gathered to discuss the unforgivable misogyny of Burton not including Helen's name on the matchboxes—it was thoughtless, insensitive, typical of our patriarchal society and bordered on a war crime. No, it was *worse* than a war crime!

I wanted to bring Shaun on the trip, but quite rightly Christine thought he'd been through enough upheaval, plus she didn't want to disrupt his schooling. Not that the latter would have mattered—he was super bright in his own singular way. One dusk when a friend was loudly admiring a sinking sun, six-year-old Shaun coughed politely at her elbow and offered a gentle correction. 'Actually, the sun is not sinking, Claire. It stays in one place. The earth is rotating, creating that impression.'

I DIDN'T ENJOY ENGLAND. PARTLY because I was missing Shaun terribly, and partly because it was bleak and freezing in the terrace house in Whitstable by the sea, it was bleak and freezing in the apartment block nestled amongst Oxford's dreaming spires, and it was bleak and freezing in the Georgian manor house set amongst skeletal trees in flat Surrey countryside. The common denominator seemed to be clanking Califonts, damp sheets and burnt toast.

Phil Melchior was working for Reuters and over some boozy lunches he introduced me to his Fleet Street chums. Two newspapers were interested in hiring me. The pay was pitiful and I could be a writer or a cartoonist, but not both. I wanted to be both. I submitted samples of my work to *Punch*, the once legendary, now deceased weekly humour and satire magazine. I got a letter from the late, great Alan Coren, whose brilliant columns were the only enjoyable thing about sitting in a dentist's waiting room, in which he offered me a job. I was elated—but not because I wanted to work there. I didn't. I just wanted proof that I was good enough to do so. It meant I could go home. My homesickness was crippling.

But first there was a trip down the Grand Union canal, which I enjoyed despite the bitter cold. In the absence of roads, motor vehicles and other signs of civilisation we glided along languid waterways, down staircases of locks and through serene landscapes that seemingly hadn't changed for centuries. Then it was off to the south of France in a swaying, groaning campervan to where Helen's sister Debbie, her partner Roy and their two children were living in a stone fort atop the Île du Levant off the coast of the Riviera, near Toulon.

Before we left I went into Michael's study to phone Shaun on his sixth birthday. There was no answer from Christine's house. I rang around her friends, mindful that Maggie, Michael's second wife, would be timing me on a stopwatch in the next room. I got uncomfortable, cagey answers from everyone I spoke to—Shaun was fine, they just weren't sure of his precise whereabouts. I widened my search and finally got to speak to him. He was staying with neighbours. His quavering voice broke my heart. I told him I would be home soon and he was relieved. It turned out Christine had gone on another trip to China. I got off the phone and dissolved in tears recounting this to Helen. She said I didn't really care about Shaun—I was crying for myself.

It was one of those cockpit-warning moments—'Whoop! Whoop! Pull up! Pull up! Low terrain! Low terrain!' There was nothing to be done. Helen was pregnant with Sam—one of the great joys of my life along with darling Rosie, the daughter Helen and I had next, and Will, Averil's beautiful boy who feels like mine as well, and of course big, quirky Shaun, a constant source of astonishment and laughter. They have all grown into sensible, caring, considerate, creative, amusing adults, curious about the world around them and their obligations to it. I blame their mothers.

I went to France counting the days until I could return to

Aotearoa. I don't tan, and even if I did the nudist beaches on the Île du Levant were frequented by aging British homosexuals. As they were about to leave the surf they turned their backs to the sands and worked frantically on their genitals until they approached porn-star dimensions. I couldn't compete with that, and if I tried it could easily have been misinterpreted. I didn't want the embarrassment of being hit on by some perfectly decent gay bloke who through no fault of his own got the wrong idea—or worse still, being completely ignored by the loneliest homosexual on the beach, who averted his gaze and shuddered when I waddled past.

Instead I found a shady spot on the stony ramparts and wrote the first draft of my second book, *Overseizure*, a mock travel diary that I also illustrated with ink and pencil shading. Published by Whitcoulls, it sold very well and was reprinted several times to meet demand. A character not dissimilar to Michael Forlong featured prominently—and not always in a flattering light.

His first wife, Elizabeth, Helen and Debbie's mum, an elegant and beautiful lady, came to stay on the island with us. Elizabeth could be a prickly flower and easy to offend but I grew very fond of her, and she of me. After dinner in the cool of the evening, when I regaled everyone with the work in progress, Elizabeth led the laughter—which gave me permission of sorts to continue.

WHEN WE RETURNED TO NEW ZEALAND we lived for a time with the brilliant, revolutionary, vastly entertaining architect Ian Athfield and his gorgeous, spirited wife Claire, a gifted interior designer in her own right, in their extraordinary cement block and white plaster Greek village of a home slipping and a-sliding, ducking and a-diving down a Khandallah hillside above the Hutt motorway and Wellington harbour. In the distinctive tower with its bulb and round windows for eyes, I finished the illustrations for *Overseizure*, and it was launched lower down the hill in the Khandallah Arms, a drab cube of a house to which Ian had added a double verandah and dazzlingly transformed it into a Wild-West saloon. Pooling our resources, Helen and I were able to afford a half-renovated house in Wadestown backing onto the town belt. There was a tennis court tucked up in the pines. Friends with children the same age as ours lived within easy walking distance. And I returned to the *Listener*.

When hiring me, the new editor, Tony Reid, made a point of telling me that circulation had gone up when I was away. I knew I was home. Ed Hillary told me that after climbing Everest in 1953, walking down London streets, cabbies and pedestrians would yell out, 'Congratulations, Ed! You've done very well for your country!' Back in New Zealand people would yell out, 'Congratulations Ed. You've done very well for yourself.'

In my absence, Karen Jackman wrote a splendid column on politics for the *Listener* and I played no part in the coverage of the 1978 election—save for participating in a live television interview on election night while attending a Wadestown party.

The reporter was Simon Walker, who had recently been called a 'smart alec' in a testy studio exchange with Prime Minister Rob Muldoon. Simon's crime was to call Muldoon 'Prime Minister' with such mock respect it was obvious he didn't consider him worthy of the label. Simon went on to work for David Lange, British Prime Minister John Major and Buckingham Palace. When Her Majesty, unaccountably immune to the charms of the Sultans of Swing, decided to forego a Dire Straits concert at the Albert Hall she lent the royal box to Simon and whomever he wished to include. I was in town editing a documentary on Ed Hillary for Channel 4 in the UK and made the cut. At interval we exited a grand rear door and crossed a wide corridor into a chandeliered reception hall where liveried staff treated us as if Her Majesty were in attendance, gliding amongst overwhelmed guests with silver trays laden with champagne and canapés. Forget the mud and overflowing toilets of Woodstock and Glastonbury—this is how you attend a rock concert!

On election night 1978, despite Labour winning most of the popular vote, National won most of the seats. For a while early in the evening it looked like a close-run thing as Muldoon's majority in the House was reduced from seventeen seats to nine. My live-to-air interview with Simon Walker, who looked about twelve, went as follows.

> SIMON: Here's a man who must be disappointed with the result.
>
> ME: I was worried satirists would go out of business. It was touch and go there for a while. George Chapman was dousing himself and his wife with petrol outside the bunker, and Muldoon was rolling cyanide capsules around in his mouth, but they managed to hold on.
>
> SIMON: So you'll be back in business next year?
>
> ME: I'll be back in business next year.

CHAPTER FIFTEEN

BREAKING BAD

I WAS BACK IN BUSINESS next year. In 1979 I got a bit careless. An article I wrote on the PSIS started the worst month I experienced on the Hill. The piece is of no particular interest now, except for the fact I was sued for libel by Muldoon as a consequence. Some of the key details were incorrect. Journalists shouldn't make mistakes—especially when writing about heads of government.

The first I knew of my transgression was when Kevin Hyde, my lawyer friend, came round late at night looking sick with worry. I thought he was about to tell me his marriage was on the rocks so I poured him a huge whisky. He took a large slug then told me that the PM had retained the services of the much-feared Des Dalgety of the Wellington law firm Bell Gully, with the express intention of hitting me with a writ for defamation. I was terrified at first but this soon subsided into callow self-pity. I didn't mind defaming the PM so much—politicians must expect that sort of thing. I figured he would soon get over it, if indeed he was ever hurt to begin with. After all, he was only demanding $10,000 in damages, which meant either (a) he felt sorry for me, or (b) his reputation wasn't too severely impugned, as (c) my own reputation was so low any charge of libel from whatever source would be hard to sustain. But I did feel bad about my editor. I had let Tony Reid down.

He was very decent about it at first, which only made me feel worse, but as the plot thickened he took to shaking his head sadly, rolling his eyes at the ceiling and muttering darkly about things being pretty grim on the third-floor executive row.

'What do you mean?' I would enquire nervously.

'Don't ask, pal, don't ask. Trust me. You don't want to know.'

Ignoring my feeble suggestion that we defend the matter in court, the *Listener* suspended my column one week and published a full apology in its place. Being only the second defendant, being in disgrace, and with the BCNZ paying all the costs, I was not consulted on the wording—which was largely the work of the Prime Minister's people anyway. BCNZ's default response to litigation was capitulation and in this instance I didn't have much choice. Still, I winced when I saw the printed grovelling apology. I took some comfort from the fact that while they were at it they at least refrained from blaming me for the Great Fire of London.

The more immediate problem was that the National Party annual conference was about to begin in Christchurch. Tony told me he would understand if I preferred to give it a miss. It was tempting, but there was no escaping the ignominy. It would be better to get it over and done with.

The joshing began shortly after I landed at Christchurch airport—waiting for my baggage, dozens of National Party delegates wandered across to chat.

'I guess Rob got you there, Scotty?'

'Yeah, I'm afraid so.'

'Gidday, Tom, got ya cheque book on ya, mate?'

'No, the bank confiscated it—I'm ten thousand dollars overdrawn.'

'Hey, say something nasty about me next week. I need the money!'

'What a good idea—we could go halves on the damages.'

And so it continued for most of the weekend. A triumphant Muldoon asked me to stand and take a bow during his speech. I obliged, to great applause. It reached a crescendo the night of their social in the Town Hall. I joined a group of colleagues at one of the bars serving free liquor. We stood in a sullen huddle watching the Nats whirl by in their finery. I had an almost constant stream of people coming up to clap me on the back and wink at me, and I started asking for double whiskies, but somehow, rather than dulling my senses, they seemed to intensify my irritation.

A group of young Nats sauntered up, saying, 'I suppose you're too famous to talk to us.' An awkward conversation ensued but eventually I asked to be excused as I was with friends.

'Oh yeah,' sneered the ringleader. 'Done your bit for the masses! The famous person doesn't find us interesting enough to talk to! He wants to get back to his famous friends!' The awkward conversation staggered on a bit longer until I could stand it no more and I turned away, ordering another double whisky. 'See!' and 'Thought so!' they shouted over my shoulder. The pretty girl behind the counter smiled and shrugged in sympathy.

Near the end of the evening someone came up and shouted in my ear, 'Want to go to a party?'

'Why not?' I replied.

'Good.' He beamed. 'It's in your room!' It was news to me but the word had gone out that I was holding a stir of some sort. By this stage I had decided that the pretty girl who'd been pouring me whisky all night was my only real friend in the whole world. I enquired casually if she would like to come to a party. She smiled sweetly and to my secret relief she said she couldn't—her husband was at home babysitting the kids.

When I got back to Noah's Hotel there were already a dozen people in my room. Someone had got a key from the desk. As I forced my way into the crush I was hailed loudly. No one had brought grog. I was obliged to be a good sport and ring room service for some whisky, gin and beer.

'Don't worry,' brayed a red-faced young Nat in a checked sports coat and cravat. 'We're going to take a collection.' They did. It barely covered half of the bill. The crowd swelled. To escape the din, I went out into the corridor, where Ian Fraser and some journalists were talking quietly and swapping yarns. It was decidedly more pleasant out there, laughing and passing around the wine.

The scrum in my room didn't begin to abate until some time after three. What I didn't know then was that the cabinet minister Hugh Templeton and his wife Natasha had the room on one side of me, and another cabinet minister, Police Minister Air Commodore Frank Gill and his wife, were on the other side. Natasha apparently begged Hugh repeatedly to get up and complain about the noise, but he remained in bed, indirectly contributing to the catastrophe his intervention might have prevented.

When the crowd thinned, I returned to my dishevelled room. There were only a handful of people left, including senior cabinet minister Jim McLay, who I have always got on well with, and his first wife, Jenny. She was sprawled languidly across my bed and appeared most reluctant to leave. I busied myself stacking bottles and glasses and emptying ashtrays while people thanked me profusely as they left. Finally, there was only the BCNZ's Neil Roberts left. Neil was a bit the worse for wear— just minutes before he'd had to be stopped unwinding a fire hose in the corridor. It seems he'd wanted to wash the last of the stragglers out of my room. He was a decent bloke like that.

I was moaning about the state of the room when suddenly he barked, 'Jesus, don't those young Nats just give you the shits!' Slumped on a low table I concurred moodily, and looked up to see Neil pluck a heavy black armchair off the carpet and hurl it through the plate-glass window. There was a terrible explosion, followed by another crash as it disintegrated on something far below. We were twelve floors up and a strong, icy wind surged through the splintered wound. Sheer horror left me momentarily paralysed. I was thinking, first a libel suit and now this shit! I came out of my trance when Neil threw the telephone directory out the window and began looking about the room for other missiles.

Roberts was a big strong boy, but I managed to get a table lamp off him. Wrestling him to the floor, I dragged him by his heels out into the corridor. Just opening the door was an experience. The breeze became a howling gale, flattening the curtains against the ceiling. The whirlwind subsided once I'd locked Roberts outside but he immediately began pounding on the door. I had no choice. I had to open the door again. My advice to him that he had to behave himself was lost in the maelstrom, as bending double into the head wind he surged past me and started dragging the double bed towards the window. I restored a modicum of calm by shutting the door, then raced after him. I had to knock him over and drag him by the legs back to the door again. I was wondering just how often this cycle would need to be repeated when hotel security burst in.

I said as calmly as I could that there was no cause for alarm and everything would be paid for. They didn't say much. They could have got very heavy but obviously they assumed I was a government MP or a highly placed National Party apparatchik and things were best hushed up. Neil, who had become unaccountably meek all of a sudden, was led away gently. The man in charge surveyed the carnage and asked me menacingly if I wanted another room. I shook my head and said I'd caused them enough trouble. He grunted agreement and reached for the door handle. The curtains billowed like spinnakers and he was gone. I stole this pantomime for my screenplay *Separation City*.

It was so freezing I got into bed fully dressed. Sleep when it came was fitful and tormented. I was awakened early by a phone call. It was Jim McLay, talking in hushed tones. His wife's handbag was missing—had I seen it? I told him I would ring him back, and searched through the debris with no luck. Finally, I pulled the bed out from the wall and something thudded to the carpet. I rang Jim and he said he'd be down in a tick. No kidding.

Barely had I put down the receiver when there was a soft tap on the door. Peering anxiously up and down the deserted corridor, Jim had one hand tucked into the small of his back, palm open. I pressed the purse into his trembling fingers and he was gone in an instant.

The incident was the talk of the hotel. Some thought it had been a terrorist attack. There was a rumour going round that the pressure of the libel suit had been too much for me and I had jumped to my death. I decided to skip the conference and spent the day with my old friend A.K. Grant and his wife, Liz. I returned to the Town Hall for the evening session and a burly farmer who'd been at the party came up, grinning broadly.

'By Christ, this senior whip bloke Friedlander has got his knickers in a twist. He was giving me the third degree. He wanted to know if any MPs were there.'

'If he asks again,' I joked, 'tell him you didn't recognise anyone because no one had their clothes on.'

'Jesus.' He beamed. 'I just might do that. He'd go apeshit!'

Feeling that the worst was over, I wandered into the house bar at Noah's later that night and was having a chat to television producer Derek Fox and reporter Amanda Millar when Frank Gill sighted me, leaped up from his seat and came charging across, shouting angrily that I owed him and his wife an apology—the noise of the chair going through the glass had nearly given her a heart attack. I replied that I was sick and tired of apologising for something I hadn't done. He got even angrier, shouting that as Minister of Police he could order an inquiry and I could find myself in deep trouble. I replied heatedly that I didn't take kindly to threats. At this point Derek intervened and led me away.

The next morning, I rang Air New Zealand to see if I could get an early flight north. There was one about midday and I booked myself on it.

Almost as soon as I had put the phone down, it rang.

'Hello,' purred a woman's voice.

'Who is it?' I enquired cautiously.

'It's the barmaid you spoke to the other night. I couldn't come to your party, remember? My husband has gone to work and the kids are at school. I could come to your room now if you want.'

'I'm so sorry,' I lied. 'I'm literally heading out the door to the airport ...'

I hung up, checked out, and headed out to the airport two hours early. 'Where was she,' I asked myself, 'when I was nineteen?'

CHAPTER SIXTEEN

INDIA, BUT NOT CHINA

BEFORE THE OLD PARLIAMENT BUILDING was closed for earthquake strengthening, the Press Gallery used to occupy a corridor on the second floor just a hop, skip and jump from the debating chamber. Every office had a radio tuned to the parliamentary broadcast frequency, and at the first hint of a headline we could be leaning over the balustrades in seconds flat. The back corridor was the horizontal equivalent of a fireman's pole, and as an added bonus Government MPs had to walk down it to attend their weekly caucus meetings. Journalists merely had to prop themselves in office doorways and thrust out microphones to conduct interviews.

My office was a desk in the 'smoko' room between Radio New Zealand and BCNZ. I shared it with a teleprinter, a coffee machine, a fridge and an ominously stained couch. I have always maintained that if parliamentary couches could talk they would have a bad stammer. Late in the afternoon the sun poured in, rendering me drowsy. Only sheer terror kept me awake when an article was due.

I was slumped at my desk one day in 1980 when the BCNZ's chief political reporter, Dennis Grant, strode in for some coffee and mentioned casually that he'd just completed costings on his forthcoming trip to India and China with the Prime Minister.

I responded wistfully that the *Listener* never sent me on trips like that. Dennis almost dropped his coffee.

'No one sends you on these things out of the goodness of their hearts, you daft bugger,' he snapped. 'You have to submit a proposal. You make a case for why they should send you.'

He told me I could use his costings and insisted that I got on to it right away. I did as I was told and about half an hour later handed the document to Dennis.

'No, no, no . . .' he sighed. 'I wouldn't give you a taxi chit for this. For Christ's sake, you've got to sell them the idea. Build it up a bit. Make it sound absolutely imperative that you go. Don't pussyfoot around.' With him yelling advice at me to stress how the unique grouping of world leaders in India and Muldoon being the first Western leader to visit China since its major leadership shake-up provided the *Listener*'s loyal readers with an unprecedented window into the normally closed world of geo-political intrigue, I typed away furiously, producing two pages of hyperbole that I found deeply embarrassing, but which Dennis insisted would do the trick nicely.

He knew what he was talking about. The new *Listener* editor Peter Stewart got very excited and came close to writing me out a cheque on the spot. The only conceivable hitch would be getting the Prime Minister's approval to be part of his official party.

The next morning, quite fortuitously, I ran into his deputy Brian Talboys in a corridor and I told him I wanted to follow his 'boss' around Asia, not as a satirist but as a serious journalist, and did he have any good advice?

'Drop him a note telling him just what you've told me.' He grinned. 'Good luck.'

I dispatched a suitably sober and craven letter off to the PM's office and two days later his press officer Gerry Symmans told me that as Muldoon had scrawled 'seen' on the bottom of the note it could well mean I would be allowed to come. At the very least he hadn't rejected the idea outright.

Over the next week, however, the news from the ninth floor was not good and time was running out. Dennis suggested I sound Muldoon out personally by giving a note to a parliamentary messenger to take in to the chamber requesting a quick word in the lobby. I wasn't all that keen.

'Go on,' urged Grant. 'He can only say no.'

I handed the note to a messenger and waited nervously for the man himself. He came out a short while later, scowling. His voice was sharp and deliberate when he spoke. He told me I wouldn't be going to China or India if he could help it. My usual response to authority is casual insolence. (It must be genetic. My own children do it to me.) I enquired if he was serious or if this was just another tantrum. He assured me that he was deadly serious. I conceded that refusing to have me in his official party meant I couldn't go to China, but I doubted whether he could stop me going to India. He jutted his jaw and told me that he could and he would.

Going back upstairs to the gallery I suddenly felt weak at the knees and in a daze told the others what had happened. Within minutes they were thumping away on their typewriters—Prime Minister threatens to ban *Listener* journalist from China. It was a slow news day. I don't know how he found out, but within half an hour, Radio New Zealand's Richard Griffin came dashing into my office to alert me that Muldoon had already been on the phone complaining about my rudeness to the BCNZ chairman, my former editor and mentor Ian Cross. The new editor, mild-mannered Peter Stewart, not long at the helm, suddenly found himself embroiled in a controversy he could have done without. He was very good about it, however, and as the media storm gathered momentum he issued a cautious press release.

I regret the Prime Minister has not given
approval for Mr Scott to join the official

New Zealand party attending the Commonwealth
Heads of Government conference in Delhi
next month and afterwards visiting China. The
Listener intends sending Mr Scott to the New
Delhi conference independently. The situation
regarding China is different and Mr Muldoon
is exercising his prerogative although I disagree
with that use . . .

In print and on radio Muldoon and I engaged in a bizarre war
of words. He claimed that I wrote garbage and I riposted that
it was garbage of the very highest quality—hardly Oscar Wilde,
but enough. Then it became a battle of Chinese sayings, with
Muldoon claiming that his reluctance to have me along could
be explained by the old Chinese proverb that one rat dropping
spoiled the soup. I replied with a quote from Chairman Mao
that you couldn't smell the flowers from the galloping horse—
but you could smell the horse and that was good enough for me.
It was all very silly. The *Dominion* interviewed me for a front-
page story.

BANNED SATIRIST MOURNS WORLD'S LOSS

Listener satirist Tom Scott was unfazed last night
after the Prime Minister rejected his application
to accompany Mr Muldoon on next month's visit
to India and China. Scott said that he was not
upset for himself but for a quarter of the world's
population who would miss out on the chance of
meeting him.

The Press Gallery, the people who had once debated whether
I was a suitable person for membership, put out a statement.

The Press Gallery Officers met the Prime Minister,
Mr Muldoon, this morning to discuss his decision
not to allow *Listener* columnist, Tom Scott, to

accompany him on this forthcoming overseas
trip. Gallery Chairman, Alastair Carthew, pointed
out to Mr Muldoon that Mr Scott was entitled as
a journalist to cover the Delhi conference but the
only way he could cover the China leg of the trip
was to be included in the official party. 'However,'
Mr Carthew said, 'Mr Muldoon stuck to his
earlier decision saying he could not afford to
have Mr Scott on the trip in view of the delicate
nature of these missions.'

Privately Muldoon took journalists aside to tell them I threw
chairs out of hotel windows—the implication being that you
couldn't take me anywhere. While the latter was true enough,
the former was incorrect. Then, as good as his word, he wrote
to the Commonwealth Secretariat asking them to ban me from
the Commonwealth Heads of Government Meeting. They
replied it was out of their hands—the Indian government was
solely responsible for journalist accreditation. The Indian
government, to their credit, opted to accept the untouchable.

The Commonwealth Press Union condemned Muldoon's
actions. Editors and leader-writers across New Zealand came
to my defence. Murray Ball did a cartoon on the issue for the
Sunday Star. Eric Heath did a cartoon for the *Dominion*. Dear
old Sid Scales from the *ODT* drew one. Nevile Lodge drew two
cartoons in support in the *Evening Post*. Talkback-radio callers
and letters to the editor ran overwhelmingly in my favour.
The Northern Journalists Union urged the Prime Minister to
reconsider his stand.

We believe your attitude raises important issues
for press freedom and deprives a recognised
political journalist of the right to work.

And the debate was still raging on my return from India. On 23
October 1980, the *Southland Times* ran correspondence from a
Mrs M. Quinn, a self-declared friend, confidante and adviser to

the Prime Minister, that took up almost all of their letters page. One paragraph in particular intrigued me.

> In respect of the Tom Scott affair there was an unpublished reason why it was in the national interest for the *Listener* columnist to be left in New Zealand. Instead of criticising Muldoon for trying to get him banned from the Delhi conference, right-thinking people would admire and respect the PM for his stance if they were aware of the facts.

I would have dearly loved to know what the unpublished reason was, what national interest was at stake and what these facts were. I should have asked the Director of the GCSB if he knew when we had afternoon tea together. I assume that 'national interest' meant protecting New Zealand from the possibility I might hurl an armchair from a twelve-storey New Delhi hotel room.

IT WAS ACTUALLY A RELIEF to finally board the Air New Zealand flight at Auckland airport and get away from it all. At the end of the air-bridge the Prime Minister's official party, which included his staff, foreign affairs wallahs and journalists, turned left into first class. I turned right into economy. Speakers hummed to life and the pilot came over the intercom:

'Good afternoon, ladies and gentlemen. We're just waiting for clearance from the tower and we'll be closing the door and pushing back from the apron. Our flight time to Singapore is ten hours, forty-five minutes. We should have you on the ground at Changi at six o'clock local time. We're very privileged to have a special guest on board today. It's Tom Scott from the *Listener*. He's down the back!'

I'm told that Muldoon, who had been almost purring seconds earlier, went dark with fury. But that wasn't the worst part. The worst part was the tsunami of cheering and applause that raced up the plane and smacked into the first-class compartment.

It was pitch black when we landed, and by the time I got

through customs Muldoon's motorcade with its police outriders and wailing sirens had long departed. I emerged into the frangipani-scented sauna that is Singapore, envious and clearly agitated. A local scam artist with no English but fluent in body language offered me a cheap taxi ride into the city. I followed him and should have twigged things weren't right when we crashed through two hedges and across a garden to an unlit car park and a battered car with no meter. Feeling committed, I clambered into his vehicle and he drove out of the car park with his lights off, only switching them on when we hit the freeway. There was no air-conditioning that I could detect. He refused to drop me at my hotel, pulling up a quarter of a mile from it, telling me he was a poor man and demanding an exorbitant sum of money in cash. I paid up limply and stepped out into air so humid it was close to being submerged.

I was staying in an older, less salubrious wing of the same hotel as the official party. Muldoon had already held a press briefing. Australian politician Joh Bjelke-Petersen famously called these sessions 'feeding the chooks' and he wasn't wrong. Reporters compete for miserable scraps of information. Back in Wellington newsrooms they were more interested in my stumbling progress, and scribes were waiting in the lobby for me to arrive, sweat-sodden and trailing tropical vegetation. They recounted a tale of a bedraggled, bewildered yet curiously heroic figure doggedly pursuing his craft.

That very same night, by incredible coincidence, my mother was staying in another, less sumptuous Singapore hotel on the return leg of her trip to Ireland—her first since immigrating to New Zealand in 1949. In those days before cell phones and the internet she knew nothing of the controversy surrounding my trip, which was a relief because it would have sent her into an extreme panic state, clutching her throat and asking people with poor English to fetch her angina pills—which in her Irish accent came out sounding like 'vagina pills'. Still, as a freelance worrier when it came to her offspring, doubtless she was sending out anxiety vibes which I unwittingly picked up. I'm sure that it was because of her unknown proximity that I slept fitfully with my passport and wallet tucked under my pillow and had to fight the urge to stack up all the furniture against the securely chained door. The next morning the local paper *The Straits Times* printed a small piece on the saga, which thankfully she missed.

DELHI INTERNATIONAL AIRPORT IS now vast, elegant and state-of-the-art. In 1980 it was a teeming, exotic, chaotic shambles. By the time I had weaved my way from the rear of economy, across the tarmac, through the customs and immigration halls, to the barn dance of the arrivals hall, only a New Zealand High Commission staffer in charge of Muldoon's luggage was left. He nervously offered me a ride in their panel van, but I would have to crouch in the back with the suitcases. I accepted. It proved to be only marginally cooler than the surface of the sun.

It was a relief to get to The Ashok Hotel, a majestic, imposing edifice built in the Mogul style. It had a tatty splendour, suggesting a glory from centuries gone by. It was in fact barely 30 years old. English is an official language of India, as are Hindi, Urdu and Punjabi. In addition, hotel receptionists speak fluent Air Traffic Control. When I gave my name on arrival as 'Scott', the tall, handsome Sikh behind the marble counter beamed happily.

'Sierra, Charlie, Oscar, Tango, Tango.'

'No,' I explained patiently. 'Scott.'

He beamed even wider and nodded violently. 'Sierra, Charlie, Oscar, Tango, Tango!'

'No,' I replied, slowly and loudly. 'SCOTT!'

He replied in kind, shouting in frustration. 'SIERRA! CHARLIE! OSCAR! TANGO! TANGO!'

We continued back and forth in this fashion for quite some time, but I eventually got to my palatial room. It had dark drapes, dark walls and dark carpet so badly laid it rippled like waves. It smelled deliciously of sandalwood and incense.

I had barely settled in when there was a knock on the door. It was a big, loud, brash, broad-shouldered, lantern-jawed

Australian reporter, Bill Darcy from 2UE, working out of Canberra.

'So you're the joker the Pig didn't want?' he said after he had introduced himself. 'I'm going to do a report straight down the pipe to Australia.' He started bellowing into a microphone. 'Today, Piggy Muldoon flew into Delhi and, metaphorically speaking, stamped his cigarette out in Indira Gandhi's carpet!' It didn't matter that our Prime Minister didn't smoke. Speaking metaphorically allowed Bill to speak colourfully and forcefully about anything without the need for a factual basis. He was a man after my own heart.

Bob Jones has always maintained that in India there is a Booker Prize-winning novel waiting to be written every four hundred paces in any direction you care to walk. In Delhi, life in all its sordid glory abounds on every spare patch of ground. The air is thick with the heady aroma of incense, spices, wood smoke, diesel fumes and human faeces. On our first morning I accompanied Dennis Grant and his stringer crew to film Muldoon being driven through the grand gates of 7 Lok Kalyan Marg, the official residence of the Indian Prime Minister, for a private audience with Indira Gandhi. Dennis's man on the ground recommended a beater, very cheap, very good. Dennis had no idea what he was talking about, shook his head and indicated to the cameraman where to place the tripod. Denny would stand before it in his khaki safari suit and do one of his authoritative pieces to camera as Muldoon's convoy swept into the magnificent grounds. But no sooner had the camera been set up when an excited crowd about a thousand strong materialised out of nowhere, blocking all view of the gates.

Dennis's man on the ground pushed some burly men forward, armed with long batons. 'Beaters, sahib. Fifty rupee.'

'I'll take two,' hissed Dennis. Flailing wildly, they waded into the crowd, who didn't seem to mind unduly and parted like the Dead Sea with just seconds to spare.

Back at The Ashok I had early evening drinks with a man who I had long admired as a rugby fan, but had never met before: Chris Laidlaw, the former All Black, Rhodes Scholar, author and personal assistant to the Commonwealth Secretary, Shridath 'Sonny' Ramphal. After downing three quick beers, Chris abandoned his professional guard and began pouring his heart out about the nightmare of dealing with Muldoon and confided that one day he hoped to return to New Zealand and become a Labour Party Prime Minister.

Muldoon wasn't the only problematic leader in attendance. Singapore's stern and domineering Harry Lee Kuan Yew sent organisers into a spin with his strict stipulation of no smells—an impossible request in India. He was staying on the same floor as me. Half a dozen soldiers, sweating in heavy khaki uniforms and armed with old Lee-Enfield rifles, were guarding his door. Those not squatting on their haunches lay full stretch on the carpet. They had taken off their boots and socks.

The smell was something else. Back in my room I got a call from Jim Kebbell. His boss Tupuola Efi wanted to know if I felt like a nightcap. We sat outside on a wide balcony overlooking the Lodi Gardens with the great temples and the sprawling city beyond, knocking back industrial quantities of gin and tonic. On the flight up from Singapore Jim had been entrusted with Muldoon's reading glasses, which he'd accidentally left behind in the airport VIP lounge. My advice was to smash the fucking things and reduce Muldoon to a stumbling Mr Magoo figure at the conference table. Efi demurred. He liked Muldoon. Our Prime Minister was kind and respectful to leaders from small Pacific Island states. This warmth did not extend to the towering Australian Prime Minister, Malcolm Fraser, or Sonny Ramphal, of whom Muldoon would bark that where he came from, secretaries kept the minutes. Off the record I was told about deep hostility and blazing rows.

Well after midnight I tottered through the dimly lit foyer of The Ashok only to have NZPA's nuggety Bruce Kohn come hurtling out of the shadows, asking, 'What's the guts? What have you heard?'

'Nothing,' I lied, and kept going.

When the leaders went off to their traditional retreat, Bill Darcy invited Richard Griffin, Dennis and me to join the

Aussie media and the crew of Malcolm Fraser's Australian Air Force VIP jet on a bus trip to Agra, 204 kilometres south, to visit one of the wonders of the modern world, the Taj Mahal. The flight crew organised a packed lunch and bottled water for everyone and the Aussie press organised the alcohol—chilly-bins running the length of the aisle filled with cans of Foster's. The hired bus came with a guide and a crackling, hissing sound system. The guide started gabbling at great speed with great pride every time we passed a temple or ruin, which unfortunately was every few minutes. Imagine the home straight of the Melbourne Cup with an Indian race caller and the lead constantly changing between horses with names like Brahma, Vishnu, Shiva and Ganapati. The three Kiwis nodded politely at every incomprehensible thing he said, but behind us the Aussies started complaining loudly, which forced us to nod even more furiously by way of compensation.

'For fuck's sake! Will you bastards stop it!' yelled Bill Darcy. 'You're only encouraging the prick!'

Bill had a point, but we didn't want to hurt the guide's feelings —he was already on the verge of tears. He stoically refused to leave his post when they started throwing empty Foster's cans in his direction. When a full can glanced off his temple he sensibly called it quits and retreated to the front of the bus, convulsing with sobs.

The driver's seat was actually in a separate open-air compartment outside the main body of the bus. The driver sat at the wheel behind a low windscreen exposed to the elements like a rider on a motorbike. Our broken guide climbed out and squeezed in behind him, clinging to his shoulders like a baby koala as bugs, dust and all manner of flying debris whipped past.

It was terrifying enough inside the bus. They don't drive on the left-hand side of the road so much as favour it slightly. When two vehicles approach each other from opposite directions they both stay in the centre of the road, blasting their horns in a game of chicken, until at the very last second one of them loses their nerve. The side of the road was littered with scorched, crumpled wrecks.

Halfway to Agra there was a comfort stop. In the middle of a wide, turning circle was a toilet block sitting in a small lake of raw sewage. If you were desperate you had to take off your shoes and socks, roll your trousers up to your knees and wade through a moat of shit. None of us were that desperate. A local approached with a threadbare bear and prodded it with a stick. It rose up on its hind legs and shuffled listlessly in a tragic approximation of Mr Bojangles while its master held out his hand for money. We all duly parted with our loose change.

Appetites blunted by the smell of the toilet block, some of the Australians began feeding their unfinished lunches to the bear over the shrill protestations and manic gesticulations of the keeper. The bear knew what was happening and gobbled them up ravenously. His envious keeper gave the bear a tongue-lashing in a tongue I didn't recognise, but I'd put money on the gist of it being 'Save some for me, you bastard!' As we drove off, the keeper was lashing the bear with the stick. I'm no David Attenborough but, eyes closed, head lifted towards the warm rays of the sun, the bear had a post-coital, I-don't-give-a-shit look of utter contentment on his face.

When we finally got there, the Taj Mahal exceeded all expectations. It was breathtakingly beautiful and brought a curious moisture to my eyelids—but then again that could have just been air pollution so toxic it is eating into the majestic white marble mausoleum. Bill Darcy was moved to bellow, 'Any nation who can build this is a great nation.' People selling ganja swarmed around us. 'Is that dak? Can I smell dak?' he asked, even more excited.

ON THE LAST NIGHT OF the conference, Sonny Ramphal hosted a farewell cocktail party for everyone in an impossibly grand ballroom of an impossibly grand hotel. On hearing that I had been invited, Muldoon boycotted proceedings. A Commonwealth leader came up and asked, 'Are you the guy Muldoon doesn't like?' I said I was. He grinned. 'Can I shake your hand?'

The Australian Foreign Minister Andrew Peacock wanted to

shake my hand also. Resplendent in a safari suit so iridescent a white you could feel it bleaching your retinas, silver-haired and tanned like an orange, continuously threading worry beads through his hands and scanning the room for more important people to talk to, Peacock filled in time telling Dennis and me about the time he was in bed with Shirl in the Waldorf Astoria and there was knocking on the door, and it was Hank. It was clearly meant to be an amusing tale so we laughed dutifully. Then it dawned on us that he was boasting to journalists that he'd only just met about bonking the actress Shirley MacLaine and being interrupted by Henry Kissinger. Spotting other strangers he hadn't told yet he moved off.

Dennis and I were chatting to some Indian officials when we got the gob-smacking news about the East Coast Bays by-election back in New Zealand—National had just lost the safe, blue-ribbon seat and it was partly my fault. Muldoon's treatment of me was the last straw for many disaffected National voters. While I was digesting the shock result, an Indian official beamed with delight. 'It couldn't happen to a nicer chap.'

The by-election, which National could have done without, was made necessary by the resignation of Frank Gill and Muldoon appointing the well-past-his-use-by-date old warrior to the post of New Zealand ambassador to the United States. Both major parties are guilty of treating diplomatic postings as halfway houses between the chamber and retirement villages for politicians they want to reward, or in some cases get well out of the way. Former Prime Ministers Bill Rowling and Jim Bolger fell into the latter category and were exemplary in the execution of their duties in Washington. The witty and engaging Paul East and the more dour and diligent Russell Marshall fell into the reward category, and both did their country proud in Westminster. The portly Jonathan Hunt not so much. Fondly referred to as the Minister for Wine and Cheese by both sides of the House, he famously refused to get out of his chauffeur-driven limousine at a Remembrance Day ceremony at the Cenotaph in Whitehall because it had started to rain and he wasn't dressed for it. Interviewed about the embarrassing incident by *The New*

Zealand Herald, his boss, Helen Clark, tartly advised him to buy a coat. Mind you, in Jonathan's defence, if all armies refused point-blank to fight in inclement weather the world would be a much safer place and there would be less need for cenotaphs.

The Commonwealth Heads of Government Meeting produced very little that was newsworthy, but I was taken with the line of one Indian economist talking about the urgent need to bridge the gap between the world's rich and the world's poor: 'You cannot take two steps across an abyss!' This applies equally to climate change today.

WE ALL FLEW OUT TO Bombay, the Muldoon party flying on to Beijing and me flying alone to Sydney and on to Canberra to cover Australian politics. The first indication that Muldoon had changed my public profile exponentially came in King's Cross. I was loitering in the doorway of a dirty bookshop trying to pluck up the courage to go in when a bunch of teenage girls from New Zealand on a school trip started yelling, 'OOOH! TOM SCOTT! THAT'S DISGUSTING! YOU SHOULD BE ASHAMED OF YOURSELF!' I protested feebly that I was trying to purchase a copy of *Newsweek* but my flaming cheeks gave me away.

Then I ran into a National Party dominion councillor and soon into party president, the lovely Sue Wood, and her husband, getting away from the East Coast Bays madness and recrimination. Sue insisted on taking me to lunch and gave me the inside story on the defeat. Muldoon blamed it on their candidate—the tall, gaunt, bespectacled economist, merchant banker and less than effervescent Dr Don Brash. Certainly, on the hustings he was no match for Social Credit's complete unknown, Garry Knapp, handsome in a poor man's Elvis way and more charming than a Mississippi paddle steamer card-shark. Sue said the government's raising of the tolls on the Auckland Harbour Bridge hadn't helped either, and their own polling showed that Muldoon's heavy-handed treatment of me coupled with his bullying insistence that only he knew how to run the economy was losing its charm both within and outside the government.

Further proof of my new status came when I sneaked back into Wellington and my good mate Barry Soper was waiting at the airport to thrust a microphone in my direction, asking for my thoughts. Helen had brought our toddler with her when coming to pick me up. Jiggling gorgeous wee Sammy on my hip, I just kept walking, telling Bazza I was going home to play with my kids.

There is a very fine line in New Zealand between being an accidental centre of attention and wallowing in it. After scoring a try under the posts, our All Blacks back then knew better than to celebrate wildly—instead they trudged back to halfway as if they had done something they were deeply ashamed of, much like an old dog that knows it shouldn't have pissed on a rug.

Additional confirmation came on our way to a wedding in Waikanae. I pulled into a service station at the bottom of the Ngaio Gorge and filled up the van.

'Sorry mate, no cheques or credit cards,' said the owner when I went to pay him. I assured him the cheque wouldn't bounce. 'Oh yeah, well, I've heard that before.' I produced a wad of ID cards and press passes that left him unmoved. He seemed quite prepared to siphon the petrol back out, should the need arise. I started to get desperate. 'I was the guy Muldoon tried to have banned from India.'

He grinned and patted me on the shoulder. 'No worries, mate.' Then, turning to the kids, he added, 'Help yourself to some drinks from the fridge.'

AS IS OFTEN THE CASE, simmering discontent with Muldoon's leadership came to a head when he was absent overseas. If you could plot caucus bravery on a graph it would confirm that fearless courage soars exponentially in direct proportion to any leader's distance from Wellington. It eventually spilled over into what the plotters themselves proudly called the 'Colonels' Coup', after Colonel Gamal Abdel Nasser, who toppled the Egyptian monarchy in 1952. Rob Muldoon found himself flying home to face an unprecedented leadership challenge.

Shocked and stunned by the vehemence of the criticism and

the suddenness of it all, a jet-lagged Muldoon began fighting back on pure instinct alone. He went on television, appealing directly down the barrel of camera lenses to members of the National Party who supported him to put pressure on openly disloyal or wavering electorate MPs. It helped him that the Colonels' preferred leader, Brian Talboys, was overseas.

When he should have been full of steely resolve like Lady Macbeth, Talboys turned into a hand-wringing Hamlet. On flights between European capitals he poured his tormented heart out to my chum, Phil Melchior from Reuters, the only reporter covering his lobbying for continued access for New Zealand agricultural products to the EEC. Mindful of the need for future headlines, Phil did what any responsible journalist would have done in his position—he urged Talboys into battle. Of his own volition he even wrote a press release and short acceptance speech for Brian to help tip the scales.

The scenes in the back corridors of the second floor of Parliament the morning Muldoon attended his first caucus on his return were quite amazing. I hadn't witnessed anything like it since the Labour caucus met six years earlier to pick a successor to Norm Kirk. There was the same sense of dramatic possibility in the air. Every journalist, television cameraman and newspaper photographer in the building milled about, feeding off and contributing to the tension and excitement. For some of them it was too much. Thrusting tape recorders at others to hold, they shot off to the toilets, demanding they should be called immediately if anything happened. It soon became obvious that many in caucus felt the same way. Assorted members emerged to race into the same toilets, unbuckling their belts. Muldoon had that effect on people's bowels.

Speculation and those strange jokes journalists make at these times ripped through the throng. When Hugh Templeton dashed past carrying a plastic lunchbox one wag observed that the crusts had been cut off all the sandwiches and they were pre-masticated—surely a bad sign for the Brian Talboys lobby. There were suggestions that Muldoon was planning yet another television address to the nation and his staff had been dispatched to find a puppy or some kittens he could cuddle live on air.

The caucus ran way beyond its normal length and it was a very subdued Muldoon who emerged and told a crowded press conference that he was still Prime Minister. The challenges to his leadership were far from over and he no longer enjoyed the full confidence of caucus, but he thought he could still lead National to victory in 1981. 'I really do think I can,' he added wistfully, sounding for the first time in his long career diffident and insecure.

He was saved when news came through that his deputy wasn't running and the coup wilted for want of a challenger. The conspicuously decent Talboys had no stomach for what he knew would have been total war and announced that he would be retiring at the next election.

One deeply cynical senior MP told me later that the Prime Minister's humility and contrition in caucus was an acting performance worthy of an Academy Award. He said Muldoon never absorbed criticism willingly and sooner or later, unable to help himself, he would go back to his rogue elephant ways. At his press conference Muldoon likened himself to another wild animal from the plains of Africa—he doubted that a leopard could change its spots but he would give it a try.

I decided to put this to the test and went along to his next press conference. I had been banned previously on the grounds that they were for daily-accredited journalists only. Muldoon looked up when he saw me seated near the back of the Beehive theatre and in a gravelly voice intoned solemnly, 'Oh no, Mr Scott.' Then asked one of his staff to escort me out. His junior press officer, Sue Elliott, barely in her twenties, looked sick at the prospect of having to manhandle me to the door. Being held in a headlock by Sue was a tempting proposition, but to spare her that indignity I rose from my seat and walked—asking plaintively as I went if this was an example of the Prime Minister's turned-over new leaf.

Many of my colleagues were later furious with themselves for not getting up and walking out with me. For ages their friends and neighbours accused them of being cowardly and gutless while I became, briefly at least, a fearless and saintly

Top Me and my twin sister, Sue, on a Sunday drive, Manawatū, 1950. Before I fell into an empty swimming pool and needed glasses.

Above Cartoon exhibition, Wellington, 1979. Back row: Nevile Lodge, *Evening Post*; Eric Heath, the *Dominion*; Burton Silver of *Bogor* fame; me in the glory days of my 'afro'; Bob Jones, who I would soon resemble; and Bob Brockie, *National Business Review*, one of my early heroes since his *Cappicade* days. Disappointingly his hair remains thick and luxuriant to this day.

Top A hand-drawn, hand-painted animation cell from *The Dog's Tale*, the Footrot Flats movie. Washing the Dog and Horse out to sea, I was able to bring my recurring childhood nightmare to the big screen.

Above My tense fortieth birthday at Emerald Glen. Noam Pitlik pretending to be shocked, me pretending to be sober, and Helen wryly amused.

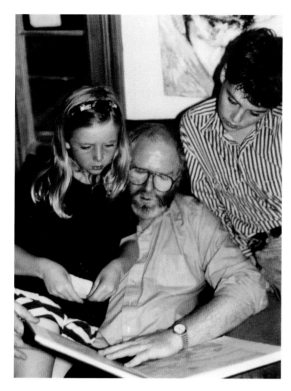

Left With my daughter, Rosie, and son Sam, Kotinga Street, 1989. To curious people under the age of thirty: I am holding something called an atlas and I am showing them maps that don't come with a voice.

Below Trapped in peak commuter rush hour, en route to Lublin, Poland, 1990.

Top Me and Barry Soper, Prague Castle, 1990.

Above On the hill trail above Khumjung, with the Everest massif in the background, Nepal, April 1991.

Top Averil and me, Kotinga Street, 1993.

Above George Lowe and Ed Hillary at Lukla, en route to Khumjung for the 40th anniversary of the conquest of Everest, Nepal, 1993.

Top Presenting two of
my cartoons to Nelson
Mandela at the 125th
Anniversary Dinner of
the Press Gallery,
Wellington, 1995.

Above Will and Shaun,
the whānau bookends,
at Kotinga Street, 1995
or thereabouts.

Top John Carlaw, Mike Single, Ed Hillary and me at the South Pole, filming *View from the Top*, January 1997.

Above Averil, me, Ed Hillary, June Mulgrew, Maharaja of Benares, John Carlaw, Mike Single and Haresh Bhana, Varanasi, India, February 1997.

Above Me and John Clarke, celebrating the successful season of *The Daylight Atheist* at the Melbourne Theatre Company, 2004.

Right I was overwhelmed when I first saw this poster. It's a shame the production didn't live up to the billing, sigh . . .

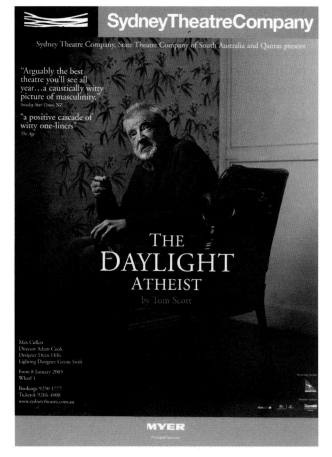

figure worthy of being mentioned in the same breath as Joan of Arc, Thomas Becket and Che Guevara. I mentioned them anyway, whenever the expulsion came up, and if the expulsion didn't come up I made sure that it did. Every time a significant anniversary of television broadcasting in New Zealand comes around they replay this clip—with me looking silly with my thinning afro and blue jacket with absurdly wide lapels. It reduces my heartless children to hysterics.

One of the Prime Minister's press officers told me that in the days that followed Muldoon got heaps of mail critical of his treatment of me and only a handful of letters in support. Muldoon was shocked by one letter congratulating him warmly—it was from my father. It was brief and to the point. 'Egghead had it coming!'

I might be drawing a long bow here, but I got the impression that Muldoon's attitude towards me softened after this. His own father, Jim, contracted syphilis while serving in France in World War One. Jim's health declined after his son was born. He lost the use of his right arm and his left leg and the power of speech. Confined to Carrington mental hospital he degenerated into a pitiful wreck, playing no part in the life of the small, bright boy who visited regularly with his mum.

CHAPTER SEVENTEEN

1981

THE SPRINGBOK TOUR DOMINATED THE political landscape for much of 1981. I found it impossible to ignore, and even more difficult to rein in my own feelings. I was passionately opposed to the tour and yet had to sit down at the typewriter and force myself into an artificial state to write about it calmly and fairly. Often I didn't make it. It was easier if I stuck to pure farce, like the following piece. It provoked a lot of angry letters from pro-tour people complaining about how I had insulted Errol Tobias, the only black player in the touring party. I was even the subject of a complaint to the Race Relations Conciliator, and in due course got a silly little letter from Hiwi Tauroa advising me to be more careful.

The offending piece was a tour diary from an Afrikaner Springbok called Okkie, writing letters to his younger brother.

Dear Danie,

We are settling in here nicely. I went shopping
this morning and got cheered later in a pub when
I said that I supported racial equality, and as far
as I was concerned all black people were equal.
There has been a lot of talk about South Africans
and New Zealanders dying alongside one another
on Italian battlefields. This is true. And, as I have
told some Kiwis, it wasn't easy for people like our
Uncle Heemie. Afrikaners like him, imprisoned
for their pro-Nazi sympathies, had first to break
out of South African jails, smuggle themselves
across the South African border, hitchhike up
the African continent, cross the Sahara on foot,
swim the Mediterranean, joining the Allies and
fighting for the side they didn't agree with—
surely the supreme sacrifice in anyone's book.
I must retire now. Our first practice run was
gruelling. Claassen had the forwards running
repeatedly head first into an iron girder. Still,
I suppose I can count my lucky stars I wasn't
a Springbok back in the grim, unimaginative
win-at-any-cost days.

Your brother, Okkie

LATER THAT YEAR A FULL Commonwealth Heads of Government
Meeting was being held in Melbourne. I thought it important
that the *Listener* attend this meeting as well. At first Peter Stewart
enthusiastically agreed, but as it drew nearer he seemed less
keen and ducked the subject when I brought it up. Eventually he
left on a trip to the United States without saying a word, instead
leaving it to others to instruct me that I wasn't to attend. Peter was
never the bravest of men. Even the way he sat in a chair, floppy
and loose-limbed, implied less calcium than other people. He

eventually quit the editorship to run a motel on the shores of Lake Taupō with his wife. Brilliant author and poet Vincent O'Sullivan, who worked for the *Listener* at the time, wrinkled his nose in distaste at this news. 'Ooooh, can you imagine anything worse? Emptying out adulterers' ashtrays!'

I was angry with Peter on a number of counts. Had he told me to my face that the Melbourne trip was off I would have been surly and deeply disappointed, but accepting. In advance of the conference some African leaders denounced Muldoon for allowing the Springbok tour to proceed. In retaliation, Muldoon said that unlike their countries New Zealand wasn't a dictatorship and didn't have their appalling records of human rights abuses. I thought the *Listener* was opting out on a confrontation with huge implications for the New Zealand election, which was only a few weeks away. On a more personal level I thought that in not sending me to Melbourne the *Listener* was in effect apologising for sending me to India the year before.

In the Press Gallery I complained bitterly to my colleagues about this infamy. I said that if I had somewhere else to place an article and get paid for it, I'd take annual leave from the *Listener* and go to Melbourne anyway. Radio New Zealand's Trevor Henry suggested I ring Martinborough publisher Alister Taylor, which I did immediately. Within minutes the deal was done and the die was cast. He would bankroll me and I would write an eight-page article for his glossy magazine *The New Zealander*.

As I was boarding a plane for Melbourne, Alister's partner and the editor of this publication, Deborah Coddington, released a press statement to the effect that I was now on assignment for them. The gloating tone, while perfectly understandable, was hardly the ideal homecoming present for twitchy Peter Stewart, so it came as no surprise a few days later when Helen rang me in Melbourne to read out a letter that I'd just received from Stewart arguing that as I had not sought to renew my *Listener* contract (previously it had rolled over automatically, with me none the wiser), they would not be renewing it. It had only a few weeks to run anyway and no further work was required from me. Included was a cheque for $1800, effectively a full and final payment.

In the same post there was a letter from our bank demanding that we do something about our $1900 overdraft. I was the main breadwinner for a whānau of seven. I no longer had a job, I was a hundred bucks in arrears, and my thirty-fourth birthday was just days away. I felt sick.

It was a worsening of a queasy feeling that had begun flying in at night. Melbourne has been described as the largest lawn cemetery in the world, and flying in over Port Phillip Bay after dark provided little evidence to the contrary. Unlike Sydney or Los Angeles, where a foul incandescence lights up the horizon, Melbourne, at least from our jumbo in 1981, looked like a glow-worm cave on strike. Was it a sign? I was coming to Melbourne in reckless pursuit of a big story. What if it didn't eventuate? What if nothing happened? I was going to look pretty foolish.

TO GENERATIONS OF MELBOURNE CHILDREN, the Royal Exhibition Building was a dread and terrible place. Within its vast interior thousands of schoolkids from all across the city gathered to sit certificate examinations. The Commonwealth Heads of Government Meeting was being held here. CHOGMs are a form of exam where every leader goes home with a pass. In 1981 one leader failed and came close to being expelled.

That first morning at the REB we had to pass through an impressive security cordon, rare for this side of the world at that time, but once inside journalists swarmed through the halls with the brainless ecstasy of children at a trade fair—pausing at any one spot only long enough to snatch whatever was free before moving on. Facilities included a news agency, bank, duty-free shop, post office, two pie and sandwich counters, two bars, several lounges, three television studios, a number of radio- and television-editing booths, a 24-hour telex service, a shop selling Aboriginal arts and an exhibition of Australian photographs. In a separate enclave, leaders would enjoy even more elegant lounges and their own coffee bar.

The innermost sanctum was the vast, hushed, circular conference room itself. It exemplified the Australian Prime Minister Malcolm Fraser's 'no expense spared' approach to proceedings. So there could be no distractions, the walls were covered in soothing dark brown suede, the only splash of colour being the specially woven carpet in the centre of the room, where a green map of Australia was emblazoned with a gold CHOGM symbol. The leaders would sit at plush, high-backed chairs. With its subdued lighting, it reminded me of the war room in *Dr. Strangelove*. The Commonwealth Secretary-General, Sonny Ramphal, saw it differently. Calling for good sportsmanship in his opening remarks, he trumpeted that the circular table was 22 metres in diameter. 'Providentially, the exact length of a cricket pitch!'

The one leader capable of bowling underarm and not averse to a little ball tampering, Rob Muldoon, was running late for the conference's first press conference. The assembled media would forgive him if he provided good copy and they were not disappointed. He moved swiftly to the microphone and, although pale in person, the close-up face on the TV monitors around the room exuded a ruddy authority. He began insisting he would be raising the Gleneagles Agreement on sporting contacts with South Africa, warning that if there was not acceptance of his view that New Zealand had fulfilled its obligations, then his government would pull out of the agreement altogether.

It was a gritty, taking-charge performance spoilt only by a very sharp response to an ebony-coloured journalist in a tribal kaftan who nervously ventured that sporting contacts with apartheid-practising South Africa was an emotional issue to many African countries. Muldoon leaned into his microphone, jutted his big jaw, and barked, 'There are some people who think only folk with black faces have feelings!' You could hear air being sucked in all across the room and the poor man half-vanished into his robes. Asked whether he would be producing his now infamous dossier on the shabby human rights records of some Commonwealth countries, Muldoon growled ominously, 'Let's see what happens.' Challenged on New Zealand's record on human rights, he took a moment to smile then conceded that we had deficiencies in this area—the major one being whether boys and girls should get separate prizes in painting competitions. The auditorium, which was looking for something to ease the electric tension, erupted in laughter. He was able to swat away all questions with ease after this, like Don Bradman at the crease facing an opening spell from the Queen Mother with a rib injury.

IF AUSTRALIA HAS ONE PLACE of worship every bit as sacrosanct as the Taj Mahal, it is the Long Room at the Melbourne Cricket Ground. With its twenty-five-year waiting list and nine-year probationary period before you become a full member, it is one of sport's holiest shrines. Linseed-stained, yellowing, autographed cricket bats line the walls along with scores of framed sepia photographs of heroes from yesteryear and notices advising that ties or cravats must be worn at all times—not that the CHOGM media managed this the night the Australian Prime Minister hosted us to drinks. High above the famous oval, a vivid jade in the dying light, the room above all else symbolised the enduring value of 'mateship'.

By constantly and knowingly upstaging his host, Muldoon was not being a good mate. Fraser was ferociously committed to ending apartheid and it was no secret that his impatience with Muldoon bordered on loathing. While we stood sipping gin and tonics and nibbling canapés, Fraser worked the room like a whale swimming in a shoal of herrings. When the New Zealand news media quizzed him about Muldoon, he sighed and rolled his deep-set Easter Island statue eyes that perfectly matched his Easter Island statue face and giant frame, nodded and quickly moved on.

Two South African journalists asked me in a low whisper if I wanted to duck away and shoot out to Monash University with them to hear Zimbabwean President Robert Mugabe give a speech. They made it sound slightly illicit. In the car, one of them, named TJ, explained, 'To be born a white South African is to know original sin. Even though you hate the fucking place, man, you are condemned to spending the rest of your life in perpetual atonement.' For them, going to hear Mugabe was a step on the long road of guilt exorcism.

With the other journalist, Bruce, at the wheel, a huge map spread across his lap, we were soon hurtling down a wide motorway, not sure if we were going in the right direction. Then a racing motorcade with police outriders, sirens and flashing lights shot past us. 'That'll be him!' screamed TJ. 'Don't lose them!'

Bruce dropped down a gear, veered into the fast lane and planted his foot. Racing up behind the last car in the motorcade aroused suspicions. Mugabe's security men turned around to see who was chasing them and I got a small whiff of what it's like to live in a police state.

'Pull back! Pull back! Jesus!' screamed TJ. 'Those bulls probably think we're BOSS agents! They'll shoot our fucking tyres out, man, and we'll end up wrapped around a power pole. Pull back!' Their paranoia was palpable and contagious. The motorcade accelerated through a series of intersections against the lights and left us far behind and I wasn't sorry.

I declined to go with the South Africans again the next night to hear Margaret Thatcher. Instead I caught up for drinks with Bill Darcy and some of his media mates in a hotel off Swanston Street in the central city. One of Bill's mates was supposed to be covering the Thatcher event. Word came through that her car had been surrounded and was being rocked by angry students. Bill's mate was due to report live to a Perth radio station in a few minutes' time. No worries, cobber. We all shot up to Bill's room, someone opened the windows to let in traffic and street noise and someone else passed around a joint the size of a didgeridoo. I passed. I'm not musical.

When Bill's mate picked up the phone to talk to Perth the others all started chanting 'THATCHER OUT! THATCHER OUT!' Bill's mate had to shout into the mouthpiece to be heard. He painted an astonishingly vivid picture of the student demonstration and Thatcher's bodyguards having to bundle her to safety—it was almost like being there. I think some of the guys completely off their faces really thought they were there. I have never been prouder of my profession.

ONE BRIEF ENCOUNTER MADE THE CHOGM trip worthwhile irrespective of what had gone before and what would follow. At a cocktail party at the Hilton the long-time, legendary African correspondent for the *Observer*, Colin Legum, guided me across a crowded atrium towards the tiny Tanzanian President Julius Nyerere.

'*Mwalimu*,' said Legum, removing a semi-permanent cigar from his mouth. 'I want you to meet a New Zealand journalist who is an enemy of Mr Muldoon's.' Nyerere's intelligent, surprisingly boyish face broke in half with a wicked grin, his top teeth filed to points like the blades of a saw. He gripped my hands in his.

'I want to thank you. New Zealanders must be the nicest people in the world. You have done so much for the black man.' When I demurred and apologised for the Springbok tour, his sing-song delivery rose in pitch. 'Look what happened during the tour! All across Africa, black men, women and children are listening to the BBC World News. And what are they hearing? White people on the opposite side of the world, white people who have so much, are sitting on motorways for the dignity of black men. The dignity of black men they will never meet. How can we punish New Zealand after what you have done for us?' He hugged me. I was close to tears.

I INCORPORATED THIS EXCHANGE INTO *Rage*, the telefeature on the 1981 Springbok tour that I wrote with Averil's brother, Grant O'Fee, a 'good bastard', to use the highest compliment Grant can pay anyone. He joined the police as a sixteen-year-old cadet and retired as Commissioner of Police in the Kingdom of Tonga. Along the way he was head of the Armed Offenders

Squad, District Commander of the Tasman Police District and Superintendent in charge of security for the 2011 Rugby World Cup held in New Zealand.

As befits a top cop, Grant had a great eye for detail and photographic recall of events tense, tragic and comic, but more than this he had a genius ability to re-create the tone and subtext of these moments. He was a delight to work with, except when coming to grips with scriptwriting software on his computer. When things went wrong, which they frequently did, his temper would erupt like a volcano. He would leap from his desk screaming, 'I would like to drive a red-hot frigging railway spike right down the eye of Bill Gates' penis!'

We also wrote *Tiger County* together, which holds up remarkably well today due to the raw authenticity Grant brought to the table. He was adored on set because he quietly worked his way around the cast and crew and by the end of the first week was able to greet everyone by their Christian name, and they could tell that he was genuinely interested in what they did.

It helped that he had a great turn of phrase. He was particularly fond of one television newsreader—he couldn't watch her without sighing, 'I would crawl on my belly across broken glass to stick toothpicks in her poop!'

In the middle of the night in 1995, Averil and I were watching Jonah Lomu single-handedly demolish the English rugby team at the World Cup in South Africa. Jonah had just run over the top of their fullback, Mike Catt, when the phone rang. There was no introduction, just someone screaming joyously at the other end of the line. 'DID YOU SEE THAT? DID YOU SEE THAT? JONAH MUST HAVE MUSCLES IN HIS SHIT!' And with that, Grant hung up.

CHAPTER EIGHTEEN

THE MONEY LENDERS

AFTER THE BITTER, BRUISING AND divisive Springbok tour, Muldoon won the bitter, bruising and divisive 1981 election by the narrowest of margins. At the risk of sounding like a *Game of Thrones* trailer, his aura of invincibility was punctured, the authority of his government was haemorrhaging badly, the skies over the Beehive were growing dark with economic chickens coming home to roost, malevolent forces were on the prowl, winter was coming. The only good news for National was that Bill Rowling, desperate for vindication, wanted to stay on as Leader of the Opposition for a fourth crack at winning an election. Logic and electoral mathematics decreed that he must surely win next time, and many in his party were sentimental enough to want him to have that chance.

The brutal pragmatists surrounding Roger Douglas, however, didn't want to leave anything to chance and pushed for his deputy,

David Lange, to take over. I witnessed an electric exchange in the House after one evening meal break that made this inevitable. Muldoon, a bit the worse for wear, as he often was after dinner, weaved to his seat and slumped onto the green leather sofa, abdomen bulging, watching the Deputy Leader of the Opposition stride confidently towards his seat like a Spanish galleon under full sail.

'Hah! Lange!' snorted Muldoon. 'Your belly is bigger than mine!'

'That may well be so,' bellowed Lange, 'but mine is higher off the ground!'

The Labour benches hooted and brayed with laughter and even government members grinned discreetly. It signalled a bellwether change. National's chief government whip, Don McKinnon, told me later that when he looked back at his troops, most of their heads were down and their smiles wan. They knew what Muldoon knew also—his days of effortless dominance were over. The spell had been broken. Rhetorically at least, Muldoon had finally met his match.

Six months after the tour and the 1981 election I published a book called *Snakes and Leaders*. While in Christchurch on a book-promotion tour I was interviewed by *The Press*, which elected to splash the article across their front page in pride of place below the masthead. It wouldn't happen today. Unless I was Justin Bieber.

> Before the satirist, Tom Scott, left for Melbourne to cover the Commonwealth Heads of Government Conference, he drew a cartoon of what he thought would happen. It shows the Prime Minister, Mr Muldoon, walking up the path to the conference building and all the other world leaders diving for cover. 'In the event, that was substantially what happened. They ignored him,' said Mr Scott in Christchurch yesterday. 'He was lonely and isolated.'
>
> Although Mr Scott has had some very public problems trying to cover the Muldoon administra-

tion, banned from the Prime Minister's press conferences, banned from the press party covering Muldoon's visit to India and having difficulties covering the Melbourne [CHOGM] and general election, he does not seem to feel that Muldoon really has it in for him. 'I have the belief, rightly or wrongly,' he said, 'that while I may irritate him from time to time, he's not that opposed to me.'

He thinks his troubles stem from the fact that Muldoon does not like being laughed at and that he is sensitive to criticism and particularly to ridicule. 'I don't have strong feelings about him,' Mr Scott said. 'I have a personal regard for his political skills. He's a very genuine New Zealander, a true nationalist, he really does care about New Zealand but at the same time I am disgusted in some of his behaviour and ashamed of some of his behaviour in Melbourne. I actually felt embarrassed to be a New Zealander. I'm sure if the roles had been reversed and I'd been going on like that, he would have been just as ashamed of me. I suspect he might be a bit ashamed of himself, but there was one thing you cannot do and this has scarred his Prime Ministership. He has an inability to apologise and admit his mistakes. It is significant that the thing missing from all his books is any acknowledgement that he has any human or political frailties. He's got to see himself as a winner. He has got to rewrite history endlessly to prove that point.'

But where would Tom Scott be without Rob Muldoon? The satirist readily admits the Prime Minister is perfect material. 'When there was a leadership challenge last year I don't think anyone was more worried than the cartoonists and satirists of New Zealand.'

—

MULDOON HAD ONE LAST MISSION to complete before his work here on Earth was done—the setting up of a new Bretton Woods agreement designed to solve many if not all of the world's economic ills, and more particularly New Zealand's, which were mounting daily. For those of you not familiar with the old Bretton Woods agreement, for nearly three weeks in July 1944 over 700 delegates from the 44 Allied nations gathered together in the colossal, brooding Mount Washington Hotel in Bretton

Woods in remote, upstate New Hampshire (imagine the sinister hotel in Stanley Kubrick's *The Shining* on steroids) to decide on a new set of rules for the post-World War Two international monetary system. To avoid the chaos and destructive anarchy of the pre-war years the agreement, which bears the name of the surrounding forests, set up the World Bank, led to the setting up of the International Monetary Fund (IMF), and agreed to fixed exchange rates tied to gold. When the cost of the Vietnam War began bleeding America's coffers dry, President Richard

Nixon abandoned tying the US dollar to gold, effectively killing off the Bretton Woods agreement. Muldoon, who never met an economic regulation he didn't like, wanted to bring it back from the dead, and with it the New Zealand economy.

In 1983, possessed of a cool intelligence, calm and independent (all sufficient grounds for Muldoon to veto him for the top job), the Deputy Governor of the Reserve Bank Dr Rod Deane (Sir Roderick since his investiture in 2012) suggested to me that there was sport and mischief to be had covering Muldoon's visit to the IMF annual meeting—US President Ronald Reagan would be giving a keynote address and I would find Washington fascinating. The *Dominion, New Zealand Herald,* Radio New Zealand, the BCNZ and NZPA were sending reporters, so the *Listener* consented to me going as well. When I confessed to Rod that I knew absolutely nothing about economics he said not to worry, I would have something in common with most of the ministers of finance who would be attending. He recommended that I read Anthony Sampson's book *The Money Lenders*—it would tell me more than I needed to know.

Unfortunately, I came down with a bad dose of flu two days before I was due to fly out. I took to my bed sweating, shivering and shaking. I should have pulled out but instead went to my doctor and got a horse syringe full of antibiotics injected straight into a buttock and flew non-stop from Wellington to Auckland, Auckland to Los Angeles, Los Angeles to Atlanta, Atlanta to Washington, apart from brief intervals sweating, shivering and shaking in transit lounges—where people gave me a wide berth.

That first night in the American capital Rod and his supersmart, kind and vivacious wife Gillian had arranged a ticket for me to accompany them to The John F. Kennedy Center for the Performing Arts on the banks of the Potomac River to a black-tie concert by the renowned violinist Itzhak Perlman. The music was stunningly beautiful but a deep fatigue overwhelmed me. I struggled desperately to stay awake until it became physically painful to do so. In the end I succumbed. It was a dreadful waste and a terrible shame. If I snored, Rod and Gillian were too decent to say anything.

Rod was right. Washington was fascinating. I was moved by Lincoln's memorial, wowed by the Smithsonian and impressed by Capitol Hill. I went along to Reagan's opening address to the IMF expecting to detest him, but the man Gore Vidal once famously described as having gone prematurely orange and being a triumph of the mortician's art, knew how to please an audience. Someone had written a very good speech for him and the former actor delivered his lines word-perfect first take.

When the other reporters told me that Muldoon was holding a briefing in his hotel suite that afternoon I sounded out his press officer about attending. Beverly said she would get back to me. She did and I could.

The security at Muldoon's hotel, the swanky Washington Sheraton, was astonishing. We had to go through X-ray machines and have our IDs checked and double-checked just to get into the lift taking us to his floor. My name had been added to the list so I was allowed up with the others. A big black Secret Service agent was waiting for us when the lift arrived. He had a clipboard and checked our names and IDs again. When we were good to go he led us down the long corridor to Muldoon's suite, past another room that had been taken over by the Secret Service. Banks of screens showed black-and-white footage from cameras monitoring the inside of lifts, the stairs, the hotel foyer and other strategic vantage points. He knocked on Muldoon's door. Beverly opened it. A few paces behind her, Muldoon took one look at me and growled, 'Aaah, no, Mr Scott, you can't come in.' I stood awkwardly in the corridor as the other reporters entered sheepishly, closing the door behind them.

The Secret Service agents with earpieces and dark shades were taken aback. 'What the fuck, man? You're on the list, what's happening?' I said I didn't know. Clearly feeling sorry for me, they walked me back to the lift. Passing their room, I saw on a colour monitor that *Australia II* was leading in the last race off Rhode Island—the America's Cup was about to head down under.

'Do you mind if I watch this?' I asked politely. 'I'm from New Zealand. We're neighbours.' They readily consented and

I was enjoying Australia's victory when their boss, a big angry white guy, turned up.

'What the fuck is he doing here?' he snarled, pointing at me. Embarrassed, they tried explaining that I was a New Zealand journalist who at the last minute wasn't allowed to attend his own Prime Minister's press briefing. Not placated, he turned on me.

'I don't give a fuck. You can fuck off right now.' I was frog-marched to the lift and bundled into an elevator going down. I punched the air when the doors closed. I knew I had a better story than anyone in the room with Muldoon.

The elation was short-lived. When I got back to my room in a seedy hotel on Washington Circle I got a phone call from Beverly; the Prime Minister was embarrassed about changing his mind and he would grant me a twenty-minute, one-on-one interview the next day at 11 a.m. Horrified, I grabbed Anthony Sampson and started devouring it madly—especially the section on Bretton Woods. I stayed up well into the night devising questions that would give me some semblance of economic credibility.

When I returned to his corridor the next day, the Secret Service guys were surprised to see me again. 'Good luck, man!' Muldoon let me in and sank onto a sofa. I sat bolt upright less than a metre away on an armchair. I had never been this close to him before for this length of time in broad daylight. He looked far older than his years. He had turned 62 two days earlier. His staff had got him an 'Oscar the Grouch' birthday card and a cake. The Secret Service demanded that one of his staff eat a slice first just in case it was poisoned.

When he spoke to me, his breath was sour. I was struck by the number of tiny warts he had running along his heavy, leathery upper eyelids. It was a curiously reptilian setting for astonishingly beautiful cornflower-blue eyes.

I began by asking him some patsy questions about Bretton Woods, much like a tennis warm-up, followed by some decent returns of serve that showed I could play a bit. He was agreeably surprised. My twenty minutes stretched into half an hour. It was quite extraordinary. It was almost pleasant. I left the room wondering if the Prime Minister was as surprised as I was.

I was not alone in detecting a new mellowness. His staff commented on his distracted, preoccupied air. On long flights, instead of burying himself in official papers or sleeping, as was his usual practice, he spent many hours just staring out at the clouds. He became philosophical. The visible decline in his powers was misleading. Any depletion needed to be measured against the original stockpile, which was formidable. And the authority he appropriated by sheer force of will was still staggering. There was only a minimal diminution in his ability to inspire psychic dread in those who dealt with him on a regular basis. Alastair Carthew, TVNZ's senior gallery journalist, admitted to me once that he had no problem dealing with Muldoon if he primed himself beforehand, but meeting him without warning in a corridor could send his heart pounding.

From a distance I once watched him cross Bowen Street from Parliament to the Reserve Bank on foot. He virtually brought traffic to a halt and had pedestrians scattering out of his path. It was as if there had been a police warning issued about a pear-shaped man on the run with gelignite strapped to his chest who wasn't to be approached under any circumstances.

After the IMF meeting his press conferences became curiously understated affairs. The scolding of the news media wasn't entirely abandoned but his reprimands had a half-hearted air about them. If he didn't come out in a fluffy sweater and sing 'Moon River' he got close.

I suspect that he knew the end was coming and he was getting his grieving, resignation and acceptance in early. Bill Rowling was facing the same fate. It took him a while but he eventually bowed to the inevitable, and at the end of 1982 announced his intention to stand aside to have a new leader elected by the Labour caucus in February 1983. I went to interview him and his bitterness took me by surprise. On three election nights I had been in the room with him and felt for him when he displayed commendable courage and dignity after stinging defeats.

'Your cartoons have really hurt my feelings,' he said quietly. He knew I liked him and he thought that guaranteed him some immunity. I think I know which cartoon hurt him most. I even winced when drawing it, but it was true and needed to be said.

Bill had three war medals pinned to his chest. One reads 'Runner up '78', another reads 'Also Ran '75', the third reads 'No 2 in '81'. Bill is saying, 'I'm the only one battle-hardened enough to lead the Labour Party.'

MULDOON'S WELL-INTENTIONED BUT ULTIMATELY catastrophic King Canute response to the economic forces beyond his control has been well documented. For fresh accounts, I commend the brilliant Tony Simpson's wise, elegant and feisty memoir *Along for the Ride*, written from a left-wing perspective, and Dr Michael Bassett's somewhat drier *New Zealand's Prime Ministers*, written with a neo-liberal slant. Both are excellent in quite different ways.

When I was studying physiology I learned that the heart muscle behaves as a functional syncytium. Every heartbeat, millions and millions of cells act as if they are one entity, contracting at precisely the same time, every time for a lifetime. If they don't, you need a pacemaker. This makes the cardiac muscle unique. It marches to the beat of a different drum—its own. In the late 1980s, writing and researching a short film for Electricorp, *Our Future Generation*, I came to appreciate that it was a functional syncytium as well.

All its power stations, from Manapouri in the deep south, to the Clyde dam station, the upper and lower Waitaki stations, the Tongariro River stations, the Taupō geothermal stations, the Waikato River stations, and the fuel-burning Huntly thermal station, made up a concrete and steel syncytium as sweetly and beautifully synchronised as cardiac muscle. At Manapouri, thanks to routine maintenance work, the film crew and I were able to shoot footage inside the base of one of the penstocks. It was a slightly unnerving feeling walking inside a giant steel snail shell leading to massive turbine blades knowing that normally zillions of tons of icy water from the lake above us would be thundering through here. It was equally unnerving at Huntly, where again due to maintenance we were able to stand inside a giant fire-box where normally coal as fine as talcum powder was blasted into a furnace with a core temperature of 1200 degrees Celsius, turning water flowing up the myriad pipes lining the walls into super-heated steam—a giant Thermette, essentially. Even more wondrous was the control centre beside the Atiamuri Dam, just off Highway 1 north of Taupō. In a plain building behind high-security fencing is a room that looks like a kids' version of mission control in Houston.

Every day, starting with low-cost hydro-electricity first and leaving expensive, polluting fossil fuels to last, Electricorp orchestrated power generation in precisely the right amounts at precisely the right time. You could tell when their timing was slightly off—your lights dimmed or flared. They called diminutive Lake Rotoaira just south of Lake Taupō the 'breakfast lake'. It tops up overnight and that water is run through the Tokaanu power station turbines the next morning the instant Aucklanders step into their showers and put on their kettles.

Our film was exquisitely shot and directed by Waka Attewell, one of New Zealand's finest cinematographers. Big, brilliant Shaun and Helen's golden-haired, golden-natured Ned, both still teenagers, did some amazing animation for me on a primitive home computer. It was fronted by multi-award-winning nature-show presenter and producer—and my old chum from Massey—Peter Hayden, and edited by a very young John Gilbert, who recently won an Oscar for his work on *Hacksaw Ridge*. He made no mention of *Our Future Generation* in his Oscar speech. I can't speak for Peter or for Waka, but I personally found this omission hurtful.

Our little film won a prize or two in boutique film festivals, but ultimately it made no difference. Despite a number of overseas experts admiring Electricorp and advising that it be kept intact, it was carved up into separate competing entities, and subsequently these entities were sold off. This was the master plan all along. Consumers who used to own an electricity grid that supplied them with the second-cheapest electricity in the world (after Norway) are now held to ransom.

If you must sell people something, ideally it's a product they simply cannot do without. That's the aim. Electricity and toilet paper are good examples. The trouble with toilet paper, though, is that there are many brands and variables within brands to choose from. On a whim in a supermarket, consumers can switch allegiance to competing rolls—embossed, patterned, softer, tougher, double-ply or perfumed. For manufacturers it's a pain in the arse compared to selling electricity, which comes one-size-fits-all. The size just varies slightly from country to country.

The great World War One humourist and pen-and-wash cartoonist Captain Bruce Bairnsfather's most famous cartoon is of an older soldier crouching in a bomb crater with a young infantryman. Bullets whizz past uncomfortably close and shells explode over their heads. To the younger man, who is clearly unhappy with their location, the old guy is offering this advice. 'Well, if you knows of a better 'ole, go to it.' That's the choice facing electricity consumers in New Zealand who want to change suppliers—a better 'ole. And good luck with the move. The mega-wealthy covet power utilities above all other investments for this very reason. As long as steam continues to billow out of the ground, wind continues to blow, rivers continue to flow and turbines continue to spin, all they have to do is count the money.

If Muldoon's first act in office hadn't been taking a wrecking ball to Roger Douglas's far-sighted if imperfect compulsory superannuation scheme there would have been enough money in the kitty today to make the selling of state assets unnecessary and unthinkable. By this one measure alone Muldoon failed to meet his modest goal of leaving New Zealand no worse than when he found it.

CHAPTER NINETEEN

LANGE TAKES THE REINS

RIGHT FROM HIS ARRIVAL IN Parliament, Lange was burdened with the expectation that he was a leader in waiting and the corollary accusation that, try as he might, he would never be battle-hardened enough for the top job. Just how ready he was, we were about to find out. The scenes on the morning of his elevation to the top job on the third floor of the old Parliament Building were almost without precedent. Not since the early '70s when these rooms were part of the Prime Minister's Department had there been such heady excitement.

More than 40 of us congregated in the long corridor. Red and black power cables feeding four television crews ran like the entrails of a terrible beast down to the old cabinet room where the crucial caucus meeting took place. Under the heat and glare of the television lights, Labour MPs gathered nervously at the tea urn for a last hit of caffeine before the vote. Russell Marshall, who had bravely tossed his hat into the leadership ring, glided past calm and serene in the knowledge he didn't have a shit-show. Bill Rowling attempted light conversation with a solemn David Lange, who didn't want to be engaged. Party president Jim Anderton looked like he hadn't slept. His preferred choice for deputy leader, Ann Hercus, wore a rictus smile. Grinning sheepishly, Mike Moore conceded that he was the ugliest contender for deputy leader. The man who would eventually beat him by one vote, Geoffrey Palmer, arrived looking quite unruffled, jacket draped casually over his shoulder—he'd just done twenty lengths of the Beehive pool and looked like a man who either knew he had it won or genuinely didn't care either way. Eventually the Opposition chief whip, Jonathan Hunt, fussily shepherded his flock into the caucus room and ushered us back down the corridor.

We listened to distant bursts of applause much like doctors listening to a heart murmur. What did it mean? Forty-five minutes after they'd gone in, the door flung open and a jovial Rowling, flanked by a less pleased Anderton, led out Lange and Palmer. Lange expressed his relief that it was all over. Genuinely dazed, Palmer could only give a silly grin and say he felt humble. Unable to conceal her hurt, Ann Hercus dashed tearfully to her room where staffers guarded the door. Mike Moore, who had wanted the number-two spot just as desperately, hand-delivered a gracious press statement around the Press Gallery offices, congratulating both Palmer and Lange, lingering to add sorrowfully, 'You spill your guts for the party and this happens.' Russell Marshall, a former Minister, exuded the Methodist equivalent of Zen calm. He had just wanted the record to show Lange hadn't been elected unopposed, something he pointed out repeatedly in years to come.

Lange appeared delighted with the leadership mix when he and Palmer held a first press conference together in the Beehive theatre. 'The pairing,' he said, 'could have come straight from a manual and the chemistry was immensely attractive.' Compared to the government's top two the combination exuded vigour, youth and optimism, and Lange fielded questions with an awesome battery of quips. It was a lively, hugely entertaining start, even if it did feel like a child's birthday party—lots of sugar and food colouring but precious little nutritional value.

A *Newsmaker* television special taped a few hours later with Ian Fraser was considerably less assured. Lange sounded fine. It was what he said that was disturbing. He claimed that his greatest political strength was his ability to articulate a vision so Ian invited him to do just that, then shrewdly sat back and let him go without interruption. Lange began saying he had a conviction that New Zealand was a richly endowed country with an unmatched population mix, adding that this vision wasn't really a vision because he could see it already in the schools in his electorate. 'If I talk about these things in terms of a vision it's because they are rooted in me.'

He went on to explain that this vision came partly from the fact that the state intervened to give him free school milk. A little worried, he then asked what many were wondering. 'Can a vision be communicated rationally?' Ian didn't answer. Lange boomed that he wanted to be a person who really wanted to say something for himself and for the people he cared about. 'These things are emotional and not necessarily coherent but I tell you, it's what the Labour Party is all about!' Then he tossed in the towel altogether and admitted, 'I'm simply saying, accept me as a person with a soul and not just a mechanic.'

It was too late. Small wonder that Palmer, who had earlier been describing himself as the backroom boy and Lange as the great communicator, was within hours intervening politely with, 'What I think David was trying to say was …'

The confusion continued when it came to articulating his stance on visits by American warships. I wrote a *Listener* piece called 'The philosophy of the philosophy of confusion' that in part went like this:

> Studio lights dim, throwing a small but excited
> audience into darkness. The floor manager
> raises one arm and conversation stills. All eyes
> are on the black swivel chair that seems to float

in the centre of a single shaft of light. To one side illuminated by another spot sits the ageless, blond quizmaster, Peter Sinclair, nervously licking his thin lips and shuffling papers. The floor manager gives him his cue.

SINCLAIR: Good evening and welcome to *Mastermind*. Our first contestant is Reon Mudgeway, a Dargaville beekeeper and amateur gynaecologist. Mr Mudgeway has chosen as his specialist subject the policies of the Opposition leader, David Lange, on the nuclear threat and visits of nuclear warships. You have two minutes starting now. What, in Mr Lange's own words, has characterised the recent debate in New Zealand on the nuclear threat?

MUDGEWAY: Confusion.

SINCLAIR: Correct. And what sort of confusion is it in Lange's view?

MUDGEWAY: Unfortunate.

SINCLAIR: Correct. And where does Mr Lange think this unfortunate confusion has come from?

MUDGEWAY: It arose in the heat of debate.

SINCLAIR: Correct. And who provoked that debate and ensured it was heated by advocating changes at variance with existing Labour Party policy?

MUDGEWAY: (screwing up his face and closing his eyes) Oh dear. I don't know. I'll have to guess, the people of Mangere?

SINCLAIR: So close but I can't accept it. The answer I wanted was David Lange. You knew that all the time, didn't you? (Close to tears, Mudgeway can only wring his hands despairingly.) Now, in March Lange called for a review of Labour's official policy on the visits of US warships and he warned his party not to get sidetracked by what?

MUDGEWAY: (still rattled) Loose women?

SINCLAIR: No. He warned against getting sidetracked over whether the vessels were nuclear-powered as well as nuclear-armed.

MUDGEWAY: Of course! (He strikes himself a blow with some force to the side of the head.)

LATER THAT YEAR THE LABOUR PARTY held its knees-up in a windowless convention centre on Auckland's beautiful water-front overlooking the glittering harbour—not that anyone would have known. I picked up a copy of the *Auckland Star* en route to the opening session on a Friday evening and read a long piece on David Lange on the eve of his first conference as party leader. In the piece he revealed that one of the worst aspects of political life was having to deal with people he despised, and he named me in that category. I must admit I was a little taken aback, but I didn't have time to brood for very long as I ran into him just minutes later in the conference foyer. He strode towards me bellowing, 'Tom! Tom! I was misquoted! It was taken out of context!'

I replied, 'Don't worry about it, David. I get to say critical things about you in print—you can say critical things about me.' He looked visibly relieved.

'As long as you see it in the spirit of tit for tat.'

Over the two days he kept coming up, cracking quick jokes then wheeling away again. It was quite touching in its own way.

On the last afternoon he lingered a little longer.

'Are you heading home tonight?' When I said I was, he reached into a pocket of his jacket. 'Here! Have these.' He pulled out half a packet of Griffin's Chocolate Wheatens. The heat of his body had melted the chocolate, fusing everything into a brown gelatinous mass. It resembled a bag of dog poop scooped up from a park. Given how dear chocolate was to David's heart, this was the equivalent of giving me a knighthood. There was no higher compliment.

'No thanks, David,' I demurred.

'Go on! Take them. Bring them home to the kids.' When I declined again he asked how I was getting out to the airport. I said I was catching a cab.

'Come with me in the LTD.' As the Leader of the Opposition he had his own chauffeur-driven limousine.

I said it wasn't necessary but he was still desperately seeking to make amends, so I accepted. When we parked outside his modest house in Mangere I opted to stay put in the car, but David insisted I come in with him. I soon discovered why. Having a stranger in the house would prevent his wife letting him have it with both barrels.

We walked down a driveway past knee-high grass and a rancid Para pool. Inside the house it was all clamour and clutter. Pots boiled on the stove, dishes filled the sink, folded washing was piled on chairs, kids delighted to see their dad hugged him and wanted to tell him things. Petite and pretty Naomi, clearly harassed, shrilly demanded her husband's input on all manner of domestic matters before he shot out the door again. Back in the car Lange sagged in his seat and mopped his brow, looking relieved to be heading back to Wellington and he wasn't even in power yet.

IN THAT REGARD HE WAS helped when Malcolm Fraser called a snap election in Australia. I covered it for the *Listener* and caught up with Bill Darcy covering Labour leader Bob Hawke on a walkabout through a crowded Sydney shopping mall. The diminutive man they called the silver budgie, obviously very proud of the Liberace pompadour shimmering high above his scalp, was wearing a dapper, nattily cut, powder-blue new suit. 'The Jewish tailors in Melbourne have done a number on you, Bob,' whispered Bill proudly as Hawke swept past, looking insufferably pleased with himself. And why not; the polls predicted a big Labour win. The crazy grazier's plan had badly backfired.

Two nights later in Melbourne, Aussie journalists snuck me into a surprise birthday party for Fraser in his hotel suite. The big man knew he was done for. His deep-set eyes were full of sorrow and regret. Earlier that day he'd been on ABC Radio talking about his stern father and his tough childhood in the Outback. It was a plea in mitigation. Unconsciously he was saying 'I know I can seem arrogant and patrician, but I have suffered. Don't judge me harshly.' It was too late. He lost.

Back in New Zealand, Muldoon declared that he wouldn't be making Malcolm Fraser's mistake. Hell no! His government would serve out its full term, giving Lange as much time as possible to shoot himself in the foot. As it happens, he made *exactly* the same mistake as Fraser—calling a snap election—and he made a nearly *identical* plea in mitigation on the campaign trail.

I was in the audience the night he addressed an election rally on the shores of Lake Rotorua. National's sitting MP Paul East and his team toiled mightily to ensure that the hall was booked out well in advance. A room full of party faithful guaranteed a decent hearing, looked good on camera and kept hecklers to a minimum. In the event National voters stayed away. When it should have been full, a good third of the hall was empty. Muldoon was confronted with a disheartening crescent of empty yellow seating. He swallowed and began telling the people who had turned up that he came to Rotorua often as a small boy. His mother put him on the train in Auckland and he walked to his grandmother's house when he arrived at Rotorua station. He described getting off the train one night and walking through swirling steam from thermal pools in the wrong direction until he was thoroughly lost. His voice cracked. He was that terrified child again. I knew that *he* knew he was going to lose.

I WAS BY THIS STAGE working for the *Auckland Star*, covering my first election in real time. As well as writing and illustrating a weekly column for their Saturday paper I wrote a daily campaign diary accompanied by a pocket cartoon. The former NZPA photographer, the kind and conscientious Ray Pigney, who had a bushy white beard with no moustache that made him look like an Amish elder in mufti, was my driver and minder who photographed my cartoons and columns then wired them both back to the *Auckland Star* office. Jumping back and forth between Labour and National, Social Credit and Bob Jones's New Zealand Party I was seldom in bed before midnight and always up again before dawn.

I had anticipated leisurely reflections in tranquillity for the *Listener* but yet another editor, this time David Beatson, had fired me. There was a degree of provocation involved. I had just been approached by the *Auckland Star*, who offered me a job for twice what the *Listener* were paying. I told David I would stay if the *Listener* gave me a rise that split the difference. He became apoplectic and said he wasn't going to be blackmailed and I could leave forthwith. I cleared my desk and did just that. No drinks. No thanks. No farewell. My *Listener* colleagues were more stunned than I was when I walked out.

My new desk was in the *Auckland Star* office in Parliament. It was a delight to share it with the doyen of the Press Gallery, the supremely knowledgeable, utterly charming, ever thoughtful and helpful Ian Templeton. I was working harder than ever, but I felt less like a solo yachtsman than before so it was a lot of fun until it stopped being fun, and a lot of that had to do with my home life. Helen was holding the fort, which was only half renovated, while I was trying to justify the huge investment the *Auckland Star* had made in me.

I accompanied Lange on his first trip as Prime Minister to the UN in New York. It was raining when we arrived and the famous skyline was veiled in low overcast. The travelling press party hit Chinatown that night, where we tested our noughts and crosses skills against a hen in a cage. RNZ's Richard Griffin and private radio's Barry Soper got beaten soundly. I was relieved to battle the hen to a draw. They were inconsolable until I theorised we were playing a computer and when it was the hen's turn it got a zap of voltage through its feet and pecked a fake keyboard.

Afterwards we spilled happily out into the night and I saw a sight from a science-fiction film: two impossibly tall ladders of light stretching up and vanishing into cloud. It was the first I had seen or heard of the Twin Towers. They were dazzling, awe-inspiring advertisements for American might, know-how and can-do. When my alarm radio came on automatically on the morning of 11 September 2001 and I heard the slow, deliberate baritone of former US Secretary of State Henry Kissinger intoning gravely, 'Der verld vill never be der same again!' I rushed to switch on the television in time to catch the second plane hitting the second tower. You could see immediately why Osama bin Laden had long had them in his sights.

Back at the UN the next morning, it was Lange's turn to dazzle at the General Assembly. The room started to empty as soon as he was introduced but his sonic boom of a voice and soaring anti-nuclear rhetoric had people scrambling back to their seats. Afterwards, trailed by admiring journalists, he made his way to his next appointment down wide UN corridors. A cluster of Japanese diplomats bowed at his approach.

'Excuse me. Are you the Finnish?'

'No,' roared Lange. 'We're from Neeeew Zeeeeealand!!! We're the pits!'

His mega-decibel ebullience and dancing wit on that trip was astonishing. Later that same day, at his grand hotel over the road from the UN building, I observed him emerge from a meeting with the normally granite-faced US Secretary of State George Shultz, who was grinning broadly. In a corridor crowded with press and wary Secret Service agents, Lange did all of the talking, cracking jokes and laughing loudly, but rather than looking peeved at being upstaged Shultz wore the look of a proud uncle in the presence of a precocious nephew. I saw this phenomenon repeated a few days later in London, in another corridor in another swanky hotel, overlooking the Thames. Labour leader Neil Kinnock, small, sandy and pasty, looked on in frank admiration as Lange amusingly described their talks.

Clearly this did not happen on his visit to Chequers, the sixteenth-century official country residence of the British Prime Minister, Margaret Thatcher, who was displeased with New Zealand's stand on nuclear weapons. Asked about this visit by the assembled UK press at a press conference in New Zealand House just off Trafalgar Square, Lange's irreverence got the better of him when he said Thatcher spoke to him as if she were addressing a Nuremberg Rally. Gasps and shocked laughter filled the room. Likening a British Prime Minister to Hitler in a city that had endured the Blitz was borderline unforgivable but he was saved by the fact she gave everyone the shits.

FIVE YEARS AFTER THE PREVIOUS debacle, in 1984, I was back in Delhi again with Dick Griffin, this time as an accredited member of the New Zealand Prime Minister's official party. Unlike Muldoon, David Lange had a deep affection for India and a prodigious knowledge of its recent history. He had visited the subcontinent as a young law graduate on his OE, staying in shonky backpackers' and youth hostels. This time he was a guest of the Indian government in the former residence of the last Viceroy of India, Lord Louis Mountbatten, 1st Earl Mountbatten of Burma, and Edwina, Countess Mountbatten of Burma. With unabashed glee David led the press on a tour of their vast and sumptuous private quarters.

'Edwina's bedroom. After mounting the balcony late at night, Nehru would mount her! Naomi will be in here!'

'Stop it, David.' Naomi giggled.

Lange led us through the adjoining bathrooms, small palaces in their own right, to another grand bedroom.

'Lord Louis's bedroom—where he would entertain lithe young naval ratings!' he shouted to more laughter.

THE NEXT DAY, INDIRA GANDHI, daughter of the first Indian Prime Minister Jawaharlal Nehru and now PM herself, hosted a state lunch for David and Naomi in the Hyderabad grand banquet hall, to which the New Zealand media were also invited. Prior to this we were granted a small audience in an antechamber with Gandhi. I was surprised to find her smaller and more beautiful that her photographs allowed, with a disarming smile and unflinching gaze. She gave each of us a small, exquisite white marble box inlaid with brightly coloured stones arranged in a flower pattern from the Taj Mahal.

During lunch she expressed admiration for New Zealand's anti-nuclear stance and the courage of our young Prime Minister. This time it was David's turn to beam, the adored nephew in the presence of a favourite aunt.

That night we were her guests again on a rickety viewing platform along with a million-strong crowd at Diwali festivities at the Red Fort in old Delhi. Fireworks rat-a-tat-tatted like rapid gunfire. Flames and sparks from giant, four-storey-high papier-mâché representations of various gods leaped high into the crimson night sky. There seemed to be no security in place. Barely a year earlier, in a bloody climax to years of fighting with Sikh separatists, Indira Gandhi had ordered Indian army troops to storm the sacred Golden Temple in Amritsar. Vengeance hung in the air like a million question marks. I had flashbacks to newsreel footage of Egyptian leader Anwar Sadat being assassinated while reviewing a military parade from a viewing platform not dissimilar to this. I shouted into Dick Griffin's ear to be heard above the deafening cacophony.

'I smell assassination. I'm getting out of here!' Dickie went a whiter shade of pale.

'Bloody hell, you're putting the wind up me now, I'll come with you.' We pushed through the teeming, delirious throng and caught a battered Morris Oxford taxi back to our opulent hotel. Later, sipping ice-cold Kingfisher beers in the calm and quiet of the plush house bar, I felt sheepish and apologised to Dick.

Two weeks later, in the grounds of her official residence, while Peter Ustinov and a BBC film crew were waiting to interview her, Indira Gandhi was gunned down by her favourite Sikh bodyguard. I'm not sure that David Lange ever really got over her loss. He flew to Delhi numb with grief and sat in the front row at her cremation beside George Shultz. David told me the heat from her huge funeral pyre was searing and unbearable— good training for the blowtorch that Shultz and the Reagan administration would soon be applying to the soles of his feet. Drenched in sweat, with tears and perspiration streaming down his face, he braced himself for her brain to boil. When it did, her skull exploded with a gunfire crack that freaked out the Secretary of State's already twitchy Secret Service.

CHAPTER TWENTY

LANGE IN REPOSE

AFTER HIS RETIREMENT IN 1996, David Lange and I were once guest speakers at a black-tie dinner in Auckland. It was before the blood disorder amyloidosis began sapping his strength. He'd just delivered a rollicking speech, without notes as usual, to a hugely appreciative audience. The waiters were serving coffee and chocolates.

When the chocolates reached our end of the table, I piously raised my hand and said, 'No thanks, my body is a temple.'

'Pass them along here,' boomed the former Leader of the Nation at my elbow. 'My body is a warehouse!'

Neither of us knew then that our respective careers in politics and journalism had one last round to play. For the twentieth anniversary of Lange's elevation to the prime ministership, Television New Zealand asked me to make a documentary on him.

'What's the name of your documentary?'

'Reluctant Revolutionary.'

'What's it about?'

'It's about David Lange.'

'Who's he?'

The phone call was from someone at Television New Zealand, the very company that had commissioned the documentary in the first place. The caller was from sales and marketing and was working on publicising our contribution to their Saturday-night New Zealand Festival documentary series.

It was twenty years ago. She was probably one of the two million New Zealanders born since David Lange's Fourth Labour Government won the snap election of 1984 and flipped this country over like an old, stained mattress that needed airing. If you could transport back in time all the New Zealanders who weren't alive then, and for that matter many of us who were, the chances are that none of us would recognise the place. The past wouldn't be a foreign country so much as a different planet.

Michael Cullen, a callow young cabinet minister and republican in Lange's second cabinet that tore itself apart, wrote for a symposium on the first term of the Fourth Labour Government that New Zealand was undeniably a more dynamic, varied, exciting, colourful place in 2004 than it was in 1984, and this could be attributed in good measure to this government—as could the fact that we are now a more socially divided country with greater extremes of wealth and poverty.

The changes did not come without huge cost, and in the end few paid a higher price than the man at the centre of the maelstrom: David Russell Lange. One of the lesser costs was being ridiculed in print.

Cartooning is a foul business. Our job is to mock and find fault from the sidelines. Over the years David Lange probably wanted to strangle me. He is not alone.

In 2002, when David turned 60, because I admired him greatly, even though there were times when I wanted to strangle him too, I sent him a tribute cartoon where all the faces carved into Mount Rushmore were his. I got a letter back that was wry, witty, wise and brave:

Life has fallen into a languid pattern, my voice is unreliable and my blood count chronically low and I tend to spend a lot of time asleep. I had three transfusions in the last fortnight and the fourth round of chemotherapy on Friday. One spends lots of time in hospital. I went there for a transfusion a couple of months ago in a government car and the driver was told to wait. They spotted an infection, whipped me off to a ward and discharged me four days later. The driver had gone. You can't get good help these days.

I remain hopeful of some significant remission. I met a chap in the hospital who had four years under his belt, and remember another who had his first chemo with me and died a fortnight later. We were both mortified. There is for all the morbid self-centredness a curious pleasure about being released from the banality of political theatre ...

THIS RELEASE CAME JUST AS the twentieth anniversary of the snap election loomed. With not a lot of energy to squander and far better things to do on his rare good days than retrace his time on the boards for the cameras, David declined to take part in our documentary, apart from the briefest of cameo appearances filmed in the cosy study of his Mangere home. He was tired, his shoulder muscles had wasted, his clothes hung off him, and the once great sonic boom of a voice was reduced to a croak, but the legendary wit and warmth were still intact. We all wanted to hug him but you weren't sure you wouldn't break something. When it was time to go he came out to the verandah to see us off. He'd perked up and we got the impression that provided we kept off politics we could have stayed and chewed the fat all afternoon. He stood watching us drive off, solitary, stooped, fragile and somehow majestic.

David appeared in my documentary in archive footage, but the actual retracing of his steps was left to others—his siblings, former members of his parliamentary staff, old political comrades in arms and old political foes, though this distinction blurred over the course of his career as comrades became foes and vice versa. In the end David's absence was a curious bonus. It put an extra responsibility on the other participants to contribute to the larger truth and not simply air old grievances or settle old scores, and people were more candid and less self-serving than we dared hope for.

I was particularly fortunate to interview Richard Prebble on the eve of him quitting the leadership of the ACT Party, though he had yet to make the announcement. He was relaxed, jocular and engaging. Having just weathered months of caucus disloyalty he was more able to appreciate the nightmare to which he and others had subjected David Lange in the last months of his prime ministership. Prebble had some stinging criticisms of his former boss, but these were laced with regret and frustration. Mostly his recollections were fond and filled with genuine admiration.

This is how many of his former colleagues spoke about Lange. Awe and affection were mixed up with exasperation and sorrow. His intellectual brilliance, speed of wit and oratorical power were without equal. Mike Moore described David as being gifted almost to the point of insanity. When he heard the scathing jokes Lange told about him, Moore just sighed. 'Why does he do that?'

My guess is he couldn't resist saying things the moment they occurred to him. David used humour both as a shield and as a weapon, to attract attention and to deflect attention, to put some people at their ease and to put some on their guard—but mostly he used humour because he could, even when it wasn't always diplomatic. Asked if the French government, in the wake of the *Rainbow Warrior* prisoner release debacle, was getting any closer to the negotiating table in New York, he snorted, 'Continental drift finished some billions of years ago.' When the French finally showed remorse, Lange was asked if the government apology to New Zealand had been made public. To which he replied, 'I suspect it was available from the fourth customs officer on the left somewhere in the Alps.'

John Clarke couldn't have said it better.

Enough books—both gushing and incensed—about the Lange government and its radical economic reforms have been published to fill a small library. Books about the Palmer, Moore, Bolger, Shipley or Clark governments would fit in a shoebox and still leave room for the shoes (and the radical innovations and sweeping reforms of the Key government could be written on the head of a pin and still leave room for the angels if they switched to a slow waltz). But in all of this literature, despite all the hurt and anger, it is hard to find instances of David Lange and Roger Douglas resorting to personal denigration of each other. Douglas, who gives the appearance of having iced water flowing in his veins, was close to tears talking about the breakdown in his relationship with David. At the end of our interview, he asked after him. Had we seen him? How was he? How could he contact him?

Other colleagues were much the same. Boy, if there was ever a platoon that needed a reunion it was these guys. I tried to get David and Roger to meet on film, but they quite properly declined to share this private moment. They were the Lennon and McCartney of New Zealand politics. Roger wrote the lyrics; David was the lead singer. They had hit after hit. They took the country by storm. Everything was perfect until Yoko Ono—in the form of Margaret Pope—entered the picture and David decided to leave the group, for which some fans will never forgive her.

Pope contacted me, offering to take part in the documentary. David's former speechwriter, now his widow, was a very reserved and intensely private person. She did not give interviews and was extremely nervous at first, but ended up acquitting herself very well. Gary McCormick didn't want to talk to us about his friendship with David, but did so eventually because David asked him to. He told me that Pope was a very amusing person at home with David, and there were tantalising glimpses of that side of her in the interview.

When Jim McLay sat opposite him in Parliament, David used to regularly punish him with the accusation that he was snuggling up to the bomb, with taunts like 'The present Leader of the Opposition would go into a hot flush if he had to pick three pizza toppings out of four' and 'Why does he insist on grinning like a 1954 DeSoto radiator grille?' Yet, when David retired from politics and Bob Jones threw a farewell dinner, David not only insisted that McLay be invited, but also that he make the only speech. McLay walked away from politics making a covenant with himself that he would never look back or talk about that time. He broke that vow for my documentary and his contribution is as gracious as the speech he made at that dinner. (To this day I receive Christmas cards from Jim and his family from various exotic locales. They are Yuletide circulars and newsletters, but I am still on the mailing list!) I also spoke to Gerald Hensley, the former head of the Prime Minister's Department. When he describes David, the courtly and elegant Hensley could almost be describing himself. 'He was unfailingly nice, unfailingly charming, and for that I liked him a great deal. He was by far and away the easiest Prime Minister I ever dealt with, and I dealt with a lot. No civil servant could have asked for more.'

Senior civil servants like Hensley, working along the corridor from their political masters, probably get to spend more one-on-one time with them than their cabinet colleagues, spouses and children are able to. They see them in the best of times and the worst of times. Someone once wrote that no general is a hero to his batman, but this is not true of David. Hensley got to know him very well.

> His quick intelligence enabled him to grasp
> situations quickly, with a minimum of paperwork.
> Too much paperwork for the Prime Minister and
> he contrived to lose it anyhow. His restlessness
> made him impatient of formality and lengthy
> sittings. He preferred the personal to the
> procedural approach, to rely on his empathy
> for people, rather than his consultation with
> his colleagues.

Hensley tells a wonderful David yarn. It was in the wake of the terrible East Coast floods in 1988 (the same floods that prompted Geoffrey Palmer to famously reply when asked if he had any special message of comfort for his beleaguered fellow citizens, 'We must all accept that New Zealand is an indubitably pluvial country.' Stern and principled to the point of pathology, Geoffrey is indubitably pluvial himself. He continues to write cogent, learned tomes on the need for constitutional reform, for which I am delighted and honoured to provide cartoons and illustrations). Hensley and David were in a helicopter delivering supplies to farmers trapped by the flooding.

> We took lots of fresh bread, orange juice and milk
> and things for isolated places. On the way home
> at the end of the day, there was one carton left
> in the helicopter. It seemed a shame to take it all

the way back to Gisborne, so I said to the pilot, find an isolated farmhouse and drop it off. We were halfway down over the backblocks, and he pointed down and there was a farmhouse that had been completely cut off by a rising river.

We landed in a paddock outside the back door. The farmer's wife, who of course was secure in the knowledge that there was no one within 20 kilometres except her husband, came out of the back door to see what this clattering noise was. She was wearing a short pink nightie and gumboots. When she was confronted by the sight of the Prime Minister of New Zealand advancing upon her with a carton of milk and orange juice and other things, she did the only possible thing in the circumstances—she burst into tears.

Kindness and patience were recurring themes in the stories that David's staff told. His principal private secretary, the dashing and urbane Ken Richardson, has worked for seven Prime Ministers and two Governors General and is the keeper of many secrets. He had never spoken to the news media before, but made an exception for David and my documentary.

Richardson is proud of the amusing postcards that David sent from all parts of the globe. Many are filled with cryptic references to 'KTK' moments. When pushed, Richardson explained that David once committed the cardinal sin of falling asleep during a gala Kiri Te Kanawa concert. There was outrage in some circles, so after that, whenever Richardson saw David trapped in some conversation or other with his eyelids drooping, he would sidle over and say, 'I think we might have a KTK situation on our hands, Prime Minister.'

David's capacity for thoughtfulness is probably best illus-trated by this story. Shortly after David became Prime Minister, Richardson, who was in charge of his appointments and travel diary, informed him that he had to go to the UK and the US on official business.

I said to him, 'Which way do you want to go, east or west?' and he said to me, 'I think we'll go east, because you have a mother in California and I'm sure you'd like to see her.' And I didn't even know that he knew that I had a mum in California. So we went and I arranged for her to come to the hotel, and she arrived and she came to my room. We sat there and David was in his suite with Naomi and lots of other people. Mike Moore was there, too. And one of the Secret Service guys came along and said, 'The Prime Minister wants you', so I went down and he said, 'Where's your mum?' I said, 'She's in my room', and he said, 'I want to meet her.' My mother and brother were all trembling because they'd never met a Prime Minister before, and he asked, 'Has he given you coffee?' and she said, 'No.' He said, 'What a son! You've got to have coffee,' and then he jumped onto the piano stool and played the piano. They were absolutely stunned by this, and I had to remind him he had an appointment, so he left us in the suite and said, 'Have what you like.'

I also talked to David's brother and sister, Peter and Margaret —smart, funny, down-to-earth twins to whom David was just their beloved older brother, albeit an older brother who blossomed into something that they never predicted. As kids, they used to steal thermometers from their father's surgery, which was attached to their grand family home in the Auckland suburb of Otahuhu (now the offices of a money lender—the final insult of Rogernomics), break them open and play with the slippery contents.

To nearly everyone I spoke to, David was as bright, as shiny, as inviting and as difficult to pin down as a blob of mercury. He brightened the political landscape like no one else before or since. At times, his oratory made us fiercely proud to be New

Zealanders. He was wickedly funny, he was endlessly fascinating, he was baffling, he was infuriating, he was wonderful.

I WAS FORTUNATE ENOUGH TO see him in Middlemore Hospital just a few days before he died. Gary McCormick told me that he was asking to see me. At the desk there was a list of approved visitors. My name wasn't on it. Margaret had just ducked out. The nurse said she'd check with David. She came back smiling. 'You'll have to be quick.'

One leg below the knee was dark and swollen from the onset of gangrene. His belly was distended because morphine-based painkillers had slowed his alimentary tract to a halt. The muscles of his chest and shoulders had wasted from diabetes, his emaciated arms wore a welter of bruises and sores from nursing staff giving injections and inserting drips, and he had a thin plastic hose up his nose delivering oxygen. His hair was plastered to his head with sweat. Yet he lit up with a grin when he saw me.

'Have you seen Jonathan Hunt lately? He's huge. He's going to be the first High Commissioner to the Court of Saint James's to explode in office! How are your kids? How's your mum— how's Joan?'

CHAPTER TWENTY-ONE

EMERALD GLEN

MEANWHILE, BACK IN THE MANAWATŪ my father's heart was threatening to explode inside his ribcage. Corrective measures were needed following coronary bypass surgery and he was transferred from Palmerston North Hospital to intensive care in Wellington Public.

My relationship with him at best was fraught with inhibition and apprehension. It was easier for both of us if I took someone with me when I visited.

Allan Grant happened to be in town so I dragged him along. Dad was a big fan of Allan's writing. He grinned and told Allan that he was a daylight atheist.

'During the day I don't give a fuck about God. God can get fucked as far as I'm concerned, but at night, when it's pitch black outside, the lights are dim in here, and all you can hear is the sound of nurses' plimsolls on linoleum and the building's creaks and groans, I believe in God like you wouldn't believe. I'm a daylight atheist!' I was impressed and quite proud of him. I could see Allan was impressed too. He was less impressed with what my father had to say next.

'Why are you wasting your time with McPhail and Gadsby? Don't bother with them! They're shite.' Allan got huffy on their behalf.

'I beg to differ, Mr Scott.'

'Yew can beg all ye like. They're shite!'

David McPhail and Jon Gadsby did good work together and were household names, but some of their finest work was done separately—Jon was a terrific writer and David was a brilliant actor on stage and screen in both comic and straight roles. He was fabulously accomplished in an Auckland Theatre Company production of Edward Albee's *Who's Afraid of Virginia Woolf?* and pitch-perfect in the lead role in *Seven Periods with Mr Gormsby*, which I co-produced with Danny Mulheron, who also directed, and co-wrote with Danny and Dave Armstrong.

While my father was in intensive care, a teenage boy on oxygen and various arterial drips, trailing tubes, cables and catheters, was wheeled in and placed next to him. Forty-eight hours earlier this boy had been a highly promising rugby player. A gash in his leg became infected, pumping streptococci into his bloodstream. In a case of mistaken identity that can sometimes happen with antigenic responses, his white blood cells attacked his own heart valves, all but destroying them. To save his life a Skilsaw was taken to his sternum, his ribcage pulled open, his heart bisected and his wrecked valves replaced. His rugby dreams in tatters, he just wanted to die.

I was at a tennis tournament in Lower Hutt a few years later when this boy's mother approached me tentatively. She knew I didn't have the best relationship with my father but she had something she needed to tell me—something she thought I needed to know. She remembered the man with white whiskers, missing teeth and the *Goon Show* voices in the bed adjacent to her son. He was so different, so eccentric and so continuously funny about everything, he'd restored her son's spirits and helped save his life. She would be forever grateful.

It was a bittersweet moment. I was proud of my father, pleased for her son and envious that I never saw this side of him. I know my brother Michael did, and he was standing next to me. As real estate agents attest, location is everything. We start out as one cell, then millions of divisions later cells with identical DNA, based purely on location, have transformed into nerve cells, heart muscle and so on. They look different and have different roles and responsibilities forced on them by location alone. Small wonder then that siblings living under the same roof at the same time can have quite different parents.

DAD CONVALESCED WITH US IN our Wadestown house before returning to Feilding. He was interested in the children, who found him mysterious. He was polite with me. He adored Helen. She was an attractive woman and as his photograph album attested he loved attractive women. Helen was so beautiful, in fact, that a drunken colleague, apologising in advance, asked me once what she possibly saw in me. I think it was a question she was increasingly asking herself. I told him that I had lied to Helen about my looks. There had to be some explanation and he seemed perfectly satisfied with this one.

Helen was kind and patient with my father. They enjoyed each other's company. They had things in common. He was a brilliant man, a comic genius at times, denied by fate and circumstances the chance to express his creativity, which left him deeply frustrated. Helen, hugely creative in her own right, feared her life was going the same way. They shared another bond. I got on their nerves.

My career was going well. I did some of my better journalism for the *Auckland Star*. With the help of Rod Deane and Don McKinnon in particular, and many others who wanted the whole story told properly, I wrote two lengthy pieces on the snap election, the currency crisis that left New Zealand teetering on the edge of insolvency, and the constitutional crisis that left us with a power vacuum when we needed someone to take charge. When Treasury officials eventually compiled an official account of the currency crisis, my name and someone called 'ibid' appeared repeatedly in the endnotes. Ian Fraser wasn't handy, so I had to look up what 'ibid' meant in the dictionary— it was Latin for 'same source or place'. It was slightly unnerving knowing I was the mother lode for this turbulent chapter in recent New Zealand history.

HELEN WANTED THINGS TO BE different. She embraces change while I shy away from it. She had been talking for some time about us living in the country, but I wasn't keen. Every time we drove up-country out of Wellington she would ask if I had changed my mind yet. Just north of Paekakariki, at MacKays Crossing, on the opposite side of the railway line, there stands a beautiful two-storey colonial homestead with double verandahs just visible through tall trees. My stock answer was always, 'I'd consider it if that place ever came on the market at a price we could afford.' It seemed a fairly safe thing to say, but to make absolutely certain I added a caveat—it needed to have a pond with an island in the middle of it with ducks and geese. Helen would sigh.

'So if it's for sale at a price we can afford, has a pond with an island in the middle, with ducks and geese, you'd buy it?'

'But of course!' I lied. 'Who wouldn't?'

In the summer of 1985 we were renting a bach on the beach at Paraparaumu. One day it was too cold and overcast to swim, there was nothing worth watching on television, no curling paperbacks in the bookshelves worth reading, we were sick of Trivial Pursuit, and the smell of burnt toast and wet sea-grass matting was getting steadily more oppressive, so Helen suggested we pile into the van and go for a drive. She wanted to take a closer look at the homestead that we had both long admired from the main road.

Little warning bells began to ring as we drove up and parked at the gate of a property named Emerald Glen.

'Look!' said Helen excitedly. 'There's a little lake with an island in the middle!' Too frightened to open my eyes, I asked in a dry whisper if there were any ducks or geese.

'YES!' chorused the kids.

Helen was all for driving up and offering to buy the place from whoever owned it. I argued that would be a vulgar invasion of their privacy and was about to turn the van around when one of the kids spotted the sign saying that free-range eggs could be purchased at the back door.

'Are we going to buy some eggs?' asked the kids.

'No!' Helen laughed. 'We're going to buy a house!'

I felt sick.

Up close, the old house was run-down. Guttering sagged from the top verandah, it badly needed painting and some of the weatherboards were rotten, but it was still elegant and beautiful. It reminded me of the farmhouses of Vermont I had coveted as a boy while reading *National Geographic* in dentists' and doctors' waiting rooms.

We knocked on the back door, and Barry the owner came out. He was solidly built and craggy-faced. You just knew he would have been a filthy rugby player in his day. And he was voluble and extremely loud. Handing over the money for the eggs, I commented neutrally that it was a lovely old house.

'WANNA BUY IT? I DECIDED TO SELL IT LAST NIGHT. MY BLOODY HIP IS GIVING ME GYP! THROBBED SOMETHING AWFUL LAST NIGHT. YOU WOULDN'T CREDIT THE PAIN I'M IN! THE QUACK RECKONS I'LL BE A CRIPPLE IF I DON'T SELL THE PLACE. SO I RUNG THE REAL ESTATE AGENT THIS MORNING. HE'S A DUTCHMAN BUT HE'S OK. I SAID, "GERRY, PUT THE BLOODY PLACE ON THE MARKET!" YOU'RE THE FIRST BUGGERS TO KNOW! APART FROM GERRY, THAT IS!'

'Well, that is interesting . . .' I stammered.

'We'll buy it,' said Helen calmly.

I RAN INTO NATIONAL'S CONVIVIAL Warren Cooper, the MP for Clutha, in a parliamentary corridor shortly after we had moved in.

'I hear you've bought a farm, Tom. How many acres?'

'Eleven.'

'Hundred or thousand?'

'Eleven as in eleven.'

'Bloody hell. How many sheep?'

'Ten.'

Warren rolled his eyes and sighed deeply.

'What are their names?'

I grew up in the country. I had forgotten how dark the nights can be and how bright the stars. And I had forgotten how much sheer hard work farming involves.

The property had many moods, none better than dawn on a good day. The sun rising over the Maungakotukutuku hills scattered delicate mists and turned the dark blue hillsides and valley floor a brilliant golden green. It was bucolic and idyllic, but impossible to fully appreciate when you had to rise early to chop kindling for the wood range or there would be no hot water, you had four acres of inkweed to clear by hand with a slasher, you had hens to feed and pigs to feed (some of whom were carnivorous, and some mornings all that was left of the peacocks that foolishly slept on the wooden gate beside the pig-pens were their bloody legs, their talons embedded like staples into the timber). Everywhere you looked there was work that needed to done and money that needed to be spent. Mercifully, our small flock of sheep looked after themselves pretty much. And our two steers, Short and Tall, were no problem—apart from when they escaped and they were worse than Charlie Upham. And you couldn't blame them for making a bolt for it—the grass *was* greener on the other side of the fence.

There was a good reason for that. Barry told me proudly he'd sold the topsoil off the two bottom paddocks for a small fortune, and the new pasture was struggling to take hold. He also told me that the hens scrambling around the barn were mostly for show—he got most of his 'free-range' eggs from a mate who had a battery farm in the next valley. If you threw a piece of straw into a carton with the eggs most people were thrilled to pay a hefty premium. His mate was keen to continue the arrangement if we were. We weren't.

We also inherited a pregnant sow that presented us with a

litter of sixteen piglets. One piglet, Runty, was so tiny we didn't think he'd survive. For the first six weeks of his life he was the same size as a pound of butter and had to be hand-fed. According to Darwin he was the least fitted to survive, but it worked in his favour when it was time to take his siblings to the Levin saleyards. Right on cue, the moment he knew he had escaped becoming a Christmas ham, Runty inflated like a dirigible to gargantuan proportions.

When he was small he used to slip through the fences like a cat and run to the back door to be fed scraps. When he grew truly massive he pushed his way casually through the fences as if they weren't there, poked his great pink snout through the cat-flap and honked like a foghorn for attention. If he saw the door was open he picked up speed and careened into the pantry, where he drilled holes in sides of sacks of flour and sucked up the contents with the brainless ecstasy of a Hollywood producer snorting cocaine. My patience ran out the night we came home late and found he'd devoured half a sack of spuds, two bags of apples and a bag of flour, and had been stricken with a sneezing fit while snorting it. A fine white powder covered the walls, the ceiling and the floor of the kitchen. Well almost *all* the floor— Archimedes' principle decreed that he had to make room for this extra cargo and there were giant glistening circles on the floor where pig urine and pig poop held the flour at bay.

I knew I was taking a risk, because Runty was very popular, but I told the family that either the pig went or I would. They asked for a couple of hours to think it over. Runty and I were sent out onto the verandah, like contestants on *MasterChef*, while they deliberated. The first vote was a draw. I won on a recount. Runty was gifted to a farmer who had a small-holding next to the Big Tex restaurant on Highway One. The first evening, when the deep fryer warmed up and the smell of sizzling French fries reached Runty's nostrils, filled with an insatiable curiosity of Christopher Columbus proportions when it came to food, he just had to check it out. Again, fences were no obstacle. Runty raced in the back door of the kitchen, and snatching all food in his path he rocketed into the dining room. Screaming customers and sobbing children pressed against the walls while he proceeded to clean plates more efficiently than the best German dishwasher or hospital autoclave. The manager failed to see the funny side of it and warned the farmer that he had a gun and would use it if necessary. He spent much of the next day repairing and strengthening the fence. He needn't have bothered. When the siren odour of boiling beef dripping caressed his nasal epithelium, Runty went through the sturdy fence like it was a bead curtain in a harem. Seconds later a terrible shot rang out from within the restaurant. I dearly hope Runty got to swallow a few mouthfuls and died happy. Customers shocked at the sight of a giant pig convulsing to death at their feet could take some consolation from the fact that of all the things on the menu the pork at least was fresh.

Our steers were bloody lucky we weren't armed. One memorable evening, while driving off to a flash dinner party in the city, we caught Short and Tall sneaking up the road. Despite being dressed in her finery, Helen insisted on chasing them home. Holding her shoes and stockings in one hand and pulling up her white frock with the other, she plunged bravely into the ditch and herded them back the other way. Lit from behind by the headlights of our van, the steers cantered off into the gloom pursued at speed by a mad woman holding a skirt over her waist, exposing her knickers.

THROUGH ALL OF THIS I was still covering Parliament, writing and illustrating a lengthy Saturday article on politics for the *Auckland Star*. My fourth book, a collection of political columns called *Ten Years Inside*, was launched in the Beehive, in time for the Christmas market in 1985, by Prime Minister David Lange, who made a big fuss of my mother. But not as much fuss, according to Mum—who measured these things with the precision of a Large Hadron Collider particle physicist—as Jim Bolger when he launched another book of mine when he became Prime Minister. This made Jim the better man in Mum's book.

In the early days, parliamentary stories lay ankle-deep on

the ground, like wind-blown fruit in an orchard. Fourteen years on I had scooped up most of them and helped myself to all the low-hanging fruit. Fresh stories or rather fresh angles on familiar stories were harder and harder to find, or further and further out of reach. A bunch of top-notch young reporters like Greg Shand in the *New Zealand Herald* and Jane Clifton and Bernard Lagan in the *Dominion* (now with the *Listener* and *The Times* of London respectively) were turning out brilliant copy, leaving me panting and puffing in their wake. I was exhausted, physically, mentally and emotionally. Moving to the country hadn't changed things in the way Helen had hoped.

One Thursday night, after covering a late sitting of the House, I stumbled to my old heap of a car after midnight and found it wouldn't start. It was nearly 1 a.m. when I finally got it going and I had an hour's drive ahead of me before I got home, where I set the alarm for 4.30 a.m. to give myself time to write an article and deliver it back to my office at Parliament by the 10 a.m. deadline. I wrote it in a close-to-tears zombie state, drove it into Wellington awash in black coffee to ward off slumping over the wheel in a coma, handed it across in a daze and lapsed into blessed unconsciousness on the small office couch. I refused to read it again when copies of the *Star* arrived next week. I was surprised and relieved when some of my colleagues congratulated me warmly on it, but I never wanted to clap eyes on it again.

Two weeks later it happened again. This time the car never started and I ended up spending a fitful night at Parliament, tossing and turning on the office couch. Breakfast consisted of half a packet of chocolate biscuits and black coffee. Sitting in my now rancid clothing, with furry teeth and a sore back, typing a woefully inadequate article, I decided there had to be more to life than this.

CHAPTER TWENTY-TWO

THE BOLGER YEARS

A LOT OF COLUMNS FROM this period are lacklustre, but there were some diamonds in the rough. The following is a personal favourite of mine, on National coming to terms with the radical, free-market, neo-liberal economic policies of Labour's Minister of Finance Roger Douglas.

It was the leader who finally broke the oppressive silence. 'Does anyone have any bright ideas?' He was clutching the pointer so tightly in his powerful farmer's hands the blood had drained from his knuckles and MPs in the front row thought they could smell wood burning. Behind him on the blackboard someone had printed in capital letters the word POLICY with a question mark beside it. The rest of the board was bare. The blank surface seemed to stare accusingly at the room full of MPs, who just as blankly stared back.

Jim Bolger looked at his watch. The big hand was on 12 and the little hand was on 10. Back on the farm they would have been knocking off for smoko. He remembered it well. Two cups of milky tea in a tin mug and four dozen hot-buttered scones. Mind you, people earned their tucker in those days. Many's the time he and Joan would have got up before sunrise on their rugged King Country property and toiled without pause for eight or nine back-breaking hours folding nappies. Not to mention those long cold winter nights making school lunches. City folk would never have been able to hack it.

Sometimes, though, he wished that he were back on the farm. Everyone chipped in. No one complained. Unlike this lot, thought Bolger. Here they were on the second morning of a three-day policy formation seminar and half of them were wilting already. Most of them looked away when they caught his eye. Only Doug Graham gazed back at him quite unperturbed, sucking contentedly on his pipe, a cryptic smile on his face. Graham was altogether too composed and pleased with himself for a new boy. Bolger wondered what the cryptic smile meant until he realised that was the whole point—cryptic smiles weren't meant to be understood. Two could play that game. He gave the Remuera MP a wink and took some satisfaction from the fact that the pipe fell from Graham's lips and when he hastily put it back into his mouth he did so bowl end first.

'Don't all speak at once!' said the leader of the National Party tartly. 'Does anyone have any ideas that we can toss around a bit and maybe incorporate in our election manifesto?' Down the back a small, compactly built, smartly dressed young man with blazing eyes and arteries that pulsed in his temples climbed on to the top of his chair and started waving his arms about frantically to attract attention. Bolger sighed. 'Anyone apart from John Banks?' Almost immediately a familiar walking stick was jabbed into the air and an excited cry of, 'Too bloody right I do!' emanated from the middle of the room. Bolger took a deep breath. 'Anyone apart from John Banks and Norm Jones? A few policies would make all the difference to our manifesto.'

Warren Cooper turned wistfully to Venn Young, seated beside him. 'A few years back we never used to worry much about policy, did we?'

'We were the Government then, Warren,' said Young gently.

'It's a nuisance, I know,' continued Bolger. 'But people seem to expect it. At this rate we'll have to print a glossy cover and wrap it around some blank pages.'

'It worked for Labour!' shouted Paul East.

'But only once!' chimed in Winston Peters. The room chuckled but the laughter curdled when a tall, gaunt figure in the front row rose slowly to his feet. His thick head of hair was Brylcreemed neatly into place and behind wire-frame spectacles his eyes glowed with a strange cold fire. He spoke with the precision and gravity of a judge pronouncing the death sentence, pausing for up to a minute between each crisply enunciated word. It was Merv Wellington.

'I crave your indulgence, Mr Chairman, if I may have the floor?' As far as Bolger was concerned, Merv could have any part of the room he wanted. Especially the door if he shut it on his way out. He knew better though than to stop the

Papakura MP and waved him on. 'Prithee, good sir, a blank manifesto has been vouched and I say why not acknowledge openly and honestly on the cover that we have no policies!'

'I think Merv's point, whatever it was, was a good one!' shrieked Banks. 'We are going to need truth and light on our side if we are ever going to defeat these godless, atheistic socialists!'

'The trouble is, John,' said deputy leader George Gair, 'we're not dealing with godless, atheistic socialists. This lot are anti-socialist.'

'Isn't that just typical of your modern socialist,' snarled Winston Peters, his voice thick with contempt. 'They have no respect for their proud heritage.'

Cries of 'Shame!' and 'Disgraceful!' rang around the room until a cool, clear voice penetrated the babble. 'Outrage has its place, but I think we must come to terms with a number of things if we are to make progress here ...' It was their former leader, Jim McLay. Bolger noticed yesterday just how relaxed the Member for Birkenhead had become now that he was no longer in the hot seat. The worst of his shaking had died down and he no longer scalded everyone in the immediate vicinity when he poured himself a cup of tea. 'We have to accept that Labour have outflanked us on the right. They are more market-oriented than we ever dared to be. They are contemplating corporatising some government departments. They are privatising the BNZ. They believe in the user-pays principle. They have removed subsidies, floated the dollar, and are about to further deregulate the banking and finance sector. We must ask ourselves, where it will end?'

'Gentlemen, fear not, be not of faint heart, I see it not as an end but a bold beginning!' All eyes turned towards the small woman sitting to one side. It was Ruth Richardson. 'If Labour have appropriated our territory and made it the middle ground, what is to stop us moving further to the right?'

'How can we?' asked a despairing Don McKinnon. 'There's no room.'

'Nonsense!' snapped Richardson, fixing him with a gaze that only needed to be a kilowatt or so stronger to be able to burn holes in a steel girder. 'If we have the political will, and the courage to stick fast to our principles, the right kind of policies will fall into place.'

The short, pear-shaped man in the corner who had barely made a sound for two days put a little hand up. 'Sir Robert.' Bolger swallowed. 'I wondered when we'd hear from you.'

'It's perfectly obvious, Mr Chairman,' said Muldoon evenly, 'that the National Party has been outmanoeuvred by the Labour Government on the right. There is nothing we can do about that now. But we could get our own back by outflanking them on the left.

'What exactly do you have in mind, Sir Robert?' asked Bolger cautiously.

'Well, for starters we could socialise the means of production, distribution, and exchange.'

'Brilliant, absolutely brilliant!' shouted Banks. 'I hope someone is taking notes!'

FOR THE RECORD, JAMES BRENDAN BOLGER, whose election slogan was 'create a better society', became Prime Minister with a huge parliamentary majority. Promising a kinder, gentler country, his government delivered precisely the opposite. As jokingly predicted in my column, Ruth Richardson's neo-liberal zealotry became the new order. She cemented Roger Douglas's reforms in place and went even further, until today New Zealand has the widest and fastest-growing gap between the rich and the poor of any country in the OECD.

It must be galling to Jim Bolger today that his tenure is remembered mostly for Ruth Richardson's self-styled 'Mother of all Budgets'—a shock-and-awe attack on the welfare state, named after Iraqi President Saddam Hussein's 'Mother of all Battles' boast before the first Gulf War in 1991, which was only marginally more destructive and cruel. At the time a television commercial for Drive concentrated laundry powder featured PAC-MAN-like cartoon red dots carnivorously devouring stains on clothing. A voiceover exclaimed that these wondrous dots were 'hungry enzymes'. Lange quickly dubbed Ruth the hungry enzyme.

It was cruel and it was perfect. It fitted her shape and her Panzer-tank approach to politics. Ruth always spoke with authority. She didn't appear to have a scintilla of doubt, which to people racked with indecision gave her huge appeal. When she was wrong she was inevitably wrong at the top of her voice, so if you weren't paying attention you hardly noticed.

She had no dress sense when she first arrived at Parliament. She wore tweed skirts that looked like they had been woven from marmalade and sagging stockings the colour of cocoa. While serving as the country's first female Opposition spokesperson on finance, then the country's first female Minister of Finance, she began hitting the gym and underwent a complete style makeover, getting into power dressing in a big way. She wore jackets with shoulder-pads so wide that front on it made her look like an aircraft carrier. Meanly, I still drew her short and dumpy with her feet placed wide apart like the legs on a grand piano—the pelvic girdle of a ruminant, essentially. (Some of my Irish relatives have them. As a consequence, the second stage of labour is very short. Two coughs and you need someone with the reflexes of a slip fielder to catch the baby in one hand and the placenta in the other.) One of her press officers, understandably fed up with this mean and terribly unfair portrayal, rang me one day to say that Ruth had a fantastic body and was prepared to disrobe down to her underwear in her office to prove this to me. I declined. I couldn't take the risk. What if I was smitten?

When Ruth stepped down from Parliament I drew her trim and slim in a tight-fitting *Star Trek* bodysuit, standing in a transporter pod, asking to be beamed up as her mission on earth was complete. Her office was on to me in a flash, requesting a copy of the original.

The most enigmatic thing, the most cryptic thing about Jim Bolger, the thing that baffles and perplexed most political commentators, the thing no one could fathom, not even his colleagues, was his complete and utter lack of mystery. Obviously very intelligent, he was nevertheless self-conscious about his lack of formal education—he left school at thirteen to work on the family dairy farm. As a result he had an understandable tendency to exaggerate his achievements. I asked him once how a one-on-one meeting with British Prime Minister John Major had gone. Jim puffed his chest, tilted his head back and intoned grandly, 'Well, Tom, it was the usual world leader stuff …'

He hated being mocked in my cartoons. Dick Griffin hated it as well. He tried to slip quietly away from the ninth floor of the Beehive if my doodles were unflattering, but was often waylaid by an anguished howl.

'GET IN HERE, GRIFFIN!' Flushed with rage, jabbing his massive King Country paw at the offending page, Bolger would bellow, 'YOUR MATE, GRIFFIN! YOUR MATE! DOESN'T HE REALISE THAT WHEN HE MAKES FUN OF ME HE IS MAKING FUN OF THE NATION?'

DICK IS ONE OF THOSE truly blessed people who can get blind drunk, sleep in his clothes in a rubbish skip and emerge in the morning and go straight to a GQ cover shoot without wardrobe or make-up having to lift a finger. I can purchase a new suit, shirt and tie, walk from the store and within sixteen steps look like a homeless person and have people give me money. It was a nightmare for him when he accompanied Bolger in the United States. Everyone assumed the pencil-slim, elegant man with the splendid mane of silver Bobby Kennedy hair was the New Zealand Prime Minister, and that the burly unmade bed beside him was his diplomatic protection squad bodyguard.

This confusion sometimes worked in Dick's favour. In 1995, Sir Edmund Hillary was in Phaplu, high in Nepal's Solukhumbu District, visiting one of his school projects, when he received a phone call from Buckingham Palace informing him that he had just been made a Knight of the Most Noble Order of the Garter. Membership of the Order is made at the sole discretion of the sovereign and is limited to 24 living companions at any one time.

It was a great honour, but it came at a price. Ed rang me in an agitated state on his return. He would have to purchase his own ermine robes and commission his own coat of arms, which didn't come cheap, on top of travel and accommodation costs for himself and his wife, June. I said confidently that he should leave it with me, then promptly rang Dick in desperation to see if the Prime Minister could help. Dick rang me back a few days later. It was all sorted. The Reserve Bank, Brierley Investments and Air New Zealand were happy to pick up the tab.

At a function in Parliament's banquet hall some weeks later I sought out the Prime Minister and thanked him warmly for helping Ed. When I saw complete incomprehension and an irritated curiosity sweep ominously across his features, I backed out of the conversation. Clearly Dick had never spoken to Bolger, but everyone he rang assumed that he had, and that he was ringing them expressly at the Prime Minister's behest. When I challenged Richard on this he flashed his naughty altar-boy smile. 'Did I give them that impression? How remiss of me. Oh dear, never mind.'

CHAPTER TWENTY-THREE

RAIDERS OF THE LOST DOG KENNEL

I WAS A PRIMARY-SCHOOL BOY sitting on a plank of wood on the muddy sideline and didn't realise it at the time, but I first gazed upon Murray Ball one winter's afternoon in 1959 at the Palmerston North showgrounds when the Junior All Black and son of an All Black marked the great, snorting, prancing British and Irish Lions winger Tony O'Reilly, who was half man, half racehorse.

'Mostly O'Reilly beat me with sheer pace on the outside,' sighed Murray years later, when I reminded him of the thumping Manawatū received. 'Other times he sidestepped inside me. And then, when he got bored with that, he just ran over the top of me.'

Most rugby players get better and better in fond recall, but not Murray. Typically his nostalgia trod a fine line between lacerating honesty and mocking self-deprecation.

I remember still the exhilaration I felt when I stumbled

across Murray's early editorial cartoons in the now long-extinct *Manawatu Times*. They were nothing like the stolid, insipid, reactionary offerings in other newspapers. They burst off the page with a rude energy and undeniable humanity. Imagine a Giles cartoon if Giles had dropped acid. And they were drawn by somebody from my hometown! If you wanted to be a rock star back then it was a hopeless cause unless you came from Liverpool. Actually, if you wanted to be anything, coming from Feilding made everything a hopeless cause, until quite literally at the stroke of a pen, Murray opened up possibilities.

Those possibilities expanded exponentially when strips by Murray began surfacing in British publications. Stanley the Palaeolithic Hero, who graced the pages of *Punch* magazine for many years, was clearly the work of someone of astonishing wit and fierce intelligence. The black shearer's-singlet-wearing Bruce the Barbarian, who appeared in a left-wing journal, was clearly the work of someone fiercely egalitarian. If it is possible to be too egalitarian, Murray most certainly was. Injustice and unfairness burned him, and as a consequence the fruits of his success always made him uncomfortable. When the imperfections of the real world bore down on him he departed England and retreated to a remote and beautiful part of New Zealand where he created a perfect world of his own, 'Footrot Flats'.

Mike Robson, the editor of the *Evening Post*, saw the strip's potential and snapped it up. Other newspapers followed suit. Seemingly overnight the strip was enjoying phenomenal popularity across New Zealand and Australia. A transplanted Northern Irishman, Pat Cox, a former newsreel cameraman and film editor, running his own production company making snazzy commercials in Wellington, fell hopelessly in love with the strip and the world it captured and approached Murray about making 'Footrot Flats' into a full-length animated feature film.

Murray had never written a film script before and recommended to Pat that I co-write the screenplay. I had only written one television play, *Inside Every Thin Girl*, but in Murray's eyes that made me a veteran.

In truth it was a Victorian marriage. We were both innocents. We shared a rural Manawatū background. We both knew the sound sheep make when they cough at night, and the creak macrocarpas make in the wind. We'd heard weka call each other at dusk, roosters crow at the break of dawn and chained dogs howl at the moon. And we knew each other.

A friendship based on mutual respect and trust deepened over the next two years. Money was never mentioned. It was a passion project. We both had families to support and other paying jobs demanding our attention, but together and separately we devoted all of our spare time to the task. Sometimes Murray came to work with me in my attic office in Wadestown or I went to stay on Mikos, Murray and Pam's slice of paradise just over the hill from Gisborne. One summer we met halfway and worked in a Palmerston North motel.

No matter the location, Murray insisted on breaking the day up with a sporting contest of some sort, usually involving eye-hand coordination, like golf, ping pong, squash or tennis—which put me at a huge disadvantage. To make the tennis interesting, we would play five sets, starting with me leading two sets to love and five games to love in the third set. Despite this seemingly unbeatable advantage Murray would chase me down and win three sets to two, barely breaking a sweat. Long before Dean Barker was caught from behind and humiliated by Jimmy Spithill in the 2013 America's Cup, Murray was doing it to me on a regular basis. His teasing was merciless. I don't think I have ever laughed as much. He had a genius for including my children in games and making them great fun. Dear little Shaun burst into tears when a game of backyard cricket in Palmerston North had to be called off because it was pitch black and we could barely see each other, let alone the ball.

It took a year just to plot a rough storyline. Murray was astonishingly fecund. With every new plot suggestion he would sketch out on the spot more sight gags than we could possibly use. I soon realised that my major role would be to pare back the flood of material accumulating each scripting session and keep the storyline moving forward. I suggested ransacking his brilliant back catalogue for gags, but ever honourable and never one for short-cuts Murray insisted on all new material. He wanted the screenplay to remain absolutely faithful to the 'Footrot Flats' world, but he also accepted the need to introduce some external menace to sustain a feature-length plot. He came up with a new character, Vernon the Vermin, the King of the Rats, and during one weekend session he worked on the croco-pigs overnight, arriving the next morning with the characters fully developed, fully rendered, lurking in the muddy waters of the script as if they had always been there. Remembering the terrifying wild boar in Battersby's bush, I loved the idea. It was my suggestion to include the storm and flooding, and consistent with my fear of water I was the instigator of the Dog and Horse being washed out to sea at the film's climax.

Pat gave us extensive notes on pacing and structure and we toiled away for the best part of another year completing a storyline to everyone's satisfaction. I remember the exciting moment in my attic when I finally wound a sheet of A4 paper into my small portable typewriter and typed in the magic words:

RAIDERS OF THE LOST DOG KENNEL
A dog's life, 1st draft

Murray and I were just kidding with the title, but it can't have been too far off the mark. As I was going I would read it out loud to the kids. Cute little Ned listened enthralled and squealed, 'This is more exciting than *Raiders of the Lost Ark!*'

I still have that manuscript. It's huge. Including Murray's attached cartoons to clarify the action and copious quantities of my white-out, it is bulky enough to derail a train. I am particularly fond of one scene that Murray, for all his brilliance, could never have written. With his superb aerobic capacity it would just never have occurred to him. It needed to come from me. It required someone with negative buoyancy:

EXTERIOR, DAY. RUGBY GROUND.

It is half-time and the two teams are huddled at
either end of the muddy paddock. The grandstand
crowd is stretching and standing up. The
scoreboard still reads 12 to 0. At one end Irish
Murphy is berating the Mill team.

MURPHY: Geezzz what are ya? Playing with the
wind and only twelve points up against that pack of
girls! You should be murdering the sods. I wanna
see some effort this half. I wanna see some driving!
I wanna see some sweat! I wanna see some blood!
I wanna see some guts! I wanna see a priest being
called onto the field to administer the last rites.
Is that clear? Yeah and do that Footrot joker, he's
getting on my nerves!

At the other end it is Wal's turn.

WAL: The trouble . . . (choke) with you lot . . .
(gasp) is . . . (gasp) . . . you're . . . not (gasp) fit.

When the project stalled at the lights, Pat brought Wellington film producer John Barnett on board and together they got it funded and made—never easy with an animated film. Dave Dobbyn backed by Herbs launched the film with the magical song 'Slice of Heaven' and the movie was a box-office triumph on both sides of the Tasman.

John was to come to my rescue on two more of my dramas: the television mini-series *Fallout* that I wrote with Greg McGee, which John rescued when he became head of South Pacific Pictures, and *Separation City*, which only got New Zealand Film Commission funding after his gutsy intervention on our behalf after what he considered unfair treatment.

John let slip once that his dad won the Military Medal for bravery at Ruweisat Ridge in North Africa in World War Two. There is no question in my mind that John inherited all of his father's chromosomes for courage. He is an articulate, relentless campaigner for causes he believes in. It is wonderful having him in your corner in a fight. It is much less fun being on the receiving end of a scolding, which I have been from time to time. He is a good mate. I owe him a lot. And Pat Cox is a wise and trusted confidante.

I owe Murray even more. Being invited to co-write *Footrot Flats* was an honour in itself and to have it succeed beyond all expectation gave me the courage to write feature screenplays and stage plays of my own. I'm proud to have known him. Through all weathers, in all seasons and over time, in 'Footrot Flats' Murray created a world every bit as delicate and true as a Katherine Mansfield short story, every bit as visceral and unsentimental as a Ronald Hugh Morrieson or Barry Crump novel, every bit as whimsical and nonsensical as a John Clarke or Billy T. James comedy routine (both of whom appeared in his film), and visually every bit as arresting and instantly recognisable as a Rita Angus or Toss Woollaston painting. To borrow from Dave Dobbyn, Murray gave us a slice of heaven.

CHAPTER TWENTY-FOUR

A THOUSAND MILES BEHIND

FOR SOME MONTHS, MIKE ROBSON from INL had been continually wooing me to join the *Evening Post* as an eventual replacement for the venerable Nevile Lodge, who wasn't in good health. In mid 1987 Mike took me to lunch to formally ask for my hand in cartooning matrimony. It was at the Museum Hotel in its former location before they shifted it to make way for Te Papa. Rod Deane had advised me beforehand to ask for an inducement payment and nominated an eye-watering sum. 'If they really want you, they will pay' was his mantra. I waited nervously for the right time to drop it into the conversation, but it never came, so I just blurted it out like a burp. Mike went apoplectic with shock and outrage, turning white then purple without making a sound. He was vibrating like a tuning fork at one point. I think the shock waves shifted the Museum Hotel a few centimetres well before the big move. He eventually said yes in a low, strangled croak.

WHEN THE *EVENING POST* CELEBRATED its one hundred and thirtieth birthday in 1995, the paper's publishers and senior editors made a fuss, probably because they knew full well that if they waited until it turned 150 it would have been dead for thirteen years. For the big birthday I was asked to write what I especially liked about New Zealand's largest evening newspaper:

> I like the obvious things about the *Evening Post*—
> the look and the feel. By rights, being an evening
> paper, we should be a downmarket tabloid but
> instead the layout, the graphics, the use of colour
> and the quality of the writing make it consistently
> one of the most stylish papers in Australasia.
>
> I like the less obvious things even more. One
> morning I was at my desk in the illustrations
> department when one of the photographers
> arrived breathlessly with colour shots of a body
> being fished out of Wellington Harbour. Several
> days earlier, after leaving a nightclub, a young
> man had gone missing and here he was now, face
> darkened and belly distended by decomposition,
> bobbing like a cork just out of reach of a
> policeman's gaff. One shot had two attractive
> young women in a rowing skiff approaching to
> take a closer look. The angle of the boat, the light
> on the water and the grim smudge in the bottom
> corner made it a great composition. And we were
> short of a good front-page pic that day.
>
> Acting editor Karl du Fresne shook his head.
> 'That body has parents who must be fearing the
> worst by now. I wouldn't want to see my child as
> a piece of meat.'
>
> We published a picture of a body wrapped
> in a sheet on a stretcher being loaded into an
> ambulance.
>
> The *Evening Post* is thoughtful without being
> unctuous, intelligent without being highbrow,

careful without being anal retentive, and lively
without being gormless.

In 2002 the *Dominion*—the paper you would have an affair with—
and the *Evening Post*—the paper you would marry—merged
to become the imaginatively named *Dominion Post*. I am still
there. It is my intention to be carried out feet first in a simple
pine casket. The editors assure me there is no hurry, though they
have taken to running a tape measure over me once every three
months rather than annually, which used to be the case.

ALMOST INSTANTLY, CARTOONING WAS VASTLY more fun and
much easier than writing. For starters, everyone can write but
far fewer people can draw. Right away you are a one-eyed man
in the land of the blind. But you have to settle for a different
relationship with your readers. They spend seconds on a
cartoon, while they have to commit five to ten minutes on an
article. Cartoons are casual sex, articles are marriage. Woody
Allen once wrote that sex without love was a hollow experience,
but as hollow experiences went it was one of the best. Cartooning
is a hollow experience that is hard to beat.

Every night I would set the alarm for six o'clock, leap out of bed
at the first bring-bring, creep downstairs to my office, shut the
door quietly and listen to Geoff Robinson on Morning Report,
sipping coffee, with a brand-new day all to myself. When I had
settled on an idea I left my desk to help Helen make breakfast
for the kids and concentrate on my specialist subject: school
lunches. (Over the years I have received numerous heartfelt
requests from my kids for less elaborate sandwiches and for a
week or so, sulking badly, I would oblige with white bread and
peanut butter before falling back into my bacon and avocado
bad habits.) Back at my desk doing the cartoon, I delighted in the
sight of towering Shaun, willowy Jacob and Ned in their Kapiti
College uniforms striding down the meadow through waddling
ducks and white geese, heading for the school bus at MacKays
Crossing with baby brother Sam half-running to keep up with

them, their happy laughter floating in the onshore breeze from the Tasman Sea glittering in the distance.

Drawing a daily cartoon is only slightly more onerous than shaving with a dull razor. Part of its charm is that it is so disposable. You can't luxuriate on your triumphs or brood over your disasters, as they both vanish within 24 hours. Some Monday mornings, standing under a drumming shower, I would think of a week's worth of drawings in a matter of moments, and if my hand was working well I could dash them off in less than an hour each, which editors over the years suspected and understandably deeply resented. It meant I had more time to work with Helen restoring the house, which Barry and his missus had badly buggered. In the kitchen they had glued red vinyl panelling over beautiful tongue-and-groove timber. In the upstairs bathroom eight different kinds of tiles in eight different sizes and in eight different colours competed for attention. On the landing of the magnificent kauri staircase they had glued hideous mirror squares to the wall—creating a cheap bordello look. They couldn't be peeled off. I had to destroy several dozen of them with a hammer. Standing precariously on the top of a stepladder, I did the sums. I would have to live seven lifetimes to use all the bad luck I was generating for myself. And it felt like that at times.

IT WASN'T ALL GRIM—the first summer was glorious. We invited all of our friends and their children to a picnic in the grounds. It was like the scene after the grain harvest from one of my favourite films, the Russian masterpiece *Burnt by the Sun*. And *Footrot Flats* premiered to great acclaim. When John Barnett rang me somewhat ruefully to say they couldn't justify the expense of flying me to the Australian premiere because no one had heard of me over there I immediately got on the phone to Bill Darcy and Dennis Grant, who was working in the Canberra Press Gallery, and between them they arranged sufficient radio and press interviews for me to tag along. Murray Ball was relieved. Naturally shy, he was more relaxed when he had me around to joke with and tease unmercifully.

Together we went on Channel 9's show *Midday* with Ray Martin. Ray loved the film and commented that New Zealand farm fences had five strands of wire while Australian farm fences had only three—why was this? 'Our sheep are smarter than your sheep,' was my response. The audience roared. It was my biggest single contribution to the Anzac spirit since Muldoon borrowed my line about Kiwis migrating to Australia.

Another television crew interviewed us at our hotel on William Street just off Hyde Park. The reporter was blunt, cheerful and matter-of-fact, as only Australians can be. 'Jesus Christ, mate. What the fuck happened to all your hair? You've got shitloads in the publicity stills!' It was true. Just a few years earlier the photographer Paul Roy was commissioned by Pat Cox to take press stills for the upcoming film. In these I am sporting an afro, albeit thinning at the temples. My hair was going to fall out anyway, but instead of abandoning ship gradually over ten years it walked the plank in eighteen months, accelerated by stress. I was also in one of my fat Elvis periods. Given my unkempt beard and remaining hair it would probably be more accurate to say I was in one of my fat Charles Darwin periods.

One of the consequences of feeling unloved is you become unlovable. Helen and I had been going to relationship counselling in Wellington, which more often than not made for long, frosty drives back to the farm. As Bob Dylan would say, Helen was right from her side, I was right from mine, but we were both just one too many mornings and a thousand miles behind.

Helen began spending more and more time in Wellington, taking sweet little Rosie with her. One day the van wouldn't start for her. It refused to crash start when I pushed it down the long, sloping driveway. I had to push it some more along Emerald Glen Road. It wasn't light. It took several more Herculean efforts for me to finally get it up to enough speed to roar into life when Helen slipped it into gear. Gasping for air, I leaned against the driver's window while she revved the engine.

'I can't do this much longer,' I croaked.

'Neither can I,' responded Helen crisply, and drove off.

I was speaking metaphorically. She was speaking literally. Not long after that she took the children and moved back into town for good.

I remained at Emerald Glen on my own and prepared it for sale. We had made many improvements to the house, including replacing weatherboards and painting it. It looked a treat. I walked every day to the top of the property where the creek babbled down from the ranges. I sat and looked at the sea in the distance. Through spreading oaks, sinewy gums, slender poplars and gnarly macrocarpa I watched smoke curling up lazily from brick chimneys and knew I would miss it despite being desperately unhappy there at times.

An elegant transplanted English stockbroker zoomed up the drive one day in a Bentley, Audi or BMW (or quite possibly all three), expressing keen interest in purchasing the house. We sold it privately for a considerable capital gain. We were incredibly lucky with the timing. Like every other stockbroker in the world he never saw Black Monday coming—the 19 October 1987 fall of the Dow, when the New York Stock Exchange lost $500 billion in a single day—the biggest fall in its history. A few months later and he would have tramped up the drive with all his worldly possessions in a sugar bag and asked if he could sleep in the barn for free.

Helen bought a large, nicely appointed house in Wilton. Dividing the chattels was easy. Out of guilt I had given Christine everything. Out of exhaustion I did the same with Helen. I was the last of the Mohicans when the moving firm arrived at Emerald Glen with a huge furniture truck to take everything to Helen's place. They packed it expertly to full capacity and the Māori foreman asked me cautiously where my stuff was. I pointed into my office where books, records, a typewriter, an anglepoise lamp, pens and pencils, original cartoons and clothes were stacked in a modest pile. I said I could handle it and not to worry. He whistled softly and patted my shoulder gently. 'Geez, tough, bro . . .'

I followed his truck into Wilton and assembled Rosie's and Sam's beds for them as an endless stream of Helen's friends arrived bearing gifts of maidenhair ferns, quiche and wine. The kids seemed settled and Helen and her friends looked to be having a good time when I walked out to my car and drove off. I was 41 years old, a second-eleven celebrity and everything I owned fitted into the back of my Toyota Corolla. Not for the first time the needle on my self-pity gauge was jammed on full.

CHAPTER TWENTY-FIVE

KOTINGA STREET

MY FAVOURITE JOURNEY IN THE whole world is driving out to Island Bay and taking the long and winding coast road around the Miramar Peninsula back into the city—past plunging hillsides, wild rocky shores, fierce seas with huge swells, crashing breakers, lacy foam and drifting phosphorescent spray. The first glimpse of the rugged Orongorongo Ranges across the harbour heads never fails to make me think of *King Solomon's Mines*, a book I loved as a child. Regardless of the weather, I force all houseguests to take this journey with me. If none are available I go on my own at least once a month. Its hold on me never diminishes. It is my turangawaewae—my spiritual home. It doesn't belong to me—I belong to it, which is vastly more special. I dream about it when I am overseas, which is why an artist's loft in New York, a mews house in London or a maisonette in Paris hold no particular appeal for me.

I can say this with some confidence. When I was reconfiguring my Hillary documentary *View from the Top* for Channel 4 in the UK, I stayed in a grand, five-storey Regency house just off Berkeley Square in London as a guest of Don McKinnon and Clare de Lore (now Sir Don and Lady Clare). Don was Secretary-General of the Commonwealth at the time. They were hugely entertaining and absurdly generous hosts. It was a splendid house that shared fabulous park-like private gardens with surrounding mansions. From my bedroom I had Dickensian views across gabled rooftops and extraordinarily elaborate chimney-stacks with gleaming spires in the distance, but I ached for the first rays of the morning sun creeping over dark blue hills and turning Evans Bay a liquid silver.

On one of my very first pilgrimages shortly after settling in Wellington in 1972, I rattled around a bend in Evans Bay in my old Ford Cortina and spied an intriguing colonial home nested all by itself in the town belt high above Kilbirnie. It was so alluring I went in search of a closer look and was hugely frustrated when I couldn't get anywhere near the place. Maddeningly, no roads led to it. For years when I drove around the bays it remained ever beckoning and tantalisingly out of reach, until one day I got a phone call from a dear friend, Chris Hampson, who produced and directed the voice performances for *Footrot Flats*. Chris can do just about every job in moviemaking except play the female lead, but I reckon with the right make-up, the right wardrobe and dim lighting the bastard could probably pull that off as well. Chris told me on the phone that he was contemplating buying an old house up in the trees above Kilbirnie. 'I know it! I know the house!' I shouted excitedly. After that he had little choice but to invite me to come with him and have a look.

We approached from another suburb, on the opposite side of the ridge, through a dark forest of geriatric pines up a half-hidden track of pitted clay and gravel. My heart was beating fast. The house, when it loomed up through the trees, even in a state of considerable disrepair, was magnificent. The verandah was rotting, the stairs leading up to it were lopsided, finials and bargeboards had fallen off, paint was peeling and windowpanes were cracked. Inside rooms had been divided into cubicles with olive-green hardboard and Pinex partitions, yet it was still beautiful. It was originally a farmhouse then, according to local legend, a secret hideaway for pregnant nuns waiting to give birth, and for a time was a hippie crash pad.

I urged Chris to buy it. He is a Renaissance Man when it comes to renovating homes as well. He is pretty much his own architect, draughtsman, quantity surveyor, chippie, joiner, glazier, plumber, plasterer, electrician, tiler, painter and interior decorator. Then at his house-warming parties he pulls out a guitar and entertains his guests. He is a charming and gracious host into the bargain. It is any wonder none of his friends can stand him? In just a few years Chris and his then wife, the equally dynamic and vivacious Ruth Jefferies, utterly transformed the place.

It was to this house, through a dark corridor of brooding conifers, that I drove in my Corolla with my share of the marital spoils bouncing around in the back. I seem to remember a gathering darkness and rain falling as I unloaded the car, but this might be a figment of my imagination and my tendency to embellish every story. It was certainly raining in my heart.

Chris and Ruth had been going through a painful separation of their own. Chris moved out. Then Ruth moved out. Then Chris moved back in. For two years we were middle-aged bachelors together on the hill, me rising at dawn to draw a cartoon and, if Chris was awake, making him a cup of tea while he checked my spelling. More often than not he emerged from his bedroom closer to noon, then sat at his desk for hours in his dressing gown playing *Leisure Suit Larry* on his computer, one of which I was years away from owning. He also had one of the first cell phones. It was the same size and weight as a brick. And he introduced me to lattes at Caffé L'affare. These truly were days of miracles and wonders. We were a remake of Neil Simon's *The Odd Couple*. Mostly I was the uptight, fastidious Felix Unger and Chris the more relaxed, slovenly Oscar Madison, but to be fair we occasionally swapped roles.

Big Shaun came to live with me permanently. He was now producing testosterone in industrial quantities, which meant his socks breached the Geneva Convention on chemical weapons and had to be transferred to the washing machine with tongs. There were now three bachelors on the hill, two of them playing Oscar.

When Shaun was in London flatting with my brother Michael's first-born, the effervescent and gorgeous Milly, she came home from shopping one sunny Saturday afternoon to find him in the curtains-drawn lounge watching a soccer match on television. He hadn't shaved in three days. His long, lank locks were a stranger to hair products. He wore a stained T-shirt covered in pork scratchings and potato-chip crumbs. His shorts were baggy and frayed. His socks didn't match. He was sipping beer. Barely looking up, he said one or more of her beautiful friends had to come across soon as he was getting very little action in the sack. Milly adored Shaun, and in exasperation said he needed to tidy up his act.

'Take a good look at yourself, Shaun,' she said, not unkindly. 'You need to get in touch with your feminine side!'

Shaun took another sip of beer.

'Trust me on this, Milly,' he drawled. 'If I had a feminine side, I'd be touching it all the time.'

Rosie and Sam came to visit every second weekend. Often I collected them midweek from Wadestown School, took them out for afternoon tea, a play in a park or early dinner at my place, then dropped them back at Helen's house. It wasn't ideal but it was the best I could do.

Chris threw great parties, but finding myself a single man again I reverted to my Massey University single-man mode— mania alternating with bouts of wretched melancholia. As those wise philosophers the Brothers Gibb asked so presciently, how can you mend a broken heart? How can you stop the sun from shining? What makes the world go round? I had no answers. My self-pity gauge was still reading full.

TVNZ approached me about being in the pilot of a proposed show called *On the Couch*, where prominent people would be interviewed about their childhoods by a psychiatrist—a dumb idea, so of course I agreed to take part. I had a strict proviso:

it was never to be broadcast. Shielded by this and blinded by self-pity I told raw stories about my father's drinking and our grim upbringing. TVNZ was delighted and immediately commissioned a series, but wisely none of the other guests were blabbermouths, or at least not in my stellar class. TVNZ said my episode was easily the best and begged for my permission to broadcast it. Vanity got the better of me and I consented. I shouldn't have. I was so hard on my father some of Mum's friends assumed he must have died and rang her offering their condolences.

He was alive all right. He never rang me. Not once in the twenty years I had been gone from Owen Street, Feilding, nor I him, for that matter. But shortly after it went to air I got a phone call that was quite impressive. It was icy cold, calm and composed, with no traces of a stammer.

'Is that you, Egghead? It's your father here. I see you're quite the man these days. You'll be in a lot of demand, driving back and forth to Auckland. It's a long trip. You'll need to break your journey. If you're thinking of calling into Feilding for a refreshing cup of tea, don't fucking bother!'

Three years earlier I had dedicated *Ten Years Inside* to him.

> To my father, from whom I inherited my sense of
> humour and bad table manners.

Much like him, I suppose, I had to add a dash of vinegar in with the oil. He didn't attend the Beehive launch—he didn't attend his children's weddings so he was hardly likely to attend a book launch. Plus his health wasn't the best, so I posted him a copy, adding a hand-written inscription—again adding a splash of vinegar.

> To Tom Scott Senior
> Who I love but can't remember why.
> Cheers
> Tom Scott Junior

He must have been following proceedings closely. He cut a story about the launch out of the *Dominion* and stapled it to the page facing the inscription. The press clipping included a photo of me standing with the Prime Minister David Lange and Mum. All three of us are beaming.

Within days of *On the Couch* going to air, the book was posted back to me. In the photo Lange has 'FATSO' scrawled in capital letters on him. Mum is labelled 'DINGBAT'. An arrow points to my mouth: 'NOTE BIG GOB'. In giant letters he has scrawled 'HORSESHIT' over my inscription and smeared the bottom of the page with something that looked and smelled like excrement.

I was taken aback but I still didn't get it. I was hanging out with Carol Hirschfeld that summer and one evening I proudly slipped a VHS copy of the programme into the player and sat down to watch it again with her. Three minutes in she rose from the couch. 'I can't watch this! It's too cruel!' I drove her back to her place in uncomfortable silence. I still didn't get it.

Murray Bramwell, my comrade-in-arms from *Masskerade* and *Chaff* 'Long March' days, now a professor lecturing on theatre and film at Flinders University in Adelaide, happened to be holidaying in New Zealand and we spoke on the phone.

'Did you see the show?' I asked expectantly.

'I read your father's hurt response in the papers,' he replied cautiously. 'Everything you said was undoubtedly true, but that's not the point—you punished a powerless old man in a public forum with disproportionate force. Not everything that can be said needs to be said. Sorry...'

I wasn't sorry. Expecting fulsome commendation for my candour I was instead all wounded indignation. Murray is the sweetest man, who would rather detour a thousand miles if he thought a direct route might cause hurt or offence, but this time with uncharacteristic force and bluntness he had said what I needed to hear, even if I wasn't listening.

Despite living in Adelaide for nearly half a century, and despite not driving, he makes annual pilgrimages home laden with books, CDs and DVDs of television shows and distributes them like John the Baptist to his old chums across the land, keeping us all connected with each other. In 1970 he introduced me to Miles Davis's masterpiece *Bitches Brew* and is still introducing me to new sounds to this day. I don't block my ears to them.

A few years later, when Averil arrived in my life like a shaft of pure sunlight, I showed it to her. Averil is beautiful within and without. She didn't want to watch it all. She didn't need to. She didn't chide me, she just said quietly that it was unnecessary and unfortunate, but it was done now and I should put it behind me.

I finally got it.

Had my father been still alive I would have driven to Feilding and apologised to him in person, but it was too late for that. It sounds easy to say after the fact, but apologising in person is one of my strengths. I've had to do a lot of it over the years.

CHAPTER TWENTY-SIX

WALLS COME TUMBLING DOWN

ON 2 NOVEMBER 1990, JIM BOLGER'S National Party defeated Mike Moore's Labour Government in a landslide. On election night I was a comments man for TV3 in its Auckland studio. Afterwards I ended up at a party in Neil Roberts and Karen Soich's townhouse on Parnell Rise. I briefly toyed with the idea of throwing an armchair out of their lounge window, but it would only have landed on their patio and that wouldn't have been anywhere near dramatic enough to justify the damage.

At this party a striking Māori woman arrived late. She was wearing a white blouse, a natty black bolero jacket, a tan, knee-length skirt and stunning high-heeled black boots. She was lovely, quirky and charming. I didn't catch her full name. It was Eliza something. Back in Wellington I thought about her a lot. I rang Neil asking for her full name, phone number and advice.

'Yeah, Eliza's lovely. Dude, don't ring and tell her you're

coming to Auckland to see her. That'll freak her out, man. Say you're gonna be in town next weekend and it would be cool if you could catch up for a drink. Keep it casual. Rock on!'

(A true original and a charismatic force of nature, Neil was cut down by cancer in 1998. He was just 50 years old. The night before the funeral I met up with Bob Jones and TVNZ's Richard Harman for drinks. Bob was trying to tell me about his latest project, but I was more interested in what Richard was telling me about his last visit to Neil in hospital. 'His last words to me,' said Richard, on the edge of tears, 'the very last words he said to me were, "Harman, Harman—"'

'Oh for fuck's sake!' interrupted Bob. 'Stop going on and on about Roberts. He was a good bastard. None of us dispute that. But he's dead. He's dead! We all live and we all die!' There was no disputing this either.)

I followed Neil's instructions to the letter, sounding as relaxed as I could. I couldn't believe how easy it was. She would love to catch up. She laughed at my jokes. She nominated a time and a place—6 p.m., CinCin On Quay, on the waterfront. I got off the phone feeling lighter than air.

I was still lighter than air boarding my cheap flight to Auckland. I had arranged to have lunch with some friends at Prego on Ponsonby Road. I have a theory that lonely guys in need of female company have a flashing sign above their heads saying 'desperate for sex'. Only women can see this sign and their first instinct is to turn on their heels and walk briskly in the opposite direction. Their second instinct is to turn on their heels and run like the wind, never looking back. Men who are fully sated sexually have a sign saying 'Not in service—testicles empty' and women hurl themselves at them. It is one of the cruel ironies of nature that the best way to get invited to an orgy is to look like you have just come from one.

So I hit Prego brimming with confidence. I don't want to get too technical here, but I was exuding pheromones like I had extractor fans in my armpits. My self-pity gauge was low and my smugness readings dangerously high. I was sitting outside in Prego's courtyard when a tall, strikingly attractive woman came striding in. She was six foot in her boots, wearing a black leather jacket and tight denim skirt that came dangerously close to breaking my friend Kerre McIvor's cardinal rule that a woman's skirt should never be shorter than her tampon string. Heads swivelled, men's mouths gaped and women's lips pursed. Her eyes met mine. She joined our table. (It wasn't exactly random. She knew someone.) She sat next to me.

'You are a Scorpio, yes?' I confirmed this.

'October twenty-nine, yes?' I confirmed this as well. Her delighted laughter pealed out and she nestled into me. She was Katia Pavlak—a Polish actress who had been to a Polish film festival in Melbourne, decided to defect and had escaped her minders. What Churchill had famously dubbed the 'Iron Curtain' was still in place. Poland was under the cruel yoke of the Soviet Union. Fearing that Poland's secret police, the hated SB, were searching for her and would abduct her if they could, she fled to Auckland. She'd been in New Zealand a few weeks and was looking for work.

When she heard I was doing nothing that afternoon she invited me to come with her to play snooker. I don't play snooker. I went. Trying not to look when Katia bent low over the pool table was agreeable torture. When she asked me what I was doing that night I told her I was going to CinCin to have drinks with a woman friend. Clutching her throat, she exclaimed excitedly, 'Oh my Got! This is amazink! Katia going to CinCin tonight also. I start my first job. I am maître d' and waitress at CinCin. I wheel see you!'

When I arrived at CinCin, Katia was at the door looking absolutely stunning in a figure-hugging, ankle-length jade green frock. 'I miss you! I miss you!' she squealed, kissing me lightly on the cheek. She seemed to know intuitively who I was there to meet and led me around the corner to where Eliza was sitting at a high table, also looking gorgeous. Katia lingered longer than was strictly necessary, looking wistful. 'I will see you later.' She smiled shyly.

Eliza cocked a quizzical eyebrow when she had departed. 'Who is that?'

I explained nonchalantly that it was just someone I had bumped into recently, as if beautiful women were constantly attaching themselves to me. As my good friend Mark Sainsbury says, 'Hey, they're only human!'

Eliza was every bit as lovely as I remembered. She reached out to take my hand. She had booked a table for two at an Indian restaurant in Ponsonby. We were due there in an hour's time. My heart skipped a beat. But first she had something important to tell me. She was getting married in a few weeks' time. I tried to be cool. 'Congratulations, that's wonderful . . .'

Before devastation had time to sink in, Katia, who must have had hearing that could give sonar on a nuclear submarine a run for its money, was at my side.

'Getting married?' she hissed. 'You are having drinks with Tom and you are getting married? This is not right. You should not be doing this. This wrong!' She shot away again, watching us like a hawk when we ordered more drinks, unnerving Eliza.

'I think we should split this funky scene . . .' she muttered. 'Let's take off now.' Out on the footpath she hailed a cab. As we were opening the rear door Katia, minus her white apron, raced up. 'I tell manger I haff to come weeth you. I have to look after my friend, Toma Scott. He famous writer. He innocent. Toma need looking after.' She squeezed in between me and Eliza, who was too shocked to say anything.

At the restaurant Katia sat between us again like a stern chaperone, asking Eliza pointed questions about her upcoming nuptials. Before the food arrived Eliza rose, smiled tightly and said she would leave us to get on with things.

I wasn't hungry. Nor was Katia. She took me to a friend's party. They were all in their twenties and thirties, dancing frenetically and passing around joints. I felt out of place and told Katia it was great meeting her and I would just slip away. She insisted on coming with me. Under a starry sky we walked through narrow Ponsonby streets to Sam and Barbara Pillsbury's beautiful old villa on Beaconsfield Street. At the back, nestled in palms, they had a hot tub, a swimming pool and guest cottage where I was staying. Katia looked at the double bed and said she would sleep with me, but nothing would happen. I had to promise. I promised. I would sleep below the top sheet. She would sleep above it.

Sam and Barbara had exquisite taste. Separated by fine 600-thread-count Egyptian cotton, Katia lay beside me in just her bra and leopard-skin knickers. In the morning the movie star kissed me lightly and stepped into the shower while I pinched myself to make sure I wasn't suffering the effects of second-hand cannabis smoke.

We had breakfast with Sam and Barbara on their deck overlooking the pool. Sam could barely contain his excitement. 'You tinny bastard! She is so beautiful!' he grinned when she had left. I assured him that nothing had happened. He took this as absolute and irrefutable proof that it had and was stricken with envy.

I called in to see her at CinCin on my way back to the airport. The manager had forgiven her and she was back at her post. She hugged me when I was getting back into my cab. 'I miss you,' she said with tears in her eyes. We arranged to meet again in Wellington. A few weeks later she came down for an indefinite stay.

SHE MOVED INTO A CUTE little attic room at the top of the stairs. We went to a Miles Davis concert together. Miles was frail but with surprising force and great delicacy played classic tracks from his *Kind of Blue* and *Bitches Brew* albums. We walked on beaches. We went to art galleries, museums, movies and Wellington City Library—an embarrassing first for me. She wanted me to read the translated works of her favourite Polish playwright. She had read some of my journalism and urged me to write stage plays—something I had never previously considered. I took her to a supermarket and she got enraged in the fresh fruit section. Holding up an orange plucked from a huge bin of the same she cursed loudly. 'FUCKING FUCK! FUCK! CHRISTMAS PRESENT IN MY FUCK! FUCK! FUCKING COUNTRY!' It was the same feeding Lady, my black Labrador dog, sausage. Katia would wave it like a shillelagh and swear,

'THIS IS WHAT HUMAN BEINGS EAT IN MY FUCK! FUCK! FUCKING COUNTRY!'

All that passion, I noted ruefully to myself, should not go unrequited. I turned to Chris for advice. 'Thomas Joseph, as a gentleman and a scholar it behoves you to make the first move.' That night, after she had gone to bed, I waited a decent interval then crept up the stairs with a bottle of Baileys Irish Cream, which she loved. She was fast asleep. I didn't want to startle her, so I placed the bottle by her bed and tiptoed away. I was making coffee in the morning when she came downstairs wearing one of my shirts as a nightie and waving the bottle, puzzled and alarmed.

'What is theees? I don't remember . . .' I mumbled an explanation. She smiled softly. 'Oh, so you want Katia to come to your room tonight?' I stared at the floor. 'Yes please . . .'

She did, and rarely left for the rest of her stay except to bring me avocado and Marmite on Vogel's toast, 'To build up your strength, my darling.' Or to fetch red wine, which she swigged straight from the bottle before thrusting the neck at me. It was different. 'If you want, my darling, Katia will marry you.' She said this often. It was both exhilarating and terrifying. I had already failed at one marriage and the shock waves from my break-up with Helen were still radiating across the universe like X-rays from the Big Bang. I adored Katia, but what if the relationship evolved into something enduring then fell apart further down the track? It was heartbreaking enough living across the city from Sam and Rosie, just as it had been torture with Shaun before. How would I cope with a child living in Łódź if homesickness pulled Katia back to Poland?

And there were already signs. She was a gifted pianist. She loved Keith Jarrett's free-form jazz classic *The Köln Concert* and could play a little like him. Some nights I woke to find myself alone. When I went looking for her she would be at the piano in the lounge in the dark, naked in spite of the chill, a half-drunk bottle of red wine on the floor beside her, playing Chopin pieces with tears streaming down her face. She did some modelling for the fashion pages of the *Evening Post* and Sharon Crosbie wrote a terrific piece on her for the *Sunday Star-Times*, but she was unable to get much acting work and began missing her family terribly. With the Soviet Union fragmenting into its constituent parts and the authoritarian Communist regimes of Eastern Europe facing collapse it was safe for her to return, so she did. From time to time she sent me letters and postcards from Łódź sweetly imploring me not to forget her. 'I miss you, my darling. I hope you are having a good life.'

One package included an alluring black-and-white photograph of her in lingerie. It might have been a publicity still taken on a movie set. She was back with her husband Charles and working in films again. She looked gorgeous. I collected it from my Kilbirnie P.O. Box and quickly smuggled it into a bottom drawer in my office desk. I had to. Helen had moved back in.

She said the children missed me and she was willing to give it one more try. I owned the house on Kotinga Street by now. When Chris and Ruth decided to sell it they very generously gave me first option. With my share of the sale of Emerald Glen I was just able to afford it.

One of the first things I did when it was mine was get council permission to cut down the tall, aging pines leaning menacingly over the house. It was lucky that I did. A wild storm later that year toppled giant trees like skittles. Every year winter storms send more and more sullen conifers crashing to the ground and a soft green native forest is slowly taking its place. The transformation is transcendent. Sunlight filters through where shadows used to fall. There is more birdsong, and slithers of the inner city are visible through gaps left by retreating trees.

Carol Hirschfeld always felt there was something tapu about the house. When I cleaned out the basement I found a marble cherub with a broken wing. Was it stolen from a cemetery or did it belong to one of the pregnant nuns? There was no way of knowing, but it was mine now. I cleaned it gently as though I were bathing a child and placed in the back garden, surrounded by the flowers and warmed by the sun. I could be imagining it, but the house felt lighter and happier after this. I restored the broken chook house and we got hens. It was a joy collecting eggs in the morning with Rosie. Projects were Helen's thing—she was good at them—and we set about renovating the attic rooms, adding bigger windows, a dormer and a skylight.

For a time things were great. Then they weren't. The old demons that we both hoped had been exorcised for good returned. We went back for more debilitating, depressing rounds of counselling. Sometimes Helen came into the front room where I was reading, stood in front of me and said accusingly, 'You have nothing to say to me, do you?' It's hard to think of anything when you are put on the spot like that. I could hardly tell her that just before falling asleep I thought often about Carol or Katia. I started falling asleep at night with my right arm hooked over my face—the way you shield your eyes from the sun when you are lying on your back. It was a return to how I fell asleep most of my childhood—using the crook of my elbow to block out the world.

CHAPTER TWENTY-SEVEN

MORE WALLS, AND BRIDGES

CLOSE TO MIDNIGHT ON 9 November 1989 the Berlin Wall came down. Not literally—the wall would not be demolished for months—but psychologically it ceased to exist. This was not through some ringing, Gettysburg Address-like exhortation—as Americans believe happened after President Reagan's 'Mr Gorbachev, tear down this wall' speech made two years earlier before the Brandenburg Gate—but rather through poor sentence construction in a press statement from the Central Committee entitled 'Immediate Granting of Visa for Permanent Exit', issued at a Ministry of Information press briefing.

For several years a steady trickle, then a surging stream of East Germans had been crossing the border into the Czechoslovak and Hungarian republics. When this stream grew exponentially into a raging torrent, causing huge problems for the terminally ill regimes in Prague and Budapest, the humiliated East Germans thought easing travel restrictions at *all* border crossings might relieve the pressure. The foreign press at the briefing wondered if this was a mistake, and the hapless politburo spokesman repeated that private travel and permanent exit from the German Democratic Republic (GDR) was now permitted. He wasn't absolutely sure but it was probably effective immediately, and he stressed it was only a temporary measure.

While the other journalists present were mulling over exactly what this meant, the Associated Press reported explosively that East Germany was opening its borders. This instantly led to news bulletins around the world. Within hours, thousands of East Berlin citizens who paid close attention to Western media outlets began jamming border crossings into West Berlin, demanding access before the press statement could be rescinded. Border guards and the hated Stasi couldn't shoot them all, and capitulated to this human tsunami. It was effectively game over for the Honecker regime. Lech Wałęsa's Solidarity movement had already assumed power in Poland and the Soviet Union, which had problems enough of its own, was in the process of switching off life support for politburos in Czechoslovakia and Hungary.

Labour's lateral-thinking and irrepressible Minister of Overseas Trade Mike Moore saw opportunities for New Zealand in this chaos. The man once described by David Lange as behaving like a pinball machine assembled by a colour-blind electrician had been using one of the Defence Ministry's Boeing 727s to take trade delegations around the word. Mike announced his intention to lead an exploratory trade delegation to Warsaw, East Berlin, Prague and Budapest in the New Year. It was too good an opportunity to pass up, and the *Evening Post* quickly agreed to send me along.

Łódź is just over an hour from Warsaw by road and I asked Helen if she would mind if I caught up with Katia and her husband for a drink in the Polish capital. She said icily that I could do what I pleased—it made no difference to her. It was an extremely thoughtless thing to ask when things were already tense at home—so tense in fact it was a huge relief in late February 1990 to join my old mate Barry Soper and the others on the long, noisy and uncomfortable flight to Poland.

Our aging 727 had the fuel capacity of a two-stroke motor-mower and flooded when the pilot pulled the starter cord too vigorously. We had to stop for gas in Brisbane, Darwin, Changi, Mali, Bahrain and Cairo before arriving in Warsaw three days later on a freezing, overcast afternoon. John le Carré could not have scripted it better.

On the bus into the city I told Barry about Katia and possibly catching up with her and her husband for a drink—adding that I had sought Helen's approval first. 'You're an idiot!' he barked. My response was that it didn't really matter as I hadn't heard back from Katia and they were highly unlikely to show up in any case.

We drove through endless, bleak and depressing suburbs to Aleje Jerozolimskie (Jerusalem Avenue) in the city centre, where two monuments, one to communism and the other to capitalism, stood opposite each other. The former, the Palace of Culture and Science built in Stalin's wedding-cake style, grand and ornate in a vulgar, heavy-handed way, loomed oppressively over its surroundings. Locals wanted to live in it because that way they wouldn't have to look at it. Across the plaza was capitalism's rejoinder—the gleaming, brand-new, 40-storey Marriott Hotel. Immaculately built, elegantly designed, dripping with chandeliers, fine furnishings, classy watercolours and good restaurants, it was a tourist attraction in its own right. Many Poles came to marvel at what their world could be like. For some the contrast was too painful. I met people who refused invitations to step inside, let alone dine on culinary delights the likes of which they could never afford unless they set aside their life's savings.

I had barely settled into my luxury suite when the phone rang. It was Katia. She was in the foyer with her husband. I rounded up Barry and some of the other reporters to act as protective ballast and headed downstairs. She was in high heels and a short skirt and wore a fur coat and scarf—she looked incredible. Her husband was very tall, very handsome and very fierce-looking. If they'd had an honesty session when she returned home she had clearly forgiven him, but I don't think he'd forgiven her.

Katia hugged me warmly. Charles crushed my offered hand in a vice-like grip—it was a moment equivalent to boxers touching gloves at the beginning of a grudge bout. Unbidden, an old joke came into my head.

Question: What is the biggest book in the world?

Answer: Famous Polish axe murders.

Katia declared that we must all go to a famous nightclub, and taking my arm swept me out to the forecourt and bundled me into a cab. I suspect she told the driver to go as fast as he possibly could. We accelerated away in a cloud of Trabant smoke while Barry, her husband and the others were still hailing their cabs. We raced through Warsaw being chased by them, all ending up in a noisy, basement nightclub, the Krokodile, where a burly bouncer on the door demanded a million zlotys each in cover charge. Barry immediately got huffy and said he didn't come down in the last shower and wasn't going to put up with this shit. Then Pattrick Smellie from *The Press*, who is good with sums, calculated the exchange rate and said it came to less than five New Zealand dollars each. Inside, Katia somehow managed to position me alongside her at one end of a crowded table, while Barry was stuck at the other end doing his best to make small talk with her husband, who was clearly building into a pathological fury.

The service was first-class. Barry's voice was so deep and gruff, everywhere we went people assumed he was a Russian general and snapped into action. The downside was that out in the kitchen there was the very real possibility that chefs and waitresses were lining up to drop their underwear and urinate or worse into the borscht.

As a healing gesture, I offered Katia and Charles my hotel room for the night, insisting they help themselves to my mini-bar and catch an early train back to Łódź in the morning. All suites came with two double beds. I would crash with Barry and see them off at dawn.

In Barry's room, he whistled softly in the dark. 'Oh mate, she's gorgeous.' Then he giggled. 'He hates your guts.'

I sighed. 'He's terrifying. Thank God they're going in the morning.'

I was in a deep sleep when the phone rang. I snatched it before it woke Barry. It was Katia. I assumed they were leaving for the train, got dressed clumsily in the dark and stumbled down the corridor to my room. Katia opened it, wearing a skimpy hotel bathrobe.

The room was a shambles. There were empty miniature bottles of alcohol, empty potato-chip packets, salted peanuts and chocolate wrappers everywhere. Her clothing and his had been flung onto a sofa. The mattress from the bed nearest the window was half off. Tangled sheets, pillows and bedding were strewn across the floor. I have never been on the set of a porn movie but I imagine it would smell like my room did at that point.

I saw that my suitcase had been opened. A Madonna watch that I had bought in Bahrain's souk and had specially gift-wrapped for Helen's lovely daughter Emily was now on Katia's wrist. She was twirling around and waving it excitedly in the air.

'Thank you! Thank you!'

I smiled wanly.

A towel around his waist, Charles, sexually sated and fractionally less fractious as a consequence, pointed at me and intoned gravely, 'You have the eyes of a child!' He said this over and over again. 'You have the eyes of a child! You have the eyes of a child!'

How far away is their fucking train? I thought. Then I caught a glimpse of the bedside clock. Dear God! It was only three-thirty in the morning. Their train didn't leave for another four hours.

I couldn't go back and wake Barry, so I got into the spare bed fully dressed and pretended to be asleep while they quietly had sex again. I think. I didn't want to check. It was a huge relief when dawn finally came.

In the corridor as they were leaving, Katia said she needed to use the loo and ducked back into the room. Then I walked with them to the nearby station. The lightening sky was a sepia smudge. Brown haze from lignite-fired power stations hung over the city like a duvet. Noisy trolley buses lumbered past, chased and overtaken by swarms of Polish Fiats and antiquated lorries spewing diesel smoke.

At the station Charles shook my hand almost fondly and Katia hugged me a final time and they were gone. I skipped with relief back to my suite. In the bathroom mirror Katia had drawn a heart with lipstick and written 'I love you' in the centre. She had left her scarf neatly folded on the edge of the hand-basin. It filled the room with her perfume.

LATER THAT DAY, WALKING PITTED, uneven pavements, I came across kiosks selling soft porn—badly printed publications filled with smudged photos of flaxen-haired, busty girls draped uncomfortably over tractors and ploughs—old men selling coloured pencils and old women selling daffodils. Polish women seemed to come in two types—leggy supermodels and squat grandmothers in headscarves, both sweet and endearing in their own way.

After the assassination of President Kennedy, Chairman Mao was asked what might have happened to the course of human history if the Soviet leader Nikita Khrushchev had been shot dead instead of JFK. The Great Helmsman paused for a moment before saying he didn't think Aristotle Onassis would have married Mrs Khrushchev.

On the walls of various government ministries dissenters had scrawled 'FACK OOFF'. I had difficulty accepting that much of Warsaw was younger than me. Buildings approximating the grand style of pre-war Warsaw, the beautiful medieval city that retreating Germans in a final act of savagery systematically dyna- mited to the ground, were built in a rush after the war and already looked more tired and worn than the centuries-old structures they had replaced. Taking advantage of buildings being razed to the ground there were many tiny, pocket-handkerchief parks, bare rectangles of soil surrounded by high-sided mesh fences that looked like cages in a zoo. Seeing mothers inside rocking babies in prams only reinforced that impression. Black-and- white German newsreels record a time when this city was literally an animal cage for most of its inhabitants.

Certainly that is how the Nazis saw the Poles. Their barbarism went further with Jews. They weren't any animal; they were vermin. You got some idea of what Warsaw must have suffered when you pressed the button for 'sites of martyrdom' on the light-board map in the Palace of Culture and Science and the whole thing lit up like a Times Square Christmas tree. It was the same when you pressed buttons for cemeteries and battlefields. It seemed that every square inch of the city was soaked in blood before the Wehrmacht soaked it in petrol and put a torch to it.

A short documentary film on the destruction and the later reconstruction of Old Warsaw shown in another museum across town to an audience of teenage British backpackers had them muttering, 'Oh my God! Oh my God!', heartfelt and disbelieving in the dark. The old city square had been rebuilt using red bricks reclaimed from the rubble, but locals told us it was not the same. You can't re-create in a few years what took seven centuries to build. Katia had warned me: 'It's a fucking, fuck, fuck film set. Disneyland! An illusion; like all of fucking, fuck, fuck Poland, a dream!' Small wonder many Poles we met were apprehensive about German reunification.

Only a handful of journalists were allowed to accompany Mike Moore to the seaside city of Gdańsk for his meeting with Lech Wałęsa. Leigh Pearson from Radio New Zealand reported later that they could have been twins. Both men were manic and spoke English like it was their second language.

The rest of us had a whole day to ourselves and organised a trip to Majdanek concentration camp in Lublin, a city close to the Russian border. It was a three-and-a-half-hour bus journey south across flat, unfenced, featureless Polish countryside, misty like a van Gogh painting. Our progress was made slow by the horses and carts that farmers insisted on trundling down the centre of the narrow tarseal. The roadside store we stopped at sold cheap vodka and steak tartare crawling with flies, prompting Pattrick Smellie to comment that it was incredible that the entire country didn't die from bowel cancer. There was nary a hill in sight. If ever a country were designed by God for cavalry and tank warfare, it was this one. Apart from the steak tartare there were no natural defences. Poland was a tempting corridor for armies hell-bent on conquering Russia, as Napoleon and Hitler found to their cost.

It was early afternoon when we pulled into Lublin, a beautiful medieval city that had once been the seat of the Crown Kingdom of Poland. Home now to a large university, its streets teemed with cheerful, well-dressed students. We expected to drive well beyond it out into open countryside to Majdanek camp but instead found it cheek-by-jowl with the outskirts of town.

As our bus approached the camp the streets seemed to empty and the sun disappeared behind dark clouds. We parked at the front gates near a great monolithic memorial and stepped out into a bone-piercing cold. I was wearing the Savile Row black woollen coat that John Clarke had found for me in Cuba Street, but it provided scant protection from the freezing wind racing in from the Russian steppes not that far to the northeast of us. How did prisoners cope in their wooden clogs and thin cotton striped pyjamas?

The camp was the same as it ever was. At the end of the war, Russian troops overran the camp so swiftly the Nazis didn't have time to destroy their bestial handiwork. It remains fully preserved within its high perimeter fencing, with sixteen guard towers.

The icy, chill wind made the wire hum a mournful dirge. We walked in stunned silence between rows and rows of creosoted huts, at the end of which backyards with clotheslines were clearly visible. Pity the poor mothers of Lublin hanging out their baby's nappies during the war. They would have had to watch out for wind-shifts like America's Cup tacticians lest soot from other mothers and babies being incinerated suddenly swirl in their direction.

On the far side of the camp there was a Catholic burial ground. While good Catholics were getting a full Catholic burial, children of a lesser god were being slaughtered without ceremony and having their ash emptied like the contents of a vacuum-cleaner bag into a pit.

I was struck by the concrete walls of the gas chamber being as crudely boxed and poured as a Depression-era Taranaki milking shed—clearly these were people who had a lot of killing to do and had no time for anything fancy. Next door in the crematorium there were crude concrete morgue tables with low rims and a drain in the middle. Our guide told us that because some people were given to swallowing their wedding rings, bodies were routinely disembowelled in search of jewellery. These split corpses were then rolled onto mechanical litters and pushed into roaring ovens like pizza.

Visitors before us had tossed popsicle sticks into the dusty furnaces. I supposed they thought they were being tidy, though how you could walk through the dimly lit and echoing showers, gas chambers and crematorium while licking an ice cream was beyond me.

A vast storeroom was floor to ceiling full of shoes. In an adjacent storeroom, behind chicken mesh, was a mountain of human hair, waiting to be spun into thread then woven into socks for U-boat crews. Apparently, when you are a mile under water nothing can beat the warmth, comfort and durability of socks made from human hair. Now that I am bald I can confirm that it has thermal qualities the hirsute take for granted.

At the rear of the camp, a huge memorial dome bearing the inscription 'Our destiny is your fate' protected a giant circular sand-pit filled with seven tons of human ash. Beside it, winding back and forth like an intestine to make the most efficient use of space, was a deep trench. Nazis made Jews—who made up the vast bulk of the prisoners—gypsies, communists, homosexuals and dissidents line up in here to be shot. On one particular day, 3 November 1943, the SS, in a single twelve-hour frenzy, accompanied by loud music blaring from speakers to drown out the screaming and gunfire, pausing only for a tea-break, shot 18,000 people. Lublin parents reading their children bedtime stories would have had to compete with this grim cacophony.

On the bus back to Warsaw I was angrier than I have ever been in my life. So were all the guys. The girls sat at the front of the bus weeping. This sharp difference in their reactions was a foretaste of something haunting and disturbing that I read in a historical account of the camp purchased from a bookshop in Lublin. It had been translated from the original Russian into English.

Separated by barbed wire, men and women lived in identical barracks. They endured identical freezing snows in winter and searing heat in summer, they ate the same foul food, they were subjected to the same brutalising, dehumanising treatment, and they were slaughtered at the same rate—yet their lives differed in one profound way. In the men's huts, if you were too weak to hold your bread other men stole it from you. In the women's huts, if you were too weak to hold your bread other women held it for you and hand-fed you the pieces. Women are better human beings than men.

THAT NIGHT MIKE MOORE HOSTED a cocktail party for Warsaw's movers and shakers in one of the Marriott's many splendid reception rooms. A prominent New Zealand businessman and Dutch Honorary Consul, Alex van Heeren, was one of the guests. We knew each other and he stepped forward smiling warmly, extending his long right arm inside the sleeve of a beautifully cut bespoke suit palm down. This technique obliged people shaking his hand to approach him palm up, like a spacecraft returning to a mother ship. Donald Trump sometimes does it.

At my elbow Barry hissed, 'Is that the owner of Huka Lodge?' I nodded and began exchanging pleasantries with Alex when Baz hissed at me again, 'Introduce me!'

Fearing the worst, I said, 'Alex, have you met Barry?' Barry's hand attached itself like a limpet to the mother ship and could not be shaken loose.

'Soper. Private radio. How about a free weekend?'

Mortified, I reeled away to the drinks table. They were pouring me a hefty vodka and tonic when Barry approached with a grin. 'Got it!'

We flew to East Berlin's Schönefeld airport next afternoon. There was a small reception for us in the VIP terminal. Erich Honecker had kissed Khrushchev, Brezhnev, Chernenko, Andropov and Gorbachev smack on the mouth when they arrived here. Mike Moore had to make do with a handshake from a lowly official, but wore his disappointment well.

We drove into the heart of East Berlin at dusk. From the high windows of our bus I could look directly into orange rectangles of light and observe ordinary people relaxing after work, preparing meals and watching television. Television sets must have fetched a good price on the black market in East Berlin back then. The small, flickering set in my room at the Palast Hotel in Potsdamer Platz was chained securely to the wall, as was my desk lamp and the bed itself, though how you smuggled a bed out of a hotel in a suitcase was beyond me.

Within seconds my phone rang. It was Barry, kindly advising me that there were two free channels of slightly out-of-focus Filipino porn that didn't need English subtitles. I was too busy to look. I was feverishly writing a ten-page piece on Poland that I needed to fax back to the *Evening Post*.

The next morning I walked the short distance to Museum Island and the famous Pergamon Museum, home to all manner of glorious Islamic and Babylonian treasures, and most spectacularly of all, an almost entire second-century-BC Hellenic temple purloined from what is now Turkey by German archae-ologists. The altar included a sculptural frieze over 150 metres in length. In awe and admiration, I studied it closely. The level of detail was astonishing, right down to veins on the back of hands and tendons in wrists. Fifteen hundred years before the genius of Michelangelo, scores of artists with equally superb appreciation of musculature and bone mechanics would have needed to work together in harmony over many months to carve it out of stone. After the foul and cloying evil of Majdanek it was uplifting to see what human beings at their best were capable of.

Museum Island was spared from Allied bombing until the very last months of the war, when the German capital was pounded around the clock. Thankfully the most precious antiquities had been removed to salt mines for safekeeping or walled in for protection.

The next day we visited Cecilienhof Palace, the site of the July 1945 Potsdam Conference where over the course of two weeks Winston Churchill, Joseph Stalin and Harry Truman, plus their small armies of advisers, decided the fate of post-war Europe. The huge Tudor-style house, once the home of Crown Prince Wilhelm, was carefully selected because it had three separate entrances of equal grandeur so that none of the leaders would feel slighted on their arrival.

Growing up in Feilding, I was obsessed with nuclear weap-ons. It was an eerie feeling walking through the dark-panelled, elegantly furnished reception rooms knowing that in one of these rooms, in great secrecy, President Truman ordered the dropping of the atomic bomb on Hiroshima and less than a week later, on 6 August 1945, in a coastal Japanese city of no great military significance thousands of men, women and children were vaporised in an instant.

THE NEXT DAY A SMALL group of us headed out for a quick look at West Berlin. At the Brandenburg Gate crossing, beefy German border guards and a smattering of pimply Russian soldiers in ill-fitting khaki greatcoats awkwardly cradling Kalashnikovs mustered advancing pedestrians into two streams—tatty locals who were waved through quickly, and sleek Westerners who needed their passports stamped. *Listener* columnist and economist Brian Easton, with his heavy horn-rimmed glasses, fleshy Slavic face, swept-back thick, oily hair, short stubbly beard and penchant for polyester, has always resembled a Soviet physicist or chess grandmaster down on his luck. Border guards took one look at him and assumed he was kith and kin and waved him into the rapidly moving 'no questions asked' queue.

Before vanishing from sight, Brian turned to give the rest of us in the stationary queue a triumphant wave. It was a different story later that night. He was refused entry back into East Berlin because he could not furnish proof that he had ever left the place.

Our queue had to show passports and negotiate a maze of bleak corridors watched by remote-control cameras before negotiating a second gauntlet of hawkers on the other side. Poles and Czechs wanted to change our money. Locals had chunks of the wall for sale. Turks were flogging off Russian military wristwatches and military uniforms which, judging from the greasy lining inside the hats, were probably authentic.

I phoned the only Germans I knew, Manfred and Anneke. They used to live in the Coromandel, where Manfred painted landscapes. He hadn't got New Zealand out of his system. Somewhat incongruously, glorious depictions of wild surf and pōhutukawa in full bloom lit up the gloom of their artists' loft.

Over lunch, Manfred told us that he was born in East Berlin just as Russian troops were blasting their way into the outskirts of the besieged, ravaged capital of the Thousand Year Reich. The Cold War followed, and when that escalated his father moved his small leather factory to West Berlin. While Manfred finished his high-school education they continued living in East Berlin. They had two residences.

On 13 August 1961 he went to his girlfriend's sixteenth birthday party in the East. He could have spent the night with her or stayed on his own in the old family home at 78 Bornholmer Strasse, but for reasons he can't explain he decided to return to West Berlin on the midnight U-Bahn. He noticed an unusual level of troop activity in the street near the station and woke up next morning to find that just minutes after he had gone through, the border had closed behind him. He never saw his girlfriend or any of his other friends again.

In the 30 years since, he had travelled all over Europe, Asia, the Americas, Africa and even spent an agreeable week in Bluff staying at the Foveaux Hotel. But he had never made the short trip back across the city to his old home. Not until Barry convinced him to drive back with us.

We eased slowly through famous Checkpoint Charlie, Anneke steering with one hand and patting Manfred's trembling arm with the other. Barry thrust a microphone between them and asked him how he felt. Manfred joked that he was a typical German—he wasn't happy or unhappy, just cool. Which of course he wasn't—his voice was close to breaking.

We threaded our way through the concrete chicane, past the strobing orange lights, barbed-wire coils and barrier arms that we had all seen re-created in spy movies, out into East Berlin's streets. Manfred marvelled at the extensive renovation. Much of what had been rubble when he was a boy now gleamed, but he cautioned against being overly impressed with downtown East Berlin. He was right. While the grand and tidy boulevards were filled with Trabants and smoking Wartburgs, the side streets were largely empty, bumpy and strewn with rubbish. Every building needed maintenance. There were few shops and only a handful of pedestrians, nearly all wearing black nylon jackets and blue-grey denim jeans. Manfred's old family home on Bornholmer Strasse looked especially neglected.

'Nothing has changed,' said Manfred, close to tears as we moved through the dark foyer of the apartment and out into the grim, sour-smelling courtyard. 'It was rotten when I left thirty years ago. It's still the same.'

To cheer ourselves up we drove out into the countryside to find the village of Wandlitz, built specially for the politburo members and their families. Honecker, and before him Reich Master of the Hunt, Field Marshal Göring, enjoyed luxurious hunting lodges dotted throughout the surrounding forests. According to legend, when Honecker hosted lavish hunting parties for visiting VIPs, deer were drugged to make them easier to shoot.

In the end we couldn't find Wandlitz. That was the whole point. Quite deliberately, there were no road signs. Communist bosses constantly fearing uprising had designed it not to be found. It was hidden behind a high security wall and camouflaged by specially planted trees and vegetation. The people responsible for the Berlin Wall lived nervously behind another secret wall.

Still, we enjoyed the drive through seemingly unspoiled countryside. There wasn't a cattle beast in sight on any farm.

'They're all indoors. They are battery cows,' joked Manfred, 'looked after by battery farmers living in a battery society.'

Back in East Berlin we bought ice creams and took a stroll in the sun. The cones looked and tasted like recycled cardboard but the ice cream itself was delicious. Manfred grinned. 'This isn't so bad. I may come back every weekend from now on.' Anneke smiled and patted his arm. It was no longer shaking uncontrollably.

—

THE FOLLOWING MORNING, CHECKING OUT of the Palast, I was presented with a bill for US$1000 for my faxed articles. I didn't have US$1000 and was nearly in tears. I whimpered something to Barry.

'Leave it to me,' he said. He leaned across the counter and grabbed a middle-aged man by the tie, rasping, 'Oi! Squire! This is a fucking outrage. I demand to see the manager!'

He was the manager. A loud, heated exchange followed. I blocked my ears and fled. Barry was headed for the Gulag Archipelago and couldn't be saved, but I felt if I distanced myself sufficiently from him the Stasi might let me off with a pistol-whipping and a caution.

Barry eventually came running after me, grinning from ear to ear. 'Tommo, I got the prick to shift the decimal point. You owe them a hundred bucks!' It was still extortionate but it stopped me from having to sell my blood or a kidney.

Next stop was Prague. We flew in to the capital of the Czech Republic on a golden autumn afternoon. We caught a cab in from the airport and sucked in our breath in collective wonder at our first glimpse of the glorious medieval city. Barry, who is from Southland and fiercely loyal, conceded it was even flasher than Gore. Our driver, his kind, weathered face suffused with civic pride, turned and beamed.

'Is this your first visit to Prague?'

Barry leaned forward and barked, 'NO! WE WERE HERE LAST WEEK, SO DON'T TRY RIPPING US OFF, MUSH!' The details are hazy now, but I think he may have paid Barry when we got to our hotel.

That night at a lavish cocktail party hosted by Mike Moore I met the new Czech Foreign Minister, a very sweet, unassuming man who just a month earlier as a disgraced opponent of the previous regime was shovelling coal in the boiler room of one of the hideous apartment blocks that framed the most picturesque city in the world. When I asked him what the worst thing was about life under communism he paused for a moment then said sadly, 'They took away our Shakespeare.' My mother would totally understand.

Last stop was Budapest, the glorious Hungarian capital straddling the Danube. We stayed on Margaret Island in the middle of the river in a modern hotel with thermal baths.

Pattrick Smellie and I were allowed to sit in as observers at Mike Moore's trade talks with his opposite number. The frenetic pace of the trip was catching up with him—the black rings under his eyes were more panda-like than normal and the syntax had fallen out of his language altogether. He made very little sense. He was given to saying things like 'Rice. Tapioca. Singapore—same size as Lake Taupō—think about it!'

The Hungarians listened politely and shook his hand warmly in one of the courtyards of their truly wondrous Gothic revival Parliament building as a car approached to whisk him away. I was depressed but Pattrick, who had worked previously as a press officer for several cabinet ministers, cheerfully assured me that he had seen far worse. This was one of the better bilateral talks he had witnessed. This depressed me even more. He wrote a piece for *The Press* about this meeting which was headlined 'Moore Puzzles Hosts'.

The next morning we went to the Peto Institute, pioneers of 'conductive therapy' designed to enable children with cerebral palsy to lead more independent lives. Kiwi mums had brought children with varying degrees of disability to the institute, hoping desperately for a miracle but in their heart of hearts not really expecting one. They were thrilled to see us. It was humbling to observe their patience, kindness and resilience in the face of grinding daily heartbreak.

'What choice do we have?' asked one of the mums, cuddling her daughter, who hadn't moved or spoken since being accidentally deprived of oxygen during a routine surgical procedure.

I was there when a previously immobile five-year-old in callipers took his first steps. The delight of his therapists was one thing. The astonishment of his parents was another. The rapture on his face was something else altogether. I had flashbacks to when I was roughly the same age and wore a calliper. Without warning I needed a weeping bowl. I had to dash to a toilet and plunge my face repeatedly into a deep basin of freezing water until my chest-heaving sobbing slowed to a halt. It took ages.

That night Mike threw a cocktail party in our hotel and invited the Kiwi mums attending the Peto Institute to come along. It was a lovely gesture. Then he blotted his copybook.

'Look on the bright side,' he told some mums who had brought their children with them in prams. 'Other people's kids grow up and leave home. You'll always have them with you.' One of the mothers started screaming, 'I don't want to have my child with me forever! I don't want the rest of my life to be like this!' Crying uncontrollably, she wheeled her pretty, blank-eyed and mute daughter away. Looking daggers at Moore, the other mums went with her. Mike was genuinely baffled and distraught. 'What did I say? What did I say?'

ON OUR FINAL DAY WE drove through snow to the Austrian border via a Hungarian collective farm, which had entered into a joint venture with Canterbury graziers who were trying to convince them that electric fencing made for much more efficient pasture management, and that sheep in the wild survived winters perfectly well without five-star accommodation in barns. At long, rough-sawn refectory tables in the workers' cafeteria they served us a hearty goulash washed down with pálinka, a traditional fruit brandy that you have to keep well clear of naked flame. Locals proudly concede that it tastes like a blow across the bridge of the nose with a hammer.

Barry and I started trading toasts with two massive Hungarians, which morphed into a drinking contest. Six shots in Barry was weepily telling everyone he loved them. Eight shots in he lost the power of speech, as did one of the Hungarians and in a new language, known only to themselves, they communicated through a warm exchange of slurred vowel sounds. Ten shots in the last Hungarian in the race slid from view under the table, making me the winner.

I have never represented my country in competition before and it was a proud moment. Had I had a black flag with a silver fern emblazoned on it I would have draped it over my shoulders

Valerie Adams-fashion and done a victory lap. Instead, after Mike Moore had given a speech, I felt compelled to stand on the table and tell a joke. It was something very silly that somehow I remembered from an episode of *The Dick Van Dyke Show* in the 1960s. Dick Van Dyke's younger brother sits at a piano and announces that he is going to play the Hungarian Rhapsody No. 2 by Goulash. Dick protests that goulash is a stew. 'I don't care if he did drink, he was a damn fine composer!'

I don't know what was said in the translation but not much can have been lost because the Hungarians laughed uproariously and applauded wildly. Moore sat in po-faced silence. This was supposed to be his day in the sun, albeit watery, and I was hogging all the attention. Realising I had overstepped the mark I went in search of water. There was a crank-handle pump and a wooden trough in an adjacent shed. I filled the trough with icy water, bent over, plunged my head into it up to my collar and sucked up water like a camel. I did this until I was waterlogged, and waddled to the bus.

At the border the watchtowers were unmanned, the wide strip of raked soil there to detect footprints was sprouting weeds, and the barbed-wire fencing sagged from neglect. After discreetly emptying my bladder for what seemed like twenty minutes I set about using my topdressing and freezing worker's hands to repeatedly fold barbed wire back and forth until it heated at the hinge and snapped. I did this for everyone on the bus. I needed the exercise.

Back on board I sat with Barry, Pattrick Smellie and others, crowded at the back of the bus. We sang Beatles' songs very badly as we headed towards Vienna. Mike's wife, Yvonne, squeezed in beside Barry and me. It was a cross between Twister and Stacks on the Mill, with everyone laughing and singing 'Yellow Submarine' with wild, tuneless, gormless abandon.

The next minute Mike had pushed through the crowd and was shouting that he knew what game I was playing and he was having none of it. Barry assured him everything was above board. Yvonne shrank into the seat looking mortified.

Mike left as quickly as he came. The singing picked up where it had left off. Mike appeared again, even more enraged—he had worked on a stationary dredge, he could deal to me no trouble. Still half-intoxicated, I rose out of my chair, told Mike I didn't like being threatened, spun him around until he faced the front of the bus and told him to piss off. This he did.

Some people whooped and hollered. He had exasperated nearly everyone at some point on the trip, but had done nothing to deserve this. I sat back shamefaced.

I was still remonstrating with myself in my room in the Vienna Hilton, tapping out another long piece for the *Evening Post*, when there was a soft knocking on my door. A delegation of scribes led by Barry wanted me to do a cartoon of Mike as a thank-you present, which they could give to him at the final debriefing that evening. I protested that this would be the very last thing Mike wanted. They insisted, and I did my best.

At the briefing Mike didn't mince his words—he had poured his heart into this trip, he had sweated blood to make it happen and we were all a bunch of ungrateful, selfish bastards.

'It's been long journey, Mike. We're all tired, Mike,' ventured the deputy leader of the delegation soothingly. 'It has been a wonderful experience. The opportunity of a lifetime, Mike. And as a token of our appreciation, Mike, we'd like to give you this gift.'

He bravely handed over my cartoon. Mike looked at it briefly before hurling it away.

'GET FUCKED! YOU CAN ALL GET FUCKED!' And with that he stormed out.

We regrouped in a subdued circle in the palatial bar. The consensus was that I had done my best to make amends and that Mike had behaved poorly in response.

When the expensive cocktails eventually kicked in, a raucous evening ensued. Next door in a vast ballroom, a string quartet played Strauss waltzes to an empty dancefloor and a solitary couple siting by themselves in the far corner—Mike and Yvonne. Barry has a good heart, and went across to join them. Mike was tearful.

'I love Tom. I love Tom. I fucked up. I fucked up!'

When we met in a back corridor of Parliament a few weeks later he sheepishly invited me to his office for a drink, I sheepishly consented and we were soon laughing our heads off. Years later, when he became head of the World Trade Organization he sent me an affectionate postcard from Geneva. Mike has a good heart too. Left unspoken was the understanding that all relationships are complicated, divine mysteries that don't bear too much analysis.

Didn't I know it! Crouched low over my typewriter at small hotel desks for long stretches at a time and, when there wasn't a desk, resorting to using the corners of beds and splaying my feet at right angles to get close enough to the keyboard, I popped a disc in my lower back. ('At the time of the alleged incident, Your Honour, my client was self-medicating on pálinka . . .') The long flight home in cramped seats in the noisy, vibrating Boeing 727 was agony.

We parked at the Defence Forces terminal on the opposite side of Wellington airport, next to the breakers rolling into Lyall Bay. There was no taxi rank. Other wives, husbands, sweethearts and boyfriends were there to pick up their partners. There was no sign of Helen. As they left, people offered me rides. I shook my head. It was all arranged. I was sorted. This was before cell phones, so I asked if I could use a phone in the traffic-control office to call home just to check that nothing had gone wrong. No one answered. I left a message.

When the compound emptied I sat out on the road beside my suitcase and waited forlornly. A flight sergeant emerged, having switched off the lights and locked the place up. He took pity on me and said I could borrow their phone again.

This time Helen answered. I asked if she was coming to pick me up. There was no disguising the irritation in her voice. Had an Air Force Skyhawk written it in the sky with white smoke it couldn't have been more obvious—my relationship with Helen was failing again. It would end for sure. The only question was when.

We hardly spoke on the drive home. The kids were pleased to see me.

CHAPTER TWENTY-EIGHT

MEETING ED

LATER THAT YEAR, OUT OF the blue, I received an invitation to be an after-dinner speaker at a black-tie dinner that changed my life forever and for the better—I just didn't know it yet.

In 1990 New Zealand celebrated its sesquicentenary. Foreign Affairs dispensed additional largesse to embassies and high commissions around the globe so that our one hundred and fiftieth birthday could be acknowledged in style. When my mate Dennis Grant, at the time a widely admired senior member of the Canberra Press Gallery—and I have this on no lesser authority than Dennis himself—heard that our high commissioner was contemplating some sort of bash with sawdust on the floor where a Kiwi-born NRL player would say a few words, one of which would be 'Maaaaaate', Denny felt morally obliged to intervene and suggested a glittering dinner at the National Press Club instead, with Sir Edmund

Hillary to give the main speech. This implied a subsidiary role for another orator, and when that question arose Dennis was ready. He knew just the right man for the job.

I had no idea of Denny's involvement when the formal invitation to be Ed's warm-up act arrived. I thought it was entirely on my own merits, and that Australia was treating me with a respect and deference my own country had cruelly long denied me.

I had never met Hillary, and this made me giddy with excitement as well. When he strode purposefully into the Koru Lounge at Auckland International Airport he looked so like himself I barely recognised him. He had a physical presence and an aura that made him appear closer to seven foot than his six foot two. We sat next to each other on the plane and hardly exchanged a word. I scribbled speech notes frantically.

I lost him at the international arrivals hall. We had a connecting flight to Canberra leaving shortly from the domestic terminal on the opposite side of the aerodrome. Ed would just have to fend for himself. Lugging my big suitcase, I had a hell of a time getting there and arrived at the departure gate drenched in sweat just as they were about to close the doors. Ed was waiting for me, as cool as a cucumber. 'I was getting a bit worried. They've been paging you.'

We talked a bit more on the flight but he didn't really loosen up until the end of the evening when I bought him his first ever glass of Jameson's Irish whiskey, which he took to instantly. It had been an enjoyable night.

In my speech I said that we had crossed the Tasman at 31,000 feet, just a little higher than Everest, and it was minus 50 degrees outside, just a little colder than Everest. Ed asked for a blanket and went outside and sat on the wing. He was as happy as a sand-boy the whole journey. The air hostesses had a hell of a job coaxing him back into the cabin. 'Please, Sir Edmund. We have to land. We can't keep circling like this . . .'

The audience, a mixture of Ockers and Kiwis, enjoyed my gentle mocking of the great man, and the great man enjoyed it even more.

'I'll have to lift my game.' He beamed when I sat down. There was a steely glint in his pale blue-grey eyes. It suddenly struck me that he was deadly serious. He was 71 years old and still fiercely competitive. He disguised his ruthless streak well in his autumn years—he knew that at full force it wasn't attractive and it had got him into bitter disputes with a number of climbing companions and fellow adventurers over the years. I caught whiffs of it again in later dealings with him. It worked to his advantage this night, though. He wasn't going to be upstaged by a chubby, waddling, balding cartoonist and gave a tremendous speech, punctuated frequently by laughter, applause—and sharp, gasping intakes of breath when he recounted some of his close calls in the wild. It was a thrill discovering that hard-nosed cynical Australians held Ed in much the same affection and awe as Kiwis do.

I stayed that night with Dennis Grant and his wickedly droll wife, Robyn. Denny knew I had been working on a television drama about David Lange, who he was very close to when he worked in the Wellington Press Gallery, and he wanted to know what I thought of his idea for a movie. He proceeded to tell me about New Year's Eve 1978, when he was a member of a television news crew in the SAFE Air Argosy night-time freight delivery run that filmed a close encounter with a UFO off the Kaikōura coast of the South Island. I was stunned when he recounted the extraordinary moment a strange ball of light buzzed their aircraft as they flew north—sweeping around them, under them, over them, drawing alongside them and whizzing away from them at what science-fiction fans would call warp speed.

'I have no idea what it was,' recalled Dennis dryly, 'but it wasn't a fucking squid boat as some experts suggest. Air Traffic Control radar tends not to record fishing boats dragging nets at twelve thousand feet. Nor does cockpit radar. And it wasn't Venus. Our pilots were reasonably familiar with where Venus is positioned in the sky.'

When I asked him why he had never told me this before he responded simply that he kept the story to himself because he didn't want people to think he was mad. His Channel 10 mate, the reporter who broke the story, Quentin Fogarty, was all but broken himself by the event and the media feeding frenzy that followed.

While Dennis diligently scribbled down copious notes on a yellow legal pad I gave him the full benefit of my vast knowledge of moviemaking, which at that point consisted solely of co-writing an animated feature film about a neurotic sheepdog. As a consequence, making movies was playing on my mind when I flew back to Sydney with Ed the next morning.

All the way through the international departures terminal he was besieged by autograph-hunters and people who wanted their picture taken with him. They were of every nationality and sometimes sign language bordering on charades was required. He consented without fuss. It looked exhausting.

'How long has this been going on?' I asked.

'Forty years,' he replied, flashing the famous grin.

He insisted on buying me lunch and took me to a discreetly tucked-away white-linen and silver-service restaurant that I never knew existed. We were totally at ease in each other's company now, laughing and joking with each other. I was curious to know why a film had never been made about his exploits. He told me that he had been approached over the years by some big-name Hollywood types, but the right person hadn't asked. I blurted out that I would love to do it. He had known me less than 24 hours. He replied evenly, 'You are the right person.'

I was staggered, thrilled and terrified all at once. As is my wont in moments like these, I immediately applied the handbrake and provided him with an escape clause. I advised him to discuss it with his wife and family.

It was mid-December. We would talk again in the New Year, after he had given it more thought, and if he still felt the same way I would do everything in my power to make a movie worthy of his life.

Back in Wellington I scoured second-hand bookshops for everything I could find on or by Ed. He wrote his first, and in many ways his best, book, *High Adventure*, in longhand just months after the successful 1953 British expedition to Everest, when every lung-burning step of the ascent was still fresh and vivid. The writing is so visceral and so real, I read it that summer shivering under a blanket, fearful I might lose my fingers and toes to frostbite. It was blindingly obvious that, told well, it would make a stunning movie.

I had a book of my own out that Christmas, *Private Parts*. Ed was given a copy as a present and luckily for me he enjoyed it. The Hillarys had been holidaying in the South Island. I caught up with them at a motel on Peka Peka Beach on their road trip back to Auckland, meeting June Mulgrew, Lady Hillary, for the first time. She proved to be a beautiful, elegant, lively, strong-willed force of nature in her own right. Fortunately, we clicked as well. They had talked the movie idea through and they gave the project and my handling of it their full and unconditional blessing. My head reeled with giddy excitement and ached with the weight of responsibility at the same time.

For research purposes I needed to accompany them on their next trip to the Solukhumbu in Eastern Nepal and see for myself the 30 schools, half-dozen medical clinics, three airstrips, two hospitals and many bridges Sir Edmund's Himalayan Trust had funded and built along the hill trail to Everest. I told my mate Mark Sainsbury, a reporter on *Holmes*, that he should come as well. Taking a leaf out of the Dennis Grant playbook, Mark played the age card—how much longer could the hero of Everest keep going? Could this be his last trip to his second home—the land he loved and the people he loved, the Sherpas, who worshipped like a god the man they called Burra Sahib? He laid it on shamelessly. TVNZ bought every wild exaggeration, all of which very nearly came to pass.

MEANWHILE, BACK IN FEILDING MY father's heart was failing him again. He was so frail he had to move out of the tribal seat in Owen Street to Wimbledon Villa rest home in Manchester Street. When I heard from sister Sue that he had to be readmitted to Palmerston North Hospital for treatment I rang the cardiac ward several times to talk to him but I could never get through.

He always seemed to be sleeping or was with a doctor or nurse and could not be disturbed.

One evening my youngest brother, Rob, rang. Rob is a very funny man and just about the nicest person on the planet. I asked him how he was.

'Not very good, actually,' he replied solemnly, which was unlike him.

'Why, what's wrong?'

'I've just been talking to the old man.'

I braced myself for bad news. 'Is he OK? I can't get through to him on the phone.'

Rob's voice cracked. 'I know. He told me that just now.'

Rob then quoted what my father said to him next: '"Egghead is trying to ring me. I'm refusing to take his calls. I want my death on his conscience!"'

I sighed. What had I ever done to warrant this? My father returned to Wimbledon Villa. When friends pushed his wheelchair around the block, to give him some fresh air and some sun on his face, he told them in his still-thick Ulster brogue that he was going home. If they could see the Wimbledon Villa looming up they smiled and said, 'Yes, Tom, we're nearly there . . .' But that's not what he meant.

I got on with my preparation for Nepal, going for long walks over the Wellington hills in my new tramping boots with a pack on my back, desperately trying to lose weight and get fit, my lower back still stabbing me intermittently with searing pain. Two physiotherapists giving me treatment said there was nothing more they could do. It was my age. I would have to live with some degree of chronic discomfort for the rest of my days.

As our mid-April departure day approached, every couple of mornings I woke to find coils of fax paper spilling out of my machine—updates on Sir Edmund's already immaculate planning, hand-written in his neat copperplate. I started to feel like Ed and George Lowe on the eve of their departure to join the British expedition in 1953—except I would arrive in Nepal in a wide-bodied jet after just two days of travel. Travelling by

Sunderland flying boat, passenger liner and steam train, it took them three weeks.

I landed at Kathmandu airport in a misty, dusty, gathering dusk. When I finally escaped the teeming madness of the international arrivals hall a deep, velvet blackness had descended over the city. There was barely any street lighting. En route to the Shangri-La Hotel, my dilapidated taxi had to circumnavigate sacred cows sleeping smugly in the centre of the streets. We rattled past open fires showering sparks, and past the turmeric glow of kerosene lamps in small pavement stalls. Ghostly figures on ancient bicycles wobbled in and out of a ground mist. It was magical, enchanting and deeply mysterious. I couldn't wait to discover in the morning what sort of world I had flown into.

I awoke to the caw of large black crows on my balcony. Below me in the exquisite walled gardens of the Shangri-La a line of kneeling men in pristine white tunics and turbans cut the lawn with scissors. There was scent and incense floating in the still air.

I endeavoured to capture the intoxicating strangeness of those first days in an early draft of my screenplay, *Higher Ground*.

201 EXT. SWAYAMBHUNATH STUPA—DAWN

In a jumble of shrines overlooking a city draped
in fog, monks chant, gongs sound and monkeys
scramble over stone temple-dogs splattered
with wax and red powder.

Far below, roosters crow and dogs yelp—

Beyond the shrouded, ramshackle city, jagged
Himalayan peaks are backlit by the rising sun.
It is the start of a new day in the fairy-tale
mountain kingdom of Nepal.

Super the Title: Kathmandu—31 March 1975

202 EXT. KATHMANDU—EARLY MORNING

> HILLARY, now in his fifties, walks with LOUISE,
> now in her forties, down a narrow alley already
> teeming with cyclists, monks and merchants.
>
> Incense burns from countless small shrines.
> Baskets of brightly coloured fruits, vegetables
> and spice narrow the streets even further—

Mark Sainsbury, his nuggety cameraman Alan Sylvester and I spent four days in the Kathmandu valley acclimatising to altitude, sightseeing and meeting the rest of Ed's expedition for drinks hosted by tiny, feisty, elderly Elizabeth Hawley, a Reuters correspondent who had never gone home. She was New Zealand's honorary consul and the world's foremost authority on Himalayan climbing expeditions. Her house was Somerset Maugham meets *Casablanca*—tiled floors, thick walls, arched doorways, lots of latticework, heavy furniture, revolving ceiling fans and a much-scolded servant wearing a topi hat serving hefty gins in crystal buckets.

The trekking party included Ed's old chums, the towering Zeke O'Connor, a former gridiron player from Vancouver, and burly Larry Witherbee, a former Sears, Roebuck executive from Chicago, who ran the Canadian and US branches of the Himalayan Trust respectively, plus a cluster of wealthy donors from north and south of the border: multi-millionaire Alex Tilley, who invented the famous hat bearing his name; his attractive daughter, Alison, whose buxom breasts were always threatening to fall out of her blouse; slow-talking mega-vague, mega-millionaire Ted Lorimar, whose grandfather invented extruded aluminium furniture and tampons (don't even think about joining those dots—you'll go mad), and his wealth consultant, whose other major client was the Emir of Qatar (last I heard, this man was serving time in a US prison for fraud, where he is probably advising El Chapo); Barbara, a wealthy Canadian who had been successfully married several times and to dull the pain of yet another annulment was hurling herself into a rugged wilderness with enough creams, potions and painkillers in a belt around her waist to stock a small pharmacy, and two steps behind her a trusty Sherpa carrying a Fortnum & Mason-like hamper of exotic treats and delicacies that no intrepid explorer should be without; and Professor John Redpath, a professor of logical positivism and North America's leading expert on the writings of Ayn Rand—pretty much what you'd find on any wet Sunday in any tramping hut in New Zealand.

Nepal was due to go to the polls. Kathmandu walls were festooned with strange political logos. Due to widespread illiteracy, a government committee allocated recognisable symbols and names to the numerous political parties. The bicycle party, the bullock party and the spectacles party were happy enough. The frog party and the toilet-brush party felt short-changed.

Professor Redpath asked Mark Sainsbury and me if there was any way he could possibly address the Nepalese people live on television on the evils of democratic socialism and wealth redistribution. Sadly, the people of the second poorest country on Earth were denied this treat, as the weather cleared in the Solukhumbu and we had to head for the hills.

The King of Nepal laid on two of his Super Puma helicopters for Ed. Since it was a religious holiday, sacrificial offerings needed to be made to the gods in order for us to fly. My heart sank when six bleating goats were brought forward, prayers were uttered and a chanting *pujaree* (priest) cut their throats one by one. Still spurting blood, the twitching carcases were dragged by the hind legs around the choppers, tracing out crimson concentric circles. I will never complain about an Air New Zealand safety video again.

We lifted off in a convoy heading southeast, clattering above paddy fields, soaring over glorious hilltop temples, and sweeping past terraced hillside after hillside, until the terrain became too steep and wild for cultivation. Heading up steep gorges with waterfalls cascading down towering rock faces, the chopper ahead of us was dwarfed by the immensity of the landscape into a child's toy. A beaming Ed tapped me on my knee and pointed out the Everest massif standing head and shoulders above every other great peak on the horizon. Low sun turned the upper ramparts of Everest bronze. The taste of butterscotch filled my mouth.

Autograph-hunters surged around Ed when we landed at Lukla, the airport he had helped the locals construct in 1964, which is now named after him and Tenzing. With a short, narrow, sloping runway dropping away into a ravine at the lower end and running into a sheer mountain face at the upper end, there is no margin for pilot error and no coming back if engines falter or stall. You never know if you are going to make it. All you know for certain is the pilots have put down their cell phones, have taken their feet off the dashboard and are paying close attention. It is deemed by aviation experts to be one of the most dangerous airfields in the world. They get no argument from me.

Ed alighted as white as a sheet, his damp brow creased with discomfort, and moved urgently and distractedly through the throng. It had nothing to do with his runway.

'Ed's got the squitters,' explained June matter-of-factly.

We set off that afternoon at a leisurely pace up a winding trail through a wide ravine carved out by the raging Dudh Kosi river. We missed the rhododendrons in bloom, but glorious apple and apricot orchards were in full flower. Hens scratched in vegetable gardens. Smoke curled up from cosy Sherpa homes with timber-shingle roofs held down by stones. Above us, through forest, we caught glimpses of icy, fluted spires. It was breathtakingly beautiful.

I walked with June, behind Ed so she could keep an eye on him. He was breathing heavily. Mingma Tsering, his *sirdar* (head man), gripped the belt of Ed's trousers tightly and hoisted him up every step. From the rear, in his voluminous, baggy grey corduroys, Ed resembled an old bull elephant.

THE SMALL HAMLET OF PHAKDING was in deep shadow and freezing cold when we arrived. Ed went straight to bed. His old climbing buddy from Everest, George Lowe, was there. George and I later became good friends—he thanked me tearfully for acknowledging his contribution to the conquest of Everest in the fortieth-anniversary documentary I made for UK's Channel 4, but he was testy and difficult that night in Phakding, fed up I guess at meeting yet another bloody film crew and a writer obsessed with Hillary. He insisted on camera to Mark that Ed was the perfect man to conquer Everest, that he had used his fame to good ends and this fame would have been wasted on anyone else, but there was regret and a sadness lurking beneath the surface of his answers. He was the 'nearly' man and you could see he felt it keenly.

From all my research I am convinced that, on that particular mountain at that particular time, George was the second fittest climber after Ed—stronger even than Tenzing Norgay, who was still feeling the effects of the malaria he had caught the year before while climbing with the Swiss. But there was symmetry and poetry in having a man from the east and a man from the west stand on the world's highest point together. Had it been a brutally unsentimental All Black selector reading out the names of the first assault team the list would have been:

E.P. Hillary, Auckland
W.G. Lowe, Hawke's Bay

This is a big call, but I think I can legitimately make the claim. For *View from the Top*, my New Zealand Hillary documentary, I interviewed or spoke to all the surviving members who made it to the fortieth-anniversary celebrations in Nepal. I later interviewed on camera Charles Wylie, the expedition's organising secretary, translator and stores master, in his sunny Sussex cottage. During the war he commanded a Gurkha company. On the wall there was an oil portrait of his Gurkha batman, who the Japanese beheaded in front of him as punishment when he was a prisoner of war. After the interview the scholarly, soft-spoken Charles shook my hand and said I knew more about the expedition than anyone he had ever met. The expedition leader, John Hunt, said much the same thing when I interviewed him in Lukla the year before. I was so buoyed by this affirmation I could have skipped up Everest in plimsolls and shorts at that moment.

George Lowe's most immense contribution to the expedition was on the penultimate day. It was George who led, cutting all the steps up to Camp 9 on the Southeast Ridge. It was George who found the small, precarious ledge that Ed and Tenzing pitched their tent on. As photographs attest, he was still fresh and strong, taking off his oxygen mask and gloves to take photos. He asked Ed if there was room for another man in the summit assault team.

'Sorry, George,' said Ed. 'I've done the sums. We don't have enough oxygen.'

George returned to Camp 8 on the South Col with the English climber Alfred Gregory and the Sherpa Pasang. Gregory had a dreadful night, constipated and howling with pain at the end of George's sleeping bag, straining to shit into a tin. He descended with Pasang the next morning, leaving George alone to wait for Ed and Tenzing's return, or to come down alone if they failed to show up. For the best part of a full day he was the mountaineering equivalent of Michael Collins in the command module orbiting the moon on his own while Neil Armstrong and Buzz Aldrin descended to the dead, dusty surface in the lunar module.

Late in the afternoon George saw two specks roped together returning slowly. He made some soup, poured it into a Thermos flask and rushed up to meet them—before realising they were still at least an hour away. Spent from his efforts, he staggered back to his tent, relieved to know they were safe and well. When they got closer he walked up slowly carrying oxygen cylinders and the Thermos flask.

Everyone knows what Ed said to him: 'Well, George, we knocked the bastard off.' What is less well known is George's equally laconic, and should be iconic, reply: 'Thought you must have. Here, have a cup of soup.'

While Tenzing fell into an exhausted sleep in his tent, the two New Zealanders talked excitedly late into the night. Ed gave George some rocks that he had collected just below the summit.

'You could have climbed it easy, George,' Ed told his old

friend, which was flattering but small comfort.

The George Lowe we met at Phakding was still extremely fit and supple. Mark and I carried emergency medicinal supplies of Baileys Irish Cream and Jameson's with us, and after several glasses George relaxed and began reciting poetry. Then to demonstrate his fitness he tucked one leg, then the other, behind his neck in a yoga pose that I don't recommend.

He was gone early next morning, no doubt racing over some high mountain pass while we struggled up the gorge towards Namche Bazaar. It was steep and hard, but Mark enlivened proceedings by sprinting ahead with Alan, setting up the sticks and pretending to do pieces to camera as June approached. 'They call her the Bitch of the Snows . . . oh, hello June.'

If you arrive at the wrong time of the day the Namche hill is a killer even for fit climbers. Infra-red radiation reflecting off surrounding peaks turns it into a 2000-foot-high microwave oven. I was well cooked that first trip.

Near the top, Alison somehow found the energy to approach Mark and Alan with her idea about shooting an improvised romance movie starring herself and using Sherpas as extras. She accepted the concept still needed a little work. Mark foisted her onto me, telling her that I was a really famous film producer back in New Zealand and that she needed to pitch it to me. She bounded over full of enthusiasm, but, fighting for breath, I was in no condition to respond. Spotting a babbling mountain stream she decided she needed to wash her hair, and whipped off her white blouse and got down to her black bra—I think it was black; oxygen deprivation had leached all the colour out of my world at this point. She dashed forward and proceeded to plunge her head into the icy stream. It came out pretty quickly, followed seconds later by high-pitched yelping when she had recovered from the initial shock.

CHAPTER TWENTY-NINE

EXPERIENCES NEAR DEATH

WE OVERNIGHTED IN NAMCHE BAZAAR, an ancient trading post between Nepal and Tibet, and headed over the hill to the village of Khumjung the next morning, where Ed had built the first of his schools. Sherpa children, their dusty, smudged faces and eyes bright with excitement, formed two long lines to drape white silk *karata* around his neck, chanting, 'HILAREE ZINDABAD! HILAREE ZINDABAD!'

Later Ed slumped in a chair to watch a boisterous school concert performed in his honour. When snow started to fall, softly at first, then heavily, June persuaded him to leave. With Mingma's assistance he shuffled slowly up towards his *sirdar's* home in the adjacent village of Kunde through stone-walled fields being blanketed in phosphorescent snow.

'It's so beautiful,' I commented to Ed. He smiled. I noticed that his lips were turning blue.

'You should have seen it when we first came here. Juniper and rhododendron forest swept down to the edge of the fields...'

I put some of what I was feeling into scenes in *Higher Ground*, dramatising Ed's very first footsteps into these hills.

EXT. HILL TRAIL TO EVEREST—1951

HILLARY leads at a brisk pace uphill—

They pass a *chorten*, a long cairn of carefully stacked Mani stones, all carved with the Sanskrit inscription, '*Om mani padme hum*', which translates to 'the jewel in the lotus'.

Further back, RIDDIFORD struggles, having difficulty lighting a cigarette on the move—

HILLARY stops and looks back, irritated—

HILLARY: Jesus, Earle, pull finger!

Ahead the trail rises to a stupa and a prayer pole with fluttering flags, beneath which a scruffy SHERPA MAN waits.

ANNULLU: Namaste!

HILLARY: Namaste!

ANNULLU: You Kiwi?

HILLARY: Yes, we Kiwi.

The SHERPA MAN grins as RIDDIFORD arrives panting—

ANNULLU: Shipton Sahib, waiting! Close getting.

RIDDIFORD sags with relief—

RIDDIFORD: Thank God.

ANNULLU: Come! Come!

RIDDIFORD goes to follow, until HILLARY grabs his arm—

HILLARY: Hold your horses, Earle.

Something in HILLARY'S tone makes RIDDIFORD hesitate—

HILLARY (cont'd): I stole a library book once.

RIDDIFORD can't believe he is hearing this.

RIDDIFORD: I won't tell anyone if you don't.

HILLARY waves his battered copy of *Nanda Devi*—

HILLARY: *Nanda Devi* by Eric Shipton! The man's a legend! What's he going to make of two ragged-arse Kiwis from the back of beyond?

(BEAT/anxious)

Maybe this wasn't such a good idea?

RIDDIFORD: Take a deep breath, Ed, for Christ's sake!

INT. SHERPA HOME, GROUND FLOOR—1951

ANNULLU, HILLARY and RIDDIFORD enter a dark basement full of calm, contented, steaming yaks.

A pensive HILLARY has to duck his head as they climb a flight of rickety stairs—

INT. SHERPA HOME, KITCHEN (UPPER FLOOR)—1951

In the gloom the brass on wooden barrels and jugs glows magically. Seated by a smoky stove are four scruffy Englishmen, TOM BOURDILLON, CHARLES EVANS, MICHAEL WARD and a wiry, unshaven older man. He has a pipe in his mouth. He is wearing a fraying jersey and tennis shoes with no socks.

It is ERIC SHIPTON, barely recognisable from the Alpine Club newsreel. He leaps to his feet and warmly extends his hand—

HILLARY is immediately put at ease—

RIDDIFORD stiffens—

SHIPTON: Eric Shipton. Frightfully decent of you
chaps to join us at such short notice.

RIDDIFORD bows as he shakes hands—

RIDDIFORD: Riddiford. Earle Herbert Riddiford,
pleased to meet you, sir.

SHIPTON: Likewise. It's Eric.

HILLARY (cheerful): G'day, Eric. Ed Hillary.

SHIPTON: You chaps must have motored. The
bush telegraph said you were still days away.

HILLARY's grin couldn't get any wider—

While Mingma's wife, the tiny Ang Dooli, fussed over Ed, her
deaf-mute, laughing son Temba, a brilliant painter, served us
yak stew and rice in the smoky kitchen. We drank bottles of the
local tipple, chang, along with lots of rum and Coke. Ed loved to
laugh, so Mark and I told jokes. Mindful that we were hogging
the floor, we turned to Alison and Professor Redpath and said it
was Canada's turn.

'Canadians are not renowned for their sense of humour,'
Alison said wistfully. It was certainly true in the professor's case.

Complaining of headaches and tiredness, Ed retired to
the bright-yellow tent set up for him and June on the front
courtyard. June was confident he would be fine in the morning.

When the North Americans headed out to the dormitory,
Alan set up his camera and Mark interviewed Mingma about
his friendship with Ed.

'Burra Sahib, he old getting. Burra Sahib, he tired getting...'
said Mingma sadly.

Life at this altitude is harsh. Sherpas living in the shadow of Everest are tough, stoic people not given to displaying their emotions. They very seldom cry, but when Mark asked Mingma to describe what Hillary meant to the Sherpa people, tears started trickling down his weathered, dusty cheeks, leaving trails of clean skin in their wake. 'The Burra Sahib, he is our mother . . . and our father . . .' There can be no higher accolade than that.

I WOKE UP THE NEXT morning in the crowded dormitory with the taste of butterscotch in my mouth. I was puzzled at first, then realised my back pain had vanished. Weight loss and exercise had hounded and shepherded errant lumbar vertebrae back into position and they have remained there ever since.

The news about Ed was not so good. His condition had worsened overnight. He was as grey as the skies overhead and had difficulty speaking. He was shifted into a bare downstairs storeroom, where he was joined by his younger brother, Rex, who had got crook doing routine maintenance on the nearby Kunde hospital—the hospital he and Ed had built with others in 1996.

The hospital doctor paid a visit. She listened to Ed's heart and clipped a digital pulse oximeter on one of his fingers. His pulse was too high and his blood-oxygen saturation was too low. He had altitude sickness. We were at 13,000 feet; he needed to go low immediately.

Dark clouds spilling over the rim of the Dudh Kosi valley blotted out the sun and made helicopter rescue impossible. He was put on oxygen and had another bad night. The cloud cover was no better the next day. Ed would have to wait out another night.

A gnawing anxiety infected the whole party. Professor Redpath decided he was critically ill as well. June, who is from the 'run it under a cold tap' school of nursing, asked him what his symptoms were. He described gnawing anxiety.

'You're fine,' she snapped, heading back to attend to Ed.

'This is me we're talking about!' shouted the professor, who was being neither logical nor positive.

The day dragged on. Late afternoon the doctor made a shocking admission—they were down to a handful of oxygen bottles and for some reason some of these were not compatible with the breathing mask. There was a chance Ed may not make it through the night. As darkness approached and Ed's old friends became numb and incapacitated by the prospect of his impending death, Mark Sainsbury took charge, racing tirelessly back and forth to the hospital trying to find piping and valves that would render the rogue oxygen cylinders useful—with no luck.

Shortly after two in the morning, the gauge on the last oxygen cylinder read empty. The pulse oximeter reported that Ed's oxygen saturation was 40 per cent and falling. If it fell below 30 per cent there would not be enough oxygen in his blood to keep his cardiac muscle working. We braced ourselves for the worst, but to our astonishment the gas kept bubbling—obviously, the gauge was faulty but we favoured the idea of miracles at this point.

Eventually the flow trickled to a halt and under his mask Ed's face turned grey and his lips turned blue. Suppressed grief made the room claustrophobic. I stepped out into the icy night for some fresh air. The cloud cover had lifted, a good portent for the morning, and the highest peaks in the world were silhouetted like Halloween pumpkin teeth against the brightest stars—a zillion shimmering diamonds on a deep purple jeweller's velvet.

As I was marvelling at this wondrous sight, the face of my best friend at vet school, Tom Quinlan, appeared in full colour and three-quarter profile. He was smiling his knowing smile and a celestial wind was ruffling his fine hair. Tom had died from cancer five years earlier.

I have no explanation for this. I knew it wasn't oxygen deprivation. When the doctor clipped the oximeter on my finger my oxygen saturation was a very respectable 93 per cent. I headed back into the storeroom and blurted out something that again I have no explanation for: 'My father has just died, but Ed will live!'

As the words came out of my mouth I was hearing them at the same time as everyone else and it occurred to me that I sounded mad. I told myself to keep quiet. Upstairs, Temba prayed at a beautiful and surprisingly elaborate Buddhist altar and thrashed away on cymbals, oblivious to the racket he was making. On the floor directly below him, at the foot of Ed's bed, his father rocked back and forward, repeating a mantra in a trance-like state.

Ed's old mate, the fearless climber Murray Jones, headed off to bed deeply distressed. Sheer exhaustion overtook June as well, leaving Mark and I doing a shift on our own with the two ailing Hillary brothers.

Ed suddenly decided to get out of bed, strictly against doctor's orders. We didn't know him very well then and were reduced to pleading politely, 'Please, Sir Edmund. Sir Edmund, please, could you get back into bed, Sir Edmund.' He ignored us.

'I have to pack my bags for the chopper,' he rasped, reaching for things. Even assuming it would arrive at first light, that was still hours away. Mark and I were getting desperate. Rex Hillary, who had barely said a word the past two days, suddenly sat up bolt upright and barked, 'GET BACK INTO BED, YOU DAFT BUGGER!' Ed meekly obeyed his younger brother, which was a huge relief because somehow he was as weak as a kitten but still strong as an ox.

At his best, Ed's strength, stamina and iron will were almost super-human. In his terrific book on the 1953 expedition, *Coronation Everest*, the *Times* correspondent James Morris (who became the celebrated travel writer Jan Morris after a sex change) wrote clipped, economical pen-portraits of all twelve men in the climbing party, save for Ed; Morris devoted a full page to the New Zealander, waxing lyrical and effusive in a manner no one else could ever match. Here is a fragment:

> [Hillary] worked in the half light, huge and
> cheerful, his movement not so much graceful as
> unshakably assured, his energy almost demonic.
> He had a tremendous, bursting, elemental,
> infectious, glorious vitality about him, like
> some bright burly diesel express pounding
> across America . . .

Twenty minutes later, Ed announced he needed to take a leak. It was snowing heavily outside; besides, he wasn't supposed to move. Mark spotted an empty can of Edmonds 'Sure to Rise' baking powder on a ledge and grabbed it.

'I'll hold the tin if you do the honours with the plumbing.' I did the honours and, with nary a second to spare, urine was soon drumming into the Edmonds tin. Ed and I both felt a little self-conscious. 'Quick, get the camera for the blackmail photographs,' joked Mark. Despite being desperately sick, Ed started laughing under his oxygen mask. I was confident then that he was going to make it.

Murray Jones returned, and it might have been him who suddenly remembered that the Hotel Everest View, several miles away on the ridge high above Khumjung village, had oxygen in every room for guests. Mingma and another son raced off down the valley in the pitch black through shin-deep snow to fetch some.

When the first rays of the new day hit the tops of the distant peaks I joined June in the courtyard.

'Where are they?' she whispered. 'They should be back by now.'

Sherpas have great eyesight. Beside her Temba grinned excitedly, tugged her sleeve and pointed. Barely visible in the deep shadow, two specks were racing up between stone walls— his father and brother shouting and waving in triumph. June wept silently.

The colour returned to Ed's cheeks within seconds of him being attached to fresh oxygen. Word came through from Kathmandu that the king's Puma was on its way, but the good weather wouldn't last.

Being the biggest, Mark and I took an arm each and propelled Ed to the landing spot marked in the snow. He was a dead weight and it took some effort. Then a respected Sherpa elder, the tall, handsome Kumbo Chumbi, resplendent in traditional Tibetan costume, took Ed lightly by one hand, like he was leading a debutante onto a dancefloor for a supper waltz, and somehow, without support, Ed glided with him.

Blackening skies were closing in. Then we heard the clatter

of the Puma's rotors as it approached up the Dudh Kosi gorge under a ceiling of low cloud. It would be touch and go.

In the end it wasn't even touch. The Puma didn't land. It hovered above the snow with its doors open while we unceremoniously bundled Ed in and scrambled in after him. We wheeled away and dropped down to Lukla. The relief and release was intense. We all shed some tears.

At Lukla, wearing a mask and holding an oxygen cylinder in his lap, Ed sat on the runway in an olive-green plastic chair a safe distance from the Puma while it was refuelled. We formed a protective cordon from tourists and trekkers who pressed close to take pictures of the famous mountaineer laid low. Mark and I got aggressive with some Americans, telling them to fuck off when they tried to engage the still woozy Ed in conversation.

The weather was dicey, so as soon as we could we took off for Kathmandu. Ed improved dramatically as we descended through the hills and, by the time we reached the Kathmandu valley, at a pinch he could have run a half marathon. Jokes and banter started whizzing back and forth again.

In our taxi back to the Shangri-La, Mark remembered what I had said in the middle of the night. 'So, your dad has died?'

For some reason I jutted my jaw stubbornly. 'Yes. And the manager of the hotel will walk across the foyer and hand me a fax confirming that!' I said this with uncharacteristic force. Mark and Alan exchanged looks and let it go. My vehemence took even me by surprise. It was time to shut up again.

We grabbed our packs from the boot and walked out of the heat, noise and smells of the busy street into the cool, incense-laden calm of the foyer. The manager in a tuxedo came dashing across, bowing apologetically. 'So sorry, Mr Tom, so sorry . . .' and he handed me a fax. The fax said that my father had died. Mark and Alan were stunned.

'See! I told you!' I hissed with the grace that is my hallmark.

'Jesus, mate, what are you going to do?' asked Mark quietly.

'I dunno. I'll go upstairs . . .'

They hugged me and I went to my room and lay on the bed staring at the ceiling. I felt nothing. Nothing at all. There was no need for a weeping bowl. Every tear I had for my father had already been shed.

I shrugged and went downstairs to the bar in the beautiful garden, where Mark and Alan were enjoying a gin and tonic in the cool of the evening. They were surprised to see me, surprised to see me so dry-eyed.

'Mind if I join you, gentlemen?'

ED AND JUNE HAD A beautiful bach right on the dunes at Waihi Beach. Averil and I rented baches nearby and spent a number of glorious summer holidays with them. On the morning of 5 January 1999, I rose early and got dressed, telling Averil I had to go into town to buy something. 'It's not even seven o'clock yet,' she protested sleepily. 'Nothing will be open.' I could not be dissuaded; I suddenly had an urgent need to write to my friend Michael Hirschfeld. I ended up parked in our car for nearly an hour, waiting for a stationery shop to open so I could purchase a writing pad and some envelopes. Back in the car again, I scribbled Michael an affectionate note, and then had another wait for the post office to open.

When I got back to Waihi Beach, Averil and the kids were strolling along the sands. It was already building into another perfect day. I was strangely relieved I had got my letter away. Then my cell phone rang. It was Daniel Hirschfeld, Michael's lovely son.

'How is it going, Daniel?' I asked jauntily.

'Not very good,' he replied quietly. 'Dad died this morning …'

It was five days before Daniel's wedding and two weeks before the scheduled heart bypass operation that had been hoped would make Michael strong enough for the kidney transplant he desperately needed.

I was one of the speakers at his funeral service, which filled Wellington's Town Hall with a who's who of political, cultural and media people. I said that his beautiful wife, Vivian, made the small decisions—like where they would live, what car they would drive, what schools the children would attend and what insurance they would have—and Michael made the big decisions—like should Israel return the Golan Heights to Syria. I described how whenever I did a cartoon critical of Israel Michael would indulge his enjoyment of silly voices and ring me up to say in a thick but poorly executed Middle Eastern accent, 'This is the president of Hamas. Keep up the good work.' I recounted how he once whipped out a syringe at a critical stage in a tight tennis match to inject himself with insulin, at which point I fainted at the sight of the needle and Michael served over my unconscious body to win the game, the set and the match. John Barnett in his eulogy said that Michael was an agnostic who was very proud of his Jewishness. Michael may have been without faith himself but he understood and respected the important role it played in lives of others. I loved and often repeat his definition of the doctrine that guided his behaviour: 'The world is my church. To do good is my religion.'

AFTER MY FATHER DIED MY brother Michael rang Mum to discuss what to say in the death notice. She knew immediately what it had to be: a line from one of her favourite poems in one of her favourite selections of poems—the *Rubaiyat of Omar Khayyam*:

The bird is on the wing . . .

Such a delicate avian metaphor for the man who, when Mum announced at the dinner table one night that a little bird would eat more than her, responded acidly, 'Yeah. A South American condor!'

The Scott clan gathered for a private funeral service in the chapel of a Feilding undertaker. I was still in Nepal but I'm told my father was wearing black-and-white pyjamas with wide stripes and looked like an escaped convict from a chain gang in America's deep south. When Sal commented to Sue that she barely recognised him, the undertaker looked very pleased with himself and said proudly, 'Yes, didn't he scrub up well!' It was Sue's suggestion that they should try putting his horn-rimmed specs and his Panama hat on him to see if that made a difference. It just made him look like he was sunbathing.

From all accounts, Michael ad-libbed a wickedly funny, highly irreverent eulogy. Then people who my siblings barely knew rose and respectfully described a man they barely recognised—a man of infinite kindness, patience and jest. Sister Sue said it was a bittersweet, wistful moment. She was relieved and happy for our father that he'd had friends who loved him and who he loved in return. It was just a shame they didn't include us.

When I came back from Nepal the Scotts assembled at Kowhai Park in Feilding to scatter his ashes. Someone was running late, so Rob suggested a game of touch footy using his wooden ashes urn as a ball. We ran up and down the park laughing helplessly, stopping when it became obvious that soon someone would drop the ball. Mum sat in the shade by the cricket pavilion, giggling and saying things like, 'You're wicked and awful the lot of ye!' Rob assured her that the old bugger would have loved it—and he would have. He would have loved it even more if someone had dropped the ball and his ashes had sprayed across the grass. It would have been just like his topdressing days spreading slag and superphosphate. Not that he would have made very good fertiliser. His bones must have been saturated in weed-spraying toxins because every plant, flower and shrub within a huge radius subsequently wilted and died. Sue visited the site a year later and was quite shocked to find a near perfect circle of dead soil. I have never been back.

After the ceremony we retired to Michael and Jan's place in Nelson Street for refreshments. There was a pile of our father's books in a corner of the living room. I idly picked up a photograph album that I had never seen before. It had a heavy, dark yellow-green embossed cover. Michael tried to snatch it from me. 'I wouldn't look at that if I were you!' He looked sick and apprehensive.

Curiosity aroused, I turned black pages filled with family photographs. Every picture of me, or every group picture with me in it, had been dealt to very carefully with a scalpel. My face was missing. I was absent. I was a small, round window on the blackness beneath. And he had taken such care. Two lines from The Beatles' masterpiece 'A Day in the Life' swum around my head. John Lennon just had to laugh. He saw the photograph.

I put it down. Michael grabbed it and I never saw it again. When Michael died it wasn't among his effects. I think he destroyed it.

IN THE WAKE OF THESE events my relationship with Helen foundered once more, and she suggested I might like to temporarily move out of my house so the children wouldn't be traumatised by yet another shift. A mutual woman friend and lawyer could see that I was demoralised, weary and about to consent to this and she told me in no uncertain terms that I had to stay put, so Helen moved with the children into her own home across town. This left just Shaun and me again—Oscar and Felix round two—and it was fine. It was better than fine. It was fun, especially when sister Sue's boy Brendan came to live with us for a while. It was certainly less tense.

Helen and I had a final round of counselling, this time at the well-regarded Family Centre in Lower Hutt, where a Māori woman called Tui watched our interactions through a one-way mirror. Her insights were acute and chilling. I'm paraphrasing here, but she said the de facto marriage was stuffed and I was Norman Bates in *Psycho* keeping the preserved corpse in a rocking chair in a back room of my mind. Far smarter than me in many things, Helen had known for some time that it couldn't be revived and had moved on, literally and emotionally. I was the person one too many mornings and a thousand miles behind.

The only time I ever read my horoscope is on my birthday. The *Dominion* horoscope used to carry a prologue: Your Birthday Today. On my forty-fifth birthday it advised me as follows:

End a relationship that causes more pain than pleasure.

For some reason I cut this out and kept it in my wallet.

My counsellor, Charles Waldegrave, a truly wonderful, decent man, took me aside for some final words of advice. He said that I prided myself on explaining politics and complex issues for my readers in my cartoons and in print, I was good at it, and it was driving me crazy trying to figure out why things went wrong with Helen. Charles said there were many mysteries in life that we just had to accept. After what had recently unfolded in Kunde I was now in full agreement with the Bard when he wrote in *Hamlet*, 'There are more things in heaven and earth, Horatio, Than are dream't of in your philosophy.'

I could hardly argue with Charles. Still, it drives me mad when people say some misfortune or tragedy happened for a reason. Sports stars and celebrities who fall from grace are particularly prone to this. 'I was up to my eyeballs on methamphetamine and Quaaludes and totalled my new Ferrari for a reason.' When friends trot out this pabulum I bark, 'What about spina bifida? What did any child do in the womb to deserve that?' Life is not entirely random, there is cause and effect, but things don't need a *reason* to happen.

Having said that, if there *was* a reason for my final, painful and irrevocable break with Helen, it was to set me on a path of finding Averil.

CHAPTER THIRTY

FALLOUT
FROM
FALLOUT

THE MORNING AFTER AN INTOXICATED Rob Muldoon called a snap election on the night of 14 June 1984 I drew a cartoon for the *Evening Post* depicting Muldoon in the marital chamber with his good wife. There are balloons and party hats attached to a bedpost. Something is troubling the hungover Prime Minister. 'Did I mention anything about a snap election last night, Thea?' (I dubbed it the schnapps election, which quickly caught on.)

Muldoon had been hitting the bottle all that evening— before, during and after a blazing row with rebel National MP Marilyn Waring. The Governor-General, the suave and hospitable Sir David Beattie, happened to be hosting a black-tie dinner for editors at Government House when he got word that the Prime Minister was on his way for a private audience. Barry Soper, private radio's political editor, knew this could only mean one thing—Muldoon was going to the country and needed the Governor-General to formally dissolve Parliament and set a date for a general election. Barry made sure he was standing at the front door next to a fairly comprehensively pissed Sir David when a chauffeured limousine pulled up and Muldoon toppled out onto the ground. Stepping forward, Her Majesty's official representative bent low, offering his hand and uttering the immortal words, 'This man needs a drink!' One of the guests, Labour's Deputy Leader Geoffrey Palmer, shot back to Labour's rooms at Parliament in his tux, squawking excitedly like Chicken Licken that the sky was falling on Muldoon. The formal proclamation was bashed out on a typewriter by another dinner guest—*Listener* editor David Beatson. When Muldoon returned to the Beehive with this document he held a stand-up press conference in a corridor.

RNZ's Dick Griffin thrust a microphone at him. 'Four weeks doesn't give you much time to organise an election campaign, Prime Minister?' Like a person in two minds at a sushi train, Muldoon selected his words slowly, slurring. 'Doesn't give my opponents much time either, does it, Mr Griffin?'

Hours later, in the Prime Minister's office, National's president Sue Wood, who was furious with Muldoon's precipitous, unilateral act, was talking lowly and quietly with equally dazed and dismayed senior cabinet ministers when there was a loud crash from the Prime Minister's private dining room. Sue dashed in. Muldoon was on the floor. She helped him to his feet. There were tears in his eyes.

'I have done the right thing, haven't I, Madam President?' Sue told me later there was such fear and vulnerability in his gaze, compassion overwhelmed logic and fury. She had to lie. 'Yes, Prime Minister . . .'

I knew it would make a great television series one day, I just didn't know who I would write it with, because it was too complex, sprawling and ambitious an undertaking for me on my own. It needed to be someone good.

IN 1971 THE TOURING BRITISH and Irish Lions played a New Zealand Universities fifteen at old Athletic Park and a fleet of us from Massey drove down for the game. Catering in those days consisted solely of hot pies. An ag student mate of mine, Ross Stanway, happened across a wide, flat, greasy cardboard box of them parked on the grass at the halfway line. 'Carpe diem!' thought Ross, and grabbed the box. He jogged along the front of the Millard Stand, shouting, 'HOT PIES! HOT, HOT PIES!' People yelled and hundred of hands waved frantically. Ross hurled them like a discus thrower into the packed stand where they exploded on impact, splattering patrons with pastry and hot mince shrapnel. No one seemed to mind, or perhaps their screaming was lost in the general din.

On the way back to Palmerston North, some of us stopped in a pub in Levin where a talent contest was taking place. As was mandatory in those days, several of the contestants were Māori boys wearing sunglasses pretending to be blind. Friends led them to the low rostrum where they belted out stunning versions of Ray Charles and Stevie Wonder songs. Another university chum, Alistair Williams, tall and handsome in a Jane

Austen's Mr Darcy way, got up and sang Bob Dylan's 'Quinn the Eskimo (Mighty Quinn)' in a deep baritone. Every woman and girl in the place voted for him and he won first prize—a hamper of dressed hogget. The hostility from the local men was such we had to abandon the hogget and hightail it to Alistair's old Jag.

We could have done with the services of the towering, rangy, raw-boned, fast, furious and filthy, sandy-haired bastard who played at number eight for New Zealand Universities that afternoon. Had he been with us they would have formed a guard of honour and applauded us to our car, maybe even insisting that we take a couple of their women as well as the hogget.

This big rig went on to write a seminal New Zealand stage play, the acclaimed *Foreskin's Lament*, and the equally acclaimed television drama series *Erebus* about Air New Zealand Flight TE901 slamming into the slopes of Mount Erebus while on a sightseeing trip to Antarctica in 1979, killing all 257 people on board—Greg McGee. I researched and wrote the four-hour television series which became known as *Fallout* with him.

We were the perfect combination. For those of you familiar with *The Wind in the Willows*, he was tall, reliable, sensible Badger to my yapping, bloated, blowhard Toad.

We were funded at one stage in that endeavour by Auckland film producer, distributor and exhibitor, the late Barrie Everard, and former journalist, PR consultant and more latterly philanthropist, crusading environmentalist and guardian angel of Antarctica's heritage sites, Rob Fenwick (now Sir Robert). Under their aegis the project, provisionally called *1984* then *End Game*, progressed for a while, then stalled and died. This is no disgrace. Every writer and producer I know has a movie script, play or novel going mouldy under their mattress, which at one point came within a whisker of being filmed, staged or published.

When their option expired Greg and I chose not to renew it. It seemed like the only sensible course of action for us. In a switch on the usual film and television operating procedure, where the producers blithely sack the writers with nary a second thought, we sought to change producers.

—

HOWEVER, IN MARCH OF 1991, just as I was about to board a plane for Nepal to research another film project on Sir Edmund Hillary, I got a menacing letter from Barrie Everard's lawyer, Jim Kingston, hinting darkly that our refusal to renew their option would be resisted. Good lawyers are skilled in drafting letters so authoritative and menacing your bowels turn to water when you read them. My first response was to go into flight or fight mode. Both wrong, so I opted for dismissive sarcasm. It was a lot of fun to write. I would have loved to have been there when he got it. I'm told Jim ran from his office screaming expletives after reading it. I hope so.

20 MARCH 1991

James Kingston
J.R.B. Kingston & Co

Dear J.R.B.... no, too impersonal.
Dear Jimmy baby ... no, far too familiar.
Dear James ... close, but still cold.
Dear Jim ... yes, that's much better.

Jim,

RE: *END GAME*
   Thank you for your warm and endearing fax of yesterday. What a thrill it was to hear from Barrie and Rob again, albeit indirectly via your good self.
   I must say it is frightfully decent of you to act as an intermediary like this. I have some recipes and holiday snaps I'd like to share with them, can I forward them on via you? Could you tell them that the kids are settling in well at school and autumn down here is proving delightful. Please pass on my regards while you are at it. I trust they are both fit and well.
   Incidentally, Jim, I hope you are keeping good

health yourself. It would be a terrible blow to lose an intermediary at a critical time such as this.

I must say my initial perusal of your letter conjured up visions of some sort of terrible fate befalling Barrie and Rob. I'm assuming that you received your instructions while pressing your ear to their lips in some grim hospital ward. Certainly this would account for much of your fax's incoherence and the slipping into and out of reality.

The reality is cut and dried. Barrie and Rob had an option on *END GAME*. They were unable to get it into production. Their option has expired, as you know full well, since you yourself drew up the documents calling for it to be extended. It will not be extended.

I can see no point in a meeting unless it is to negotiate the expenses that would be picked up as a first charge should the project go into production with another party. If the project, to use your quaint language, is to be 'resisted' then of course, Barrie and Rob will do all their dough, plus your legal fees, Jim, which I'm sure won't be inconsiderable.

In any event no meeting is possible for the next month as I will be overseas. Should you need to contact me urgently my forwarding address is care of the Thyangboche Monastery at the base of Mount Everest in Nepal.

Cheers,
Tom Scott

PS I really enjoyed your prose style—law's gain has been literature's loss.

—

IN 1992 I HAD TWO drama projects dear to my heart on the go: *Higher Ground*, a feature film on Sir Edmund Hillary that I was still researching, and *End Game*, which was written but still needed a production company and a broadcaster to fully commit to it. I thought both projects would benefit if I could come up with audio-visual proof that I had actors who could play the respective lead roles.

Helen and I had separated for the third and final time and it was my turn to have the kids in the school holidays, so I took Sam and Rosie with me to Melbourne to put the two possible leads on tape. Back then I favoured the tall, rangy, shock-haired William McInnes to play Hillary—he was a terrific actor and looked and sounded a lot like Ed—and the burly television comic Mark Mitchell to play David Lange. Mark was brilliant as Con the Fruiterer in *The Comedy Company*. I had a hunch he could do justice to the warmth, brilliance and fragility of the David Lange character that Greg and I had written.

To save money, we stayed in a cheap motel in north Melbourne halfway between Queen Victoria Market and the Melbourne Zoo and walked everywhere, including to the recording studio in Fitzroy. Rosie complained of sore feet much of the time. She was diagnosed a few years later with over-mobile joints and had to wear corrective orthotic shoes, poor angel.

William McInnes was reeling from a recent family bereavement and wasn't up to acting, so just spoke on camera—which was just as effective. Mark Mitchell proved to be a delightfully funny, engaging, brilliant polymath steeped in history, philosophy and mysticism. With coaching notes from me he was soon booming and orating like the real thing. It was an incredibly exciting moment. I knew I had my David Lange.

Sam offered good advice, candid as always. From birth almost, Sam has never tempered his opinions to please other people. He's not rude, just polite and fearless. On his first day at Wadestown School, when the infant mistress handed out blue chair-bags to the boys and pink chair-bags to the girls, Sam felt it was his duty to inform her, 'Some of us don't agree with that sort of thing.' At around about the age that I was lying about taking rocket trips to Mars, Sam was chiding adults on gender stereotyping.

I flew home elated and passed the VHS audition tape on to Greg, who rang me sheepishly a few days later to say that one of his boys had recorded an NBA basketball game over the top of it. I now had no proof that Mark was perfect for the part.

We had had some interest to produce the project from South Pacific Pictures, but they were never entirely convinced until they saw the first rushes and were blown away with what director Chris Bailey and Mark were achieving. In pre-production, Chris and I made a special pilgrimage to Prime Minister Jim Bolger's office seeking his permission to film in the chamber of Parliament itself—not the old chamber, as it was being gutted for earthquake strengthening, but the temporary chamber in a high-rise building across the road from Parliament in Bowen Street. It wasn't perfect but it would be more authentic than any set we could build.

I get on well with Jim now and I have a lot of respect for him. When he was Prime Minister he very kindly launched *The Great Brain Robbery*, a book I illustrated with my own cartoons and co-wrote with Trevor Grice with the sole intention of informing teenagers, their parents and teachers about how drugs work, with a particular emphasis on the adolescent brain. We accepted that people of all ages took mood-altering drugs because they enjoyed altering their moods, but we cautioned that for every high there was a low, and for every trip a return journey. Sir Edmund and Lady Hillary, Jim Anderton and Mike Moore attended the launch in Parliament's grand old legislative chamber. The news media gave it a swerve. There is a pharmaceutical chauvinism when it comes to cannabis. Many of my chums in the press who partake of the exotic cheroot were privately scathing about the book. When their kids got into trouble they sheepishly sought me out, asking for a copy. The morning Chris Bailey and I went to meet with Jim Bolger in his office on the ninth floor of the Beehive the one mood-altering substance that should have been coursing through his arteries was in short supply—his blood sugar. There is no polite way of putting this: he was a grumpy prick that morning. I suspect his staff knew this. While he barked and snarled at us, a crouching staff member gingerly pushed a plate of sandwiches along the armrest of his seat towards his beefy Taranaki cowcocky fingers. He couldn't for the life of him see why we were bothering to make a drama about Lange and Muldoon, both of whom had ignominious departures from the political stage. I suspect he knew there would be no dramatic re-creations of his glorious reign in office. (He was not immune to self-aggrandising. After a meeting with the British Prime Minister I asked what had been discussed. 'The usual word leader stuff,' he replied evenly.) Nor was he convinced that *Fallout* would be fair and accurate—in his experience the news media invariably got things wrong. I bore the brunt of this tirade. Looking sideways at Chris for support I saw that he had somehow managed the neat trick of vanishing almost completely into the pattern of the fabric on his chair.

In desperation I said that I had shown the script to his Minister of Broadcasting, Maurice Williamson, and that Maurice had loved it and thought it deserved to be made. I didn't realise that the two men were not close. Bolger snapped that this didn't carry any weight with him. He finally got to nibble a sandwich and his mood lightened appreciably. He became almost affable but didn't grant us permission. Eventually we filmed in the long-abandoned old High Court—which had some of the grandeur we needed.

The drama went to air in the winter of 1994 in two parts as *Fallout* (Helen's clever title) and triggered a firestorm of wounded and righteous indignation from the likes of Brian Edwards, Helen Clark, Geoffrey Palmer and others who were smarting about how they had been depicted or how their major contribution had been minimised, compromised or ignored altogether. David Lange sued TVNZ for libel in a case that dragged on for years before dribbling to some sort of feeble settlement. Richard Prebble was quite sanguine. 'It's a drama,' he said, cheerfully. 'Of course they are going to dramatise things.'

The most interesting response came a few years later from

the former US Ambassador, Paul Cleveland, who was posted here in 1985 and tasked with cleaning up the broken crockery left by his predecessor—the hapless, hopeless, harmless H. Monroe Browne. Cleveland was an American diplomat straight out of Central Casting—tall, silver-haired and handsome. We all assumed he was Texan. He was in fact Boston Brahmin, a State Department career officer with a reputation as a tough and extremely capable trouble-shooter in East Asian affairs.

In a long and candid 1996 interview with the Foreign Affairs Oral History Project he revealed that he didn't always approve of the heavy-handed approach his political masters took in dealing with New Zealand's stance on nuclear weapons, and he was a better friend to us behind the scenes than we appreciated at the time. A few years after his posting he was back in town and asked National cabinet minister Max Bradford to arrange a lunch with me at the Wellington Club. I was a little bit nervous. I suspected the former ambassador didn't warm to me much when he was here. He confirmed this when shaking my hand.

'I never liked you. I thought you were a pinko bleeding-heart liberal!' He grinned. 'I've been given a copy of *Fallout*. I must say I was agreeably surprised. It's pretty accurate and even-handed. Richard Armitage thought I'd like it.'

Richard Armitage was a former naval officer who served in Vietnam, an Assistant Secretary of Defense under President Reagan and Deputy Secretary of State under President George W. Bush. A lifelong Republican, he declared publicly that he was voting for Hillary Clinton in the 2016 presidential election.

Greg and I interviewed him in an upmarket black suburb of Washington, DC. Built like a Sherman tank, with a shaved head shaped like a heavy artillery shell, he had a huge, framed and autographed photograph of Hulk Hogan on one wall.

'In case you're wondering,' he roared, 'I live in a black neighbourhood because I have black and Asian kids. It makes it easier for them.' He clocked Greg for a jock and they got on really well. It was impossible not to like the guy. He admired Lange's wit but was scornful of his timidity. He had even less time for Geoffrey Palmer. 'Deep down, Geoffrey Palmer is really shallow!' He summed up New Zealand's importance on the world stage in one pithy sentence. 'New Zealand is a strategic dagger pointed straight at the heart of Antarctica!' Who cares if it was Henry Kissinger's line originally?

That night, when I wanted to pore over the interview notes, the normally workaholic McGee insisted we go to a good Georgetown steakhouse and knock off a bottle of red wine, arguing, 'You must enjoy every step of the journey because you may never arrive.' I repeat this dictum with tiresome frequency to suitably impressed people. Who cares if it was Greg's line originally?

A YEAR AFTER *FALLOUT* SCREENED, Barrie and Rob went to the Auckland District Court seeking summary judgment for a substantial sum of money that they felt they were owed. Again, like all legal arguments that present only one side of a case it seemed open and shut—they had been wronged and were entitled to compensation.

Greg wrote an elegant, comprehensive, coolly factual reply, leaving me free to treat Judge F.W.M. McElrea like someone reading an article of mine in the *Listener* or the *Auckland Star*. I wrote a long, discursive, conversational colour piece. I wanted him to know just how much blood, sweat and tears are shed in getting a script to screen.

In conclusion, I wrote:

> In the final analysis, *Fallout* was never going
> to be an Everard film. Everard did not have the
> production skills or industry contacts necessary
> to get such a project up and running. When
> there was a chance to make it as a wholly New
> Zealand funded mini-series his keenness to take
> inflated producer's fees off the top of the budget
> denied him that option. Despite everything
> I remain grateful to Everard and Fenwick for
> sending Greg and I to the US to conduct research

and I regret that Rob Fenwick and I are no longer friends. There was a time when I hoped they would get some of their money back but I no longer hold that view. The brutal reality was that back in 1989 Everard Films took a punt along with Greg and I and it did not come off. Fenwick became a financial partner with Everard in this venture after the partnership arrangement had expired. That was another punt that did not come off. When consideration is given to the thousands of unpaid hours Greg and I put into this project, and the expenses we never sought reimbursement for, it is we who are out of pocket, and for considerably more than the plaintiffs are claiming.

On 10 May 1995, in an oral decision, Judge McElrea ruled that the plaintiffs' application for summary judgment in respect of rights and services payments was declined. Greg and I were hugely relieved, but it was a bittersweet moment, and a pyrrhic victory. The repercussions were terribly sad. Twenty years on, my relationship with Rob remains irreparably damaged. A once boisterous friendship has been replaced with a cool, detached politeness—an outcome I deeply regret. Rob is a good man, a passionate and articulate advocate and activist for a range of pressing environmental causes. If not for Rob and his funny, vivacious, stylish, mischievous wife, Jenny, I would never have met the love of my life, Averil Mawhinney. Forget the development costs for *Fallout*—that is the real debt that I can never hope to repay.

CHAPTER THIRTY-ONE

AVERIL

I DIDN'T KNOW HER NAME but I remember seeing her in Toad Hall, a tiny hole-in-the-wall, hot muffin and caffeine joint on Bowen Street that legendary Wellington restaurateur Jeff Kennedy opened in the '70s. It was opposite Parliament, where I worked, and down the street from the Reserve Bank, where she worked as a junior accountant. From the privacy of my booth I took note of a beautiful, willowy girl in her early twenties making her friends laugh out loud. She was radiant. She didn't see me, or if she did she didn't recognise me. Come to think of it, I had cut small peepholes in my newspaper and all she would have seen would have been newsprint.

It turns out she was a fan of my columns, delighting once to read that we shared the same three favourite books—*The Wind in the Willows* (Toad Hall was a sign!), *Three Men in a Boat* and *Catch-22*. I finally got to meet her at 3 p.m. on the afternoon of

8 October 1992 in the French farmhouse kitchen of Rob and Jenny Fenwick's Remuera home. When I am completely gaga and can barely remember my own name I will never forget this date—it started the best years of my life.

It could have been six months earlier. Jenny had been insisting for months that I should meet a friend of hers called Averil—I would just adore her. She was gorgeous, funny and clever. To this end she organised a dinner party in her own home and invited us both. I duly flew up from Wellington and knocked on the door at the appointed hour, clutching wine and roses. Jenny let me in ruefully, biting her lip. Single for a year, Averil had met someone the night before. I hardly spoke to the poor woman who came off the subs bench and returned to Wellington wondering what might have been.

Months later Jenny rang me, very excited. Averil had broken up with this guy. If I was coming up to the Auckland launch of Sir Edmund Hillary's book *Sagarmatha* she would arrange for Averil to come as well, and we could all meet beforehand at her home.

In the end Jenny was strategically absent and I was on my own when Averil walked into their kitchen and into my heart. Lithe and lovely with a confident physical grace, she wore a natty linen trouser suit with a belt tied like a judoka dan at the waist. (This was years before Hillary Clinton almost singlehandedly destroyed the concept of the trouser suit for women.) I felt at ease with her instantly and if I wasn't madly in love with her at the beginning of the joke she told, I was at the end . . .

I forget the precise preamble, but a man in a bar is telling his friend that he's had one of those dreadful days where his tongue wasn't working properly and everything he tried to say came out sounding wrong. His mate nods sympathetically. 'I know how you feel. I was sitting with the wife at the breakfast table this morning and I meant to say, "Could you please pass the marmalade, dear," and it came out, "You fucking bitch, you have ruined my life!"'

We both started laughing and Averil blew a blob of mucus out of one nostril and had to dash for a paper towel, which reduced us both to hysterics. We rocked up to the book launch in Parnell in good spirits.

Mark Sainsbury of course was both thrilled for me and insanely jealous at the same time—exactly how I would have felt if the roles had been reversed.

'How is that rash? Is the cream working?' he asked loudly. 'Has the VD lab managed to isolate the pathogen yet?' and 'I would sue Regaine if I were you. It's clearly not working!'

At dinner later in a restaurant next door it was Lady Hillary's turn in the barrel when she asked what we were doing later.

'Well, unlike *some* people, June,' boomed Mark, 'we're young with our whole *lives* ahead of us!'

'You cheeky bugger!' exclaimed June, joining in the laughter.

Afterwards Averil drove me back to Rob and Jenny's place, where I was staying. She parked her old dunger VW in the drive and we talked, laughed and even got damp-eyed at one point. I didn't want to go inside. She didn't want to leave, but she had to. She had to go to work in the morning. A demure goodnight peck seemed only right and proper. Our lips touched lightly. The taste of butterscotch flooded my senses. Things that you never thought would come to this, as Hot Chocolate sang, started with a kiss.

Twenty-one days later in the Your Birthday Today section of the *Dominion* horoscopes there was this prediction:

A romance you think temporary could prove surprisingly durable.

I cut this prediction out and put it in my wallet as well. I never read horoscopes now. I decided to quit while I was ahead. They are mumbo-jumbo, voodoo and superstition, but when I read that prediction my heart skipped a beat.

AVERIL AND I HAVE BEEN together ever since. For a short time we lived in two cities—Auckland and Wellington. Then, Averil and her bright, delightful son, Will, and her extraordinary, lovely mum, Claire, came to live permanently with me and Shaun in the big house in the forest on the side of the hill. The house filled like a tidal pool on the weekends Sam and Rosie came to stay too.

Averil adored my children and they adored her in return. It was the same with Will and Claire. Six-foot-five Shaun and tiny Will, bookending the whānau, formed a special bond that was magical to observe. One day Will told Shaun a joke that reduced them both to helpless laughter, Will laughing for much longer than Shaun.

'Hang on there, Shorty,' boomed Shaun. 'You're not as funny as you think you are.'

Will grinned back. 'Aaah, you may be right, but you don't know just how funny I think I am!' Guffawing as only he could, Shaun threw in the towel. Will was seven.

Shaun's guffaw can remove wax from ears at four hundred paces. One time, flying back from a family trip to Sydney to celebrate Rosie's birthday (she was living there at the time), he sat across the aisle from Averil, Will and me, thank God, and watched a Mr Bean movie, laughing and rocking so violently the pilot had to come on and ask people to buckle their seats securely as we were experiencing some turbulence.

Will recently married Sanae, his beautiful, super-smart, utterly delightful Japanese girlfriend, on Australia's Gold Coast, a halfway point for both families. He made a point of asking big Shaun, who had flown directly from London with his knees tucked under his chin, to sit at his elbow at the wedding breakfast, a spot traditionally reserved for the best man. As a consequence, honestly, I don't know who was most radiant on the day, Shaun or the bride.

AVERIL'S FIRST JOB IN WELLINGTON was managing a personnel company. I used to pick her up most evenings. One night she was still finishing up and she suggested that I sit a short multiple-choice personality test while I waited. I scoffed—what could that possibly prove?

Averil giggled when she looked at the results. I was the client from hell. I was unemployable. No jobs matched my personality profile. I was good for nothing. The algorithm concluded that I should work on my own or if I worked with others I had to be in complete control. I was Hitler. In the corporate world I had to be CEO of ExxonMobil or the self-employed guy who came in once a week to wax the leaves of the aspidistras in the boardroom. Essentially, I marched to the beat of a different drum and I was most probably out of step with that as well.

There was no denying it. It was true. Apart from brief stints in the freezing works and teaching I have been self-employed all my working life. I like working my own hours and not being beholden to anyone. I hate being ordered around. In that regard I am identical to my father, though I never took it to his lengths of refusing to pay for high-school uniforms if they were compulsory.

CHAPTER THIRTY-TWO

IN SEARCH
OF HIGHER
GROUND

BY THIS TIME MY MOTHER was living with my sister Sally, her husband, Bruce, and their brood on a small-holding outside Hamilton. Mum had been a tremendous help to Sally and Bruce when the kids were young. They were grateful, but Mum wasn't always the easiest person and they needed a break from her and vice versa. Mum needed some independence and a home of her own, but where?

There was a huge basement under our house. It wouldn't be cheap, but after giving it a great deal of thought and discussing it with our respective families, Averil and I decided to build two granny flats under our house. We commissioned Athfield Architects to design it. The one binding stipulation was that the new basement flats had to perfectly match the same colonial style as upstairs. They had to look as if they had always been there—or more precisely as if they had been there since the 1890s.

JOAN, THE PLAY I WROTE about my mother, is not the reverse side of the coin of my play about my father, *The Daylight Atheist*. Nor is it an antidote—though it will have medicinal properties for anyone still reeling from that confronting piece. It is first and foremost, front and centre a stand-alone work that requires no a priori knowledge of my family history. All that is needed to appreciate *Joan* is to be of woman born—to borrow from *Macbeth*, my mother's favourite play.

Tolstoy said that all happy families are alike but unhappy families are unhappy in their own way. That was certainly true in our case. When you are growing up you have no initial basis for comparison but it gradually dawned on the Scott children that both our father and our mother were singular and utterly unique.

Joan follows the arc of our mother's life from a humble but magical and mystical childhood in Southern Ireland between the two world wars, to raising six children in gruelling, reduced circumstances in small-town New Zealand with an angry, alcoholic husband, ending in a measure of qualified peace and contentment in a genteel retirement home in Hawke's Bay.

Joan is a piece for two performers, who share the narrative load and are in constant conversation with each other—Joan, wounded, disappointed and cynical, who feels robbed by life, and Johanna, her younger self, who is full of fun and optimism. A continuing tension throughout is that Joan knows what is coming but in the natural order of things cannot reveal them to her younger self—Johanna must find these out on her own. The play ends with past and present resolving and folding into each other.

EXT. WELLINGTON

Strains of John Coltrane's 'TOO YOUNG TO
GO STEADY' from *Ballads* comes up—

JOAN: Tommy and Averil offered to build two
granny flats under their house in Wellington's
Town Belt—one for me and one for Averil's mum,

Claire. They flew me down to Wellington to talk it over. Tom picked me up at the airport. I'd not met Averil in person yet. It was hard keeping track of Tom's love life. This was the complete reverse of high school when he had plenty of hair, but no girlfriends.

JOHANNA (as AVERIL): I'd heard a lot about Joan of course, from Tom, and was looking forward to meeting her. She got out of the car—and before I could say a word—walked briskly back down the driveway and stood stock still for a few moments.

JOAN walks to the far side of the stage, pauses a moment, ponders something, then walks back—

JOHANNA (as AVERIL/amused): Then she came striding back, shook my hand and smiled.

Sorry about that, darling. I thought I was about to fart.

IN 1993 I WAS STILL in Hillary screenplay-research mode, and with Averil's blessing I returned to Nepal with Ed and June again for the fortieth anniversary of the first ascent. Many of the surviving members would be in attendance, so it was too good an opportunity to miss. Mark Sainsbury came back as well, with independent award-winning director and producer John Keir on board to make an hour-long documentary on Ed for TVNZ.

At a function in the ballroom of the Kathmandu Hotel the expedition climbers sat on stage at a long table, like disciples at the Last Supper. There was no disputing the god amongst them. Ed had a commanding physical presence that put him head and shoulders above his climbing companions.

The leader of the expedition, Sir John Hunt, pointed at me and asked George Lowe questions. When the formalities were over, he made a beeline in my direction.

'Tom Scott, what a thrill to meet you, I've heard so much about you!' In 1953, Ed resented Hunt replacing his hero, Eric Shipton, as expedition leader, but when they met he was immediately won over by his charm. I now knew why.

I was able to interview all of the surviving climbers and returned to my desk in Wellington with screeds of notes, jottings and interview transcripts. Hemmed in by mounds of reference books, and to put myself in the right mood listening to CDs of beautiful Nepalese folk music by Sur Sudha, I spent every spare second of the next year fashioning such a sprawling treatment that you risked rupturing a lumbar disc if you picked it up without bending your knees first.

WITH NO REAL IDEA WHAT to do next, I set off in 1995 to the American Film Market (AFM) in Los Angeles, bumping into a number of Kiwi film-makers who had their travel and accommodation paid for by the New Zealand Film Commission. I remember looking at them with awe and unabashed admiration, thinking, wow, how do people do that?

To steal a line from a sports writer and crime novelist I admire, Paul Thomas, the AFM had all the charm of a third-world zoo in a heatwave. Like a little old lady holding a racing guide, I made appointments with every company whose name or logo hinted at anything mountaineering—Crampon Pictures, Frostbite Films, Pulmonary Oedema Movies. You get the picture.

On several occasions I would be halfway through my pitch when producers would interrupt me kindly, 'Hey, dude, this would make a great film. You're in the wrong place. We make shit!' When I protested feebly, pointing to posters of what looked like great films being made, they confessed that many of their movies started with the poster and worked back.

I was staying with Sam Pillsbury at the time, and noting my growing despair and despondency he decided I needed a change of scenery. One evening he took me up into the Hollywood Hills to meet a producer friend who might be interested in making a film about the conquest of Everest.

Jim—I'll call him Jim—was a short, angry guy with a headful of very strange crinkly orange hair. I tried my best not to look, but it was impossible.

'You're staring at my fucking hair, aren't you?' he barked.

'Not really, no . . .' He then insisted on explaining that he was an ugly Jew whose receding hair had been forcing him to have sex with women his own age.

'Imagine that? Women my own age! In this town!'

He gagged, and for a moment I thought he was going to be sick. He went on to explain that he'd recently had a hair transplant. The dermatologist wanted to do the plugs in stages but he insisted on doing them all at once. They ran out of hair on the nape of his neck so they harvested his armpits, and when that wasn't enough they took pubic hair to fill in the top of his scalp. You couldn't help thinking that his head would look better wearing underpants. Then against all medical advice he went straight back to work. His scalp got infected, turning into a seething, pussy cap. The infection got into his bloodstream, spread through his body and lodged in his lower spine. He was facing paralysis. They had to operate. They accidentally severed nerves to his dick. Now he had a full head of hair and a dick that didn't work. It was a total bitch.

You gotta like a guy who shares that sort of stuff with you. We met up a couple of times in Santa Monica coffee bars.

'Does this Hillary guy *have* to be a New Zealander?' he asked.

Not wanting to sound negative, I replied, 'Why? What do you have in mind?'

'I see him as a big guy from Nebraska. What if he was a lanky guy who comes from Nebraska? Just a thought!'

I thought it best not to tell Ed and June about Jim. I was wondering what my next move should be when I was rung in the middle of the night by a young producer and hot-shot rock climber, Kevin Cooper, who had heard about the Hillary film project. He liked the sound of what I was doing. He flew me back up to Los Angeles for a scriptwriting conference and I flew home with more notes to add to my growing pile.

In the meantime, the fortieth anniversary of the first motorised crossing of Antarctica by the 1955–58 Commonwealth Trans-Antarctic Expedition was fast approaching. Ed was deputy leader of that expedition and famously upset the British by beating them to the South Pole. Inspired by Mark and John Keir's example, I tentatively suggested to TVNZ a one-hour documentary commemorating this event. To my delight and terror they agreed. I had never made a television documentary before in my life.

I was still digesting this when American Zoetrope flicked Averil and I business-class tickets and invited us to a meeting in LA. By sheer chance, also in business class were TVNZ's commissioner of programmes, the giant Aussie Mike Lattan, and his trusty sidekick, the diminutive Andy Shaw. At one point in the journey Mike came back to our seats, crouched down and said, 'What are we fucking around with one hour for? This guy is on the five-dollar note, for fuck's sake! He's gotta be worth four hours, surely? I wanna know why he's on the note! Give us four episodes!'

View from the Top was conceived then and there, high above the Pacific. I had been panicking about making a one-hour documentary and now I had to make four. Holy Jesus! Holy Jesus!

Buoyed by this, Averil and I went to lunch with Fred Fuchs and Kevin Cooper in a plush Santa Monica restaurant. They sipped mineral water from a mountain spring. I swigged wine straight from the bottle and regaled them with tales from my travels in the Solukhumbu with Sir Ed, full of bravado and derring-do. They were suitably spellbound.

Fred disappeared to make a phone call and came back flushed. Francis Ford Coppola himself, no less, wanted Averil and I to have lunch with him the next day. They would fly us to San Francisco in the morning, a limousine would pick us up at the airport and whisk us over the Golden Gate Bridge to Geyserville, and we would dine al fresco with the great man under a spreading oak in his vineyard.

It was finally happening. A feature film on Ed Hillary by the genius director who made *The Godfather* trilogy and *Apocalypse Now* was just one pasta meal and two bottles of zinfandel away.

We were too excited to sleep that night. I gave up counting sheep and instead counted my chickens. Big mistake.

Some time before dawn a despondent Fred Fuchs rang us with bad news. Kenneth Branagh, the filthy bastard, who was acting in as well as directing *Frankenstein*, was bonking his female lead, Helena Bonham Carter, the filthy cow. His wife, the lovely, pure Emma Thompson, found out and was demanding a divorce. A shit-fight of epic proportions was brewing and Francis had to fly off to London to hose it all down. Lunch was off.

We flew back to New Zealand with mixed emotions. The Ed movie would have to wait, but the Ed documentary was happening, and happening fast. Filming and assembling that soaked up the rest of 1996 and most of 1997.

Easily the best part was the week Averil and I spent with Ed and June in their sunlit Remuera home going through boxes and boxes of newspaper clippings, photograph albums, old magazines, cards and letters. I did the picture research and Averil went through the newspaper clippings and personal correspondence between Ed and his first wife, Louise, who, along with their daughter, Belinda, was killed in a plane crash in Kathmandu in 1975. Ed set up a desk for Averil in the washhouse, where she worked furiously, making copies in longhand of everything that might be relevant. I have read those notes several times since in the course of writing screenplays and I am always dazzled by the sheer amount of hard work she put in and the astonishingly acute story judgement she displayed.

Ed must have discerned this as well. There was a cupboard on the wall labelled 'Louise's papers', unlocked but protected by an invisible force-field. Ed opened it one morning and, reaching in, pulled out an envelope wrapped in plastic.

'Gosh, I haven't seen these in years,' he remarked calmly. He proceeded to show Averil charred photographs of the Hillary family. They were from the small photograph album Louise carried with her everywhere. Ed had picked them up from the smoking crash site, just feet away from the blue tarpaulin under which lay the scorched remains of his wife.

Averil and Ed shared a special bond. Belinda would have

been close to Averil's age had she lived.

Of the five trips I have made to Nepal, my favourite was the one where there was only Ed and June, George and Mary Lowe, Averil and me. We detoured off the trail to Everest to the remote village of Beni. In a hamlet en route, the only toilet was a Dr Seuss-like structure cantilevered precariously over a wild river. Undeterred, George strode towards it purposefully, returning quite some time later when we were on our second rough Nepalese rum and Coke.

'How was the toilet?' enquired Averil, expecting a report that was structural and engineering in tone and content.

'Well,' said George matter-of-factly, 'I went into my usual squat and after a very great deal of effort managed to produce a pellet you could sell to any army in the world as an armour-piercing shell.'

In Beni they baked a birthday cake for Ed. A monk seated beside Ed wanted to know who Averil was. Ed explained.

'Ah, many young!' Ed nodded and smiled. Then the monk wanted to know who I was. Ed did the honours again.

'Ah, big fat!' I made the mistake of telling John Clarke this and it became his email greeting for many years.

DURING THE MAKING OF *View from the Top* we also took Sir Edmund back to his old climbing haunts in New Zealand's Southern Alps. We accompanied him on a fundraising tour of North America. We took him to the holy city of Varanasi, where he had undergone a life-changing religious experience while leading a fleet of jet boats up the Ganges. We were with him at the unveiling of a commemorative statue of Tenzing in the hill-town of Darjeeling. Best of all, we took him back to the South Pole, the place he had driven to overland in 1957–58 in a convoy of humble farm tractors.

Denis Harvey from the TVNZ sports department was the producer, Haresh Bhana was the sound recordist, Mike Single was the camera operator and the late John Carlaw was the director. John was a heavy drinker and could be brusque to the point of rudeness. Ed asked me once why I hadn't smacked him one on the nose. In truth, I knew very little about documentary film-making and John was savagely bringing me up to speed. In the end he trusted me enough to do the paper edit, which was really his job. He accepted I knew the story, and how to tell it, much better than anyone else, and to the surprise of us both we became mates.

After the first episode went to air I got a very generous congratulatory note by fax from Peter Jackson, which I was chuffed about. I should have photocopied it because it has since faded into non-existence. I turned to Peter for advice when American Zoetrope asked me to trim my bulky storyline down to a succinct treatment. He invited me around to his zany house on the Seatoun coast and spent several hours with me going over the three-act structure and explaining how the treatment should reflect that division in no more than thirteen pages. Impossible, I thought, but no! Peter patiently explained that if I couldn't do that I didn't have a tale that could be told cinematically—I had a book or, worse, a small library.

I went home hugely inspired and encouraged and spent weeks rendering my Moby Dick of a manuscript down to a single chalice of real oil, and dispatched this to Fred Fuchs. He immediately flew me up to Los Angeles to pitch the project to Hutch Parker at 20th Century Fox, Alex Gartner at Fox 2000, Gareth Wigan at Columbia Pictures and Betsy Newman at TNT. I was often the oldest guy in the room, babbling rapidly to confident young men in Hawaiian shirts and cowboy boots that they placed on the table when they leaned back in their chairs. They didn't seem to see any need to take notes, which was disconcerting.

Things looked up at Columbia. For starters, Gareth Wigan was older than me, which made a nice change. As co-vice chairman he had a huge corner office on the top floor. He couldn't wait to tell me that as a young university student he was part of the huge Coronation crowds lining the streets of London. He remembered how they stood in the drizzle and cheered when they heard the news over loudspeakers that Everest had been conquered by a New Zealander, Edmund Hillary, and the Sherpa Tenzing Norgay. I thought, We're quids in here, and I set off on an emotional spiel that reduced me and everyone else to tears. When Gareth had finished dabbing his eyes he took us to lunch at The Commissary. His parting words rang in our ears like church bells on Coronation Day: 'I want to make this movie!'

As we drove out the gates, an ecstatic Fred Fuchs told me it was the best pitch he'd ever heard. He was absolutely convinced that our long quest was over.

I think we might have passed the new owners of the studio as they were sweeping in. Within days Gareth was gone. In the end they all passed, though Betsy Newman at TNT did say they didn't actually need to make my film; they just needed to film me making my pitch—my passion was amazing and my accent was adorable.

Back home I got a wistful fax from Fred.

> Although they seemed fascinated by the idea,
> I think there was some hesitation regarding
> your experience as a screenwriter in tackling this
> unique subject. I have hopes that the right script
> would attract Francis as a director as well as a
> producer. Not unlike many great films we should
> not be dissuaded by the initial response . . .

It was time to stop telling people what a great script it would make and make it into a great script. It was time to piss or get off the pot. I had spent four years accumulating more and more data. I was using the research process as an excuse not to start.

WHEN I FINALLY SAT DOWN to write I found it an exhilarating, cathartic experience. Whole days flew by in what seemed like a flash. I resented sleep because it interrupted my flow. It seemed to take no time at all. As promised, I dropped off a copy at WingNut Films for Peter Jackson.

A few days later the phone rang. It was Peter.

'Congratulations. I'm quite surprised, to be honest. It's very good. Fran wants a quick word.' Peter's wife, Fran Walsh, came on.

'Hi, Tom. Fran here. I'm surprised too. It's very good.'

Fran came around to my house with script notes for the next draft and they were intimidatingly brilliant. Phew! These people are smart! I predict a big future for them both. You heard it here first.

I got another phone call from Peter. Could he direct it and produce it after *The Lord of the Rings* or even instead of if—God forbid—*LOTR* didn't happen? At that time things were wobbly with Miramax, who wanted one movie only and something reasonably modest. Peter and Fran were desperately searching for new production partners who would allow them to make two movies grand in scale, which they felt they owed to the much-loved books.

I wished him luck, got off the phone and promptly went on an odyssey lighting candles, igniting joss sticks, laying flowers and making offerings in every church, chapel, mosque, synagogue, monastery, temple, gompa and Masonic lodge in the lower North Island, praying fervently that Peter and Fran would fall arse over kite.

They didn't, of course. Their one-picture deal with Miramax became a three-picture deal with New Line, which I must say has left me pretty disillusioned with religion on the whole.

This pushed any shooting date for *Higher Ground* well beyond 2005, by which time Sir Edmund would be hitting 86. Peter understood that I wanted to make this movie while Ed was still alive, and he was candid with me—while he would like to make *Higher Ground* he could not guarantee absolutely that it would be his next project. Anything could happen in the five-year interim—priorities change, other utterly compelling movies could scream out to be made. I understood that. We agreed that I should try to get it up with someone else. What happened after that belongs in another book.

—

THERE WAS A WONDERFUL UPSIDE to all of this. A few years earlier, Chris Hampson asked Averil to be the accountant on a small first film written and directed by Anthony McCarten—*Via Satellite*. It was Averil's first film as well.

Since his BAFTA award and Oscar nomination in 2015 for his screenplay *The Theory of Everything* Anthony, a good chum and brilliant writer—you could publish his emails—has deservedly been farting through silk. For a long time it was sackcloth and ashes. He will never have to make a small film again. It's blockbusters only for Anthony from now on. Nothing less will do—and he may well work with Averil again. Peter's bold gamble with New Line meant she got to work as the accountant on the *LOTR* trilogy, then *The Lion, The Witch and the Wardrobe*, *The Water Horse*, *Avatar* and *The Hobbit*. She has just finished a stint as the financial controller on *Mortal Engines*, the Peter Jackson-produced big-budget action drama set in a dystopian future (is there any other kind?), and is about to start work on *Mulan*, a live-action remake of the animated classic. Like her brother Grant, she is a terrific team leader and gets the very best out of people who work for her, all of whom would take a bullet for her (again, just like Grant, which he greatly appreciated when he was head of the Armed Offenders Squad).

I was about to quote Oscar Wilde and say she lacks a single redeeming flaw, but I should put on record that she suffers from hay fever and at the height of the pine pollen season she goes through multiple boxes of tissues in a single night. As a consequence our bedroom floor can resemble a snowdrift some mornings. Wading ankle-deep to the door en route to the bath that I have run for her, she can spot a sock of mine buried in a crevasse of scrunched, damp tissues and will roll her eyes at the ceiling in exasperation. 'Do you have to do that?'

There's no point arguing with her. She runs rings around me. She has a prodigious memory, she is a fabulous cook, a generous friend, hates gossip, refuses to judge people, is a wry and witty storyteller—mostly against herself—is super-fit, always dresses elegantly, takes care of my appearance as well, reads voraciously, is just as obsessed about world affairs as I am, loves travelling, doesn't mind losing luggage occasionally, loves going to movies, hates bullies, insists on drinking good wine, hates eating leftovers, wins most board games ... but she can't draw. Hopeless! Bloody hopeless!

However, this didn't stop her arguing the toss with me when we were going over the plans for the flats we were building our mums with a fine-tooth comb, and they are all the better for it.

INT. GRANNY FLAT—DAY

JOAN: I can't believe how old, staid and stale me own children have become. I much prefer the company of me grandchildren now. They're fresh and full of curiosity. You can tell them anything without fear of being patronised or having them stifle a yawn.

Rosie, Sam, promise me this. Promise your old Nana! If you ever find me lying in me own shit, shoot me!

Do we have to talk about this at the dinner table, Nana?

Yes, Rosie. We DO have to talk about this at the dinner table. What could be more appropriate? We all eat. We all shit. If ye find yer old Nana lying in a pool of her own shit, put a pistol to her temple and blow her brains out. Promise me Sam you'll do dat for your old Nana!

Averil's little boy, William, is not my flesh and blood, but there's something special about that kid. So polite and considerate. Not at all rough and tumble like Stewart when he comes to stay with his old Nana.

JOHANNA (as AVERIL): One time Will went downstairs to play with Stewart and came back up almost immediately. When I asked what had happened, Will explained that Nana Joan thinks Stewart is getting over-excited and needs some time out. When I ask what Stewart was getting over-excited about, Will said he wasn't sure, but he was using the 'F' word a lot.

Maybe Stewart doesn't know the 'F' word is a swear word, darling.

Actually, Mum, Nana Joan doesn't know either.

If Averil gives up film accounting she could go into casting films. When we were auditioning guys for the role of Errol the fireman in *Separation City*, a man with anger issues who terrorises a men's group with his admission of domestic violence, she insisted I should consider a young runner and general dogsbody on *LOTR*, Mike Minogue. She told me how she went into the Stone Street studios kitchen one Monday morning after a weekend shoot. The place was awash in filthy plates and cutlery. Mike had already washed and dried a huge pile of dishes. An even bigger pile stretched out behind him, waiting to be attended to. Wearing rubber gloves, enveloped in steam, he was working furiously at a sudsy sink with a pot scrub. Just ducking in to make herself a quick coffee, Averil felt obliged to ask him, somewhat guiltily, how things were going.

'You know, Av,' he drawled laconically, 'living the dream.'

She was right about him playing Errol. He knocked the audition out of the park, and he came to the read-through match-fit and ready to rumble. Jason Hoyte, who played oily Steve from Guidance in *Seven Periods with Mr Gormsby*, did the same thing, lifting, inspiring and giving courage to all the other actors around them.

INT. THOMAS HOME, LIVING ROOM—NIGHT

French doors open onto the pool. Three couches surround a coffee table. Aboriginal artefacts cover the walls. Cushions litter the floor. Eight men are gathered in a nervous circle.

Some are husbands from the dinner, plus four others, including a powerfully built fireman, who has brought his toddler with him. KLAAS enters last—

ERROL: All quiet on the Western Front.

SIMON: I'm married to Pamela and we have three lovely children. That's about all really.

KEITH: Any issues you'd like the group to address?

SIMON: No.

HARRY grins knowingly—

HARRY: Don't be shy.

SIMON flashes HARRY a dirty look.

HARRY (cont'd): We may tell other people, but only in strictest confidence.

ERROL: Nothing, but fucking nothing, goes outside this room!

HARRY: There you go.

KEITH: Perhaps you could introduce yourself at this point, Harry?

HARRY: Harry Ronayne. Journalist. To be honest, I'm only here because my wife insisted I come.

ERROL: Good for her!

HARRY: I really wanted to go to assertiveness training but Joanne wouldn't let me.

Some of the men smile.

KEITH leans forward earnestly—

KEITH: What exactly are you trying to hide, Harry? Maybe it's time you dropped your guard and got in touch with your feminine side.

HARRY: Trust me on this, Keith. If I had a feminine side, I'd be touching it all the time.

ERROL explodes in anger—

ERROL: If you think this is one huge piss-take you can fuck off right now.

KEITH is alarmed at ERROL's vehemence.

KEITH: Ah, Errol. Perhaps you could come in at this juncture?

ERROL: No sweat. I'm Errol the fireman. I left school at fifteen. I've got one little nipper, Tracy, who is sleeping like a log in Keith's bed. Thanks, Keith.

KEITH smiles wanly.

ERROL (cont'd): I'm here because I used to

thump the missus. Every time she questioned my authority I freaked out and decked her. Put her in hospital twice. I'm not proud of meself. Why are we men like this?

KEITH is unhappy with the tenor of ERROL's introduction.

KEITH: It is certainly our intention to devote a number of future sessions to power and control issues.

ERROL smacks his fist angrily into his other palm—

ERROL: We've got to learn to express our anger without using our fists. And why are we so fucking angry in the first place?

KEITH: Quite.

After this scene was shot the German actor Thomas Kretsch-mann came up to me at the craft services table in the garage of the large house we were filming in and said that Mike was the best actor of all of them. Better than him, better than Joel Edgerton, and better than Les Hill—and they were professionals who had been doing it for years, and this was Mike's first acting role. He was just as stunning playing a cop in *Rage*, the telemovie about the 1981 Springbok tour that I co-wrote with Averil's brother Grant. I wanted Mike to play Hillary in my TVNZ drama series of the same name, broadcast in 2016, but for reasons I still can't fathom the producer and the director went behind my back to replace him with another actor. That actor did a fine job, it has to be said, but Mike would have been spellbindingly good.

Thomas Kretschmann was being too hard on himself. He was brilliant playing the lecherous Klaas. After one particularly tense scene, where his wife, played by Rhona Mitra, confronts him about his infidelity, the crew burst into spontaneous applause. The director, Paul Middleditch, ran forward shouting and clapping his hands. 'Wonderful acting guys. Wonderful!'

'Fuck off!' said Thomas, who was going through marital woes of his own in real life, 'It's wonderful writing. Tommy, come in here and take a bow, man!' I left the monitor and walked out onto the set, where he shook my hand.

INT. KATRIEN'S LOUNGE—NIGHT

KLAAS's paintings of Amsterdam line the walls.
KATRIEN's cello sits in one corner. KATRIEN
is curled up on a roll-back couch in front of an
exposed brick fireplace. KLAAS holds a photo of
their wedding and attempts light conversation—

KLAAS: Your mother was so shitty about the
paint on my hands, remember? I bet she never
hung up that painting.

KATRIEN: What is it you want, Klaas?

KLAAS: Have you told the girls about Kimberly?

KATRIEN: Kimberly? How charming. Of course
not. Give me some credit. I said mummy and
daddy were arguing a lot and needed some time
apart.

KLAAS gets tearful.

KLAAS: I behaved very badly, Kati, I know that.
I'm very sorry.

KATRIEN: Yeah, sure.

KLAAS: I didn't want this to happen.

KATRIEN (acid): It's my fault, I should never have held that gun to your head and forced you to fuck that girl.

KLAAS: Please, Kati. I don't want us to break up.

KATRIEN: How could I ever trust you again?

KLAAS: She meant nothing to me, Kati, nothing!

KATRIEN: But you fucked her!

KLAAS shrugs.

KLAAS: It didn't mean anything.

KATRIEN: You don't understand, do you? Sex is something very special and beautiful.

KLAAS (bitter): If sex is that fucking important how come we never had any?

KATRIEN has no answer—

When it came out in 2009, *Separation City* got a pummelling from a lot of New Zealand film critics. Peter Jackson saw it differently. He said it was the kind of film New Zealand should be making and was effusive about my handling of ensemble dialogue.

Evan Williams, the film critic for *The Australian*, wrote that *Separation City* was the screenplay Edward Albee might have written as a sequel to *Who's Afraid of Virginia Woolf?*, had he been raised in the suburbs of Auckland. He said the best moments of the film had an energy and exuberance worthy of Billy Wilder and some of the gags were of Woody Allen standard.

Seven Periods with Mr Gormsby also got a towelling when it was broadcast late at night by TVNZ. Some critics said it was the worst comedy ever made in New Zealand. But in Australia it was a big hit for the ABC, which repeated both series several times. My daughter Rosie, who was studying architecture in Melbourne at the time, excitedly reported back to me that fellow students were spouting *Gormsby* monologues at parties. When Australian sports fans descended on the capital for a sevens tournament that year, they cleaned out all the stores of *Gormsby* DVDs. Dozens of blogs were set up in Australia devoted to *Gormsby*, the tone almost universally one of admiring disbelief. 'Why can't we do this?' they asked.

Gormsby also garnered good reviews in the Australian press. 'Enough to make me laugh shamelessly,' said the *Sydney Morning Herald*; 'Not since *Father Ted* has there been a television series so willing to trample on every kind of sensibility and so triumphantly gets away with it,' said *The Age*; 'A devastatingly witty spoof of the New Zealand education system,' said *The Courier-Mail*.

I was in the Rumdoodle bar in Kathmandu, having just finished the sad task of filming and assembling a tribute documentary on Sir Edmund Hillary to be aired when he died, which was looking to be very soon, when a tall teenager sidled up to me. His English-born mum and Tibetan-born dad lived in Kathmandu, but he had just finished his high-school education at Geelong Grammar, just out of Melbourne. In the boarding school they compiled a top-ten list of their favourite film and television comedies of all time. The usual suspects—*Fawlty Towers, Monty Python, Blackadder, Seinfeld* and *Father Ted*—were all on it. So was *Gormsby*.

The TVNZ staff and NZ On Air apparatchiks responsible for commissioning and funding *Gormsby*, on the other hand, were deeply ashamed of it, changed their names by deed poll, altered their features with plastic surgery and denied all involvement. Go figure.

CHAPTER THIRTY-THREE

THE DAYLIGHT ATHEIST

IN 1999, AS ONE OF the speakers at Sir Edmund Hillary's eightieth-birthday bash at Government House in Wellington, I made the point that apart from the wild excitement of Ed's and Tenzing's conquest of Everest, life in New Zealand in the 1950s was stupefyingly dull. Exaggerating only slightly, I described the small Manawatū town I grew up in as being a place where you could fire a cannon down the main street at rush hour—and if you hit anyone you'd be doing them a favour. In Feilding life didn't just pass you by—it crossed to the other side of the street when it saw you coming.

Afterwards one of the guests, New Zealand's most successful playwright, Roger Hall, came rushing up and said, 'If you don't write a play about your childhood, I will!' When Roger talks like that you have to take him seriously. I went home and started work. Four weeks later, *The Daylight Atheist* was the result. I almost called it *The Weeping Bowl*, but that sounded too grim.

When asked how much of it is biographical I borrow a line from a surrealist painter who said that none of his pictures were real but all of them were true. If the play were a diamond necklace, then perhaps a third of the baubles would be real and the rest cut glass, but I have difficulty now telling the difference. Some things in the play did happen to me. Some things happened to other people. Some things could have happened to anyone. As a result, Danny Moffat resembled many fathers, including my own.

I started out with the intention of writing a play set across five countries and two hemispheres, requiring a cast of thousands. The stage would teem and swarm with characters like the concourse of Grand Central Station during rush hour and a bomb alert, but sitting at the keyboard my fingers refused to oblige. I wanted a story full of rush and clamour leading to the point where my father ends up alone in a room packed with junk, including four dead black-and-white television sets, a cockpit seat from a Harvard trainer and twin beds with threadbare burnt-orange candlewick bedspreads, getting his meals delivered on a tray. Then it occurred to me that it would be a lot simpler to set the play in that squalid room and let him tell us in his own words how he got there.

Having made that decision, the play almost wrote itself. In the process my father became Danny Moffat because the man on stage needed a childhood, and I knew virtually nothing about my father's, apart from him growing up Protestant somewhere in Northern Ireland, that he had siblings and that he had for a time lived with a childless aunt.

It's shocking really but I never knew and still don't know the day, the month or the year of his birth.

When the play was almost written I contacted Simon Prast at the Auckland Theatre Company, who was very encouraging. Yes, they would love to read the first draft. It was clumsy in places, and raw. I could hear it in my head but would other readers hear it in theirs?

Averil was still in bed one Saturday morning when I dropped a printed copy on the duvet and fled. An hour later she came out puffy-eyed and hugged me. She said it was wonderful and she was very proud of me. I was chuffed but her response was sort of compulsory.

A week later, while researching a movie project in Central Otago, I got a call from Elena Azuola, Averil's close friend and boss on *Lord of the Rings*, who before becoming a film accountant had been a dancer, an actress and personal assistant to Tennessee Williams.

'This is some powerful, poignant, funny and distressing shit,' said Elena in her confident, husky drawl. 'Tennessee would be proud of this.' I was elated, but again the response was sort of compulsory.

I was rescued by the kindness of strangers. Simon and his people liked it a lot, which wasn't compulsory. In 2001 it was scheduled for a public reading as part of the Auckland Theatre Company's Second Unit Programme. Stuart Devenie was selected to do the reading. Full of restless energy, angularity and intellect, Stuart seemingly absorbed the play by osmosis and spent much of our precious two days of rehearsal discoursing wittily and widely on all manner of matters, political and theatrical.

As the 7.30 deadline in a drab, low-ceilinged downtown hotel conference room approached, I started to panic quietly. One small notice had appeared in that morning's *New Zealand Herald*. Optimistically, a hundred stackable chairs were placed in rows under garish fluorescent lighting. In the end over 150 people showed up to see Stuart perform without benefit of props, costume, music or make-up. I sat in the front row between Averil and Elena.

Stuart played Danny Moffat with a cold, cerebral fury and was brilliant. I was relieved to hear lots of shocked laughter and even more gratified when I heard sniffing and stifled sobs. Greg McGee was sitting beside my lovely baby brother, and he reported later that Rob sobbed softly pretty much throughout. Afterwards another friend, the actor/writer/director Ian Mune, accosted me.

'You bastard! You bastard! I hated the prick right to the end, then you got me and I wept for him!'

Nothing I have done in cartooning, print journalism or television documentary-making has ever come close to the feedback I received for this small play. Strangers who were alcoholics or the children of alcoholics wrote to thank me for detailing Danny's shortcomings and then forgiving him for them. Strangers with shameful secrets—an abortion long ago, an adoption forever regretted, a handicapped sibling they battled to accept, a schizophrenic parent who constantly embarrassed them or a child they were supposed to love but couldn't—wrote to say it was cathartic having me lay bare my childhood and escape what could have been permanently wounding. For that I have to thank a saving shallowness. Even as my childhood was unfolding I was turning misery and embarrassment into anecdote. Any artistic licence lies not in the fevered imagination of my adulthood but in the fevered imagination of my youth. I rewrote history as it happened while it was still fresh and could be improved.

The reviews were universally rapturous.

> One can't help wonder at the pain endured to produce this wonderful play. Scott is our most gifted humourist. The hardest job in writing is to make people laugh and Scott pulls off the greatest trick and makes it look simple.
>
> — GILBERT WONG, *SUNDAY STAR-TIMES*, 21 APRIL 2002

> The sound of distant and ignored sobbing is a repeated image in Tom Scott's remarkable first play. Don't take it from this that *The Daylight Atheist* is a down-at-heel *Angela's Ashes* clone. Far from it. Word wizard Scott infuses Dan's story with rich humour. This is an excellent production of an outstanding play.
>
> — LYNN FREEMAN, *CAPITAL TIMES*, 8 MAY 2002

> One of the best New Zealand plays ever written. It is riddled with witty one-liners and yet it has

humour that produces not only laughter but also tears. It sounds an enigma—a serious subject so engulfed in hilarious scenes but this is theatre at its zenith.

— M. WILLIAMSON, *THE GUARDIAN*, 10 OCTOBER 2002

Plays about the irascible charm of the bog Irish have become something of a theatrical cliché, but Moffat is a disturbing, complex creation who relates a monologue rivalling Joyce and O'Casey in linguistic virtuosity and bawdy humour.

— JOHN FORDE, *SUNDAY STAR-TIMES*, 20 APRIL 2003

If there is justice in the world it will be on Broadway or the West End. Go there. Borrow the airfare if you have to. Or steal it. You won't regret it. It's the best show you'll see in years. At the end, as the one fancy lighting effect faded into black we applauded. Not polite end-of-a-play applause. It bruised the palms. Like all sincere applause it didn't say bravo. It said thank you.

— JOE BENNETT, FESTIVAL DIARY, *THE PRESS*, WEDNESDAY, 23 JULY 2003

It got similarly rapturous reviews in Australia. My chum Murray Bramwell recommended it to another expat Kiwi, the artistic director of the Melbourne Theatre Company, Simon Phillips, who picked it up and wrote this in the theatre programme notes.

This is a brave, bold, blisteringly funny play from New Zealand which seems all the braver and bolder for being drawn from life. Tom Scott had a long, difficult relationship with his father and yet he allows neither the misty tear of sentiment nor of anger to cloud his view. He has written an amazingly complex character who is genuinely hilarious and tragic.

I defy anyone not to laugh and to weep for him, especially in the charismatic hands of Richard Piper. Richard has been delighting MTC audiences for many years. *The Daylight Atheist* offers him a magnificent tour-de-force and welcomes Peter Evans to the Company for his directorial debut.

I didn't cry when my father died, but I admit I shed a few tears when I read some of the reviews.

It played to packed houses and went on to win a number of theatre awards. The Melbourne production travelled to Brisbane. The Sydney Theatre Company mounted a production of its own starring Max Cullen, which later travelled to Adelaide. I'm told that at that time it was the only New Zealand play ever performed as the main bill by the MTC and the STC.

As it happened the STC production was a nightmare. Max Cullen never got on top of the lines. Many nights the play finished anywhere between ten and twenty minutes early because large chunks of it escaped him. On the opening night, at the after-match function Max came up to me in tears to apologise for wrecking my play. It was New Year's Eve. Fireworks on the Sydney Harbour Bridge behind us were ushering in 2005, champagne was flowing, I had beautiful Averil at my elbow, but instead of being elated I was biting my lip and consoling a distressed actor.

MY BROTHER MICHAEL DIDN'T GO to the play when it came to Palmerston North in a wonderful production starring Grant Tilly and directed by Danny Mulheron. I don't blame him. It wasn't about his father. His father was quite different from mine.

Besides, he wasn't well. He was taken to Wellington Public Hospital in an ambulance when Palmerston North Hospital could do nothing to alleviate excruciating, disabling headaches. They suspected a brain aneurism. Plus his kidneys were failing him and he was put on peritoneal dialysis, a cumbersome, uncomfortable procedure, and his marriage to Jan crumbled. They sold the family home in Feilding. She moved to Rongotea, and Michael stayed permanently at the family bach at Waitarere Beach, where he cut a lonely figure walking the shore. I was shocked one visit when I joined him on the sands and he called a halt after 50 paces—he was that breathless—all the while insisting that he was fine. I remembered my father telling me once he could no longer walk to the dairy—it was too exhausting. Then Michael met the wonderful Annie, who literally took his breath away. Things got very hot and heavy very quickly.

Micky was admitted to Palmerston North Hospital after some dizzy spells. I drove Mum up to see him on a Friday. He was so in love he was more animated than I had seen him in years, laughing and joking. He told us that he had warned his cardiologist that if he wasn't discharged for the weekend he would tie sheets together like they do in prison movies and abseil the three floors to freedom.

He also told me about a dream he'd had. It bothered me on the way home but I didn't share it with Mum. In this dream he is walking along Waitarere Beach in an amazing sunset, the most astonishing sunset he has ever seen. A truly wondrous sunset. There is a ladder rising up into the sky. Michael climbs up this ladder into beautiful gold and crimson clouds.

I was at my desk on Sunday evening when my phone rang. It was Burton Silver. He was just driving north on Highway One, past the turn-off to Waitarere Beach, and the most amazing sunset he had ever seen was filling the western horizon. It was so beautiful he just had to share it with someone, so he rang me. I paid it no mind and went for a short walk in the town belt. When I got back, a worried Averil said I had to ring a Waitarere number. It sounded urgent. A good friend and neighbour of Michael's told me my brother had just died.

It was a terrible moment going downstairs and telling Mum. She rocked and wailed for twenty minutes. I hugged her but it made little difference. It was just like when her father died. Then she stopped and was astonishingly stoic and composed through the long, awful days until the funeral service held at the rugby clubrooms in Feilding's Johnston Park, just around from Owen Street where our old house was, and across from Nelson Street where Michael and Jan had lived. Sister Jane's handsome army officer husband Brian Hewson, resplendent in his herbaceous border of medals, did Michael proud as MC. Dapper as he was, Brian only barely eclipsed Mum sartorially. She wanted to cut a dash for Michael, so Averil took her shopping and bought her a beautiful deep crimson Nehru jacket, stylish black pants and smart shoes. She sat in the front row pointedly gripping devastated Annie's hand, telling everyone, 'She was the love of his life, you know!'

I delivered the eulogy. I told them that Michael was a very good guitarist and singer who exuded extraordinary confidence in the limelight. To impress Jan, he was not above appearing on stage with huge amounts of toilet paper stuffed down his tight trousers—giving the appearance he was hung like a Javanese rhino.

Michael enjoyed an astonishing ease irrespective of the occasion. As a child at posh afternoon teas at the neighbours', with everyone covetously eying the last wedge of sponge cake, Micky would reach out, squeeze it through his fingers and ask loudly if anyone else wanted it. There would be an annoyed chorus of 'Not now!' and he'd say, 'Shame to waste it' and polish it off, nosily licking his fingers.

He didn't disrespect authority so much as fail to even recognise it. Right from the outset schoolteachers found it unnerving that this undeniably bright, gap-toothed urchin treated them as equals. As his equals they were free to tease him just as much as he teased them. And he did.

One long, hot afternoon bus-trip home, Micky was goading the driver, Mr Sullivan, who was also his teacher, beyond the point of endurance. Sullivan spun around and hissed that if he didn't pull his socks up he was in for it. Micky dutifully bent down and did as he was told—hoisting up his socks. Sullivan slammed on the brakes, flew out of his seat and slapped him across the side of the face, leaving an ugly welt. The tears trickling down Micky's cheeks vanished a few minutes later, however, and were replaced by a sly grin when up ahead, as if by magic, the unmistakable figure of our mother, laden with gifts, loomed up on the side of the road. Sullivan almost shat himself. He was puce and sweating with discomfort when he pulled over and Mum bounded on board with presents of jars of jam and cream for him. Sullivan was terrified Micky would dob him in, but that wasn't his style. While Sullivan squirmed he sauntered off the bus beaming in sly triumph, pausing to say, with exaggerated politeness, 'Thanks, driver!'

Micky even had the confidence to challenge one of the neighbour's rams to a head-butting competition when he was seven. Mum called out to me as Micky, crouched down on all fours, was stamping the ground and thrusting his head at the ram. The monster took six steps back for a run-up and charged. Micky went down like a sack of shit and wanted a rematch, but Mum wouldn't let him.

Had it been a wrist-wrestle it would have been a no-contest. Michael, like our brother Rob, had forearms like Popeye. The Scotts are white Tongans.

Michael was talking once to four locals in a Texas bar when they took offence at something he said and invited him to step outside. Mike nervously took off his new jacket and rolled up his sleeves. They fled without a word.

With Michael there were no divisions or social ladders. To borrow a line from Bob Dylan, who he loved, he was better than no one, and no one was better than him.

He was with his daughter Milly at a function when he spotted Sir Howard Morrison. 'Hey, Howard! Howard! Howie! Howie! Over here!' Mike boomed, waving his large hand at the singing knight of the realm, who excused himself from his group and happily trotted over to make this excited fan's day. Mike held out his huge hand, which Sir Howard grabbed warmly.

'Mike Scott!' said Micky loudly, before abruptly turning his broad back on him, leaving Morrison stranded and bewildered in no man's land. 'That's how you treat famous cunts, Milly,' he told his shocked and appalled daughter, as Sir Howard reeled back the way he came.

He was a qualified pilot. When he was courting Jan, rather

than drive the short distance from Sanson to Whanganui to meet her parents, he thought he would cut more of a dash if they flew there in a Cessna. It was always debatable as to what was more terrifying—being in the cockpit with him, or being on the ground when he pretended to be a Spitfire pilot strafing German supply lines.

Mike's love of aircraft came from our father and was so strong that rushing Jan to hospital to have Milly, her contractions coming thick and fast, he just had to stop on the roadside at Ohakea to watch some Skyhawks land.

When the rest of the Scott clan moved away from Feilding the burden of caring for our ailing father fell mostly on Mike and Jan, which they did with grace and forbearance. In the weeks before he died we talked and joked a lot more on the phone. I was able to tell him I loved him, to which he replied, as only he could, 'I can't say that I blame you.'

ON 1 DECEMBER 2003 WELLINGTON hosted the world premiere of the third movie in the Lord of the Rings trilogy, *The Return of the King*. The Wellington City Council estimated that 120,000 people lined the streets of the capital to cheer and applaud the key film-makers and the stars as they paraded through the city in open-top classic cars. Led by Māori conch callers, the parade included hobbits, orcs, elves, riders of Rohan, Gondorian soldiers, ringwraith riders, Easterlings and Uruk-hai. The cars stopped at the western end of Courtenay Place and advanced down a red carpet towards the Embassy Theatre, which Peter Jackson had had restored and refurbished above and beyond its former glory.

Giving media interviews, signing autographs, posing for photographs, chatting with ecstatic fans reaching out from behind the barricades, the colourful, cavorting caravan took several hours to negotiate the last 500 metres. Three giant screens relayed images to massive pressing crowds. Television news crews from major international networks fed footage around the world. New Line studios had three crews and three reporters on the ground as well, providing additional coverage and conducting separate interviews: Madeleine Sami, Raybon Kan and me. I was also the MC before the premiere, introducing the Prime Minister and Peter. It was all wasted on me. I was a zombie half-numb with grief.

Michael had died barely two weeks earlier. Micky played bass in a number of rock bands. He knew that the show must go on. He would have wanted me to honour my commitment.

It was the second time I had done the honours for Peter. In 1992 he asked me to MC the premiere of his slapstick comedy-horror film *Braindead*. He was nervous. He wanted me to get the audience laughing before it started rolling to get them in a receptive mood.

He needn't have worried. I was entirely redundant. It was brilliant and hysterically funny from the first few frames.

I have no clear recollection of how things went at the *LOTR* premiere, but I did hear later from friends as far afield as Tel Aviv and Vancouver that they had seen me on CNN, so they must have switched to the New Line feed at some point. I had a small advantage over other reporters in that Averil worked on the movie. The producer, Barrie Osborne, and co-producer, Rick Porras, had become good friends. Through Rick and his then wife, Melissa Booth, (both of whom remain adored friends of mine to this day) I had socialised with Andy Serkis, Sean Astin and other cast members. When Averil learned from Sir Ian McKellen that he had long admired Sir Edmund Hillary we arranged a dinner party at our house for Ian to meet Ed and June. It was a great night. When I reconfigured my four-hour TVNZ documentary on Ed to a 75-minute documentary for Channel 4 in the UK, Ian did the voiceover, quite brilliantly, free of charge.

Plus I knew Peter reasonably well. When he advised me on my *Higher Ground* treatment I couldn't help but notice that he had shelves and shelves full of Beatles paraphernalia, memorabilia and scores of bootleg CD and concert DVDs in his study. He was more devoted to the Fab Four than I am—which is saying something.

In the street parade he shared an open-topped car with the *LOTR* composer, the hugely talented but difficult Howard Shaw. I thrust a microphone at Peter and asked, 'What is the best film soundtrack ever, Pete: *A Hard Day's Night* or *Lord of the Rings*?'

Peter is one of the smartest people I have ever met. He is razor sharp and seldom lost for words. For a few seconds, as Howard looked on, waiting for the verdict, Peter gathered his thoughts, coughed and spluttered a bit, then said diplomatically that you couldn't really compare the two. Somewhere my brother Michael was grinning, punching the air and shouting, 'That's how you treat famous cunts!'

MICHAEL'S DEATH KNOCKED THE STUFFING out of Mum. After her bravura appearance at the funeral she wilted visibly. An almost permanent sorrow and sadness enveloped her. Wellington's wet and windy weather didn't help. She had circulation problems in her hands. She wore mittens all the time and complained constantly about the pain, which I suppose you do when the pain is constant. She became very hard to please. She couldn't help it, but she started to resent us, and the life we lived if she wasn't included in it centre stage. It came as no great surprise when Mum announced she wanted to move to a retirement village in Napier.

INT. RETIREMENT VILLAGE, BEDROOM—DAY

In a shaft of light, JOAN sits in bed dressed in
a cream nightie and pink, crocheted bed jacket,
holding a blue diary in oven mitts, squinting and
scowling—

JOAN: Can't read me own fucking handwriting.
I need a stronger prescription. And I've just paid
a fortune for these!

JOAN waves her glasses in the air—

JOAN: When I told Doctor Sandhu the world was
getting fuzzy again I got the standard reply:

*What are you expecting, Mum? You are not
getting any younger.*

I tink dat when ye get to my age you know dat,
don't you? Yee've worked dat out at least. As a
matter of interest, can anyone name anything,
anywhere in the universe, dat is getting younger?
Newborn babies, for fuck's sake, aren't getting
any younger! And I wish he'd stop calling me
Mum. I don't care if it is the custom in Pakistan.

JOAN gingerly removes one hand from an oven
mitt and slowly flexes her fingers, wincing—

JOAN: Just in case yer wondering. Me diary's not
piping hot. Me hands are feck'n freezing. I'm not
a well woman! I'm not a well woman!

Doctor Sandhu tells me I have Raynaud's disease.
Something to do with poor circulation in the
extremities. Some mornings me hands are as
white to the look and as cold to the touch as a
Michelangelo marble. The pain is excruciating!
You wouldn't wish it on yer own worst enemy.

Actually, I do wish it on me own worst enemy.

And me children, who roll their eyes when I talk
about the agony I'm in.

They tink I'm exaggerating to get attention. One
morning of dis would get their fucking attention!
One of me few regrets is dat I won't live long
enough to see dem grow old and decrepit and
having to put up with the shit I'm going through!
I would pay good money to see dat, I would!

JOAN gently clenches and unclenches her fist—

INT. REST HOME—DAY

JOAN: I told Tom and Averil I was shifting to
Napier to be closer to the grandchildren I prefer.
I didn't mean it to sound like that. It came out
wrong. I wanted to be closer to Michael's final
resting place. When my time comes, and it can't
be far off, I want my ashes scattered there as
well. High in the Hawke's Bay hills, closer to the
heaven I no longer believe in.

JOAN lies back, staring at the ceiling—

FRANK SINATRA (V.O.) (singing): Blue days,
All of them gone, Nothing but blue skies, From
now on.

INT. EPILOGUE: FUNERAL HOME—NOON

JOAN, in her pink candlewick dressing gown,
cream flannelette nightie and fluffy slippers,
runs her hand gently along the top of the coffin—

JOAN: I pick dat colour. Lilac. Blue is too cold and
purple too ecclesiastical. I am very clear on the
question of religion. NO HYMNS! I don't want any
hymns at my funeral. NO SCRIPTURE! I don't want
any fucking readings from the Gospels or reciting
of Psalms at my funeral. AND NO PRIESTS! Is
dat clear? I DON'T WANT ANY PRIESTS AT MY
FUNERAL! Though if ye happen to see one cycling
past ye might like to wave him in.

CHAPTER THIRTY-FOUR

HEART MURMURS

AFTER NEPAL, JAPAN IS MY favourite destination. I can walk through Japanese cities like Kyoto, Sapporo and Nara and say to myself, 'I could live here'—something I have never felt in Nepal, or few other places actually.

My fondness for Japan began when Averil's son, Will, completed his degree in philosophy and languages and moved to Tokyo. He wants eventually to join the UN and work on their refugee resettlement programmes. Smart boy. When global warming and sea rise submerge the coastal plains where most of the world's populations live he will never be out of a job.

One trip we stayed at the Hilton Tokyo in Shinjuku-ku. The views after sunset from the New York Bar on the fifty-fifth floor were wondrous. A gaudy neon Milky Way marched off into infinity in every direction.

One evening I was sipping a cocktail, flicking idly through

the *International Herald Tribune*, when I read that 400 Japanese company employees on a junket to the southern Chinese city of Zhunhai had a three-day orgy with 500 Chinese prostitutes. These people have so much to teach the west.

I looked dreamily out the window. The last rays of the setting sun were hitting the snow-covered upper slopes of Mount Fuji and I suddenly felt ill. We were climbing it in a few days. Averil and Will were excited. I was experiencing a deep dread. Jesus Christ, it was the same bloody height as the hill up to Namche Bazaar; I'd struggled up that the last time and I was in my fifties then.

It proved to be as hard as I feared. My feet were leaden. Every step was an effort. Going up some steep sections, Will grabbed my belt and heaved me up just as Mingma had done for the Burra Sahib. I spared what little breath I could to thank him. Ever polite, he replied, 'No problem. We could rest here a bit. I could do with a break myself.' He was lying.

We reached the last lodge well after dark. They put me on oxygen but the cylinder was empty. I had seen this movie before.

We slept in communal bunks like submarine crews. At 3 a.m. alarms sound for the assault on the last 300 feet to the summit—the intention being to get there before sunrise and the start of a brand-new day. I stayed in my sleeping bag as Averil and Will scrambled up in the freezing cold and black. They made it as the sun slipped above the distant horizon. To the delight of the locals, Will stripped to his waist and did a spirited haka.

I stripped to my waist for my GP when I returned home. He needed a few moments to get the better of his gag reflex then attached a stethoscope to my ribcage. The negative buoyancy invaluable when you are stepping into rotating lawn-mower blades made it difficult to spot, but I definitely had a heart murmur.

Ken Greer dispatched me to the Heart Centre at Wakefield Hospital, where Malcolm Abernethy and his team conducted an echocardiogram—they bombard your chest cavity with ultrasound waves and scan the results. I had a thickened left ventricle wall, indicating my heart was working harder than it should. This was followed by an angiocardiogram, where they injected radio-opaque dye into a vein in my right wrist and monitored its transition through my heart on a large X-ray screen. I am not a cardiologist, but when seasoned professionals start screaming 'FUUUUCK!', pull out rosary beads or run from the room in tears, you prick up your ears. I'm exaggerating— no one pulled out rosary beads—but Malcolm did suggest very gently that I should go home and fetch my pyjamas and toothbrush, and not run any half marathons on the way.

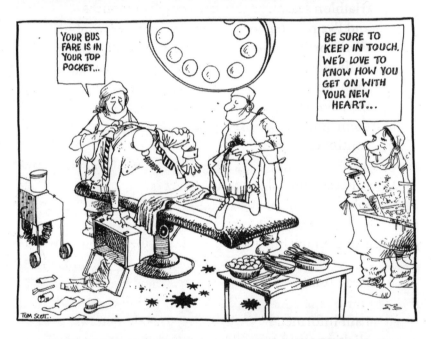

OPEN-HEART SURGERY IS NOT SOMETHING you take out full-page ads in newspapers to announce. I kept it quiet, but people found out. I got a lovely text message from All Black coach Steve Hansen wishing me a speedy recovery, and a very amusing one from the then Prime Minister, John Key, wishing me well and saying that it was highly unlikely he would ever need heart surgery because according to Nicky Hager's book *Dirty Politics* he didn't have one.

I got two emails from John Clarke that made me laugh out

loud at the time and fill me with sadness now. They are all the more poignant knowing that he died almost instantly while walking in a pristine wilderness from catastrophic heart failure.

Dear Tom,

I understand you've recently undertaken some renovations in the central thorax area and I hear that they've gone well. Excellent. I would expect nothing less and I'm delighted to hear it. The triathlon season begins in a couple of months and I've put you down for a start in the event at Warkworth in mid-December. You'll be off scratch in the 20-27 age group. Just use the swim leg to limber up a bit, sit somewhere near the front of the peloton during the bike section and mow them down in the run. We salute you and hope all continues to go well.

All best from all here,
John

And this one on my birthday two months later.

Dear Tom,

I am informed by Ginette that the odometer is clicking again today. You are to be congratulated and I understand from the makers of plumbing equipment that you are under warranty until 2046. The position will be reviewed every fortnight after that so please get everything important done in the intervening period.

Happy birthday.
Yrs,
J Clarke, Manawatu

On the Sunday evening before the Monday-morning operation, Averil and I met in turn with the cardiologist, the surgeon, the anaesthetist, and the perfusionist—the latter's job was keeping a weather eye on the fancy machine that would be doing the work of my heart and lungs while they were temporarily decommissioned. There was lots of talk and discussion about risks. I asked the perfusionist about power outages. There were back-up generators and if they failed they had batteries.

Averil was anxious and tearful. I felt strangely calm and relaxed. Like Woody Allen, I wasn't frightened of dying—I just didn't want to be there when it happened.

I had been truly blessed by Averil entering my life. Blessed with all my children, including Will, who has none of my chromosomes and is the richer for it. Sam and Jessica had gifted us with one grandchild. I had hoped to be around when Shaun, Rosie and Will had theirs. *C'est la vie*. I fell asleep knowing that I was a fortunate man who had led a fortunate life. If I woke up after surgery, everything from that point on would be a bonus.

I CAME ROUND IN A strange, grey light in a recovery room. Everything was fuzzy and in soft focus. I didn't know where I was. I knew I had been subjected to open-heart surgery but what was the outcome? Had I woken up, or was this a poorly lit dream? Or, worse, was I on the other side? Whatever that was.

A familiar silhouette with a corona of light around blonde hair leaned close. I couldn't make out the face. A gentle voice spoke and someone squeezed my hand—my darling Averil. Unless by some extraordinary and tragic coincidence Averil had died as well, it meant I was alive.

She told me that it had all gone smoothly and that everyone was pleased. I had sutures in a wound stretching from my groin to my right knee where they had borrowed a vein to replace some occluded coronary arteries. I wore pressure stockings on both legs. An aortic valve from a bullock replaced my own (Model No. TF-25A, which I thoroughly recommend), which had been steadily turning into chalk as it struggled to close properly. My sternum was stapled together. Subcutaneous connective tissue and skin also divided by the Skilsaw was glued back together. I had drainage tubes leaving my lower ribcage. I had tiny electrical jumper-leads entering my upper ribcage and running to my heart in case my blood pressure flatlined and my pump needed starting again. I was connected to a blood-pressure cuff. I wore a pulse oximeter on one finger. I had a saline drip feeding electrolytes through a catheter into one vein. I had a morphine drip feeding soothing opiate into another. I had light, clear plastic tubes delivering oxygen to my nostrils.

I was alive, and the good people at Wakefield Hospital were doing everything humanly possible to keep me that way. I would get to see my mokopuna grow up (Freddy and Gus have since made stellar entrances, and another grandson is biding his time in the green room of his mother's womb). I would grow old with Averil. Unlike my brother Michael, I had been given a second chance.

I know she is not the slightest bit interested but I would use it to take Averil to Lake Bled in Slovenia and Dubrovnik in Croatia. We both want to visit Venice and Barcelona. We both want to live and work in Paris and New York. There is so much to do and see!

Waves of euphoria and gratitude swept over me. The taste of butterscotch filled my mouth.

Then I noticed some other bastard recuperating from surgery, doubtless nowhere near as serious as mine, had the bed next to the window with a view, and I instantly felt short-changed.

I'LL LET THIS FRAGMENT FROM *Higher Ground* have the final word.

EXT. SUMMIT EVEREST—MOMENTS LATER

WIDE SHOT: We circle the New Zealander and the
Sherpa hugging on the roof of the world. Rotating
slowly below them is the brown plateau of Tibet
and the icy peaks of Nepal. Around them nothing
but sky. Above them the Indian ink of space.

Super the Title: Everest Summit—11 a.m.,
May 29, 1953

TENZING holds his flag-bedecked ice-axe aloft
while HILLARY takes a picture—

TIGHT ON: The famous Summit photo—

HILLARY takes photographs north, east, south
and west—

TENZING scoops out a depression in the snow and
places offerings of sweets, the pencil, the karta,
Lambert's red scarf and the flags from his ice-axe.

TENZING kneels and prays quietly—

TENZING: Thuji chey, Chomolungma. Thuji chey,
Chomolungma.

Super the translation: I am grateful, mother
goddess of the world. I am grateful, mother
goddess of the world.

Observing TENZING'S tribute, HILLARY suddenly
remembers something, and reaches into his shirt
pocket for the small crucifix a tearful John Hunt
gave him three days earlier on the South Col and
places it alongside Tenzing's tributes to the gods.

He quickly scans the horizon, then checks his
watch—

HILLARY: Right. We're out of here!

ACKNOWLEDGEMENTS

I WANT TO EXPRESS MY gratitude to my writing chums David Young, Murray Bramwell, Greg McGee and Dean Parker for taking the time to read early drafts and offering me prudent and timely advice on the tone and content of this book.

I am indebted to a legion of editors on the *New Zealand Listener*, the *Evening Post*, the *Auckland Star* and the *Dominion Post* for giving me the freedom to leave my office desk in pursuit of stories I thought worth telling. I am grateful to a small army of sub-editors who took pages and pages of copy coagulated with white-out and fashioned them into useable prose.

I am honoured that Murray Webb and Trace Hodgson, caricaturists whose work I have long admired, have given me permission to reprint their work. I am chuffed the Ball family have consented to the use of Murray's cartoon of me as a breastfeeding dad.

I thank John Barnett, Pat Cox and Magpie Productions for permitting me to use a fragment of the screenplay *Footrot Flats* that I co-wrote with Murray, and a cell from the finished film.

I thank my partners in crime, the political journalists Barry Soper, Dennis Grant, Pattrick Smellie, Richard Griffin, Phil Melchior and Mark Sainsbury for refreshing, confirming and correcting where necessary my memory of events.

I thank my daughter-in-law Jessica for the perfect title, and my son Sam for bullying me into using it and for roughing up an indicative layout that proved his point ... sigh.

I want to thank Jenny Hellen at Allen & Unwin for gently hounding me until I consented to write this book, then hounding me even more until I finished it, to the point where I'm wondering if perhaps she and Sam are related.

I thank Averil, who never stops believing in me even when all the evidence suggests her faith is misplaced.

Finally, I thank my sweet and funny darling twin sister, Sue, the family historian who drew up the gnarly family tree and collected and collated the few and far between Scott and Ronayne family photos. This small tome will keep her busy for months spotting errors, distortions, falsehoods and wild fabrications, none of which are her fault.

Tom Scott
Wellington
November 2017